GLOBAL ISSUES

GLOBALIZATION AND FREE TRADE

Natalie Goldstein

Foreword by Frank W. Musgrave

Ithaca College, Ithaca, New York

Viva Books

New Delhi | Mumbai | Chennai | Kolkata | Bangalore | Hyderabad | Kochi | Guwahati

First Indian Edition 2010

VIVA BOOKS PRIVATE LIMITED

- 4737/23 Ansari Road, Daryaganj, New Delhi 110 002
  E-mail: vivadelhi@vivagroupindia.net, Tel. 42242200
- 76, Service Industries, Shirvane, Sector 1, Nerul, Navi Mumbai 400 706
  E-mail: vivamumbai@vivagroupindia.net, Tel. 27721273, 27721274
- Jamals Fazal Chambers, 26 Greams Road, Chennai 600 006
  E-mail: vivachennai@vivagroupindia.net, Tel. 28290304, 28294241
- B-103, Jindal Towers, 21/1A/3 Darga Road, Kolkata 700 017
  E-mail: vivakolkata@vivagroupindia.net, Tel. 22836381, 22816713
- 7, Sovereign Park Apartments, 56-58, K. R. Road, Basavanagudi, Bangalore 560 004
  E-mail: vivabangalore@vivagroupindia.net, Tel. 26607409, 26607410
- 101-102 Mughal Marc Apartments, 3-4-637 to 641, Narayanguda, Hyderabad 500 029
  E-mail: vivahyderabad@vivagroupindia.net, Tel. 27564481, 27564482
- First Floor, Beevi Towers, SRM Road, Kaloor, Kochi 682 018, Kerala
  E-mail: vivakochi@vivagroupindia.net, Tel: 0484-2403055, 2403056
- 232, GNB Road, Beside UCO Bank, Silpukhuri, Guwahati 781 003
  E-mail: vivaguwahati@vivagroupindia.net, Tel: 0361-2666386

www.vivagroupindia.com

Published by arrangement with

Facts on File, Inc.
132 West 31st Street
New York 10001
USA

ISBN 978-81-309-1420-6

Published by Vinod Vasishtha for Viva Books Private Limited, 4737/23, Ansari Road, Daryaganj, New Delhi-110 002. Printed and bound by Anand Sons, Delhi - 110 092.

CONTENTS

Foreword by Frank W. Musgrave **v**
List of Acronyms **ix**

PART I: At Issue

Chapter 1
Introduction **3**

Chapter 2
Focus on the United States **71**

Chapter 3
Global Perspectives **94**

PART II: Primary Sources

Chapter 4
United States Documents **131**

Chapter 5
International Documents **179**

PART III: Research Tools

Chapter 6
How to Research Globalization and Free Trade **261**

Chapter 7
Facts and Figures **270**

Chapter 8
Key Players A to Z **283**

Chapter 9
Organizations and Agencies **296**

Chapter 10
Annotated Bibliography **323**

Chronology **372**

Glossary **382**

Index **392**

Foreword

The very mention of the term *globalization* appears to trigger strong emotions and political reactions. Critics of the neoliberal philosophy, the theory that has dominated economic policy in the United States and internationally during the past few decades, often view free trade as a device to enrich the industrially advanced nations that does little, if anything, to assist in problems of inadequate economic growth, poverty, health, education, or the well-being of the less fortunate populations. Although the World Bank (WB), the International Monetary Fund (IMF), the International Trade Organization (ITO), and the General Agreement on Tariffs and Trade (GATT, which later became part of the World Trade Organization, WTO) are agencies that were designed to assist in the growth and development of nations, these organizations have been, and continue to be, criticized as being insensitive to the real needs of developing nations. They are often viewed as overdemanding in terms of expectations of financial or accounting responsibilities, repayment of loans, and insistence on liberalizing trade and adopting competitive market structures. Some critics argue that neoclassical or neoliberal philosophy as a guide to policy is too simplistic, requiring completely unrestricted (by government) markets and perfect competition in order to be effective.

Although constructive criticism and unprejudiced analysis is key to improving the current system, antiglobalization advocates often oversimplify the issues, arguing, for example, that anything less than perfect competition in practice renders a laissez-faire economy ineffective. Some even advocate that domestic governments and the external agencies need to abandon free trade or free markets altogether. Critics of globalization often fail to consider the obvious benefits of trade and competitive market economies.

Given the complexity of the issue and what is at stake, a clear, accurate, and balanced guide to the economic issues that underlie globalization is a necessity. A refreshingly accurate and balanced view of globalization is brought forth in this work on globalization. *Globalization and Free Trade* is part of a series of studies on global issues. Since this book is a first step for high school students and other readers interested in gaining an appreciation, knowledge, and understanding of a major issue, it becomes paramount that it provide historical perspective, accurate economic analysis, and objective criteria for analyzing policy implications. This approach is evident in this comprehensive study.

In part I, globalization is defined as "the worldwide spread of industrial production and new technologies that is promoted by unrestricted mobility of capital and the unfettered freedom of trade." This definition not only describes globalization but also the role of resources moving through trade to the best advantage of the trading nations. The author introduces basic economic concepts in their historical context, including Adam Smith's opposition to mercantilism and his advocacy of free trade, examples of market capitalism in the 18th century, and the early world of the classical economists through the late 19th century and early 20th century of industrialization. By discussing economic issues and policies in their historical context, the author successfully unravels the complexities of globalization and draws the reader into an affair with a mystery-novel appeal. The author brings a balanced perspective to issues of liberalization of trade, privatization of national economies, and domestic control versus external institutional control. She explores the history and workings of external institutions such as the World Trade Organization (WTO) and the World Bank (WB) and analyzes their impact on the economies of less developed nations. Indeed, she allows the reader to see possible conflicts between those who criticize the practice of free trade per se and those who criticize the actions and policies of external institutions such as the WTO and WB for limiting the economic successes of less developed nations. Readers will have access to an ample and balanced set of opposing views, concepts, and interpretations from a variety of sources, allowing them to fully understand and appreciate a theory or concept.

In part II, globalization is set in the rich context of American history, starting with the later part of the 19th century and continuing to the present. This is a period of rapid industrial growth, financial crises, political upheavals, and a test of the role of government in what had become a laissez-faire economy. The author capably uses this time period to give the readers a sense of the very significant issues raised by globalization. The role of trade and its expansionary effects on the economies of the trading nations is viewed with varying interpretations. Both the voices of critics and proponents of globalization ring clearly in this book. Readers can learn not only the premises of the two sides in these issues but can also begin to see the value of research in sorting out the effects of liberalizing trade from other factors, including policies of the international agencies and the conditions present in the less developed nations that are often at odds with the demands that are attached to the promises of aid. By carefully reading this comprehensive work, students will find a veritable gold mine of material, including valuable bibliographical material. One source mentioned in the book is Nancy L. Stokey's "Giving Aid Effectively," which describes the Copenhagen Consensus project, in which a group of economists is asked what the most effective way would be to spend $50 billion over the next five years to make the world a better place. It is an excellent way to introduce students to benefit/cost analysis and how economists approach problem solving. Students would also benefit by role-playing two outstanding authors on opposite sides of the value of globalization, both of which are cited in this book: Jagdish Bhagwati and Joseph Stiglitz.

Part III reports on examples of globalization in other parts of the world. In the first case study, the author analyzes the situation in East Asia, including the region's growth in the 30 years before 1997 and the economic collapse of many East Asian nations in 1997. Capital-market speculation and its financial contagion overshadowed the roles of foreign trade and the external financial overlords (IMF, WB, and others) in response to the financial crisis. Goldstein capably outlines the links among all of these institutional, national, and international forces. Part III explores Russia as an example of a transitional economy, as it moved from a socialist economy that was part of the former USSR to a market economy in the 1990s. Unfortunately, other examples of transitional economies, such as the economy of Poland, which enjoyed some moderate successes in its transition to the market system, are outside the scope of this book. In this part of the book the author also explores the effects of globalization on China, and Cochabamba, a city in Bolivia.

Global Issues: Globalization and Free Trade is very important for its comprehensive and balanced approach to a complex and contentious issue. Besides clear and balanced analyses and historic context, readers will find a treasure trove of information and tools for further reading and research, particularly in the cited sources and annotated bibliography.

—Frank W. Musgrave, M.B.A., Ph.D.
Ithaca College, Ithaca, N.Y.

List of Acronyms

AoA	Agreement on Agriculture
APEC	Asia-Pacific Economic Cooperation
ASEAN	Association of Southeast Asian Nations
CAFTA	Central American Free Trade Agreement
CARICOM	Caribbean Community and Common Market
DSB	Dispute Settlement Body
EBRD	European Bank for Reconstruction and Development
EC	European Community
ECOSOC	Economic and Social Council
ECOWAS	Economic Community of West African States
ECSC	European Coal and Steel Community Treaty
EEC	European Economic Community
EFTA	European Free Trade Association
EMU	European Monetary Union
EPZ	export processing zone
EU	European Union
FAO	Food and Agriculture Organization
FDI	foreign direct investment
FTAA	Free Trade Area of the Americas
G-7	Group of Seven
G-8	Group of Eight
G-20	Group of Twenty
G-77	Group of Seventy-seven
G-90	Group of Ninety
GATS	General Agreement on Trade in Services
GATT	General Agreement on Tariffs and Trade
GDP	gross domestic product
GNP	gross national product
HDI	human development index
IBRD	International Bank for Reconstruction and Development

IDB	Inter-American Development Bank
IFI	international financial institution
ILO	International Labor Organization
IMF	International Monetary Fund
LDC	least developed country
MAI	Multilateral Agreement on Investment
MEA	multilateral environmental agreement
MERCOSUR	Common Market of the South
MFN	most favored nation
MIGA	Multilateral Investment Guarantee Agency
MNC	multinational corporation
NAALC	North American Agreement on Labor Cooperation
NAFTA	North American Free Trade Agreement
NAMA	Non-Agricultural Market Access
NEG	new economic geography
NGO	nongovernmental organization
NIEO	New International Economic Order
OECD	Organization for Economic Cooperation and Development
OPEC	Organization of Petroleum Exporting Countries
PPP	purchasing power parity
RTA	regional trade agreement
SAP	structural adjustment program
SDR	special drawing right
SEZ	special economic zone
SOE	state-owned enterprise
SPS	Agreement on the Application of Sanitary and Phyto-Sanitary Measures
STT	strategic trade theory
TBT	Technical Barriers to Trade
TRIMS	Agreement on Trade-Related Investment Measures
TRIPS	Trade-Related Aspects of Intellectual Property
UN	United Nations
UNCTAD	United Nations Conference on Trade and Development
UNDP	United Nations Development Program
USSR	Union of Soviet Socialist Republics
WB	World Bank
WTO	World Trade Organization

PART I

At Issue

1

Introduction

The women of ancient Rome were crazy about silk. Old and young, rich and poor, the females in and around the capital of the Roman Empire all craved clothes made out of this exotic fabric. Roman women wanted it, and they got it—hauled to them by camel all the way from China. Officials of the first century C.E. calculated that Romans shelled out more than 100 million sesterces (ancient Roman currency) for silk every single year.

The demand for silk, among other goods, made the Silk Road a heavily trafficked trade route in the ancient world. At any one time, numerous caravans, each a thousand or more camels strong, trekked back and forth from China through Mesopotamia to Rome and Venice or to North Africa. Staggering across scorching deserts and struggling over ice-covered mountain passes, the long-suffering camels carted Asian silk, spices, and jade westward and ivory, glass, and precious stones and metals, including gold, eastward.

The Silk Road was one of the earliest and most extensive avenues of trade—in a sense, a type of globalized trade, because it encompassed much of the known world at that time. It was not free trade, because the Romans imposed customs duties, or taxes, on imported goods. Completely free trade is an economic ideal that has probably never been fully realized. Free trade is the totally open, duty-free trade in all goods moving between nations. There has been free trade in specific goods—for example, two nations may agree to eliminate tariffs (customs duties) on trade in pottery—but throughout history, most nations have imposed customs duties on at least some imports.

The importation of silk into the Roman Empire in some ways resembles trade and globalization as we know it today. For one thing, it was controversial. Though Roman women had a seemingly insatiable appetite for silk with which to make their clothes, the use of this foreign, newfangled fabric threatened and angered some powerful Romans. Pliny the Elder (23–79 C.E.) railed against the silk trade, which "enable[d] the Roman maiden to flaunt transparent clothing in public."[1] Seneca the Younger (c. 3 B.C.E.–65 C.E.) self-righteously fulminated against the foreign fabric and wondered if "clothes of silk—if materials that do not hide the body, nor even one's decency—can [even] be called clothes."[2] Pliny may have been a sourpuss and Seneca a killjoy, but their argument that silk was a foreign and therefore culturally and morally degenerate influence on Rome aroused fierce debate in the Roman Senate, which tried several times to outlaw the importation and wearing of silk.

So here we have an ancient yet recognizable controversy about global trade. Some people benefited from it and supported it—in this case, Roman women and both Roman and foreign traders—and some people were hurt by it and opposed it—in this case, those who saw it as a pernicious influence on their society and, most likely, domestic Roman textile manufacturers and sellers.

Another negative aspect of the silk trade that perhaps has more resonance today than it did for the slave-holding Romans was the virtually slave-like condition of the silk workers in China. In his argument against the silk trade, Seneca pointed out the "wretched flocks of maids [who] labor" to make the coveted fabric.[3] The labor conditions that result from globalized trade are one of the main arguments against modern globalization.

As the reader can see, the trade in goods across vast stretches of the globe is nothing new. Nor are the controversies it engenders. However, though modern globalization developed from historical trading patterns, present-day globalized trade is very different—in its scale and its impact—from ancient world commerce.

WHAT IS GLOBALIZATION?

If globalization is defined simply as trade between countries on opposite sides of the world, then globalization has been occurring for thousands of years. The same is true if its definition includes the sharing or movement of technologies from one part of the globe to the other, or the cultural influences trading nations have on each other.

Globalization is a buzzword—one hears it a lot these days—yet it means very different things to different people. To some people, *globalization* means "ruthless exploitation by corporations"; others who use the word mean "bringing economic development to the peoples of the world." It is important to understand exactly what economists mean when they talk about globalization.

One economist, John Gray, stresses that modern globalization is not a fact or structure but rather a process—in his words, a process of "de-localization."[4] *Delocalization* means that local activities and networks of local relationships are broken because globalization scatters many of their functions across the globe. This becomes obvious when one examines how a great deal of manufacturing occurs today. In earlier and simpler times, global trade meant that an artisan's or even a small factory's products—clothing, for example—were made wholly by the individual or entirely locally and then transported to and sold in a distant country. In today's globalized economy, the same article of clothing is likely made in several different countries. For example, the raw material, such as cotton or wool, is produced in one country. Then the raw material may be shipped to a second country where it is woven into cloth. The woven fabric may next be sent to a third country where it is cut to a clothing pattern. The cut pieces are often shipped to yet a fourth country to be sewn together and assembled into an article of clothing. Only then is the final product put on the market for sale. This incrementalism also means that globalization "link[s] distant realities in such a way that local happenings are shaped by events occurring many miles away, and vice versa."[5] Thus, what happens in any one of the localities where the clothing manufacturing process occurs affects the textile workers in all the other places. The present-day corporate penchant for this piecemeal production method has led some economists to define modern globalization as the enormous expansion of multinational corporations (MNCs) and their investments in foreign lands.[6]

For the purposes of this book, the following represent fairly straightforward and comprehensive definitions of globalization:

> *[Globalization can be defined as] the closer integration of the countries and peoples of the world, which has been brought about by the enormous reduction of costs of transportation and communication, and the breaking down of artificial barriers to the flows of goods, services, capital, knowledge, and (to a lesser extent) people across borders. Globalization has been accompanied by the creation of new institutions that have joined with existing ones to work across borders.*[7]

and

> *[the term* globalization *describes] the worldwide spread of industrial production and new technologies that is promoted by unrestricted mobility of capital and unfettered freedom of trade.*[8]

To understand globalization today, it is helpful to know how it got to be the way it is. A bit of historical background reveals how globalization both emerged from and formed in reaction to previous economic events and principles. It also shows that there might be alternatives to some less appealing aspects of modern globalization that have worked well in the past. The following brief background will give the reader a good idea of where globalization came from, how it became what it is, and why it is controversial.

HISTORICAL BACKGROUND

The Early Evolution of Globalization

COLONIZATION

The Age of Exploration, which began in the 15th century, saw amazing technological advances in a key field of globalization: transportation. Improved design of oceangoing vessels allowed European explorers to set sail into the unknown and prowl the oceans in search of "undiscovered" lands that they could colonize. European powers colonized regions of the world that had natural resources that could feed the home country's economic engine, satisfy the greed of the imperial monarchy, and bolster the nation's power in relation to other nations.

The travels of Christopher Columbus, for example, were funded by the Spanish monarchs in hopes that he would find a route to the riches of Asia. When it became clear that he had bumped into intervening landmasses, the instructions given to him, and to subsequent explorers, were to find gold and other precious or useful commodities and ship them home to enrich its princes and the state. Native populations were certainly not seen as potential trading partners, but merely as a convenient and easily enslaved labor force for the extraction of whatever resources their homeland happened to have.

Over time, as the European imperial nations industrialized, some of them increasingly looked on their subject colonials as consumers as well as producers. This was particularly true of the British, who often set up systems of native proxy governors or administrators in their colonies. These native intermediaries often prospered, giving rise to a kind of native middle class that, nourished on the principles and values of the colonizers, sought to emulate their overlords and to acquire their goods. Thus, at least a portion of the colonized population assumed the role of trading partner in that they purchased goods imported from the home country.

Most overseas colonies were trading partners mainly to the extent that they were home to settlers or administrators from the mother country. The 13 North American colonies, for example, did a brisk trade with Britain, exchanging raw goods (timber, furs) for English manufactures. Of course, this was not free trade, as import duties were frequently imposed by the English (for example, on tea).

MERCANTILISM

Mercantilism arose in Europe during the Renaissance, beginning around 1500. Mercantilism was supported by powerful business interests within a nation, such as the early guilds dedicated to a particular manufacture. Mercantilism rested on the belief that a nation's power increases with the amount of gold or silver it has. Mercantile businesses therefore sought to bring as much money, backed by bullion (gold or silver), into their country as possible. As gold and silver are rare commodities, the nation with the greatest amount of either was, in the eyes of mercantilists, the strongest. A nation's positive balance of payments was also a measure of its power. To keep riches within a country and prevent money from flowing abroad, the state imposed high tariffs to ensure that exports greatly exceeded imports. In the view of its supporters, mercantilism was a zero-sum game; that is, if someone wins, someone else has to lose. Businesses and the state worked hand in glove to enhance their country's wealth while, at the same time, conniving to usurp the wealth of competitors. In many ways, it was a kind of economic cold war. (Mercantilism fueled hot wars, as well. Because every nation rigidly regulated trade, the amount of goods traded was viewed as fixed. The only way to increase your share of this fixed pie was to go to war to seize it from another nation. The nearly endless European wars of the 17th and 18th centuries arose partly out of this strict mercantilist doctrine.)

Mercantilism accounts for the past hunger for colonies. A nation needed a large and guaranteed supply of raw materials to feed its economic growth if it were to remain powerful. It needed more colonies and more raw materials than other nations if it were to surpass them in wealth and strength. A mercantilist nation sought above all to become self-sufficient in every respect so that it would not have to import goods from other countries and thus deplete its wealth and compromise its power.

EARLY CRITICS OF MERCANTILISM

The Scottish philosopher David Hume (1711–76) famously pointed out the paradox inherent in the notion that having lots of bullion always enriches a nation. Hume showed that in a nation that had scads of bullion, its value would decrease (excess supply lowers its value), whereas in a nation that had less bullion, its value would go up (limited supply increases its value). So hoarding gold and silver within one nation would not necessarily make that country richer than a nation with less precious metal in its coffers.

Another Scottish philosopher, James Mill (1773–1836), criticized mercantilism in his book *Elements of Political Economy* (1821). Mill argued that the mercantilist notion that only exports are good for a nation is absurd because a nation exports its goods in order to obtain money to buy imports. He wrote: "The benefit which is derived from exchanging one commodity for another arises in all cases from the commodity *received,* not the commodity given."[9]

A highly influential group of critics also arose in 18th-century France. The physiocrats were a group of French intellectuals who lobbied the government for more open trade rules. These thinkers believed that trade would prosper best if it were simply left unhindered by any type of government interference.

The physiocrats gave the world the phrase *laissez-faire* as it applies to economics. *Laissez-faire* literally means "let [people] do [as they want]," or "let it work on its own" or "leave it alone." The principles of laissez-faire economics—free trade unfettered by government interference—have had a profound and enduring impact on trade, globalization, and economics in general.

ADAM SMITH AND A NEW WORLD ECONOMIC ORDER

In 1776, British economist Adam Smith (1723–90) published *The Wealth of Nations,* and for better or worse, the world of economics has not been the same since. *The Wealth of Nations* (its full title is *An Inquiry into the Nature and Causes of the Wealth of Nations*) remains one of the most influential books of political economics ever written, and it became the foundation of most modern capitalist thought. The book also elevated the field of economics to a more "scientific" and therefore respected discipline.

Smith was a vocal critic of mercantilism, which he saw as excessively rigid, an obstacle to economic growth, and a more primitive stage in the evolution of economic systems, which, he believed, culminated in free market capitalism. Smith analyzed the policies that either encouraged or hindered economic growth. His analysis led him to the conclusion that private enterprise, driven by individual self-interest, created the greatest wealth for a nation. Enlightened self-interest was, for Smith, the essence of the economically "rational" individual. Smith argued that all people are born with the desire to better their own condition. Rather than interpreting this innate selfishness as an absolute vice, Smith believed that if it is incorporated into a system of perfect liberty, or perfect competition, then the cumulative, self-interested drive of all individuals in competition with one another will result in a kind of social equilibrium that economically benefits everyone and the state. In a famous passage, Smith explained:

> *It is not from the benevolence of the butcher, the brewer, or the baker that we expect our dinner, but from their regard to their own interest. We address ourselves, not to their humanity, but to their self-love, and never talk to them of our own necessities but of their advantages.*[10]

Smith used the metaphor of the "invisible hand" of enlightened self-interest to explain how the free market is a self-correcting mechanism that leads to a "natural" level in the prices of goods and the costs of labor. Smith's "invisible hand" refers to any free (uncoerced and unregulated) individual action that has unplanned and unintended consequences, especially in the public arena. For example, if a product is in great demand but in short supply, the price of the scarce product is high. The high price entices self-interested individuals to begin manufacturing the product. They profit, but as the supply increases, the price goes down. Consequently consumers benefit, as they exercise their self-interest and buy a desirable product at a low price. Yet if too much of the product is manufactured, there is a surplus, and the price drops too low for manufacturers to make a profit. So, in their self-interest, some manufacturers stop making the product. The price rises again—to its "natural level." Smith applied the same supply-and-demand logic to wages. The larger the population of individuals seeking jobs, the lower wages will be. In each case, the market self-corrects, and prices and costs naturalize, or become stable.

Of course, for unfettered self-interested competition to work, government and its regulations must be eliminated from the process.

> *[T]he system . . . of natural liberty establishes itself of its own accord. . . . The [government] is completely discharged from a duty . . . [in] which [it] must always be exposed to innumerable delusions, and for the proper performance of which no human wisdom or knowledge could ever be sufficient: the duty of superintending the industry of private people.*[11]

This key principle—ridding business of government intervention—has become one of the cornerstones of modern economics and globalization.

It is true that Smith was a great champion of the free market, yet Smith has been misinterpreted both by globalization's supporters and detractors. Those who oppose globalization often think that Smith advocated a type of dog-eat-dog capitalism, in which vicious cutthroat competition is the ideal. Smith, however, envisioned the invisible hand at work within a coherent social framework of laws and social institutions. Unlike many of today's neoliberals, Smith did not see society as existing for the sake of the economy. Further, Smith usually had nothing good to say about businessmen and industry, whose practices he often found abhorrent. Although he did not address corporations directly, he detested monopolies, and he would probably be apoplectic about multinational corporations. Smith excoriated "[t]he mean rapacity, the monopolizing spirit of merchants and manufacturers who neither are nor ought to be the rulers of mankind."[12] Although Smith believed in free trade insofar as "a voluntary transaction always benefits both parties," he also stated that "people of the same trade seldom meet together, even for merriment and diversion, but the conversation ends in a conspiracy against the public, or in some contrivance to raise prices."[13] In short, Smith was not the rabid and extreme laissez-faire capitalist that globalization's detractors demonize or that globalization's supporters applaud.

DAVID RICARDO AND THE THEORY OF COMPARATIVE ADVANTAGE

Four decades after Smith published *The Wealth of Nations,* an English banker wrote a volume that picked up economic theory where Smith had left off.

David Ricardo (1772–1823) published *Principles of Political Economy and Taxation* in 1817. In this work, Ricardo set forth his labor theory of value, which stated that the value of a product that is made and sold in a competitive environment is related to the cost of labor involved in its production. Ricardo was greatly influenced by the work of Thomas Malthus (1766–1834), who prophesied the doom of humankind as the population increases beyond the ability of the land to feed it. Using Malthus's ideas, Ricardo formulated his "iron law of wages," which states that because of population growth and competition for jobs (and for greater profits among businesses), in the long run, the wages laborers earn can never rise above a minimum subsistence level. This rather gloomy assessment is sometimes applied to the "race to the bottom" among corporations seeking the lowest-wage workers in the modern globalized economy. (Ricardo's idea also inspired Karl Marx's works on communism.)

Ricardo's main contribution to the economics of globalization, however, was not his pessimistic view of labor's future. Again applying Malthus's principles, Ricardo showed that the shortage of usable land available to support a growing population will force nations to prioritize its use in order to maximize its yield per unit (in other words, to get the most production out of a given unit, such as an acre of land). To illustrate his point, Ricardo set out his theory of comparative advantage. In simplified terms, comparative advantage is the notion that even if a nation could efficiently produce by itself everything it needs and uses, the country would benefit still more if it specialized in producing what it was best at making and then trading with other nations for the rest. To give a simplified example, although it is possible that parts of the United States might efficiently produce bananas, this would not be an optimum use of its land. The United States would be better off using its land to grow wheat or citrus fruit because its soil, climate, labor force, and technology give it a comparative advantage over other nations in producing these commodities. It should therefore export these foodstuffs and import bananas from a country that has a comparative advantage in banana growing. In short, a nation has a comparative advantage in producing a product if it has an abundance of the inputs that can be used intensively to produce that product.

It is not hard to see how the concept of comparative advantage promotes globalization and trade. Inputs, or conditions and resources, vary widely from place to place around the world. If each nation exploits its comparative advantage in the production of goods and commodities, then global trade increases enormously. And, theoretically, a nation that exploits its comparative advantage grows its economy. In terms of modern globalization, the main question that often arises is, *who* exploits a nation's comparative advantage? If it is the nation and its people, then the nation and citizens should prosper. If it is a multinational corporation, the country and its citizens may not reap the expected benefits.

THE BEGINNINGS OF LAISSEZ-FAIRE

The ideas of Smith and Ricardo became the bedrock of 19th-century free market capitalism. One of the first acts in response to the doctrine of laissez-faire was the British Parliament's repeal of the Corn Laws in 1832. The Corn Laws, first enacted in 1815, had prohibited the importing of corn into Britain in order to bolster the profits of domestic producers. With the repeal of the Corn Laws, the British government initiated decades of free trade largely unimpeded by government regulation.

One example of the effects of unrestricted laissez-faire policies prevalent during globalization's infancy was the British government's inaction during the Irish potato famine of the 1840s. Disease (potato blight) had killed the plants on which the Irish depended for food. Though Britain had abundant domestic and imported food, it was more profitable for businesses to sell their grain on the open market where its price was high than for the government to take measures that would divert it to save the starving Irish. For many crucial months, while people died in the famine, the government followed the principle of laissez-faire and did not act. The market was supreme and not to be interfered with on any grounds. (Later, the British government did provide food to Ireland.)

Nowhere was laissez-faire capitalism more dominant than in Great Britain during the Victorian period, in the second half of the 19th century. Hungarian economist Karl Polanyi (1886–1964) studied how market systems function in traditional and industrialized societies. He analyzed the evolution of the British economy from a land-based system embedded in the social life of the peasantry to the free market system it became in the Victorian era. Polanyi called this change the Great Transformation, and he wrote: "Ultimately, . . . the control of the economic system by the market is of overwhelming consequence to the whole organization of society; it means no less than the running of society as an adjunct to the market. Instead of the economy being embedded in social relations, social relations are embedded in the economic system."[14] Polanyi's ideas remain pertinent to the dominant role of corporations and the free market in modern societies.

Boom, Bust, and Belligerence (1890s to 1918)

CAPITALISM IN OVERDRIVE

With minimal government interference in business and with global trade booming, industrial production went into high gear. As U.S. senator William

Seward announced, "Put your domain under cultivation and your ten thousand wheels of manufacture in motion. The nation that draws most materials and provisions from the earth, and fabricates the most, and sells the most of production and fabrics to foreign nations, must be, and will be, the great power of the earth."[15]

The race to produce goods arose from several key developments. First were the inventions and subsequent improvements in communications, particularly the telegraph. Before the invention of the telegraph, it sometimes took a message two years to wend its way from India to London. Early telegraphs cut that time to about 13 hours. By the 1890s, messages reached New York from London in 10 minutes, and London could wire its colonial administrators in Bombay and get a reply back in about an hour and a half. The second innovation that propelled industrial production was improvements in steamships. Faster and larger ships could carry more cargo more quickly to and from the farthest corners of the earth. Finally, it must be said that too often the principles of laissez-faire engendered an unbridled greed among the "robber barons" of the era. The opening of global trade and the exploitation of cheap domestic labor enabled rich industrialists to accumulate wealth beyond imagining. Many workers in Western industries were often forced to work long hours for little pay. Violence was sometimes used to disperse laborers who protested against their poverty-level wages or unsafe working conditions.

In June 1873, a financial crisis struck the overextended economy of Austria, sending it into a tailspin and ripples of panic through industrialized countries. For more than two decades, the economies of the industrialized nations experienced periodic depressions. The economic downturns, some severe, had several causes: extreme protectionist measures, highly speculative and unregulated investment and business practices, and the need for strict adherence to the gold standard.

ECONOMIC DEPRESSION AND THE AGE OF IMPERIALISM

To maintain the speed of economic growth and contend for global economic dominance, nearly every industrialized nation looked to Asia as the panacea for its economic woes. The worldwide depression of the 1890s made finding an outlet for their economic troubles vital for Western industrial powers.

Relentless industrial production in Western nations led to a problem that 19th-century economists diagnosed as "overproduction." In fact, the problem was largely underconsumption. It was not that too many goods were being produced, but that the vast majority of the population labored for such low wages they could not afford to buy most products. Even basic necessities were sometimes beyond the means of the average industrial worker. Still, the laissez-faire attitude that prevailed at the time made it impossible for governments to take any steps toward more fair and equitable distribution of wealth.

In what has been called a policy of social imperialism, the United States and the industrialized nations of Europe exported not only their surplus manufactures but their domestic unemployment problems as well.[16] Social imperialism was a process in which wealthy, industrialized countries, called "metropoles," sought out poor and relatively defenseless nations, or nations of the periphery, and forced them to export their raw materials to the metropole and import the metropole's manufactured goods. Thus, metropole unemployment was kept low by high productivity, while periphery countries suffered high unemployment because their vast imports inhibited their domestic production of goods. For example, the U.S. company Standard Oil forced China to import the kerosene it produced. This kept Standard Oil's American workforce busy but destroyed the livelihoods of many thousands of Chinese workers who produced vegetable oil for lighting and cooking.[17]

Carving Up China

China, with its vast natural wealth and large population, was the supreme prize in the Western powers' plans to force open trade with Asia. China was the perfect periphery state, and it was no stranger to Western intrusion. Beginning in the 16th century, European powers had cast a covetous eye on China, and some, particularly Britain and France, had slowly but surely encroached on its land and helped themselves to its riches. In the first half of the 19th century, British and French traders were taking silk, tea, porcelain, and jade out of China and offering Western imports or currency in exchange. China refused to accept either, wisely (or so it seemed) demanding payment in gold or silver. For a while, the Europeans accepted this arrangement, but they soon found their reserves of precious metal dwindling. To reverse this worrisome trend, the British insisted that China accept opium as payment instead. (The British could easily and cheaply get opium from their colony in India.) China adamantly refused, and tensions mounted. The First Opium War (1838–42) greatly weakened China and limited its capacity to resist Western intrusion. The treaty signed at the end of this conflict opened even more of China to Western exploitation. China attempted to resist the harsh treaty conditions, and between 1856 and 1858, France and Britain again fought China in the Second Opium War. China was routed and forced to accept the legal importation of opium as payment for trade. (For the first time, opium addiction became a serious and widespread problem in China. The stereotype of the Chinese opium den came about only after the Opium Wars.) For decades afterward, all trade was controlled by the West, which imposed its own system of tariffs, implemented policies that destroyed

China's domestic textile and handicraft industries, and forced Western manufactures on the Chinese, who suffered widespread unemployment.

Japan, too, coveted Chinese wealth, and the Sino-Japanese War (1894–95) left China even weaker and easier prey for social imperialists. Alarmed that Japan might get away with the whole Chinese pie, Western powers moved in to make sure they got a bigger slice. Britain, France, Germany, and Russia all controlled important ports and lands in various parts of China. They set up mining companies to extract China's mineral wealth and railroads to move it more quickly to ships ready to carry it to Europe.

Each European power vied with all others to dominate China. Their competitive spirit was influenced by an economic theory prevalent at the time called the "Three World Empires." This theory stated that "only the three largest and most powerful nation-states would remain independent," with the others economically subservient to them.[18] It is clear why such a worldview would lead to frantic expansionist trade policies among the leading economic powers of the West.

The late 19th century is often called the Age of Imperialism, a time when free trade meant free rein for industry but protectionism when it came to foreign competition. Metropole nations prospered, controlling both the economic and political life of peripheral nations, including their labor, capital, and land. The principle of laissez-faire was applied to the multinational corporations of that era and to the accumulation of wealth by the few. It is important to keep in mind that the peoples of the periphery have not forgotten their history of exploitation, and their view of modern globalization is often deeply affected by this history.

World War I

Leaders of most of the metropole nations understood that peaceful coexistence was the best insurance for a happily humming economy. Nonagression among metropole nations allowed each to plunder its peripheries in peace. But two conditions threatened that peace. One was the rise to power of Kaiser Wilhelm (1859–1941) in Germany in 1888. Unlike his predecessor, Wilhelm pursued an aggressive campaign of militarism and expansionism; in fact, he was outraged at Germany's "Johnny-come-lately" status in the imperial game. In addition to seeking trading outposts, Germany began a huge buildup of its army. As German military might increased, the other European powers became very nervous. When Germany formed the Central Powers alliance (with Austria-Hungary and Turkey), France, Britain, Russia, and the United States united in their own defense as the Allies. The Allies felt that Germany's militarization forced them to follow suit. Soon industries in nearly all European countries were dedicating themselves to the production of armaments. The industrialization of the machinery of war only increased distrust, even paranoia, between the alliances. Add to this a growing nationalism, and the outbreak of war was all but inevitable.

The causes of World War I (1914–18) are too numerous, obscure, and convoluted to explore here.[19] Suffice it to say that World War I was one of the bloodiest and most horrific wars ever fought on this planet. About 10 million soldiers and civilians died, and the "War to End All Wars" was universally seen as the event that ended one era and way of life and began the new, modern era in which we live today.

If the economic path to war had been lined with imperialism, the road that followed the war was paved with debt. The Treaty of Versailles, which ended the war, punished the defeated Germany by requiring it to pay enormous monetary reparations to the Allies, especially France, where most of the fighting and destruction had occurred. France and the other European Allies had borrowed money from the United States to prosecute the war, and they were counting on German reparations to help them repay the loans. Unfortunately, Germany, too, had expended an enormous amount of its resources in prosecuting the war, and was unable to pay the amount stipulated in the treaty.

Protectionism (1918 to 1945)

THE GOLD STANDARD

The gold standard was a currency system in which participating nations agreed to fix the value of their currency to a specific amount of gold. Gold standard nations backed their currency by a fixed weight in gold, and paper money and nongold coins (called fiat money) were backed by a nation's gold reserves. In terms of international trade, the gold standard ensured that each country's currency could be exchanged for gold at a set price, and stability was maintained by fiscal actions taken at each nation's central bank. Because exchange rates were fixed, international currency valuations and prices moved in step with each other, mostly through automatic balance of payments adjustments. In essence, nations on the gold standard had to adjust their currencies and trade balances when conditions changed in other gold standard nations.

The gold standard, though highly controversial today, has some positive features. For one, it helps limit inflation because the value of money must be backed by scarce precious metal. In principle, a gold standard country cannot just print lots of paper money and circulate it; it must be backed by gold. This keeps inflation in check. It also checks the ability of a country to manipulate or control the value of its currency and the amount in circulation. The gold standard essentially limits uncertainties in a nation's currency and its value in international trade.

The gold standard does have its downside, however. One is that it is biased toward restraining economic growth. For example, gold standard nations that grew more quickly than others were brought back into line by other gold standard nations, which sought to restore currency and trade stability. Because all nations' economies moved in a kind of economic lockstep, what happened in one country was highly contagious to others. This was especially true for inflation and depression. In addition, mandatory adjustments constrained governments from acting unilaterally to improve their nation's domestic economic situation.

Because the gold standard severely restricts inflationary, or deficit, spending, the Allied nations abandoned it when faced with paying for the Great War. As the costs of the war increased, countries used deficit spending (that is, they borrowed money) to cover their military expenses, and inflation soared. The European nations fighting the German alliance were so assured of their victory, they counted on postwar German reparations to bring their inflation under control.

No European nation suffered greater inflation than Germany, which still had to pay reparations to the Allies. Germany's debt was so crushing that its gold reserves were wholly inadequate to cover it. Germany began printing paper money that was not backed by gold. This led to hyperinflation, which devastated the German economy: German inflation was so severe the price of goods increased *1 trillion times* between 1921 and 1924. In 1923, prices in Germany were 1.26 trillion times higher than they had been in the prewar period. The German currency (the mark) fell in value from $0.25 to $0.00000000000025. The iconic image is of German citizens carrying wheelbarrows full of money to the store just to buy a loaf of bread. Despite the Dawes Plan drawn up at the Allied Reparations Committee meeting in 1924, which set out a more manageable reparations payment schedule, Germany was never able to fully pay its reparations. Allied nations were saddled with inflationary economies they would somehow have to fix themselves. The industrialized world was in very bad economic shape, indeed.

THE GREAT DEPRESSION

Many events and decisions led to the Great Depression, which began in the United States after the stock market crash of October 29, 1929.[20] Some economists believe that U.S. adherence to the gold standard was one contributing factor that led to the worst economic collapse in U.S. history.

Though some economists disagree with this assessment, most concur that the gold standard was largely responsible for the spread of the U.S. depression throughout the world. As the U.S. economy contracted and deflation set in, American exports became cheaper, so foreign gold flowed into the country. To counterbalance the flow of gold into the United States, other nations had to raise their interest rates, which contracted their economies as well. It did not take long for the resulting declines in production and prices to send economies around the world into a tailspin.

Another cause of the depression was the widespread use of protective tariffs. After the devastation of World War I, countries sought to rebuild their industries by protecting them from the onslaughts of foreign competition. The relatively open trade of the prewar period reversed in the 1920s, and trade either stagnated or declined in most countries. Industrialized nations seemed to vie with one another to devise more restrictive and protective "beggar-thy-neighbor" economic policies. In the United States, the Smoot-Hawley Act of 1930 imposed the highest tariffs the country had ever known. Within a few years of its passage, many other nations passed retaliatory tariffs. Global trade plummeted. U.S. trade with Europe declined more than 60 percent between 1929 and 1932. A similar decline in trade with other nations followed. The already depressed world economy took a nosedive that would require another world war to reverse. The lessons seem clear now: Given the interdependence of the global economy, extreme protectionism is shortsighted, while a healthy dose of trade is nearly always recommended to lift a nation's ailing economy.

WORLD WAR II

Germany's utter defeat and humiliation after World War I left its people embittered and impoverished. Runaway hyperinflation persisted, and the life of the average German grew increasingly miserable and hopeless. As with other major world events, it is not possible to explain the causes and conduct of World War II (1939–45) here.[21] It is sufficient to say that economic devastation and the rise of nationalism led to the election of the Nazi Party in Germany and to the implementation of its policies of genocide and world conquest.

In September 1939, the German army invaded Poland, Britain declared war on Germany, and World War II began. Japan was allied with Germany (the Axis powers), and in 1941, Japan bombed Pearl Harbor in Hawaii, bringing the United States out of its isolationist mode and into the worldwide conflict.

World War II cost the lives of more than 55 million people and wounded 35 million more. As happened in World War I, deficit spending to pay for the conflict forced most nations to abandon the gold standard. Bombing destroyed large parts of Europe. By the time the war ended with the defeat of the Axis in 1945, most of the European economies were in ruins, and many of their cities and industrial centers were destroyed. In 1945, the United States adopted the Marshall Plan to help rebuild the economies of Europe. Between 1948 and 1951, the United States spent more than $12 billion on reconstruction of

European countries, including its former adversary, Germany. The United States also spent millions to aid the economic recovery of Japan.

The generous U.S. expenditures were intended to achieve specific goals. The United States understood that if it were going to prosper, it needed to support the economies of its strongest trading partners in Europe. Another key goal of the Marshall Plan was to create strong capitalist economies in western Europe to counteract the growing power of the communist government in the Soviet Union, established after the Bolshevik revolution of 1917.

Stabilization of the Postwar Economy (1940s)

Even before the western European powers staggered out of the rubble of World War II, they realized that something had to be done to create a new economic order. The old order—based on imperialism, protectionism, and laissez-faire, on which industrialized countries had pinned their hopes for peace and prosperity—had brought war and depression. Developed nations had to find a new way to establish the peace with economic growth that had so far eluded them.

In 1942, U.S. assistant secretary of the treasury Harry Dexter White and British economist John Maynard Keynes (1883–1946) began discussing the outline of a new economic plan that was to be debated—and, hopefully, adopted—at an international conference. From July 1 to 22, 1944, 730 delegates from 44 countries convened at the beautiful and secluded Mount Washington Hotel in Bretton Woods, New Hampshire. Their brief was nothing less than to hammer out a new, cooperative global economic order, including a stable international monetary system that would prevent future financial crises.

KEYNESIAN ECONOMICS

Keynes is considered one of the most brilliant figures in modern economics. In his youth, he had been a staunch supporter of laissez-faire and free trade. As a passionate and fiery young man, Keynes had written: "We must hold to Free Trade, in its widest interpretation, as an inflexible dogma, to which no exception is admitted. . . . [It should be] a principle of international morals, and not merely . . . a doctrine of economic advantage."[22] Then came World War I and its postscript: the ruinous economic policies imposed by the victors. Keynes made his reputation as the spokesman of his generation when, in 1919, he published *The Economic Consequences of Peace,* in which he condemned postwar Allied policies. His *Treatise on Money* (1930) solidified his reputation as an economist, and his views and advice were widely sought by President Franklin D. Roosevelt, among other leaders. With the onset of the Great Depression, a more mature Keynes began to doubt the wisdom of laissez-faire. In the late 1920s, Keynes argued for a limited type of protectionism that would allow countries to shield themselves from contagion by the worst global economic ills.

In 1933, Keynes gave a lecture in Dublin that was remarkable for its attitude toward laissez-faire and liberalized trade. "[F]ree trade, combined with the free mobility of capital," Keynes said, "was much more likely to provoke war than to preserve peace."[23] He added:

> *There may be some financial calculation which shows it to be advantageous that my savings should be invested in whatever quarter of the habitable globe shows the ... highest rate of interest. But experience is accumulating that remoteness between ownership and operation is an evil in the relations among men, likely or certain in the long run to set up strains and enmities which will bring to nought the financial calculation. I sympathize therefore with those who would minimize, rather than maximize, economic entanglement among nations ... [L]et goods be homespun whenever it is reasonably and conveniently possible; and, above all, let finance be primarily national.*[24]

In what could easily be a cogent criticism of modern international financial speculation, Keynes stated: "We do not wish to be at the mercy of forces working out, or trying to work out, some uniform equilibrium according to the ideal principles of laissez-faire capitalism ... [which] turn[s] the whole conduct of life [into] a parody of an accountant's nightmare."[25]

During World War II, Keynes modified his economic thought once again, cautiously adding controlled free trade to his economic prescription. Keynes had come to recognize that free trade did have an important role in economic growth. But he also came to the conclusion that when the free market fails, it is necessary for the government to take action to support the economy by creating jobs and thus reigniting economic growth. Reasonable government intervention when the free market fails to create a healthy and humane economy is the bedrock of Keynesian economics, which was the most influential economic doctrine of the 20th century.

KEYNES'S VISION AND BRETTON WOODS

The essence of Keynes's ideas was to create an international economic system in which there is free trade in goods and commodities but restrictions on the flow of speculative capital. The whole system would be managed by what Keynes called an "international clearing union," which resembled a global central bank. This union would control a "stabilization fund," capitalized with billions of dollars from member nations, which would lend money mainly to underdeveloped nations struggling with financial crises. The loans would enable these nations to stabilize their economies without having to resort to contracting them due to lack of revenue. Nations with a trade deficit would also be permitted to limit their imports from rich nations, while rich nations would be encouraged to buy deficit nations' exports. In short, Keynes envisioned a system that was radically different from the old gold standard system; instead of pressuring deficit economies to contract, Keynes's system would pressure creditor economies to expand. As Keynes saw it, nations with trade surpluses would act to aid nations with weaker economies, giving rise to a truly more equitable and just world economic system.

As an adjunct to this trade system, Keynes strongly supported the imposition of strict controls on capital moving across national borders. He firmly believed that the unregulated flow of capital around the world would inevitably lead to insupportable inequalities and from there to persistent instability, as speculators cashed in on fluctuations in foreign currencies.

Keynes's plan also set out rules permitting the clearing union and member nations' central banks to act to ensure fixed and stable exchange rates. If a country's balance of payments was negative—that is, if its imports far exceeded its exports—temporary loans from the clearing union could see it through until its exports increased and its currency regained stability. Keynes promoted the idea of establishing a world "reserve currency," controlled by the global central bank, that would stabilize currencies used in international trade.

At the Bretton Woods conference, the U.S. delegation strongly objected to this method of currency stabilization. The Americans not only disliked the idea of a powerful global central bank (which might impinge on U.S. sovereignty) but also rejected the notion of adopting a reserve currency that would supercede the one already in use—the U.S. dollar. The American delegates negotiated for and got the international currency arrangement they wanted: The U.S. dollar would remain the international currency, and it would be backed by gold at a fixed rate of $35 per ounce (28 grams). (Eliminating the dollar as the global reserve currency would have certainly weakened U.S. economic power.)

Though the United States nixed the plan for an international clearing union, some of Keynes's principles were adopted by all the delegates at Bretton Woods. Among the most important and enduring outcomes of the Bretton Woods conference were the global financial institutions that were created there.

The two institutions created at Bretton Woods, the International Bank for Reconstruction and Development and the International Monetary Fund, were intended to help countries expand their economies and assist nations in economic trouble. To accomplish these goals, nations had to cede a certain amount of economic power to these institutions. The original Keynesian plan for these organizations was too radical for the United States, and though the final structure of these organizations fell short of Keynes's ideal, they were still considered radical and visionary for their time.

The Bretton Woods Institutions in the 1950s and 1960s

THE WORLD BANK

The first institution created at Bretton Woods, the International Bank for Reconstruction and Development (IBRD), is today one part of the World Bank (WB, or simply the Bank). The IBRD was founded to assist in the rebuilding of war-ravaged economies in the short term and to finance development projects in less developed nations in the longer term.

Beginning in the 1950s and accelerating in the 1960s and into the following decade, nearly all regions that had been colonized or subject to imperial rule gained their independence. Nearly without exception, industrialization had been kept out of these regions. The peoples of newly formed and independent developing nations were optimistic about the future, and many turned to the Bank for the development loans that would finance their entrée into the modern global economy.

The United States at that time was experiencing its economic golden age, a time when all sectors of the economy were booming and the American dream seemed a reality that would go on forever. The enormous productivity of U.S. industries required increasing imports of developing nations' raw materials. The United States also wanted developing nations to prosper and become potential trading partners and consumers of American products. As the strongest member of the WB, the United States encouraged the Bank to offer the most generous loans to developing nations.

The money lent by the Bank to developing countries (which must also be WB members) is provided at interest rates below those offered by commercial banks. The IBRD, the initial WB institution, was originally mandated to lend money for the building of large infrastructural projects to aid industrialization. These included high dams, power plants, roads, and airports. The underlying principle behind WB lending was that large infrastructural projects provided the foundation without which a struggling economy could not industrialize. In its first decade, WB loans funded flood-control and irrigation projects (Iraq, Lebanon); electric power projects (Uruguay, Zimbabwe, Algeria); road-building, highway, and transportation projects (Ethiopia, Pakistan, Ecuador, Ivory Coast); and general industrial development projects (Turkey, [Belgian] Congo, India).

By the mid-1950s, it became clear that the world's poorest nations were having difficulty repaying their WB loans. Developing nations put pressure on the Bank to ease the plight of these least-developed countries (LDCs). The

Bank responded, albeit reluctantly, by establishing the International Development Association (IDA), which was charged with lending money to LDCs at little or no interest.

If poor nations continued to be in financial trouble, they could turn to what was intended to be the "lender of last resort," the International Monetary Fund (IMF). Its original charter required the IMF to stabilize exchange rates and ensure the convertibility of currency in international trade. If a nation was in financial trouble, the IMF was mandated to step in with an emergency loan to prevent the country from devaluing its currency (a policy that may lead to an economic downturn). The loans carried an interest rate that was always lower than the going rate at banks. Creditor countries were expected to repay the loans in five years.

In 1968, former U.S. secretary of defense Robert S. McNamara was named head of the WB. Under McNamara's leadership, the Bank directed most of its energy toward the elimination of poverty in the world. At his side, McNamara had Hollis Chenery, a respected development economist, who helped guide the Bank in its new mission.

Development economics is concerned with finding the best ways to enhance economic development in poor nations. It is based on the idea that developing nations are fundamentally different from developed nations and therefore need different prescriptions for economic growth. For example, the laissez-faire free trade principles that might work for an advanced economy would be ruinous for a poor one. Development economics recognizes that most poor nations rely on the relatively low income they derive from commodity exports and so have unfavorable trade balances. For this reason, LDCs may not see the potential benefits of international trade as a means of economic improvement. LDCs also suffer from what development economists call the "late-late" syndrome, which means that they are so late in entering the global marketplace that they may never be able to catch up to or reasonably compete with economically developed nations. The Bank's development economists prescribed a "Big Push" for such nations, encouraging their governments to take an active role in creating a positive economic climate.[26] Foreign development aid was also deemed essential to help these faltering economies, and this is where the WB was most helpful. The Bank assisted LDC governments in creating an economic climate conducive to growth. For the most part, this new direction for the Bank was welcomed by developing nations.

THE INTERNATIONAL MONETARY FUND

Keynes's international clearing union became the IMF, which was given the responsibility of issuing short-term, low-interest loans to nations undergoing reconstruction (postwar industrialized nations) or development (less industrialized countries). The IMF was capitalized with $8.8 billion in contributions from member countries.

One problem with the IMF that became apparent to developing nations almost immediately was the calculation method used to determine the amount of money a member nation could borrow. Each nation that joins the IMF is assigned a quota according to the strength of its economy. The quota is based on the fund's own "currency," called Special Drawing Rights (SDR). Thus, because the United States had and has the largest economy in the world, it was allotted the highest IMF quota (27 billion SDR). The higher a nation's quota, the more votes it has in the IMF decision-making process and the more influence it has on how the IMF functions and whom it funds. Needless to say, the countries that need the IMF the most are those that have the lowest quotas, the least clout, and the least foreign exchange available to them.

One bone of contention between Keynes and the American delegation at Bretton Woods has had repercussions that still reverberate today. The United States had been adamant that the IMF be required to impose conditions on nations borrowing money from its fund. The conditions were intended in part to dissuade nations from viewing the IMF as a "free lunch" but also, and more significantly, to require them to reconfigure their economies in line with U.S. laissez-faire principles. Keynes had wanted the IMF to be able to lend money to any country in need, without conditions. The Americans got their way. Instead of being a benevolent lender that extends credit to those in need, which Keynes had envisioned, the IMF was charged with being an instrument of fiscal discipline, which it could—in fact, had to—impose on borrowers.

Conditionalities are strict economic policies that a nation must promise to adhere to before it can get an IMF loan. They are written into a formal agreement between the IMF and the borrowing country. They are highly specific and often set strict targets and schedules for accomplishing the IMF's demands. Some agreements even stipulate precisely what laws the nation's legislature has to pass before a loan will be paid. This practice is highly controversial because it undermines the democratic process.

The IMF sees to it that its conditionalities are implemented by dividing a loan into parts and paying out one part only after an earlier conditionality target has been met. If the conditionality has not been met, the balance of the loan may be withheld. Typical IMF conditionalities may include dictating the type and rate of taxation, reducing a government's influence on the policies of its central bank, and requiring the government to drastically curtail spending, even if the spending would generate jobs or services for citizens. These demands are also referred to as the austerity measures a country must adhere to in order to satisfy the IMF.

A developing nation or LDC must acquiesce to this treatment because of the immense power the IMF has over international lending. A nation in need of a loan must get a clean bill of health from the IMF if it has any hope of getting a loan from anywhere. All of the world's international lending agencies and banks rely on the IMF's assessment of a debtor nation's creditworthiness before they will lend it money. Thus, if a country refuses to accede to an IMF conditionality, it is, in effect "blacklisted" as a poor risk. This ensures that no other lending institution—international bank, regional bank, Western aid agency—will extend it credit.

It is true that some debtor nations whose economies are in shambles benefit from the fiscal discipline imposed by IMF conditionalities. In Latin America, for example, steep reductions in tariffs and non-tariff barriers to trade among indebted nations in this region helped them realize modest, yet measurable economic growth.[27] In Bolivia, strict adherence to IMF conditionalities lifted that nation out of years of hyperinflation. Yet right through the 1990s, the same IMF conditionalities were applied almost universally to all nations seeking its help, and they sometimes caused more problems than they solved. For this reason IMF conditionalities provide some of the most damning evidence against modern globalization. For example, though nearly everyone agrees that an educated workforce is a boon to an economy, in many cases the IMF insists that debtor governments stop funding education and instead use that money to service their debt (this is called "cost recovery"). Governments are thus required to charge fees for basic education. Few LDC citizens can afford to pay school fees, so their children remain uneducated. Similar counterproductive directives compel governments to stop funding health care clinics, transportation, and other vital services that would otherwise help, not hinder, economic growth. As a World Bank vice president recently wrote, "there is no unique universal set of rules" that apply to all countries at all times to ensure economic stability and growth."[28]

THE INTERNATIONAL TRADE ORGANIZATION AND GENERAL AGREEMENT ON TARIFFS AND TRADE

The delegates at Bretton Woods decided to postpone the establishment of an organization that would oversee international trade rules. Not until 1948 did delegates from 57 countries convene in Havana, Cuba, to establish the International Trade Organization (ITO).

Plans for the ITO were first fleshed out by the Americans and British beginning in 1943. The intent was to create an international financial organization that promoted economic growth by constraining a country's ability to limit imports through the imposition of high tariffs except in specific situations, as when it needed to correct its balance of payments. Even under dire circumstances, any import restrictions would have had to be approved by the

ITO. The founders of the ITO did not recognize, or refused to acknowledge, the inherent contradictions between the ITO and the stated principles of the Bretton Woods agreements. The Keynesian aspects of the Bretton Woods doctrines accepted government intervention in the economy when needed to generate employment, even if this sometimes entailed tariffs on imports, yet the ITO pulled in the exact opposite direction, severely curtailing a government's ability to protect the economy.

A working draft of the ITO charter was prepared in Geneva in 1947. At the same time, the delegates produced a draft of the more limited and less draconian General Agreement on Tariffs and Trade (GATT).

The original mandate of the ITO was truly radical because it made all signatories equally responsible for enforcing trade rules; this, it was believed, would keep everyone honest. No one was happy. As happened at Bretton Woods, the U.S. representatives in Havana refused to accept the ITO charter on the grounds that Congress would never ratify a treaty that allows other countries to police U.S. actions. Less developed countries, too, objected to the ITO charter, insisting that they be given more latitude to enact protectionist policies until their industrial base strengthened. Then the British added a clause that would permit import restrictions by a nation seeking to fight inflation.

All in all, it became clear during the Havana negotiations that most nations wanted more latitude to restrict imports. Despite the bickering, in March 1948, 54 nations signed the ITO charter—though none of them was pleased about it. The U.S. State Department tried to convince Congress to ratify the ITO by pointing out that it embraced "the United States philosophy of the maximum amount of competition and the minimum amount of government control."[29] Nothing, however, could convince Congress to approve the charter, and the ITO was removed from consideration. What was approved was the more limited GATT. This "second-best" trade institution, which was viewed as a "temporary" organization, has existed ever since; and in 1995, GATT morphed into the World Trade Organization (WTO).

GATT codified four main principles of trade: (1) every member would automatically be granted most-favored nation status by every other member (in other words, trade terms agreed with one country applied to all other member countries), (2) members were expected to reduce nontariff barriers to trade, such as quotas, (3) members had to report the imposition of any tariff or trade barrier; and (4) imported goods would be treated in the same way as domestic manufactures or goods. Alas, GATT had neither the clout to enforce these rules nor an authoritative dispute resolution mechanism. GATT's authority was also limited because it dealt only with trade in manufactured goods; farm products, services, and intellectual property were beyond its purview. Many developing countries viewed GATT as favoring rich nations and bridled at the unfair trade practices it promoted (such as identical treatment for rich and poor nations). Yet because of its weaknesses and the fact that it could not directly punish nations for tariffs, GATT was relatively uncontroversial.

In its infancy, GATT performed spectacularly, reducing or eliminating numerous trade barriers. In the 1930s, world trade had contracted, but in the 25 years after the adoption of GATT, global trade increased at a yearly rate of more than 7 percent. Companies based in industrialized countries began selling their products in every corner of the globe. People migrated from regions with little employment to areas where jobs went begging. Because of labor shortages workers saw their wages increase and their standard of living improve. With their higher wages, workers bought more goods, so both domestic production and trade increased.

SOUTHERN ASSERTIVENESS

Increased trade and responsive development assistance from the WB inspired a sense of optimism and newfound power in developing nations, which today are referred to as the nations of the South, in contrast to the industrialized nations of the North. In the late 1960s and early 1970s, developing nations began to organize to increase their influence in the world economic sphere. Raul Prebisch (1901–86) was an Argentine economist and writer who studied and wrote about the discrepancies in trade between rich and poor nations. His theory of "structuralism" explained how poor nations would over time be forced to export increasing quantities of raw materials to rich nations. Yet because of the low price paid for exported raw materials, poor nations would become less able to buy Northern manufactures.[30] Prebisch recognized even then that industrialized countries were developing synthetic substitutes for developing nations' raw materials (for example, synthetic rubber) and that this would only worsen LDCs' economic situation.

Inspired by the work of Prebisch and others, developing nations formed institutions that would create programs to promote economic development. The Non-Aligned Movement, the Group of 77 (G-77), and the New International Economic Order (NIEO) arose from this movement. In 1964, with their momentum building, these organizations, and particularly the G-77, helped establish the United Nations Conference on Trade and Development (UNCTAD), with Prebisch as its first secretary general. UNCTAD's programs focused on three key elements: (1) establish a floor for commodity prices, (2) encourage developed nations to import LDC manufactures with no or minimal tariffs, and (3) increase foreign investment in developing countries. These principles were also adopted by the UN Development Programme (UNDP) and UN Economic and Social Council (ECOSOC).

One of the organizations established by a group of commodity exporting nations during this period was the Organization of Petroleum Exporting Nations (OPEC). OPEC is a cartel of those nations that derive the vast majority of their revenue from exporting oil. The mainly Middle Eastern nations that established OPEC were, at that time, relatively poor, nonindustrialized countries. By cooperating to control the supply of oil, OPEC nations hoped to increase its price and therefore the revenue they derived from their one and only asset. Other poor nations that exported particular commodities (such as sugar or coffee) attempted to set up similar cartels to lift their incomes but were not successful.

Shocks to the System: The 1970s

AMERICAN BOMBSHELLS

By the early 1970s, the United States had been fighting the Vietnam War for nearly a decade. As often happens when a nation is engaged in war, deficit spending goes up as the country borrows money to pay for the conflict. Vietnam was an expensive war to wage, and America's increasing levels of borrowing and spending caused its inflation rate to soar.

It soon became impossible for the U.S. government to maintain stable prices or control the rate of inflation. U.S. economic stability was crucial for the world economy because the U.S. dollar had been designated as the world's reserve currency and the currency of international trade. At the time of the Bretton Woods conference, the United States had pledged to peg the dollar to a given value in gold ($35 per ounce). In August 1971, the Nixon administration shocked the world by announcing that it would no longer adhere to the gold standard.

The United States was so foregone in debt that creditor nations worried that the United States would not be able to pay it off. On August 15, 1971, Nixon shocked the world again: He devalued the dollar. A less valuable dollar meant that individuals, institutions, and nations that held U.S. dollars as reserve currency or that had bought U.S. debt (U.S. Treasury bills) were now owed less money in real dollar terms. Nixon then set to work to force other nations to compensate for U.S. devaluation by increasing the value of their currencies. To accomplish this, Nixon imposed a 10 percent tariff on all imports from a country until such time as it raised its currency's value. Such was American clout in international trade that despite bitter opposition, European nations eventually agreed to the abandonment of the gold standard and to increasing the value of their currencies. The new reality was officially accepted by the signatories to the Smithsonian Agreement in December 1971.

Over the next few years, European nations tried mightily to find a way to reinstate fixed exchange rates, but all their efforts failed. At the Jamaica Conference of 1976, the regime of flexible international exchange rates was finally accepted as the new economic reality. The paucity of rules for stabilizing international exchange rates would have far-reaching and often destructive effects on the international economy, introducing global speculation on the constantly shifting value of the world's many currencies.

OPEC FLEXES ITS MUSCLE

By 1973, the WB had vastly increased its funding for loans that would help it fulfill its goal of ending world poverty. An aura of cautious optimism led many poor nations to welcome the Bank's multimillion-dollar development loans. Some developing nations began to see real economic progress.

Then, in 1973, the member nations of OPEC cut their production of oil to pressure Israel (which was supported by the West) to withdraw from the territories it had recently gained during the Yom Kippur War. As the world's oil supply shrank, the price of oil shot up. Within months, oil prices more than tripled on the world market. Highly oil-dependent Western nations suffered, and in the United States, photos depicted the mile-long lines of cars waiting for gas, or the "No Gas" signs hanging on the empty pumps at deserted gas stations. The huge increase in the price of oil caused inflation to skyrocket, and the scarcity of oil, and therefore energy, reduced Western industrial productivity. A period of stagflation ensued, in which industrial productivity *stag*nated while in*flation* soared. Economists had never seen anything like it and had no idea how to fix it. OPEC's action had effectively hobbled the economies of developed nations. The oil shortage and resulting price increase brought hundreds of millions of "petrodollars" into the OPEC countries of the Middle East, making them very rich, indeed.

Stagflation persisted throughout the period from the first oil crisis in 1973 to the second oil crisis, precipitated by similar OPEC actions, in 1979. By the time the crises passed, OPEC nations were virtually awash in money. They invested their newfound wealth in Western countries and in Western nations' currencies. OPEC was the prime mover in the creation of the modern economic system, in which trade in goods, or real assets, became melded into the once separate but now unhinged international monetary system. OPEC's ocean of money was part of a new economic phenomenon called "eurodollars." Eurodollars are foreign currencies—in this case, currencies from the Middle East—that are deposited in Western or international banks. The eurodollar market is made up mostly of U.S. dollars, which means that most foreign investment is held in dollars in U.S. banks and other American financial institutions.

SOUTHERN CATASTROPHE

If the oil crises of the 1970s were hard on industrialized economies, they were devastating to the economies of developing nations. Total LDC debt doubled to $1.5 trillion by the end of the 1980s and hit $3 trillion by 1999. These nations had been deeply in debt to the WB before the oil crises and had only just begun taking their first tentative steps toward economic development. The tripling of the price of crude led to severe financial crises in poor nations, which could no longer afford to buy oil to keep their economies going. Unable to make payments on their WB loans and bereft of fuel, struggling nations went, hat-in-hand, to the IMF or to Western banks, forced to seek yet more loans to save their economies from total collapse.

Financial institutions were only too glad to oblige. Western banks had an abundance of eurodollars that they were eager to lend out at high interest. (Interest rates were high to help control inflation.) LDCs were forced to accept whatever terms the IMF or the international lending banks imposed on them. It was during this critical period that many of the world's poor countries assumed insupportable debt liabilities that would crush them and their economic hopes for decades to come.

The Neoliberal Economics of the 1980s and 1990s

The 1980s saw the rise of what were probably the most radical laissez-faire economic policies ever developed and implemented. Perhaps they arose from the tons of money international banks had on deposit and lent out at high interest. Perhaps it was the collapse of the Soviet Union (in 1989) that made the most extreme form of capitalism seem infallible. Whatever it was, beginning in the 1980s and lasting for nearly two decades, an orthodox version of classical liberal economics was championed and became the foundation of globalization policies.

In economic parlance, *liberal* means free from government interference, and liberalized trade is free trade that is unhindered by government meddling or regulation. Classical liberal economics derives from Adam Smith. Neoliberalism, which arose at the University of Chicago in the 1950s, was an attempt to revive and refine classical liberal economic principles. The economic luminaries in Chicago, including Friedrich von Hayek and Milton Friedman, formulated their neoliberal principles in reaction to what they perceived as failed Keynesian economics. For example, no amount or type of government intervention was able to whip the stagflation of the 1970s and stimulate economic growth. Hayek's work demonstrated that centrally planned economies were impossible and that government efforts at wealth distribution often led to totalitarianism. Friedman was a founder of the monetarist school of economics that held that it was interest rates and the amount of money in circulation—and not government fiscal policies—that had the greatest effect on business and the economy. The ideology that developed from these ideas came to be known as neoliberalism. Neoliberalism advocates the greatest degree of unrestricted free trade and open markets and the free flow of capital, while insisting on the most minimal government spending, regulation, taxation, and interference in the economy. As described by University of California at Berkeley Professor Brad DeLong, a staunch supporter, neoliberalism rests on two basic tenets:

> *The first is that close economic contact between the industrial core [of the capitalist world economy] and the developing periphery is the best way to accelerate the transfer of technology, which is the* sine qua non *for making poor economies rich (hence all barriers to international trade should be eliminated as fast as possible). The second is that governments in general lack the capacity to run large industrial and commercial enterprises. Hence, [except] for core missions of income distribution, public-good infrastructure, administration of justice, and a few others, governments should shrink and privatize.*[31]

The neoliberal agenda was enthusiastically embraced by both political and economic conservatives, such as U.K. prime minister Margaret Thatcher and U.S. president Ronald Reagan, who adopted this "purer" form of classical economics. Their policy of "trickle-down economics" was based on neoliberal principles.

Neoliberal economics is based on certain assumptions: (1) the only relevant actors in economic terms are self-interested individuals; (2) in economic terms, all individuals in the world are exactly alike; (3) individuals are rational optimizers, which means they make rational, conscious decisions to maximize their self-interest at the lowest cost of themselves, and (4) individuals make every rational choice based on perfect information.[32] Neoliberal economists apply similar assumptions to free markets: (1) markets operate in a rational way based on the perfect information possessed by all actors, and (2) free markets require perfect competition; therefore free market economists defend limited government interference only when it involves action against anti-trust, anti-competitive forces such as monopolies.

Critics of neoliberalism contend that to the neoliberal economist, the economy is an abstraction that does not exist in the real world, neoliberal economists use complex mathematical models that often "oversimplify economic reality and frequently [have] no social relevance."[33] They point out that the real economy is made up not only of self-interested individuals but also of communities and societies with collective interests. Individual consumers and workers do not *ever* have perfect information on which to base their often *ir*rational choices. And actors in a free market have neither perfect information nor a perfect competitive environment.

Earlier economists regarded their field as one that had to incorporate the messy, uncertain, and imperfect world humans inhabit and act in. The neoliberal economists who came to the fore in the 1980s championed the abstract science of economics and put aside its human element, including the history, structure, and values of a society and the goals and ambitions of its citizens. As one critic has stated, neoliberal economists

> *... provide neither a history of the economy nor an explanation of its evolving nature.... [W]ithout a history ... it is hardly possible to understand the dynamics of the ... economy.... [To them] the territorial distribution of economic activity is of little consequence as long as every economy is behaving according to the law of comparative advantage.*[34]

Paul Krugman (1953–), an economist at Princeton University and a newspaper columnist, has criticized neoliberal economists because, for them, "... if there is no model available to explain a particular phenomenon, that phenomenon is of little interest ... regardless of its importance for the real world."[35]

THE IMF AND NEOLIBERAL PRINCIPLES

> *The IMF was supposed to limit itself to matters of macroeconomics in dealing with a country, to the government's budget deficit, its monetary policy, its inflation, its trade deficit, its borrowing from abroad ... A half century after its founding, it is clear that the IMF has failed in its mission ... [to] provide funds for countries facing an economic downturn, to enable the country to restore itself to close to full employment.... [D]uring the last fifty years, [economic] crises around the world have been more frequent ... and deeper.... Every major emerging market that liberalized its capital market has had at least one crisis. But this is not just unfortunate bad luck. Many of the policies that the IMF pushed, in particular, premature capital market liberalization, have contributed to global instability."*[36]

As the above quote makes clear, the IMF's original mandate was to help nations in the throes of an economic crisis resolve their macroeconomic problems, such as off-kilter balance of payments, by providing short-term loans. Macroeconomics has to do with the overall economy and its major sectors, such as employment, inflation, total economic output, monetary policy, and so on. (Microeconomics deals with smaller, individual parts of an economy, such as businesses, labor unions, households, etc.) As the debt crisis of the 1970s deepened, the IMF began making longer-term loans to poor nations and became far more involved in policies related to economic development, though that is not its strong suit, than to economic crisis relief.

IMF policies are based on neoliberal economics, or, as Nobel Prize–winning economist Joseph Stiglitz (1943–) calls it, "market fundamentalism."[37] The IMF's philosophy rests on the following concepts: (1) inflation is the most serious of economic ills; it is always and in every case bad, and must be corrected first, no matter what other conditions prevail or what the consequences; (2) the short-term effects of fighting inflation are immaterial, as what counts is the long-term result; and (3) all countries are alike and therefore will benefit from the application of the same economic prescription. The universal application of neoliberal economic policies will, the IMF believes, always be just what an ailing economy needs to get back on its feet. In some cases, the IMF's neoliberal prescriptions have effectively cured sick economies. In other cases, its one-size-fits-all approach has had less salutary effects.

CONDITIONALITIES

The Washington Consensus

Another important set of principles adopted by the IMF was formulated by economists at the WB, the U.S. Department of the Treasury, and the IMF itself. The principles were set down by economist John Williamson (1937–), who coined the phrase *Washington Consensus* because these principles reflected the agreed-upon neoliberal ideas that dominated Washington, D.C., during the 1980s and 1990s. Williamson first set forth these policies in a 1990 paper entitled, "Latin American Adjustment: How Much Has Happened?", in which he recommended these policies for developing nations seeking to reform and grow their economies. In that paper, Williamson listed the 10 policies that he interpreted as reflecting the economic orthodoxy of the U.S. capital at that time. They were: (1) fiscal discipline; (2) redirecting public expenditures toward areas that would yield high economic returns and had the potential for redistributing wealth; (3) tax reform; (4) liberalization of interest rates; (5) adopting a single, competitive exchange rate; (6) liberalization of trade; (7) liberalization of inflows of foreign direct investment; (8) privatization; (9) deregulation; and (10) securing property rights.[38]

The Washington Consensus arose from a major fiscal crisis in Mexico brought on by the oil crises of the 1970s. Lack of money to pay for oil led Mexico into insupportable debt, and in 1982, it informed the U.S. government that it could no longer make debt payments. U.S. officials wanted above all to protect U.S. banks against the huge losses they would suffer if Mexico defaulted, so short-term loans were provided to Mexico, and the IMF was charged with repairing the economic damage. When Mexico's problem was not resolved, it became clear to Washington economists that they had misdiagnosed the problem and prescribed the wrong medicine. Mexico's problem was not a short-term lack of ready cash but a lack of revenue due to basic structural problems in the Mexican economy.

The Washington Consensus was quickly adopted as the economic model for developing countries. One reason for its instant popularity was that the Washington Consensus arrived at a time when the central planning of the economy by national governments had been widely discredited. For this reason, it filled the urgent need for an economic policy framework. As economist Moises Naim explained, "The debt crisis of the 1980s . . . made it impossible for governments to sustain economic policies that were not anchored in sound macroeconomic policies or that were based on an adversarial posture toward foreign investment."[39]

Based on their experience in Mexico and bolstered by their conviction that economic prescriptions have universal application, the economists in Washington determined that economic structural adjustments would be at the heart of literally all IMF attempts to save economies in crisis. In 1985, structural adjustments were enshrined in the Baker Plan, named after Secretary of the Treasury James Baker. Structural Adjustment Programs (SAPs), which are at the core of the Washington Consensus, demand free markets, trade liberalization, and a greatly diminished role for government in debtor nations. SAPs also require that debtor governments maintain an anti-inflation monetary policy, cut spending to balance the budget, liberalize trade, and increase exports to improve foreign exchange (even if this means reducing domestic food production to feed the population). These demands are made of every poor country needing assistance, regardless of its history, social conditions, or economic situation. The results were, to say the least, mixed.

Privatization

A poor debtor country is required to direct all its energy and resources toward restructuring its economy and paying its debt. For this reason, the IMF often prohibits government expenditures on anything other than programs that bring in revenue, such as maximizing income-producing exports. Therefore, IMF conditionalities almost always insist on the privatization of what had been government services. Privatization is the sale of government-run services or industries to private, for-profit corporations or businesses.

Proponents of privatization point out that too often an LDC's or developing country's government is spending too much money on the wrong things (for example, palaces for the president, roads to nowhere) or is wildly inefficient at the things it lavishes its money on (often arising from government corruption). Further, governments are notoriously inefficient at running state-owned enterprises (SOEs), owing to corruption or, absent that, lack of competition (i.e., monopoly). In quite a few cases, the privatization of government-run services and industries has been very beneficial. One study showed that of 41 companies privatized in 15 countries (including Jamaica, Chile, and Singapore), all firms realized increases in sales, profits, efficiency, and capital expenditures. Some of these companies even expanded their workforce somewhat. When the Chilean phone company was privatized, it doubled its capacity a mere four years after the sale.[40] Other studies conducted in Latin America yield similar results. In a majority of nations studied, more than half had had SOEs that were highly unprofitable prior to privatization. Profits more than doubled in many of these firms after privatization.[41]

One serious drawback to privatization is that it almost always results in job losses. Again, Latin American nations are typical. Studies have shown that privatization of SOEs in Colombia, Mexico, and Peru resulted in workforce reductions of 24, 57, and 56 percent, respectively. Though some have interpreted these data as indicating that these nations have a "bloated" workforce, the studies show that most displaced workers reported income losses of between 39 and 51 percent compared to their pre-privatization incomes; only 40 percent of laid-off workers said they were not worse off after privatization.

Dislocations from privatization might be ameliorated by ensuring that privatization is, in fact, necessary. Immediately selling off all or most government services to the private sector is not always necessary, nor is it always beneficial. If a nation has a poor or absent regulatory structure, privatization may not be the way to go. Attempts at reorganizing the government, weeding out corruption, and implementing guidelines to ensure its greater efficiency or overseeing its domestic development programs may work just as well. This approach would also largely avoid the economic disruption that follows extensive layoffs.

One of the goals of privatization is improved efficiency, and greater efficiency may be realized when a private concern takes over a service previously run by the government. However, when governments privatize their services—such as water, energy, transportation, education, and health care—by selling them to foreign corporations, efficiency is often achieved through job cuts. With no social safety net of any kind (even short-term unemployment insurance), the masses of unemployed people may tip the country into a condition of social instability, with riots or criminality becoming more common.

Although in theory privatization may lead to greater efficiency through competition, in many cases the debtor nation lacks the infrastructure and regulations needed to ensure the smooth operation of privately run services.

In impoverished countries where few people have the resources to start businesses, competition almost never evolves. If a corporation does buy the service provision business, the lack of competition and absence of regulation often lead to its becoming a monopoly. Uncontrolled power may lead a monopoly to become corrupt, setting prices artificially high and squelching competition. Corruption is so rampant among some privatized companies in developing countries that privatization is sometimes laughingly referred to as "briberization."[42] Corrupt firms often pay kickbacks to (equally corrupt) politicians to retain their monopoly, or the politicians sell the service to a private company for far less than it's worth and then pocket the difference. And once a private firm has secured a monopoly on a service, it often disregards its mandate to achieve efficiency. Liberalized trade and investment rules also ensure that it need not be accountable to the citizens it is supposedly serving. For the new capitalists in Russia, for example, privatization is seen as an opportunity for stripping assets.[43]

When vital services are privatized, they are also often priced out of the reach of poor citizens. For example, water systems have often been privatized in LDCs at the command of the IMF, leaving poor people who cannot afford to buy it without the water they need to survive. Furthermore, if a service is deemed economically not viable, it will be discontinued even if it is seen as essential by the citizens. The IMF may even demand that a government stop providing a service when there are no private enterprises ready or willing to step in and take up the slack. Then citizens are simply left without needed services.

In general, privatization is less painful and wrenching if the service is taken over by a domestic company rather than a foreign corporation. A domestic company knows the culture in which it is operating and understands local problems. Managers of a domestic firm are less likely to fire workers because they understand the desperate situation in which unemployment leaves workers and their families. Foreign corporations, on the other hand, are ignorant of local conditions and customs and often have no compunction about large-scale layoffs to improve efficiency and profits.

Privatization also entails selling off key state-run industries, and this can have real economic benefits. Quite often, state-run industries are wildly inefficient, and for-profit control increases efficiency enormously. Selling off a state-run industry also raises ready cash that a debtor nation can use to service its debt. Yet, as with the privatization of services, the privatization of industry often results in higher unemployment as workers are laid off. And privatized industries are at least, if not more, corrupt than privatized services. Again, as with privatization of services, the IMF too often shuts down a government-run enterprise before a for-profit company is available to undertake the business. Then the industry simply disappears, and the people who rely on it are out of luck. Stiglitz recounts how Moroccan villagers were left without chickens—a dietary staple—when the IMF ordered the government to cease selling the fowl, even though no private poultry concern was ready or able to step in and take over the enterprise. According to Stiglitz, the IMF simply "assumed" that once a government enterprise was shut down, private enterprise would immediately fill the gap.[44]

In some cases, multinational corporations (MNCs) will invest in a developing country by taking over a state-run industry closed down by the IMF. Though MNC investment can be, and sometimes is, a boon to a growing economy, too often the benefits that accrue from the industrial operation go largely to the corporation, its shareholders, and its home country. The LDC may realize little benefit from the MNC investment.

The Interest Rate Dilemma

Stiglitz believes that privatization can help struggling economies if it is done in a reasonable way: "Privatization needs to be part of a more comprehensive program, which entails creating jobs *in tandem* with the inevitable job destruction that privatization often entails. Macroeconomic policies, including low interest rates, that help create jobs, have to be put in place. Timing (and sequencing) is everything."[45] The IMF, however, insists that a debtor nation keep interest rates high (in some cases, as high as 20, 50, or even 100 percent).[46] because high interest rates help reduce inflation. Yet high interest rates discourage capital investment and make it more difficult for domestic investors to borrow money to buy a privatized business or to open their own business. It is, rather, low interest rates that stimulate business growth and increase employment. With lack of capital stifling domestic entrepreneurship and the padlocking of "inefficient" industries increasing unemployment, the IMF's austerity measures may tie the hands of the government and prevent it from taking necessary steps to stimulate the economy.

In sum, though privatization has had beneficial effects in some cases, it should not be pursued without government oversight and input. Each nation is different, and government should steer privatization toward the most needed sectors, ensure that it is nonmonopolistic and affordable to all, make sure that it is regulated properly, and ease the pain of job losses. "Experience shows that it is possible for regulation to focus less on control than on ensuring access to bottleneck facilities and encouraging competition and entry, in turn encouraging innovation."[47]

Market Liberalization

There are two types of liberalization that are part of the IMF's conditionalities. One is the liberalization of trade, in which a nation opens its market to imports, increases its exports, and generally reduces or eliminates tariffs.

The second type of liberalization refers to capital, or financial, markets. In an open capital market, a debtor nation is required to rescind regulations that control the flow of currency into and out of the country.

Trade Liberalization

Trade liberalization has the potential for engendering real economic growth by increasing a nation's participation in global trade and by withdrawing resources from inefficient enterprises and investing them in a sector where the country has a comparative advantage, thus increasing productivity. Opening markets also exposes a nation's domestic industries to competition from abroad, and this may compel them to become more efficient. Noted economist Douglas A. Irwin (1962–) describes how imports into Chile in the 1970s resulted in efficiency increases in competing domestic industries of between 3 and 10 percent. Industries not challenged by imports showed no productivity increase.[48]

Trade liberalization is expected to have several beneficial effects. First, it encourages a nation to concentrate its resources on those sectors in which it has a comparative advantage. Second, it opens the nation's businesses to competition, which improves productivity and efficiency. Third, it attracts investment that should aid economic development and growth.

Supporters of liberalized trade—or an outward orientation of national economies—foresee additional benefits. These include economies of scale, as local industries achieve greater productivity and efficiency; the decline in monopolies, owing to greater competition from abroad; and government policies that are geared toward nurturing important sectors and toward maintaining the macroeconomic stability necessary for optimal industrial performance. The benefits of an outward-oriented economic policy become apparent when India and East Asia are compared. From the 1960s to the 1980s, East Asian nations adopted a free trade, outward orientation, while India turned inward to protect its industries. East Asia experienced the "miracle" of extraordinary economic growth and wealth, while India during this period stagnated.[49]

Irwin provides several examples of how trade liberalization improved the economies of developing nations. Between the early 1960s and 1999, per capita GDP increased ninefold in South Korea and threefold in Chile.[50] Other studies have used mathematical models to project the gains from trade liberalization to be between $254 billion and $2.1 trillion per year, with about 43 percent of these gains going to "low-income" countries.[51]

However, although more liberalized trade has yielded benefits—in some cases (China, India) spectacular benefits—critics point out that Irwin confines his examples of successes to "second tier" developing nations that entered the free trade fray with some advantages, such as an educated workforce or even rudimentary infrastructure and institutions that encouraged the limited industrialization they had already undergone. Similarly, the studies that delineate the benefits that should accrue to "low-income" countries do not elaborate on just how low income these beneficiaries are. Too often, the lion's share of the benefits of free trade are channeled to second-tier nations and not to the poorest nations (LDCs) that are in the greatest need of economic development.[52]

Trade liberalization is intended to enhance a poor nation's use of its inherent comparative advantage by transferring resources to high-productivity, high-efficiency sectors. Yet unchecked trade liberalization may increase an LDC's rate of trade while decreasing its overall revenue from trade and its gross domestic product (GDP). This happens because most LDCs export low-price commodities almost exclusively and import higher-priced manufactured goods from more developed nations. This leaves them with a negative balance of payments. Using the IMF's own evaluation, LDC commodity exports increased 43 percent between 1986 and 1999. During that same period, the total value of these exported commodities increased by only 26 percent, indicating a significant reduction in value per unit of exports.[53] Thus, when trade liberalization is imposed on very poor nations, it does not necessarily provide the expected income; nor does it necessarily help the debtor nation repay its debt. In fact, it may have the opposite effect, digging the hole of debt even deeper. Finally, according to a 2002 UNCTAD report, the devaluation of exports discourages foreign investment and overall economic growth:

> *A global policy shift in the developing world toward greater outward orientation may depress the price of agricultural commodities and hence worsen the terms of trade of developing countries . . . the indirect effect [of this] . . . could be of considerable significance and may entirely offset the expected gains from trade liberalisation. . . . Evidence for SAL [structural adjustment lending] programmes indicates that . . . countries with SALs do not succeed in raising their growth rates or investment rates . . . Because of this, we should not be too surprised if the gains from global liberalisation are disappointing in many low-income countries.*[54]

There are still far too many nations that have opened their markets yet remain impoverished. Yet, it also may be true that "there are no examples of countries that have risen in the ranks of global living standards while being less open to trade and capital in the 1990s than in the 1960s."[55]

Capital Market Liberalization

The capital, or financial, market is the global trade in currencies. Seeking profit from the buying and selling of currencies took off in 1971 after President Richard Nixon abandoned the gold standard, initiating the era of flexible exchange rates. Before the East Asian financial crisis in 1997–98, freeing up capital markets was seen as necessary for poor nations in order to attract foreign direct investment (FDI). Another justification for capital market liberalization was that a nation in financial trouble would be able to call on diverse sources of currency to see it through a bad patch, and this would tend to create overall financial stability. Other benefits that were supposed to result from financial liberalization included increased deposits in domestic banks, greater access to foreign credit, increases in the value of domestic bonds and equities, greater FDI in domestic industries, greater competitive advantage with foreign banks, and improvements in banking and stock market regulations.[56]

Financial liberalization in the 1990s "went far beyond the interest rate liberalization that had been recommended by the so-called Washington Consensus. To varying degrees, governments also allowed the use of foreign currency instruments and opened up capital accounts . . . international markets expanded in government and private bonds."[57] However, national governments lacking the needed financial infrastructure and controls were often extremely vulnerable. In one economist's view, ". . . opening an economy to international capital flows will be welfare and efficiency enhancing only if this step is preceded by the installation of essential preconditions: trade openness and stable macroeconomic policies, rigorous prudential supervision and regulation of financial institutions and markets, and effective corporate governance. Moreover, . . . [v]olatile short-term portfolio flows can interact with preexisting distortions to heighten financial fragility. . . . Countries on the receiving end of short-term inflows can suffer from too much of a good thing. . . ."[58]

As the East Asian crisis has shown, this policy involves serious risks. To accomplish capital market liberalization, a debtor nation is pressured to undo financial regulations implemented by its central bank that were intended to stabilize the national currency and its flow. With few or no controls on its currency, a developing nation may attract short-term currency speculation. "Hot money," speculative investments made on conjectures about how a nation's exchange rate will change, moves into and out of developing nations at electronic speed. Speculative capital investments cannot be used to build an industry or create jobs. They are used by investors solely to make a quick buck by betting on how a currency's value will change. Once the investors make their money, they pull out their capital and buy into the next currency likely to yield a short-term profit.

There are many serious consequences resulting from this type of speculation. For one thing, a poor nation that sees a huge influx of investment in its currency is advised to set aside as reserves an amount equal to the investment. This takes money that might be used for real economic development out of circulation, thus hindering economic growth. Second, as Stiglitz points out, capital liberalization will make foreign investors less likely, not more likely, to aid nations in financial trouble. If a poor nation's currency is "in play" and unstable because of currency speculation, foreign investors will consider it too great a risk and will not rescue it by plowing in their own money. This makes the nation's economic situation even worse.[59]

SEQUENCE AND PACING

One of the main criticisms of the IMF's approach addresses the timing and the sequence in which its policies are enacted in debtor nations. IMF policies would likely be far more beneficial to a struggling economy if they were implemented more carefully. In cases in which inflation must be controlled or comparative advantage exploited via private enterprise, appropriate corrective measures should be applied at the correct time and in the correct order.

Critics of the IMF approach say that before a country is forced to face high unemployment from privatization and trade liberalization, it should first put in place a well-functioning mechanism for creating jobs, as well as some type of social safety net to help the jobless. Similarly, a nation that is undergoing privatization should first get help with establishing the legal framework that will regulate the privatized industry to make sure it fulfills its function and to ensure competition. Too often, the IMF demands that its policies be instituted all at once and before any supportive or mitigating institutions or frameworks are established.

TRANSITIONAL ECONOMIES

A transitional economy is one that is undergoing a change from a communist command economy to a capitalist market economy. Russia typifies a transitional economy.

When Russia and other former communist nations abandoned communism, the IMF and other international financial institutions, particularly the U.S. Treasury, imposed a dose of "shock therapy" to hasten the economic transition. Little attention was paid to sequence and timing or to establishing the economic infrastructure required to support the new economic system. The free for all that resulted led to widespread criminality and corruption. It brought immense wealth to a few and intense misery to most Russians.

Even the conservative Strobe Talbott quipped on a trip to Russia in 1993 that "What Russia needs is less shock and more therapy." Though his remark was greatly appreciated by his hosts, it aroused the ire of the neoliberal architects of Russia's reforms in Washington.

THE IMF TODAY: CRISIS OF CONFIDENCE

The East Asian financial crisis of 1997–98 affected currencies, stock markets, and other asset prices in several Asian countries—especially Thailand,

Malaysia, Indonesia, the Philippines, and South Korea—and caused a global economic downturn. The crisis was a sobering wake-up call to lending institutions, particularly the IMF, and called into serious question the principles of neoliberal economics. The crisis underlines the "contagion" that is inherent in uncontrolled globalization.

Most developing countries of East Asia had followed IMF prescriptions and, as a result, had among the most open economies in the developing world. When their economies hit the skids, the IMF's entire approach became suspect. Capital liberalization was widely discredited, and the IMF—whose policies many blamed for the disaster—lost much of its prestige and influence as an architect of economic growth. Developing nations in Asia and elsewhere forswore their allegiance to the IMF and began to formulate their own policies for economic growth based on a greater role for government.

The IMF began to rethink and reappraise its policies. Since its formation in 1947, the IMF could point to "only a handful of successes, among them the very questionable case of Pinochet's Chile."[60] Of the numerous other debtor nations in thrall to the IMF, "77 percent saw their per capita rate of growth fall significantly," according to the Center for Economic and Policy Research. Even some of its supporters in the United States now "denounced the Fund for ... [its] irresponsible lending."[61] Stunned, the IMF's managing director, Rodrigo de Rato, initiated an internal "strategic review" of IMF policies. In September 2005, the final report was released. Many interested parties found it disappointing. To sum up the Bretton Woods Project's summary and evaluation of the report's contents, it

> *[fails to] "meet the challenges of globalisation" ... [and instead] states bluntly that "globalisation is a reality for countries to come to grips with." ... Largely missing from the discussion is the need for greater attention to the role played by the policies and institutions [that] ... trigger financial crises. ... More worrying is the description of capital account liberalisation as "a reality, a part of globalisation." ... The review fails to address debates over the degree of [conditionality] of IMF funds ... or, most importantly, the urgent need for the Fund to respond to calls from civil society ... for greater macroeconomic flexibility in its policy advice.*[62]

According to its critics, the report failed to address the most pressing issues arising from the IMF's involvement in the East Asian crisis. Calls for "more study" were inevitably made, but few or no guidelines for substantive change capable of being put into action were proposed.

The degree to which the IMF has or has not altered its rigid approach is illustrated in the controversy over its alleged role in the famine in Niger in 2005. Medical staff with Doctors Without Borders who were working there during the famine reported that the IMF and the European Union (EU) pressured the Niger government not to release food to its starving citizens. According to a news report in *The Observer,* "The Niger government under instruction from the IMF and EU, at first refused to distribute free food to those most in need," stating that "the powers that be did not want to depress the market prices that benefited wholesalers and speculators." The IMF's African department director vehemently denied the accusations, as did IMF officials in Washington, D.C. Yet such is the reputation of the IMF, with its stringent economic policies and lack of regard for the people affected by them, that this story is deemed by many to be wholly believable, even if it is not true.[63]

The East Asian and other financial crises have perhaps irreparably tarnished the IMF's reputation (Milton Friedman called for the IMF to be abolished). Since 1998, the IMF has undertaken a certain degree of soul-searching. Remarkably, though a few voices within the organization call for some policy overhauls, more prominent ones have insisted that the IMF failed, not because its reforms were too stringent but because they were only "skin deep" and did not go far enough due to "reform fatigue." In a speech, acting managing director of the IMF Anne Krueger quotes a neoliberal economist to describe her feelings about the IMF's performance. "The policies that have been undertaken are not even a pale imitation of what market economics ought to be . . . What has been implemented . . . is a grotesque caricature of market economics."[64] Similar views were expressed in a 2005 IMF report: ". . . reforms were uneven and remained incomplete. More progress was made with measures that had low up-front costs, such as privatization, relative to reforms that promised greater long-term benefits, such as improving macroeconomic . . . systems."[65]

Many other economists and analysts see the problem as residing with the IMF itself and with the Washington Consensus that underpins its policies. "In retrospect, it is clear that in the 1990s we often mistook efficiency gains for growth. The 'one-size-fits-all' policy reform approach to economic growth . . . exaggerated the gains from improved resource allocation and their dynamic repercussions, and proved to be both theoretically incomplete and contradicted by the evidence. Expectations that gains in growth would be won entirely through policy improvements were unrealistic. . . . Another mistake in the 1990s has been the translation of general policy principles into a unique set of actions. . . . 'macroeconomic stability; domestic liberalization, and openness' have been interpreted narrowly to mean 'minimize fiscal deficits, minimize inflation, minimize tariffs, maximize privatization, maximize liberalization of finance' with the assumption that the more of these changes the better, at all times and in all places. . . ."[66]

Finally, the Washington Consensus is itself being reformed, as "the term became a lightning rod for those disenchanted with globalization and neoliberalism or with the perceived diktats of the U.S. Treasury."[67] It has also been tarnished by its association with the IMF. John Williamson, who has gained unwanted notoriety for a list of policy reforms that he never anticipated would be hijacked by neoliberals and made the foundations of global liberalization, is working on a revision of his original document. "Williamson is now promoting a revised blueprint that he hopes will leave behind the 'stale ideological rhetoric of the 1990s.' What is his new agenda called? Anything but 'Washington Consensus II,' he suggests."[68]

Foreign Direct Investment and Multinational Corporations

Though not directly associated with the IMF, foreign direct investment (FDI), primarily carried out by multinational corporations (MNCs), is partly an outgrowth of the IMF's push for privatization. FDI is the buying of existing businesses or the creation of new business facilities (called greenfield investments) by a company in a nation other than its home country. Through FDI, a corporation takes control of the production and marketing of goods in another economy. FDI may occur in the overseas nation's manufacturing, services, or commodities sector. MNCs are companies based in one nation that partially or wholly own subsidiaries in one or more foreign countries.

FDI has exploded in recent decades, with 64,000 MNCs having created 53 million jobs in various countries around the world. Yet its positive impact on economic growth in LDCs has been limited. This is due in large part to the reluctance of MNCs to invest in impoverished nations. More than 74 percent of total FDI goes to the FDI top-ten nations (among them China, India, the United States, Thailand, Malaysia, and South Korea). Only 0.05 percent of total FDI finds its way to LDCs.[69]

In some cases, particularly in developing nations such as Malaysia, FDI has played a very positive role in economic growth. Studies from Asia show that FDI has created jobs and lifted workers out of poverty. However, the same studies show that FDI does not address income inequality in developing countries, mainly due to disparities in education and skill in the workforce. MNCs tend to employ more skilled workers, who are better paid than unskilled workers. This disparity creates a deepening rift of inequality between skilled and unskilled labor in the society.

A study by the International Finance Corporation concluded that FDI's impact on economic development was closely related to the sector in which the investments are made. For example, FDI in infrastructure has a strong positive impact on a nation's economy, as infrastructure is a necessary prerequisite for growth. Labor-intensive FDI, such as factories, has a more mixed track record. Though this type of FDI does put more people to work, the employees tend to be mainly women, female teenagers, and children, who are often paid considerably less than male workers (many of whom remain unemployed).[70] Child labor is, of course, an international scandal, though it continues unabated in an untold number of FDI plants around the world. The extremely low wages (often less than $1 a day) and harsh working conditions, have also made FDI "sweatshops" an international issue. In some FDI factories, employees work six or even seven days a week, 12 to 18 or more hours a day, and retire to wholly inadequate and overcrowded dormitory-like living quarters. Water and sanitation are frequently substandard or limited, and health care, totally absent. In many FDI facilities, workers are prohibited from organizing to demand better wages and working conditions, and this, too, has become an international issue of concern.

Export processing zones (EPZs), also called free trade zones, often have the worst working conditions in the developing world. EPZs are areas, usually near a port, that are set aside for MNC factories built for the production or, most often, the assembly of goods. EPZs attract FDI by granting special concessions, such as low or zero taxes on the land and on profits, the elimination of tariffs or trade barriers, limited or no controls on the movement of goods and capital into and out of the EPZ, and ease of moving money out of the host country. EPZs are often treated by the host country as if they were on foreign soil, so few regulations or conditions can be applied to them. EPZ host countries often vie with one another to grant the most liberal concessions in order to attract foreign investment. This is yet another example of the "race to the bottom" that globalization often sets in motion.

Workers in EPZs are sometimes locked into their factories and are generally paid less than workers in non-EPZ FDI plants. Studies have shown that although EPZs have increased employment in developing countries, adding about 27 million jobs worldwide, they generally do not generate significant income or economic improvement for the host country, from which they often maintain a strict economic separation.[71]

A recent conflict between China and some of its major FDI corporations underscores the imbalance in the benefits of FDI and belies the argument that FDI generates equal benefits for both the corporation and its overseas workers. In October 2006, the Chinese government announced a plan to enact a new law that would help abolish sweatshops and greatly empower labor unions to organize EPZ workers and engage in collective bargaining for a living wage, better safety conditions on the job, and policies regarding work hours, health, leave, and other benefits. The corporate reaction was predictable. Foreign corporations—including Dell, Ford Motor Company, General Electric, Microsoft, and Nike—began an intensive lobbying effort to get the

Chinese government to abandon its plan. When China did not fold, the firms insisted that they would close up shop in China and move their factories elsewhere, where wages were low and unions were outlawed or powerless. As one labor organizer acutely noted, the corporate threats "fl[y] in the face of the idea that globalization and corporations will raise standards around the world."[72]

Another notable drawback to FDI is its destruction of domestic competition. A host nation should be able to deny entry to an MNC unless it already has mature companies that can withstand the competition. Otherwise, the power and economies of scale available to the MNC will overwhelm existing domestic companies and/or prevent similar domestic enterprises from emerging. The process has been likened to what happens to "mom and pop" stores in the United States when Wal-Mart sets up shop in a community. Small, local businesses just cannot compete with a giant corporation, so they shut down.

In 2005, the World Bank issued a report on how FDI could be expanded and improved. The report reveals the influence of Western corporations and governments on the Bank and their interest in promoting FDI. Essentially, the report recommended that developing nations accept single, uniform, and worldwide standards for FDI, which would eliminate intervention or oversight by the host country—all in the name of creating a "favorable climate for investment." The "harmonized" standards would facilitate the movement of MNCs from country to country without the burden of adjusting to each nation's requirements. The codified standards would ensure the passivity and powerlessness of host countries and continue the trend toward the "lowest common denominator" in labor and environmental standards, across the board.[73]

The WB report flies in the face of on-the-ground studies that show that for FDI to truly promote economic growth, the host nation must be more, not less, involved in its regulation. According to Stiglitz and others, nations differ from one another culturally and economically and so have different needs. Thus, more, not less, flexibility should be available to governments to see that FDI fulfills its economic promise:

> *FDI may have uneven effects on development. Effects are determined to a large extent by the conditions prevailing in host countries, by the investment strategies of [MNCs], and by the policies of host governments . . . [Host nations] should retain a role in influencing the benefits that their economies gain from inward FDI.*[74]

By concentrating FDI in infrastructure and in labor-intensive industries that have adequate labor and child-labor standards, a host nation can benefit hugely from foreign investment. But it is the nation itself that must guide FDI in order to realize these benefits. Overall, more, not less, government oversight is needed to make FDI an engine of growth in developing nations.

THE WORLD BANK

In 1981, Robert McNamara was replaced as head of the WB by Alden Winship Clausen, a man more amenable to the neoliberal theories dominant at that time. The Bank continued to fund some infrastructural projects, but for the next two decades, it embarked on a program of providing mainly structural adjustment loans, with IMF approval. These loans came with their own WB conditionalities. Yet, as Columbia University professor of economics Jagdish Bhagwati (1934–) points out, "[T]he World Bank (not the IMF) is judged mainly by how much it spends. If the World Bank ends the year without lending for development, it is a failure. That creates a dilemma: if the Bank holds up spending because conditionality is not accepted or complied with, then it fails to spend; if it spends without adequate compliance, then it fails to enforce conditionality."[75] For this reason, the WB often compromises or cuts deals with its debtor nations to ease the pain of conditionalities.

Overall, the WB has a slightly better reputation than the IMF, although some of its projects (for example, the funding of high dams) are very controversial. Yet, even during the heyday of neoliberalism, the Bank emphasized and encouraged debtor-nation participation in decision making far more than did the IMF. The Bank also maintained a resident staff in the host country and so had a better handle on its social, political, and economic history and conditions, as well as the aspirations of the people it was trying to help. In contrast, the IMF had no resident staff, few local contacts, and little or no experience or knowledge of the loan-seeking nation.

In 1986, a WB report revealed that "Despite the difficult economic environment, 85 percent of all projects reviewed . . . were characterized as having achieved satisfactory results."[76] Only three years later, and after it had assumed its IMF-like role of providing mainly SAP loans, the WB acknowledged that, of 37 SAPs granted in Africa, only two (Ghana and Tanzania) were considered successful.[77]

The WB has tried to maintain more open lines of communication with host nations than has the IMF. Where the IMF banned debtor-nation officials from policy meetings that would determine their nation's future, the WB encouraged such participation. In general, the WB has shown greater respect for democratic institutions than the IMF and its externally imposed conditionalities.

THE WORLD TRADE ORGANIZATION

GATT seemed to work quite well as a framework for international trade during its first decades of existence, yet it had its flaws, including lack of authority or enforcement power and being limited to manufactured goods. Member nations recognized GATT's weaknesses and so began a series of periodic conferences, called rounds, to flesh out the structure of a new trade organization that would cover the entire range of traded goods and have dispute settlement and enforcement powers.

Principles and Structure

The World Trade Organization (WTO) officially came into existence on January 1, 1995, and it was created to promote the following principles of free trade:

- Free trade should be nondiscriminatory.
- Both tariff and nontariff trade barriers should be eliminated.
- Competition should be encouraged as a benefit to free trade.
- Free trade rules should be flexible and preferential to developing nations.

WTO decision making ostensibly occurs on a consensus basis, with all member nations having an equal part (one country, one vote) in determining WTO policy. In practice, however, most decisions are made via negotiation among a small group of developed nations. Developing countries, which are most often not invited to these discussions, have criticized this method of making decisions that often affect all members. Even during the worldwide ministerial meetings of all members, the most important decisions are made by the representatives of the developed countries, who meet behind closed doors. At several meetings, representatives of LDCs, particularly from Africa, were pointedly and repeatedly barred from meetings that were supposed to be open to all. Organizations representing developing nations and LDCs are becoming more vocal and more active in their opposition to these closed-door enclaves.

For these and other reasons, since its inception, the WTO has been viewed as an organization run for and by corporate interests in rich developed nations and as a rule-making body inimical to and destructive of the democratic process. Most of the controversies that plague the WTO have arisen in response to aspects of the different agreements in its original 26,000-page charter. The most controversial and divisive agreements, which threaten the very existence of the WTO, are discussed briefly below.

THE AGREEMENT ON AGRICULTURE

The Agreement on Agriculture (AoA) has among its mandates the regulation of agricultural subsidies. Some subsidies are permitted: Under the Uruguay Round, the United States and the EU were entitled to spend $380 billion annually on agricultural subsidies. AoA changes, engineered by the United States in 2004, have vastly expanded "acceptable" agricultural subsidies. In 2001–02, the EU and United States paid out a total of $1.6 trillion in agricultural subsidies.[78]

It is clear that the AoA permits developed nations to continue to subsidize agriculture, even though developing countries, not to mention LDCs, can in no way compete with such subsidies. Farmers in developing countries must somehow make a living trying to sell their produce at cost plus a small profit. Yet this becomes impossible because subsidies allow agricultural companies in the developed world to sell their produce for less than the cost of production.

In the EU, subsidies on "wheat, powdered milk, and sugar are fixed at 34 percent, 50 percent, and 75 percent, respectively, of their production costs." In 2002, the UN Food and Agriculture Organization (FAO) reported that "136 percent of the international price for butter" was paid as a subsidy by the EU.[79] In that same year, U.S. subsidies on cotton constituted 65 percent of the export price: The total cost of cotton production in 2002 (including shipping and other costs) was $1.068 per pound. Yet because of the massive subsidy given cotton growers, that pound of cotton was sold on the export market for only $0.37. Similar discrepancies between production costs and export price exist for numerous agricultural products coming from the EU and United States.[80]

To put these numbers in perspective, if it costs an LDC farmer 50 cents to grow one pound of a crop, but subsidies allow the farmers of the developed world to sell that crop for 35 cents a pound, there is no way the LDC farmer can compete or earn a livelihood. The skewed commodity market has a terrible impact on LDCs in general because they are so highly dependent on commodity exports to generate revenue. Thus, LDCs may get poorer even as they increase their exports.

The decline in commodity prices has had an enormous negative impact on developing countries and LDCs. Between 1990 and 1993, poor commodity exporting nations lost $2.25 billion in foreign exchange due to dumping of subsidized agricultural commodities; that figure rose to $2.4 billion in 1998–99.[81]

Developed nations do not always get their way in agricultural disputes at the WTO. In March 2005, the Appellate Body of the WTO (part of the Dispute Resolution Body, or DSB) ruled against the United States, stating that parts of its cotton subsidies were illegal under AoA rules because U.S. cotton exporters were selling their cotton on the world market for 47 percent below the cost of production.[82] The ruling is unlikely to have a significant impact on U.S. dumping of cotton on the world market; the United States will simply pay the imposed fine of $100 million or more per year and continue to do as it pleases. Protecting the interests of its agricultural sector is of far more importance to a developed nation than a few hundred million dollars in fines. Of course, fines of this magnitude would wreck an LDC's economy, so an impoverished nation that loses its case in a WTO dispute would have no choice but to alter its economic policy to align it with the WTO ruling.

WTO directives on increasing competition have pitted commodity exporting nations against one another, to the detriment of all. The disastrous plunge in the price of coffee is a case in point. Coffee is the main export of many developing nations and LDCs, especially in South America and Africa. As the demand for coffee in the West has increased, these nations have competed fiercely with one another for ever-greater market share. This competition has led to severe overproduction, which caused the bottom to fall out of coffee prices.

Though a resident of a Western city may pay $5 for a cup of "designer" coffee, and despite the fact that retail sales of coffee in the developed world have risen from $30 billion a year (1990) to $80 billion a year (2003), the income coffee growers have earned from their crop has declined from $12 billion to $5.5 billion in the same period. Such reductions are devastating for mainly coffee-producing nations such as Ethiopia, which has had to slash services in education and health to align with its drastically reduced export revenues. When translated into microeconomic terms, for every $1 of coffee sold in an upscale coffeehouse in the West, the coffee farmer receives less than one penny.[83]

Problems associated with trade in agricultural products have been intractable, though they have been addressed at nearly every ministerial meeting of the WTO. Developing countries have banded together to fight Western farm subsidies. Developed nations remain unwilling to give them up. The WTO is unwilling to set a floor on commodity prices to help LDCs. The agricultural mess has, on several occasions, threatened to destroy the WTO itself.

GENERAL AGREEMENT ON TRADE IN SERVICES

At one time, trade involved only tangible "stuff," things you could touch or weigh. With the incorporation of the General Agreement on Trade in Services (GATS) into the WTO, the concept of trade was expanded to include service provision. GATS was reportedly finalized at secret meetings during the Uruguay Round. The concept of trade in services was truly radical, and it is believed that it was pushed by the largest service MNCs in the developed world. The rationale for GATS was that it would benefit poor nations unable to provide their citizens with needed services. In essence and in practice, GATS is a WTO agreement that promotes privatization.

There are 120 services listed under GATS, among them, health and hospital care, child care, education (primary through postsecondary), libraries, museums, trash collection, transport, banking, social assistance, energy, real estate, insurance, postal services, publishing, broadcasting, telecommunications, construction, sewage treatment, and water supply. Essentially, any service you can think of that you use or that your community provides is part of GATS.

Liberalization of trade in services attempts to provide greater market access to MNCs by requiring developing or LDC nations to eliminate laws that control the service sector and/or prevent or deter foreign companies from taking over these services. GATS applies "horizontally," granting most favored nation status to all countries. This means that once a nation has allowed a corporation from one country to provide a service, it is required to open its service sector to corporations from all member countries.

For some very poor countries, allowing a foreign corporation to step in and provide a service that the domestic government cannot afford to provide itself, that it provides poorly or inefficiently, or that is not provided by a domestic company makes a lot of sense and helps citizens. However, critics of GATS assert that it is undemocratic because it undermines the authority of popularly elected governments and prevents a nation from shaping a service sector that is attuned to its needs and culture. GATS also specifically prohibits government oversight and regulation of the foreign service provider. Lack of oversight is particularly important in such vital service sectors as education and health care. No nation wants a foreign corporation dictating how its schools should be run and its children educated. In other sectors, government is forbidden to enact regulations to prevent MNCs from breaking environmental or labor laws.

With GATS, a "lowest common denominator" mentality prevails, as standards for services are generally set very low in order to maximize MNC profits. GATS operates under the WTO's "least trade restrictive" rule, which not only requires the most open market for trade in services but prevents client governments from imposing any domestic regulation on the service provider.

GATS is a prime example of the "commodification" of the world as promoted by the WTO. Critics of GATS—and they are legion—wonder aloud what, if any, part of people's public or private lives will remain outside the domain of "free trade" and "open markets."

AGREEMENT ON TRADE-RELATED ASPECTS OF INTELLECTUAL PROPERTY RIGHTS

This agreement, known as TRIPS, was added to the WTO charter at the end of the Uruguay Round, after intense lobbying by the United States. TRIPS is intended to protect intellectual property, such as copyrights, trademarks, logos and designs, patents, and confidential information such as scientific data and proprietary trade secrets. Genetically modified plants were also covered in the original agreement. Since it was first enacted, TRIPS has been expanded enormously—into highly controversial areas.

There is little controversy about the need for TRIPS in terms of protecting copyrights and certain patents. For example, TRIPS is often cited to help stem the tide of pirated music CDs and film videotapes and DVDs that are openly for sale in developing countries, particularly in Asia. Without copyright protection, the artists are not paid for their work, so pirating copyrighted material injures individuals, as well as corporations.

Yet even the pro-WTO, proglobalization economist Jagdish Bhagwati has nothing good to say about the evolution of TRIPS. Bhagwati calls TRIPS the result of "harmful lobbying by corporations" and states that copyrights and patents "[do] not belong to the WTO, which is a trade institution." Bhagwati likens the inclusion of TRIPS in the WTO to "the introduction of cancer cells into a healthy body. For virtually the first time, the corporate lobbies in pharmaceuticals and software had distorted and deformed an important multilateral institution, turning it away from its trade mission and rationale and transforming it into a royalty collection agency." He continues: "The consequences have been momentous. Now every lobby in the rich countries wants to put its own agenda, almost always trade-unrelated, into the WTO."[84]

Bhagwati may be most exercised about TRIPS being part of a trade organization, but he is also on target about its opening the WTO to excessive influence by corporations and industry lobbyists from developed countries. Yet these issues only begin to touch on the most invidious impacts TRIPS is having on the world.

To many critics, TRIPS represents the ultimate expression of the WTO's blindness to the welfare of people and the planet. One of the most controversial aspects of TRIPS is its support of pharmaceutical patents that have prevented developing countries and LDCs from obtaining life-saving drugs, such as those to treat AIDS (acquired immunodeficiency syndrome). Large pharmaceutical companies (dubbed "Big Pharma") in the United States and Europe may charge tens of thousands of dollars per person per year for AIDS drugs in some Western countries—sums far beyond what LDCs can pay. In Africa, where AIDS affects millions, Big Pharma has consistently used TRIPS to prevent domestic companies from making generic versions of the patented drugs. It was only when their behavior became a worldwide scandal that Big Pharma started to sell AIDS drugs at cost to LDCs. Still, even those prices were too high for many impoverished countries. With public opinion on their side, private pharmaceutical companies in India and Brazil began making generic versions of patented AIDS drugs in direct violation of TRIPS. In 2001, faced with unrelenting pressure from public health officials and public opinion, the WTO eased the patent requirements under TRIPS, permitting nations to produce generic versions of patented AIDS drugs for domestic consumption only. In 2003, that requirement was eased still further, permitting generic drug manufacturers to export drugs to countries with AIDS epidemics.

Biopiracy is another controversial outgrowth of TRIPS. Biopiracy is the taking of native herbs, seeds, plants, or other living organisms or parts of living organisms from a nation, usually by a foreign corporation. The corporation extracts and then must in some way alter some of the organic material (though the alteration need not be noticeable or meaningful in terms of the material's use). Then the corporation patents the living material. This practice is occurring in developing countries around the world and involves medicinal plants and traditional rice varieties grown in Asia and trees native to India. All have been altered by corporations that then patent them. The upshot of biopiracy is that, for example, people who have been using the bark of an Indian tree for its medicinal purposes for hundreds of years suddenly find that their actions constitute patent infringement. The properties of the bark "belong" to the corporation, and if the local people try to use their native plant as they have always done, they are breaking the law.

Some critics claim that patenting of organisms would be acceptable as long as it was the native people who received the royalties. Yet many people are very distressed at the whole idea of patenting life-forms. Under TRIPS, more than 150 naturally occurring plants or other organisms native to LDCs and developing countries have been patented by foreign corporations.

The patenting of life is highly controversial, and critics of TRIPS suggest that it is a first step toward turning everything on earth into a commodity that corporations can control and trade. For example, if a corporation alters one gene in an apple, it may become illegal for a person to pick the apples from the tree in his or her garden. What worries critics of TRIPS is not only that intellectual property is not trade, but that everything on earth should not, under the auspices of the WTO, become private property or a commodity for sale.

The Dispute Resolution Body

Critics of the WTO are most adamant in their concern about the way disputes are resolved in the DSB. The DSB is widely criticized because its decisions are made in private, behind closed doors, with no deliberations and documents made public, and not subject to review or appeal outside the WTO.

When one country brings a complaint against another country for supposed violations of WTO rules, the complaint goes before a Dispute Resolution Panel, or DSP, made up of three trade officials. DSPs meet in secret, do not disclose the evidence they use to make decisions, and do not even inform the legislature of the accused nation that its trade laws have been challenged. Citizen participation in the process is not permitted. The decision of the panel is binding. Once a DSP has pronounced a nation's law illegal according to WTO rules, the nation must change its law or face sanctions, including high fines. A nation that loses its case before a DSP may appeal to the Appellate Body of the DSB. Yet, despite the number of cases appealed, the Appellate Body has reversed a panel decision in only one case.[85]

Critics have pointed out that in many cases, WTO disputes involve highly technical material requiring a considerable degree of knowledge and expertise. Yet there is no requirement that panelists be experts in or even knowledgeable about the subject they are adjudicating nor that they request and use expert testimony. This is particularly worrisome for cases involving science (health, the environment) and technology. Of the many cases challenging health or environmental protection laws, the DSP and the Appellate Body have always found in favor of the complainant; that is, they have always ruled that the defendant nation's health or environmental law is discriminatory or a barrier to trade. The losing nation must therefore strike the law from its books or pay fines and face trade sanctions. Most of these cases have been filed against developed nations by other developed nations or by developing nations. A few case descriptions will illustrate some of the problems with the DSB.

In 1991, Mexico and Venezuela challenged the U.S. law banning the importation of tuna caught without protection for dolphins. Tens of thousands of dolphins are killed every year when tuna fishers fail to use special nets and procedures that allow the marine mammals to escape. The DSP and then, in 1992, the Appellate Body, struck down the U.S. law as being discriminatory and a barrier to trade. The justifications for their decision were based on their view that Article XX of GATT (which deals with environmental protection) must be interpreted as narrowly as possible to make sure it is not used to impede trade, the United States had not proven that banning tuna caught without safeguards for dolphins was the "least trade restrictive" way to protect dolphins, and—significantly—the United States could not make any law that pertained to natural resources outside its national boundaries.

Similar arguments were put forward when the United States lost its case regarding conservation of endangered sea turtles. The U.S. law required that shrimp be caught in nets that had turtle escape devices, or TEDS. Any shrimp caught with non-TED nets were banned from import into the United States. Although in the shrimp-turtle case the Appellate Body admitted that the DSP had interpreted Article XX too narrowly, it upheld the decision on the grounds that the WTO should not itself become entangled in the net of environmental law, though it reiterated that the U.S. law was discriminatory.

While it is no doubt true that nations may use environmental legislation as a cover for protectionist trade policies, critics of the DSB—particularly environmentalists—find the narrowness of the DSB's interpretation of such laws troubling for several reasons. First, DSB rulings are undemocratic. It might be argued that the very existence of a body such as the DSB is undemocratic, although a case can be made in support of having some trade resolution body. Yet when its pronouncements demand that a nation overturn environmental or health laws that citizens want, the DSB is undermining the democratic process. It is also negating laws known to protect the health and well-being of citizens. Second, rulings that reinforce the concept of environmental laws as barriers to trade discourage nations from passing such laws. Third, the DSB ruling against U.S. protections for dolphins and endangered sea turtles is particularly ominous. Based on this ruling, no nation has the right to pass a law intended to protect any part of the planet outside its borders. This judgment makes protection of the air, the global climate, and the oceans impossible.

The Need for Transparency

It is widely believed that many of the problems and controversies surrounding the WTO could be resolved if the organization's decision-making process were more open, or transparent. According to Robert Gilpin, a scholar of international political economy, transparency would entail public participation in, or at least public oversight of, WTO meetings and DSB hearings. The secrecy in which the WTO operates is the main reason that "[M]ore and more people are coming to believe that their daily lives, cultures, and social well-being are subject to secret decisions by faceless international bureaucrats."[86] The WTO's lack of transparency is also called its "democratic deficit," which refers to both its secretive decision-making process and the power it has arrogated to itself to overturn the laws and regulations of democratic nations.

There are few, even among globalization's staunchest supporters, who do not recognize that changes need to be made to make the WTO less secretive and more open. A conservative economist with the American Enterprise Institute, Claude E. Barfield, wrote:

> *All documents that governments present . . . should be made public at the time they are submitted [to the DSB] . . . Regarding the issue of open-*

> *ing the panel and dispute settlement hearings to the public, a cautious, step-by-step approach is recommended.... [I]t therefore seems sensible to provide for public access, to the opening of sessions when the panels first address a particular dispute. This would allow outsiders to hear the opening arguments of all participants, including antagonists and third parties.*[87]

The WTO's lack of transparency is so egregious and so harmful to its public image that many proponents of free trade demand greater openness to ensure the WTO's continued survival. Bhagwati states: "Today, the WTO is a legalistic body; like courts worldwide, the proceeding must become transparent, and will."[88]

The Demise of the WTO?

The most recent round of WTO talks, the Doha Round, came to a close in Geneva, Switzerland, in June 2006 with none of the most divisive issues settled. At a subsequent July 2006 ministerial meeting, WTO director general Pascal Lamy suspended all WTO negotiations for the foreseeable future, saying, "We have missed a very important opportunity . . . the progress made to date on the various elements of the negotiating agenda are put on hold . . . we must try . . . to reduce the risk that [the WTO] unravels."[89] Many WTO watchers fear that the trade organization's collapse may be imminent.

The Doha Round failed because the developed nations and the developing and LDC nations reached an impasse on the most contentious WTO agreements: the AoA and TRIPS. Neither the United States nor the EU was willing to reduce agricultural subsidies that support their agribusinesses. Developing and LDC nations, so dependent on commodity exports, therefore refused to lower agricultural tariffs, a move that, they said, would undermine their domestic food security and destroy subsistence farming. They also rejected lowering nonagricultural tariffs on imports from developed countries, as these imports would ruin domestic competitors and hinder development of domestic industries. Developed nations pushed for acceptance of Non-Agricultural Market Access (NAMA), which stipulates a 60–80 percent reduction in tariffs on nonagricultural goods, but developing nations were adamant and united in rejecting it. Disagreements over TRIPS were also intractable. Developing and LDC nations proposed that a disclosure requirement be added to TRIPS to prevent biopiracy. Developed countries, led by the United States, insisted that disclosure was unnecessary and refused to negotiate on the issue.

The Doha Round differs from previous trade rounds in the organized unanimity of developing and LDC nations' positions. No longer can the developed nations dictate the terms of trade. The inclusion of China in the WTO in 2001 and the growing economic might of India and Brazil have altered the balance of power at the WTO. In Geneva, the Group of 20 (G-20) developing countries emerged as a powerful voice for emerging economies and LDCs. The African Group (of 41 nations), meanwhile, presented to the WTO its own vision of how to grow the economies of that continent's countries. The Africa Group Initiative proposed actions that would bolster the economies of commodity-dependent nations. The initiative was not adopted.

To developed countries' protestations that the WTO has benefited developing and LDC nations, the latter cited a recent World Bank report that revealed that the projected $500 billion in economic gains the nations of the world would realize from liberalized trade in 2003 was, in fact, a mere $96 billion. Of that, $16 billion went to the upper-tier developing countries (such as China and Brazil) and the remaining $80 billion went to developed nations. Little, if any, financial benefit was gained by most of the world's developing and LDC countries.[90]

As one economist and WTO observer said at the end of the Geneva meeting, "WTO members can no longer pretend that this new evidence does not exist. . . . WTO members are facing a hard reality. The contradictions between the promised benefits at the global level and the empirical evidence on the ground are harder and harder to explain. People around the world are aware of how the liberalization of trade and finance is affecting their daily lives and are refusing to accept the current approach."[91] These contradictions and the insurmountable divisions between rich and poor countries may be the death knell for the WTO.

GLOBALIZATION AT A CROSSROADS

Those who control and support the Bretton Woods institutions and the WTO argue that free trade will ultimately bring economic growth and stability to nations and a better life to the peoples of the world. Yet, in many parts of the world, globalization in its present form is hugely unpopular. In Latin America, presidential elections during the last few years have resulted in victory for candidates who, to some degree, openly oppose or seek significant reform of neoliberal globalization. Stiglitz described how the austerity measures imposed by international financial institutions affected the vote by making Latin Americans realize that there was a "gap between what was sold and what was delivered. . . . [P]eople went through a lot of pain, and 20 years later . . . they don't see any of the benefits [of globalization] . . . [F]ew of the results in terms of incomes and poverty reduction had been [realized]."[92]

Some economists have made persuasive cases for globalization's benefits, displaying data indicating the gains that developing nations might receive as trade barriers fall. However, too often, these data are derived from those nations that were partly developed or had some initial advantage to begin with. For example, second-tier developing nations such as China, India, Brazil, Chile, and South Korea have experienced impressive economic growth in today's free trade environment. These nations entered the globalized economy with a relatively educated workforce, some degree of industrialization, and at least the rudiments of an economic infrastructure. The gains globalization supporters describe are genuine—for these countries. However, in order to make their argument, proglobalization economists must ignore LDCs in their calculations, for LDCs reveal that globalization does not, as its supporters would argue, "lift all boats." Most LDC boats are taking on water, and some are sinking.

How Developed Nations Got Rich

Many modern economists today insist that free trade is the only way for developing nations to grow their economies; however, free traders fail to acknowledge the role that governments and protective tariffs have played in the economic development of today's industrial powers. In Great Britain and the United States, especially, protection of infant industries accounted in large part for the development of a robust, competitive economy.

An infant industry is one that, if protected from international competition, will become sufficiently strong and competitive to enable it to survive when protection is eventually removed. Infant industries are most often those that the government identifies as being crucial to the economic development of the nation.

Great Britain was the home of the Industrial Revolution, and its economic supremacy resulted largely from its protection of its infant industries. As early as the 1690s, England adopted protectionist policies to shield its nascent woolen industry from foreign competition. By the time the industry strengthened and protections were relaxed, Britain was exporting woolen textiles, not just wool. Thus, protection allowed the British wool industry to evolve into a value-added exporter of manufactured goods and not just an exporter of the raw material. This is important in terms of the plight of developing nations today. International trade institutions force free trade on unindustrialized developing nations, which usually must resort to exporting raw materials. They are not given the time or the opportunity to evolve the value-added products that would significantly improve their export revenues.

British protection of textile manufacturing continued into the 1860s, though textiles were not the only infant industries protected in Britain. After woolens, Britain instituted protectionist policies to help its cotton, iron, leather, shipbuilding, fisheries, silk, and flax industries. The importation of silk and cotton from its colony in India was prohibited in order to bolster domestic manufacturing. With iron protected as well, Britain had the synergy necessary for robust technological innovation, and new textile machinery was invented and built. A steel industry arose from the protected iron industry. Both allowed Britain to lead the world in production of steam engines. In short, protecting key industries gave Britain the breathing space that allowed infant manufacturing industries to mature and become competitive in the global marketplace. By the middle of the 19th century—after *two centuries* of protectionism—Britain had developed into the world's leading industrial power. Only then, when its mature industries had a definite comparative advantage in manufactured goods, did Britain embrace trade liberalization.

The United States industrialized long after Great Britain was already the acknowledged leader in world trade. Though the United States today is the most vociferous supporter of laissez-faire, it too utilized protectionist policies to grow its economy. The Tariff Act of 1789, the first in U.S. history, taxed the import of 38 different categories of goods. In 1791, Alexander Hamilton urged Congress to protect U.S. infant industries, as European nations had done and continued to do. Hamilton's call was heeded, and Congress authorized selective tariffs to protect key infant industries.

The Tariff Act of 1816 further protected fledgling U.S. industries, particularly the woolen, cotton textile, iron, glass, and pottery industries. Where Britain's protectionist policies had persisted for two centuries, similar U.S. policies lasted only about 100 years. The high post–Civil War tariffs are generally seen as key contributors to the growth of the U.S. manufacturing sector. In the 1870s, U.S. tariffs were the highest in the Western world (a whopping 250 percent higher than those in most European nations). By the time tariffs were lowered via the Tariff Act of 1913, U.S. manufacturing industries were strong enough to compete in the global market.

Significantly, during these protectionist eras, the British and U.S. governments took an active part in providing the infrastructure industry needed to grow. Roads, waterways, railroads, and communications networks were supported by the government. Strong central banks, and later local banks, stock exchanges, and insurance services were established to oversee and protect the nation's finances and businesses, and a legal framework that established the guidelines within which business could operate was set up. Governments in all of today's industrialized nations had an active role in creating a positive growth environment for industry.

In light of all this, to say that Europe and the United States have a comparative advantage in industrial production is a gross understatement. They are so far ahead of the industrial and technological curve, and their advantage is so enormous, it is highly unlikely that today's unindustrialized nations will be able to catch up. Their task is made even more impossible by modern trade rules and globalization policy.

The pressure developing countries face to open their markets and become full-fledged members of the global marketplace does not take into account the fact that they have not had the chance to industrialize. Governments of developing countries today must adhere to a strict hands-off policy toward their domestic industries. Beginning with GATT and extending (with a vengeance) to the WTO, nearly all government intervention in trade, including the protection of infant industries, is punished by fines or trade sanctions. Because they have not had time to industrialize (in fact, were deliberately kept unindustrialized by colonial and imperial powers) and are prohibited from protecting fledgling industries, developing countries are forced to trade primarily in raw materials, not value-added manufactured goods. The trade in raw materials generally plunders the natural resource base of a developing country without bringing in adequate revenues. These countries lose yet again when their raw materials are re-imported as manufactures they must buy from the industrialized nations that bought their raw materials in the first place. Further, the exporters of manufactured goods realize a far greater profit than a developing nation does on exported raw materials. So trade becomes very lopsided, benefiting one party far more than the other.

Free trade is one important factor in a nation's economic success, yet the later a nation enters the global industrial marketplace, the faster it needs to develop its industries (the United States industrialized in half the time of Britain). Not only must it quickly and adequately protect its infant industries, it must find the revenue to provide the infrastructure that industry needs to prosper. The problem today is that the faster a nation needs to undergo these changes, the less able the lopsided free market is to provide them. Government intervention is required to facilitate these changes. Yet government intervention is prohibited in today's global free market. What is a developing nation to do? It should come as no surprise that this is one of the most contentious issues facing globalization today.

Convergence or Divergence?

Neoliberal economists are convinced that their policies will lead to an economic convergence among nations. Convergence means that as developing economies grow, they will come to resemble, in wealth and development, the economies of rich nations. Those developing countries that entered the globalized market with fairly robust, if not fully developed, industries or other advantages (such as an educated labor force) have done fairly well in the free trade environment. LDC economies, however, have generally stagnated. Some reasons for this have been described: dependence on low-value commodity exports, an uneducated workforce, a globalization structure that prohibits government-directed FDI, and a general "race to the bottom" in terms of wages, standards, and environmental and health regulations. As one economist has observed,

> *Despite the optimistic predictions flowing from the convergence theory of mainstream neoclassical economics, the growth process within and among national economies remains highly uneven.... [F]ew developing economies have converged with the developed economies, despite considerable progress that some have experienced.... The low capacity of the societies in less developed countries to absorb the knowledge required for economic development has proved to be a particularly significant deficiency.... [C]onvergence occurs only when national economies share a similar 'social capacity.'... Differences in the level of social capacity among national economies lead to an international core/periphery structure in which strong concentrations of economic wealth and economic activities (the core economies) coexist with weaker, or peripheral economies.*[93]

Social capacity is a measure of a nation's "human capital" and the institutions, such as schools and the availability of technology, that, over time, help citizens improve themselves economically. Without adequate social capacity in developing nations, the global economy reverts to the 19th-century structure of rich metropole/core countries and poor periphery nations. As in the Age of Imperialism, this structure is cemented by mutual dependence but with far greater dependence on the part of peripheral economies on the metropole economies.

Some Drawbacks of Globalization

Despite its successes in more advanced developing nations, globalization has caused some worrying trends. These are particularly apparent and serious in the world's poorest countries.

Governments in poor countries have seen their power dwindle, as the WTO and the IMF increase demands for less government interference in the nation's economic life. Lack of government control arises from the conditionalities imposed by the IMF, which dictate government economic policy, and from the WTO, which demands that governments in host nations embrace deregulation and maintain a hands-off policy toward the functioning of MNCs within their borders. In both cases, foreign institutions or corporations wrest control from governments.

Akin to loss of local control is the "democratic deficit" that results from it. Under the auspices of the WTO and the IMF, laws enacted by elected officials in response to the will of the electorate may be rescinded in order to comply with free trade or privatization policies. Thus, labor, health, and environmental standards enacted into law by a democratic government may be sacrificed on the altar of globalization. Many democratic developing nations bridle at these antidemocratic policies, which are most vociferously supported by Western democracies.

The WTO strictures against national environmental laws lead inevitably to environmental degradation and overexploitation of the commons, both global and local. Since it is in everyone's interest that the earth and the resources on which we all depend be preserved, nations should have the right to pass legislation to protect their own environment as well as the global commons, including the air, the oceans, the climate, the forests, and other threatened ecosystems. Too often under today's trade rules, foreign corporations are ceded the right to do as they please with the environment, to the detriment of every level of the commons.

The environmental degradation that too often follows in globalization's wake has revived a commitment among developing nations to sustainable development. Sustainable development is development that does not irreversibly degrade the natural environment or deplete resources, but rather nurtures them. Natural resources are used wisely, with awareness that they must be sustained to support future generations.

DEBT

Crushing debt is the main reason that LDCs and developing countries bow to the demands of international trade organizations and financial institutions. In 1970, LDCs owed about $60 billion in debt; by 2002, their debt had ballooned to $523 billion. Nearly $3 billion of that amount is owed by the poorest African nations. Of the total debt so far incurred, about $550 billion has been paid back in both principal and interest since the mid-1970s. A nearly equal amount still remains to be paid. It is not only the high interest rates but the compound interest on the principal that is crushing indebted nations. Developing and LDC countries borrowed about $400 billion in 1973. Interest owed on the debt compounded at about 20 percent per year through 1993, leaving these nations with a total debt of $1.5 trillion. As Nigerian president Olusegun Obasanjo explained, "All that we [in Nigeria] had borrowed up to 1985 or 1986 was around $5 billion, and we have paid about $16 billion; yet we are still being told that we owe about $28 billion. That $28 billion came about because of the injustice in the foreign creditor's interest rates. If you ask me what is the worst thing in the world, I will say it is compound interest."[94] Nigeria spends between 20 and 25 percent of total government revenue on debt repayment, and Malawi devotes between 30 and 40 percent of its revenues to debt service.[95] In Nigeria 70 percent and in Malawi nearly 42 percent of the population lives on less than $1 a day.[96]

POVERTY

Though the absolute number of people living on less than $1 per day decreased by about 100 million between 1990 and 2001, the degree of poverty has worsened. Between 1965 and 1969, LDC citizens living on less than $1 per day had $0.70 to spend. By 1999, their income declined to $0.64 per day. Similar reductions were seen for those living on less than $2 per day in LDCs, with a decline from $1.07 a day for consumption in 1969 to $1.03 a day in 1999.[97] The situation is even worse for the citizens of African LDCs. In sub-Saharan Africa, there are 100 million more people living in poverty today than there were in 1990. There, the 1999 average consumption for people living on less than $1 per day was only $0.59. More than 87 percent of Africans living in LDCs subsist on less than $2 per day.[98]

Does Trade Reduce Poverty?

UNCTAD data reveal that, in general, the more open a poor nation is to trade (the fewer trade restrictions it has), the greater the level of poverty and the larger the population living on less than $1 per day. UNCTAD hesitates to draw a direct cause-and-effect relationship but states that it is likely the type of economic integration imposed and not economic integration per se that deepens the poverty in nations that have the most open economies. The agency also stipulates that it is the types of goods traded (for example, commodities) that determine the degree of poverty in a country.[99] For example, a country whose revenue is derived almost entirely from coffee exports may have a far higher incidence of extreme poverty than a country that exports a commodity with a less depressed market price, even if both have equally open markets. Still, of the 22 LDCs that increased their exports between 1997 and 1999, 10 saw an increase in the number of citizens living in poverty during that period. Overall, increasing globalization has slowed the rate of poverty reduction. Today, the rate of poverty reduction is one-fifth what it was between 1980 and 1996.[100]

UNCTAD reveals the following impacts of trade liberalization on developing nations' and LDCs' exports, imports, and balance of payments:

- For every 1 percent reduction in import and export duties by a developing country, the nation realizes only a 0.2 percent increase in export growth, which is outweighed by a 0.2–0.4 percent increase in imports; for LDCs, the same reduction yields only 0.019 percent increase in export growth and a 0.012 percent import growth.
- During the postliberalization period, all LDC and developing regions (Africa, Asia, and Latin America) have seen their trade balances deteriorate.

- Trade liberalization has had the most positive impact on those developing nations that entered the regime from a strongly protectionist economy; those countries that had more open trade fared more poorly.[101]

NEW ECONOMIC THEORIES

As some economists watched the failure of neoliberal policies in the global economy, they began to formulate a new way of thinking about why poor countries are poor and what might be done to help them. One aspect of the new economic theories is their refutation of the neoliberal theory of convergence.

New theory economists proceed on the assumptions that (1) markets and competition within markets are not perfect, and, in fact, oligopolies (control by a few large corporations) predominate; (2) technology and innovation are the driving forces behind economic growth; and (3) arbitrary factors, such as a nation's history, geography, and self-image, as well as pure accident, play an important part in economic development. What follows are simplified summaries of a few new economic theories and how they might apply to economic growth in developing and LDC countries.

Endogenous Growth Theory

The theory of endogenous growth, first set forth by, among others, economist Paul Romer (1955–), focuses on technology as the driving force of any economy. It supports government intervention in economic planning to promote technology development. According to this theory, LDC governments should concentrate on narrowing the technology gap between themselves and developed nations by adopting the best technology from rich nations and using government support to develop industries and promote research and development that use this technology. Government subsidies and government-directed FDI should be channeled into high-tech economic sectors. Government should also invest in social capacity in the form of secondary technical education for its citizens. Only then will LDCs and developing nations begin to catch up with developed countries.

New Economic Geography Theory

The new economic geography (NEG) economists, such as Paul Krugman, assert that there is much more than comparative advantage that determines where a particular industry thrives. Among other things, NEG economists seek to explain why the metropole-periphery economic structure seems so persistent and so hard to overcome.

NEG theory stipulates that it is history coupled with the accumulation of random events that tend to create a hub, or core, of successful industry in a particular location. NEG economists call this "path dependence," which, in simplified terms, means that economic development depends on the accumulation of random factors, such as technology and geography, that over time may lead to the development of a powerful and competitive industry. For example, it is likely just a quirk of fate that the U.S. automobile industry grew up in Detroit. Why not St. Louis or Buffalo? Once an industry starts up and begins to make even a small profit, a positive feedback loop may be created as long as other factors are in place (cheap transportation, access to suppliers, etc.). The positive feedback loop, which tends to keep industries or economies on the path they are already on, explains why it is so difficult to undo the metropole-periphery structure: Each role is self-perpetuating based on economies of scale and low transport costs.

According to the NEG theory, free trade will only reinforce the existing economic structure. Stronger government intervention in the development and protection of domestic industry might begin to break down this debilitating cycle and lead to real growth and economic independence in poor nations.

Strategic Trade Theory

Strategic trade theory (STT), which evolved from the works of economists Gene Grossman (1955–), Avinash Dixit (1944–), and Krugman, is based on the fact that there is always imperfect competition in markets and that economies of scale will tend to elevate one or two large companies to industry dominance at the expense of smaller firms. The inevitable rise of oligopolies can create an advantage for government. According to STT, governments should invest in small successful firms in order to build them into even more successful oligopolies. Government investment and subsidies should be targeted to those industries that are most important to the nation and/or that show the greatest promise in terms of competitiveness and "spillovers" into the general economy. Companies receiving this type of help would have an enormous competitive advantage in the national economy and thus deter competitive FDI in that industry. STT even approves of the imposition of high tariffs if that is what it takes to grow a powerful, competitive domestic industry, especially in the high-tech sector.

A NEW GLOBALIZATION?

The neoliberal economic theory that has guided modern globalization has clearly not had the universally positive results its supporters had hoped for. Perhaps the new economic theories, with their emphasis on more government involvement in directing its nation's economy, will prove to be of greater benefit to struggling economies. Yet, for the new economic theories to work well, developed countries must be willing to undertake extensive technology transfer to developing countries and LDCs. Developed countries must also encourage LDC government involvement in economic development, even if that means reduced profits for the developed nation's corporations.

For globalization to succeed, it must also address the problems of local control, the maintenance of democratic institutions, and the problems of debt and poverty. The Millennium Development Goals, adopted in September 2000, committed the governments of 189 nations to the eradication of poverty through debt relief and to sustainable economic development among the world's poorest nations.

A new type of globalization with a "human face" and respect for democracy would also be less corporate and more community based. Nations would not be subjugated by international lending institutions and their conditionalities but helped to strengthen the unique products and services that can make them economically strong and stable. A nation's sustainable use of its own resources, both natural and cultural, would not be controlled by foreign firms. Globalization is a fact and must be faced, but mechanisms should be put in place to allow countries to develop and trade in their own way, free from ruinous debt and foreign corporate control.

---

[1] Pliny the Elder. *Historia naturalis.* Quoted in Wikipedia. "Silk Road." Available online. URL: http://en.wikipedia.org/wiki/Silk_Road. Accessed on January 12, 2006.

[2] Seneca the Younger. *Declamations.* Vol. 1. Quoted in Wikipedia. "Silk Road." Accessed on January 12, 2006.

[3] Pliny the Elder. *Historia naturalis.* Quoted in Wikipedia. "Silk Road." Accessed on January 12, 2006.

[4] John Gray. *False Dawn.* New York: New Press, 1997, p. 57.

[5] Anthony Giddens. *The Consequences of Modernity.* Cambridge: Polity Press, 1990, p. 64.

[6] Robert Gilpin. *Global Political Economy.* Princeton, N.J.: Princeton University Press, 2001, p. 7.

[7] Joseph Stiglitz. *Globalization and Its Discontents.* New York: W.W. Norton, 2003, p. 9.

[8] John Gray. *False Dawn,* pp. 6–7.

[9] Quoted in John Micklethwaite and Adrian Wooldridge. *A Future Perfect.* New York: Random House, 2003, p. 4.

[10] Adam Smith. *The Wealth of Nations.* Book 1. Amherst, N.Y.: Prometheus Books, 1991. Quoted in Wikipedia. "Adam Smith." Accessed on January 17, 2006.

[11] Smith. *The Wealth of Nations.* Book 4.

[12] Smith. *The Wealth of Nations.* Book 1.

[13] Smith. *The Wealth of Nations.* Book 1.

[14] Quoted in John Gray. *False Dawn,* p. 12.

[15] Quoted in Thomas D. Schoonover. *Uncle Sam's War of 1898 and the Origins of Globalization.* Lexington: University of Kentucky Press, 2003, p. 56.

[16] Schoonover. *Uncle Sam's War,* pp. 6–7.

[17] Schoonover. *Uncle Sam's War,* pp. 6–7.

[18] Schoonover. *Uncle Sam's War,* p. 73.

[19] The history of World War I and its causes are endlessly fascinating and instructive. There are hundreds of books written about the war. Among the best to begin with are Barbara Tuchman's *The Guns of August* (New York: Ballantine, 1994) and Hew Strachan's. *The First World War* (New York: Viking, 2004).

[20] The causes of the Great Depression and the human misery it caused are the subjects of countless books. An insightful look at the Great Depression might start with the following: Studs Terkel's *Hard Times: An Oral History of the Great Depression* (New York: Pantheon, 1986), Charles P. Kindleberger's *The World in Depression: 1929–1939* (Berkeley: University of California Press, 1989), and David M. Kennedy's *Freedom from Fear: The American People in Depression and War, 1929–1945* (New York: Oxford University Press, 1999), which also deals with the U.S. response to World War II.

[21] Of the thousands of books written about World War II, among the best general works are James L. Stokesbury's. *A Short History of World War II* (New York: Harper Perennial, 1980) and John Keegan's. *The Second World War* (New York: Penguin, 2005).

[22] Quoted in Micklethwaite and Wooldridge. *A Future Perfect,* p. 4.

[23] Quoted in Micklethwaite and Wooldridge. *A Future Perfect,* pp. 9–10.

[24] Quoted in Rober Kuttner. *The End of Laissez-Faire.* New York: Knopf, 1991, p. 37.

[25] Quoted in Micklethwaite and Wooldridge. *Future Perfect,* pp. 9–10.

[26] Gilpin. *Global Political Economy,* pp. 306–308.

[27] Anoop Singh et al. *Stabilization and Reform in Latin America: A Macroeconomic Perspective in the Experience Since the 1990s,* pp. 90–91. Available online. URL: http://www.imf.org/external/pubs/ft/op/238/pdf/op238_7.pdf. Accessed on November 21, 2006.

[28] Dani Rodrik. "Goodbye Washington Consensus, Hello Washington Confusion." Originally published in the *Journal of Economic Literature.* Available online. URL: http://home.harvard.edu/~drodrik/Lessons%20%of%20the%201990s%20review%20_JEL_.pdf. Accessed on November 21, 2006.

[29] Kuttner. *The End of Laissez-Faire,* p. 42.

[30] Walden Bello. *Views from the South.* New York: International Forum on Globalization, 2000, p. 37.

[31] Quoted in Art History Club. "Neoliberalism." Available online. URL: http://www.arthistoryclub.com/art_history/Neo-liberalism. Accessed November 27, 2006.

[32] Walden Bello. *Views from the South.* New York: International Forum on Globalization, 2000, pp. 51–52.

[33] Robert Gilpin. *Global Political Economy,* pp. 48–49.

[34] Gilpin. *Global Political Economy,* pp. 104–105.

[35] Quoted in Gilpin. *Global Political Economy,* p. 50.

[36] Stiglitz. *Globalization and Its Discontents,* pp. 14–15.

[37] Stiglitz. *Globalization and Its Discontents,* p. 35.

[38] Moises Naim. "Fads and Fashion in Economic Reforms: Washington Consensus or Washington Confusion?" Draft of Working Paper for IMF Conference on Second Generation Reforms, Washington, D.C., November 8–9, 1999. Available online. URL: http://www.imf.org/external/pubs/ft/seminar/1999/reforms/Naim.htm. Accessed on November 21, 2006.

[39] Jeremy Clift. "Beyond the Washington Consensus." Available online. URL: http://www.imf.org/external/pubs/ft/fandd/2003/09/pdf/clift.pdf. Accessed on November 21, 2006.

[40] Sunita Kikeri et al. "Privatization: Eight Lessons of Experience." Outreach #3. Policy Views from the Country Economic Department, July 1992. Available online. URL: http://www.worldbank.org/html/prddr/outreach/or3.htm. Accessed on November 21, 2006.

[41] Florencio Lopez-de-Silanes. "The Truth About Privatization in Latin America," p. 14. Yale ICF Working Paper No. 03–29, October 2003. Complete article available online. URL: http://ssrn.com/abstract=464460. Accessed on November 21, 2006.

[42] Joseph Stiglitz. *Globalization and Its Discontents.* New York, W.W. Norton, 2003, p. 38.

[43] Stiglitz. *Globalization and Its Discontents,* p. 58.

[44] Stiglitz. *Globalization and Its Discontents,* pp. 34–35.

[45] Stiglitz. *Globalization and Its Discontents,* p. 37. Italics in the original.

[46] Stiglitz. *Globalization and Its Discontents,* p. 59.

[47] World Bank. *Economic Growth in the 1990s: Learning from a Decade of Reform,* Washington, D.C., 2005, p. 193. Available online. URL: http://www1.worldbank.org/prem/lessons1990s/. Accessed on November 21, 2006.

[48] Irwin Douglas. *Free Trade Under Fire.* Princeton, N.J.: Princeton University Press, 2002, p. 38.

[49] Jagdish Bhagwati. *In Defense of Globalization.* New York: Oxford University Press, 2004, pp. 61–63.

[50] Douglas Irwin. *Free Trade Under Fire,* pp. 42–43.

[51] Nancy L. Stokey. "Giving Aid Effectively." *The Region 2005 Annual Report,* Minneapolis: Federal Reserve Bank of Minneapolis, p. 14. Available online. URL: http://www.minneapolisfed.org/pubs/region/06-05/essay.cfm. Accessed on November 21, 2006.

[52] Jagdish Bhagwati. "The Truth About Trade." Editorial. *Wall Street Journal,* January 18, 2005, p. A16.

[53] United Nations Conference on Trade and Development (UNCTAD). *The Least Developed Countries Report, 2002: Escaping the Poverty Trap,* p. 139. Available online. URL: http://www.unctad.org/en/docs/ldc2002_en.pdf. Accessed on November 21, 2006.

[54] UNCTAD. *The Least Developed Countries Report, 2002,* pp. 161–162.

[55] Martin Wolf. Review of *Why Globalization Works* by Terry J. Fizgerald. Minneapolis: Federal Reserve Bank of Minneapolis, *The Region,* September 2006, p. 4. Available online.

URL: http://www.minneapolisfed.org/pubs/region/06-09/review.cfm. Accessed on November 21, 2006.

[56] World Bank. *Economic Growth in the 1990s: Learning from a Decade of Reform,* Washington, D.C., 2005, chapter 7. Available online. URL: http://www1.worldbank.org/prem/lessons1990s/. Accessed on November 21, 2006.

[57] World Bank. *Economic Growth in the 1990s: Learning from a Decade of Reform,* p. 207.

[58] Peter Isard. Review of *Globalization and the International Financial System: What's Wrong and What Can Be Done?* by Barry Eichengreen. *Journal of Economic Literature* 44 (June 2006), 415–419.

[59] Stiglitz. *Globalization and Its Discontents,* pp. 64–67.

[60] Walden Bello and Shalmali Guttal. *Crisis of Credibility: The Declining Power of the IMF.* Multinational Monitor. Available online. URL: http://multinationalmonitor.org/mm2005/072005/bello.html. Accessed on January 24, 2006.

[61] Walden and Gruttal. *Crisis of Credibility.*

[62] Bretton Woods Project. *IMF Strategic Review: Reform or Left Behind.* Available online: URL: http://www.brettonwoodsproject.org/art.shtml?x=438655. Accessed January 27, 2006.

[63] Bretton Woods Project. *IMF Accused of Exacerbating Famine in Niger.* Available online. URL: http://www.brettonwoodsproject.org/art.shtml?x=351492. Accessed on January 16, 2006.

[64] Anne O. Krueger. "Meant Well, Tried Little, Failed Much: Policy Reforms in Emerging Market Economies." Speech given at IMF Roundtable Lecture, New York, March 23, 2004. Available online. URL: http://www.imf.org/external/np/speeches/2004/032304a.htm. Accessed on November 21, 2006.

[65] Anoop Singh et al. *Stabilization and Reform in Latin America: A Macroeconomic Perspective in the Experience Since the 1990s,* p. xiv.

[66] World Bank. *Economic Growth in the 1990s: Learning from a Decade of Reform,* Washington, D.C., 2005, p. 11.

[67] Jeremy Clift. "Beyond the Washington Consensus."

[68] Jeremy Clift. "Beyond the Washington Consensus."

[69] Luisa E. Bernal, Rashid S. Kaukab, and Vicente Paolo B. Yu. *The World Development Report 2005: An Unbalanced Message on Investment Liberalization.* Global Policy Forum. Available online. URL: http://www.globalpolicy.org/socecon/ffd/fdi/2004/wdrcritique.pdf. Accessed on January 30, 2006.

[70] Carl Aaron. *The Contribution of FDI to Poverty Alleviation.* International Finance Corporation. Available online. URL: http://www.fias.net/ifcext/fias.nsf/Content/FIAS_Resources_Seminar_Papers. Accessed on February 3, 2006.

[71] Aaron. *The Contribution of FDI to Poverty Alleviation.*

[72] David Barboza. "China Drafts Law to Boost Unions and End Abuse." *The New York Times,* October 13, 2006. Available online. URL: http://www.nytimes.com/2006/10/13/business/worldbusiness/13sweat.hmtl?r=1&oref=slogin. Accessed on November 21, 2006.

[73] Bernal, Kaukab, and Yu. *The World Development Report 2005: An Unbalanced Message.*

[74] Bernald, Kaukab, and Yu. *The World Development Report 2005: An Unbalanced Message.*

[75] Jagdish Bhagwati. *In Defense of Globalization.* New York: Oxford University Press, 2004, p. 239.

[76] Doug Barlow and Ian Vasquez, eds. *Perpetuating Poverty: The World Bank, IMF, and the Developing World.* Washington, D.C.: Cato Institute, 1994, p. 139.

[77] Barlow and Vasquez, eds. *Perpetuating Poverty,* p. 140.

[78] United Nations Conference on Trade and Development (UNCTAD). *Human Development Report, 2005.* p. 133. Available online: URL: http://www.sd.undp.org/HDR/HDR05e.pdf. Accessed on January 27, 2006.

[79] *Stop the Dumping: How EU Agricultural Subsidies Are Damaging Livelihoods in the Developing World.* Oxfam Briefing Paper 31. Available online. URL: http://www.globalpolicy.org/soceon/trade/subsidies/2002/10stopdumping.pdf. Accessed on February 9, 2006.

[80] Institute for Agriculture and Trade Policy. *United States Dumping on World Markets.* Available online. URL: http://www.tradeobservatory.org/library/cfm?refID=48538. Accessed February 9, 2006.

[81] United Nations Conference on Trade and Development (UNCTAD). *Human Development Report 2002.* p. 140. Available online. URL: http://hdr.undp.org/reports/global/2002.en/pdf/complete.pdf. Accessed on January 26, 2006.

[82] Institute for Agriculture and Trade Policy. *WTO Cotton Ruling Stops Short of Ending Dumping.* Press release (March 3, 2005). Available online. URL: http://www.iatp.org/iatp/library/admin/uploadedfiles/WTO_Cotton_Ruling_Stops_Short_ of_Ending_Dumpint.pdf.

[83] UNCTAD. *Human Development Report, 2005,* pp. 139–141.

[84] Bhagwati. *In Defense of Globalization,* pp. 182–183.

[85] Lori Wallach and Michelle Sforza. *The WTO.* New York: Seven Stories Press, 1999, p. 231.

[86] Gilpin. *Global Political Economy,* p. 382.

[87] Claude E. Barfield. *Free Trade, Sovereignty, Democracy: The Future of the World Trade Organization.* Washington, D.C.: American Enterprise Institute Press, 2001, p. 136.

[88] Bhagwati. *In Defense of Globalization,* p. 105.

[89] World Trade Organization. "WTO 2006 News Summary." Available online. URL: http://www.wto.org/english/news_e/news06_e/nid06_summary_24july_e.htm. Accessed on January 26, 2006.

[90] Institute for Agriculture and Trade Policy. "Why Is the Doha Round Failing?" Available online. URL: http://www.iatp.org/iatp/press.cfu?refid=89786. Accessed on January 30, 2006.

[91] Institute for Agriculture and Trade Policy. "WTO Talks Break Down—Opportunity for a New Approach." Available online. URL: http://www.iatp.org/tradeobservatory/headlines.cfm?refID=88528. Accessed on January 30, 2006.

[92] Quoted in David Rieff. "Ché's Second Coming?" *New York Times Magazine* (November 20, 2005), p. 76.

[93] Gilpin. *Global Political Economy,* pp. 141–142.

[94] Anup Shal. "The Scale of the Debt Crisis." Available online. URL: http://www.globalissues.org/TradeRelated/Debt/Scale.asp. Accessed on February 7, 2006.

[95] HIPC Initiative Update April 2005, pp. 34–36. Available online. URL: http://www.imf.org/external/np/hipc/2005/040405.pdf. Accessed on February 7, 2006.

[96] United Nations Development Program (UNDP). "Human and income poverty: developing countries." HDR 2005. Available online. URL: http://hdr.undp.org/statistics/data/indicators.cfm?x=23&y=2&z=1. Accessed on February 21, 2006.

[97] UNCTAD. *Human Development Report, 2002,* p. 58.

[98] UNCTAD. *Human Development Report, 2002, p. 58.*

[99] UNCTAD. *Human Development Report, 2005,* p. 117.

[100] UNDP. *Human Development Report, 2005,* chapter 2.

[101] UNCTAD. *Human Development Report, 2005,* pp. 201–202.

2

Focus on the United States

HISTORY

From Isolationism to World Power

Abraham Lincoln said, "I don't know much about the tariff. But I know this much. When we buy manufactured goods abroad, we get the goods and the foreigner gets the money. When we buy the manufactured goods at home, we get both the goods and the money."[1] The industrializing United States used tariffs and other types of protectionism to shield its infant industries and grow its economy. Historically, the U.S. government also used the power of the purse to invest in areas such as infrastructure that would lead to economic growth. Government subsidized the building of railroads and later the construction of airports and the interstate highway system. Government money funded land-grant colleges and technological research and development in universities nationwide. Thus, "partnerships among business, government, and schools built our economy . . . and expanded a huge middle class."[2] The economic protectionism that prevailed as the nation developed was good for the economy, but it also mirrored the American tendency toward isolationism.

The United States has always had a deeply ingrained strain of isolationism, and withdrawing from world affairs had been as frequent a reaction to world political upheavals as hiking tariffs often had been to economic downturns. This isolationist tendency was abandoned at key times when intervention was recognized as necessary to promote U.S. competitiveness, power, or wealth. This occurred most notably during the Spanish-American War of 1898, when the United States felt compelled to compete with other imperialist nations for dominance over its own periphery nations to expand its share of world trade. Several severe economic traumas preceded the U.S. entry into the imperialist club.

The Long Depression (1873–1898)

Under the laissez-faire system in the post–Civil War era, business practices were largely unregulated, and high-risk, speculative investments were not only tolerated but encouraged. Until 1873, business was booming, fed by enormous capital inputs. In the United States, railroad companies, the second-largest employers in the nation at that time, were the primary recipients of capital from speculative investments. The vast amounts of money they received fueled railroads' uncontrolled and generally financially irresponsible expansion.

In September 1873, partly as a result of the Austrian economic crash in June of that year, the most prestigious U.S. investment banking firm, Jay Cooke and Company, went bankrupt. Cooke & Co. was the primary lender to the Northern Pacific Railroad. The Cooke failure was a bombshell that resulted in a 10-day closure of the New York Stock Exchange. As the economic shock waves rippled through the U.S. economy, credit evaporated, and nearly 20,000 factories closed, leaving many thousands of workers jobless and broke. Most of the nation's railroad companies went bankrupt, and many thousands of investors lost their shirts. A panic ensued. A panic occurs when people frantically try to withdraw their savings from banks that cannot cover the withdrawals (due to business loans that cannot be repaid), so the banks fail and go out of business. An economic depression followed, and lasted until 1878. Another similar panic and economic depression occurred between 1882 and 1885.

People began demanding that the government do something to correct the situation. The U.S. government enacted laws to break up the huge monopolies, called trusts, that had developed since the end of the Civil War and that had seriously squelched domestic competition, and, therefore, trade. The monopolies exercised enormous power over their sectors of the economy, and this unregulated power led, as it almost invariably does, to unfair trade practices, such as price fixing. Anti-trust laws in the form of the Interstate Commerce Act of 1887 and the Sherman Anti-Trust Act of 1890 were intended to institute some form of regulation on big business, dismantle some of the existing monopolies, and prevent new monopolies from forming. The Sherman Anti-Trust Act, in particular, was enacted to prevent any business actions that were deemed to be "in restraint of trade."[3] John D. Rockefeller's Standard Oil Company was one of the first targets of the new antitrust legislation. Yet in these years of financial crisis and depression the United States also imposed tariffs of at least 40 percent on imported goods.[4] The tariffs restricted trade between the United States and other industrialized nations and did little to boost the lagging U.S. economy. Thus, despite these legislative efforts, another and even more serious financial crisis struck.

The Panic of 1893 resulted in the worst financial downturn the United States had experienced to that time. Since the 1830s, the United States and other industrialized countries had been using the gold standard to value their currency. Under the gold standard, every coin and bill is backed by a specific amount of gold. (All nations that used the gold standard were required to hold a minimum amount of gold as reserves.) In theory, anyone holding U.S. currency could exchange it for gold held by the U.S. government.

The speculative nature of investment, not to mention the fairly recent depressions, made people unsure of the soundness not only of their investments but of the dollar. In 1893, increasing numbers of Americans decided to play it safe, and they began demanding that the U.S. government redeem their dollar bills for gold. In fairly short order, the limit on the amount of gold the government could redeem (while retaining required reserves) was reached. The U.S. secretary of the treasury offered to redeem bills for silver, but Americans balked. They sensed that the U.S. economy was shaky, and another panic ensued. As usual, the panic forced banks to call in their high-risk business loans, which many overextended businesses could not repay. First, the Philadelphia and Reading Railroad went bankrupt. Then several major New York banks called in the loans they had made to the National Cordage Company (which then had the most actively traded stock), and the firm went belly-up. The price of silver plummeted. In total, about 500 banks and 15,000 companies declared bankruptcy, including the Northern Pacific, Union Pacific, and Atchison, Topeka, and Santa Fe railroads. Unemployment shot up to 18 percent. The country was again plunged into depression.

Many economists today point to the McKinley Tariff Act of 1890 as one contributing cause of the depression of 1893. This law levied a tariff averaging 50 percent on most imported goods. The tariff had severely restricted U.S. international trade and so caused a constriction of the U.S. economy. However at the time, the severe economic downturn of 1893 inspired calls for yet more protectionist measures. In 1897, Congress passed the Dingley Act, which raised tariffs even higher and widened the range of goods subject to import duties. Like other industrialized nations, the United States also sought to relieve its economic malaise by securing raw materials and outlets for its manufactures in undeveloped countries.

U.S. Expansionist Policies and the War of 1898

The United States had long carried out expansionist policies, from the Louisiana Purchase (1803) to the doctrine of manifest destiny, which extended the nation to the Pacific coast. Its vision of itself as an imperial power can be found in the Monroe Doctrine (1823), which declared to the world the U.S. interest in all the Americas and warned European nations against any intervention in the hemisphere. As one U.S. senator declared in 1898, "We are a conquering race, and . . . we must obey our blood and occupy new markets, and, if necessary, new lands . . . the trade of the world must and shall be ours."[5]

Like other Western nations, the United States viewed Asia as the jewel in the crown of overseas trade. Yet there remained one impediment to Western trade with Asia, and that was the difficulty of getting there. European ships had to travel all the way around the southern tip of Africa to get to India and cross the Indian Ocean to venture east from there. The United States had a definite advantage in its access to Asia from its western coast. It also was uniquely situated to create and control the Holy Grail of global trade at that time—a canal across the isthmus of Central America.

In 1898, Spain was the colonial power that controlled Cuba and the Philippines. The United States therefore viewed Spain as a major impediment to its designs on the isthmus and Asia. The Spanish-American War began in April 1898 with decisive victories for the Americans in Manila and then on the Pacific islands of Guam and Wake Island, which were taken as U.S. possessions. Fighting in Cuba lasted about one month; Puerto Rico fell to U.S. troops one week later. Senator William P. Frye of Maine complained: "The fear I have about this war is that peace will be declared before we can get full occupation of the Philippines and Porto [sic] Rico." Colonel (later president) Theodore Roosevelt urged the United States to "get Manila and Hawaii; . . . prevent any talk of peace until we get Porto [sic] Rico and the Philippines, as well as . . . Cuba." Senator Henry Cabot Lodge admitted that "there [was] no question about Porto [sic] Rico . . . the only question for us to consider is how much we should do in the Philippines. . . .the Hawaiian business [is] practically settled."[6]

The goal was accomplished, or so it seemed. A writer for the *New York Tribune* crowed: "If to [Hawaii] we now added the Philippines, it would be possible for American energy to . . . ultimately convert the Pacific Ocean into an American lake. . . . Such a possession would . . . stimulate . . . commerce and . . . add immensely to the national prosperity."[7] As a consequence of this war, the United States laid claim to Hawaii, Guam, and Wake Island. Over the next 20 years, it also acquired Samoa, Midway, and about 50 smaller Pacific islands, in addition to the Philippines. Its war in the Caribbean gave it Cuba (as a protectorate), Puerto Rico, and the Virgin Islands; it occupied Haiti, Santo Domingo, Nicaragua, and parts of Mexico and Honduras for varying lengths of time. Most important, the United States obtained a long-term lease on the Panama Canal Zone.

Despite its obvious successes, the winning of these wars was not, however, as easy and quick as U.S. leaders thought it would be. The Cuban rebellion against Spain did not stop once the United States took over. After the U.S. victory, Cuban rebels expected autonomy and freedom, and U.S. troops had to use force to quash them. Similarly, Filipino rebels had fought alongside U.S. forces, and the United States had nominally supported them. Yet once victory over Spain was assured, the Filipino fighters were not given the freedom they sought. The United States denied independence to the Philippines so it could more easily dominate it economically. As one U.S. senator observed, the United States had "crushed the Republic that the Philippine people had set up for themselves, deprived them of their independence, and established there, by American power, a government in which the people have no part, against their will."[8]

The people of the Philippines would not give up without a fight. Though the Spanish-American War of 1898 was officially over, in 1899 fighting erupted between Filipino rebels and U.S. troops. This Philippine war continued, officially, until 1902, though sporadic fighting went on for decades. By 1902, more than 4,200 American troops were dead, and nearly 3,000, injured. The exact cost in Filipino blood was not calculated, but it is known that more Filipinos were killed between 1898 and 1902 in the U.S. conflict than had died during the 350 years of Spanish occupation.

The United States did realize economic benefit from its conquests in the Caribbean and in the Philippines. Exports to Asia increased from about 2 percent of total exports (in 1896) to nearly 9 percent (in 1917); its imports from that region rose from about 5 percent of total imports (1896) to about 20 percent (1915). Immediately following the war of 1898, U.S. imports from Asia rose $40 million and exports increased $6 million; in the Caribbean region during the same period, the United States saw imports rise $14 million and exports rise $15 million. The U.S. economy stabilized, though some questioned the means to this end. "Why," wondered former cabinet member Carl Schurz, "must we own the countries with which we trade?"[9]

The Great Depression

The Jazz Age of the 1920s was a time when American optimism was at its peak, and economic prosperity seemed to be permanent. Still, conservatives in Congress believed that high, punitive tariffs made good economic sense. In 1922, Congress passed the Fordney-McCumber Act, which raised the average levy on imports to about 40 percent. Many modern economists believe that this excessively high tariff was a significant factor in causing the Great Depression. Others now assert that it was the U.S. Federal Reserve's contraction (by an astonishing one-third) of the U.S. money supply in 1929, an action taken in part to preserve the gold standard, that led to the Great Depression. The Federal Reserve had been established by President Woodrow Wilson in 1913. The primary role of the Federal Reserve, or simply the Fed, was to control the money supply by adjusting interest rates. Lowering interest rates makes borrowing attractive and increases the money supply. Hiking interest rates makes borrowing more burdensome and contracts the money supply. Economists who cite the Fed's actions as contributing to the Great Depression contend that the lack of money made it impossible for businesses to get loans, so companies were forced to halt capital investments that might have created jobs, and so the U.S. economy began to contract along with its money supply.

The Great Depression followed the October 29, 1929, crash of the New York stock market. Once the Great Depression set in, instead of freeing up trade, the United States became one of the worst offenders in the severity of its protectionist policies. On June 13, 1930, President Herbert Hoover signed into law the Smoot-Hawley Tariff Act, named after Utah's Republican senator Reed Smoot and Oregon's Republican representative Willis Hawley. Smoot-Hawley was the highest tariff in U.S. history, imposing a levy of 60 percent on about 3,000 imported products. More than 1,000 economists recognized the act as ruinous and petitioned Congress not to pass it, but conservative protectionism was triumphant. Within two years of Smoot-Hawley, more than 20 nations retaliated by passing similar protectionist tariffs against U.S. exports. The volume of global trade plummeted.

When Franklin D. Roosevelt assumed the presidency in 1933, he faced the daunting task of alleviating the suffering of millions of unemployed Americans. It is generally acknowledged that it was primarily World War II, and not Roosevelt's New Deal, that raised the United States out of the depression. Yet Roosevelt's bold actions reduced unemployment, putting money in the pockets of people who spent it on goods, which helped industrial production. Roosevelt's policies, which followed Keynes's prescription for jump-starting a flagging economy, helped lift the pall of misery for millions of Americans and began to make noticeable improvements in the U.S. economy.

Roosevelt's New Deal was the polar opposite of laissez-faire. Instead of maintaining government noninterference in economic matters, Roosevelt recognized that government had to take the initiative to get the economy rolling again. This is not the place for an extensive analysis of the depression or the New Deal,[10] yet a brief outline of Roosevelt's New Deal programs will help illustrate how government may use its power to have a positive influence on economic conditions:

- The Public Works Administration (1933) put people to work on large public works projects.
- The National Recovery Act (1933) made industries adhere to legal codes to enhance fair competition (that is, limit monopolies) and raise wages.
- The Federal Deposit Insurance Corporation (1933) provided government-backed insurance for all bank deposits up to a specified amount, to promote confidence in banks and the banking system.

- The Civilian Conservation Corps (1933) hired young people to do unskilled public service work on public lands, such as national parks, and in rural areas.
- The Civil Works Administration (1933–34) gave temporary employment to millions of unemployed people.
- The Works Progress Administration (1935) put more than 2 million Americans to work in a wide variety of fields, from construction to theater.
- The Social Security Act (1935) provided financial aid to the elderly and disabled, paid for by employer and employee contributions to a fund.

The New Deal may not have ended the Great Depression, but its programs demonstrated to most Americans that the government can have an active, if limited, role in guiding a nation's economic policies and improving the lot of its citizens during hard times. The Great Depression, the hardest economic times Americans have ever known, lasted until the U.S. entry into World War II. When Pearl Harbor was attacked by Japan in 1941, the United States was drawn out of its shell and into world war. Industrial production for the war lifted the United States out of the depression and continued to be the force that propelled it toward global economic hegemony.

The Marshall Plan

The United States and the Allies were victorious in World War II, but Europe paid a terrible price for victory. Many Allied cities and industrial centers were bombed-out ruins; European economies, too, were in tatters. The Marshall Plan, named after U.S. secretary of state George C. Marshall, committed the United States to spending billions of dollars to rebuild war-ravaged western Europe.

Perhaps the greatest impetus behind the Marshall Plan was the American fear of the communist Soviet Union. Though U.S. ambassadors in Moscow wired Washington to recommend a policy of "patience and firmness," as opposed to belligerence, diplomats pointed out that, in their opinion, "World communism is like a malignant parasite which feeds only on diseased tissue. . . . We must [therefore] formulate . . . for other nations a much more positive and constructive picture of the sort of world we would like to see . . . [In Europe] they are seeking guidance rather than responsibilities. We should be better able than the Russians to give them this. And unless we do, the Russians surely will."[11]

U.S. foreign policy toward the Soviet Union (USSR) became one of containment, or doing whatever it took to prevent what was then viewed as the Soviets' malevolent and unquenchable ambition for world domination. The United States became a passionate crusader in the cold war with the

Soviets. The fear stirred up among the American public by the threat of the "red menace" catapulted the country out of its isolationism. U.S. economic policy became intimately entwined in its foreign policy. The United States took a battered western Europe under its wing, creating a Pax Americana that turned the United States into a colossus on the world stage. The United States alone provided the capital for reconstruction and the military for security that Europe so badly needed.

U.S. government control of spending and investment both at home and abroad gave its economic policy during this postwar period a decidedly Keynesian cast. For the time being, until its allies in Europe got back on their economic feet, laissez-faire and free trade would have to wait. During this period, the United States was responsible for fully 48 percent of world exports. U.S. firms took advantage of undervalued European currencies to spend billions on opening manufacturing facilities in the slowly recovering, bombed-out cities of western Europe. The United States acted as if its European "protectorate" was essentially a single entity, a unified alliance existing in opposition to the Soviets. This view was supported by many European intellectuals and statesmen, who saw a pan-European federalism as the best way for Europe to grow economically and to prevent future European wars. (Thus was the European Union created.)

Between 1948 and 1952, the United States spent upward of $13 billion on European reconstruction. The need for oversight of this enormous project led to the creation of the Organization for Economic Cooperation and Development (OECD). The need for a unified defense against the USSR led, in 1949, to the creation of the North Atlantic Treaty Organization (NATO).

With the U.S. economy booming, the nation adopted more laissez-faire economic policies, and it encouraged other nations to follow suit. But in significant ways, the economic development of Europe did not follow the U.S. model. For example, the United States was eager for European nations to begin liberalizing their capital markets and embracing free trade, yet in the aftermath of World War II, such policies would have been disastrous for the weak European economies. Furthermore, as Europe recovered and opened trade talks with the United States, it became obvious that government support for citizens was far higher on the European agenda than was free trade.

European Social Democracy

The United States encouraged overseas investments and trade agreements with Europe. Slowly, European economies strengthened and grew, and regional trade within Europe expanded. The United States was pleased with its allies' economic progress but dismayed at the direction in which their economies were moving because of the amount of money European governments allocated to social "safety nets" for citizens. The nations of western Europe were becoming what U.S. economists pejoratively called "welfare states." By 1955, more than 40 percent of western European GDP was being devoted to social programs, such as free health care, free education, and unemployment insurance. In addition, European countries maintained tight control on their capital markets and their banks. Europeans prohibited American investment in their currencies, their governments controlled monopolies in telecommunications and other key industries, and high tariffs or strict quotas prevailed against most imports. Despite its disapproval of these policies, the United States could do nothing but grit its teeth and accept the unacceptable in order to build western Europe into a powerful trading partner and to ensure that it remained a capitalist bulwark against the Soviet Union.

U.S. unhappiness with the way European economies were organized did not limit its willingness to invest there. Between 1950 and 1969, the value of U.S. FDI in Europe increased from $1.7 billion to $21.5 billion. During this period, the United States experienced an era of unprecedented prosperity. Similarly, in Europe, per capita income grew more in these two decades than it had in the previous 150 years. And rather than hinder this economic growth, European government controls "served as the rudder" that kept their booming economies on the right track.[12]

United States Abandons the Gold Standard

The United States had become the banker to the whole of the Western world, and the dollar was in great demand in Europe. That demand grew along with the European economies. The increasing demand for dollars in Europe resulted in a deficit in the United States, and deficits lead to inflation. It is important to remember that at this time the dollar was still pegged to gold at a value of $35 per ounce. The U.S. Federal Reserve (the Fed) was faced with a serious dilemma:

> *[If the Fed] held to a monetary policy appropriate to the domestic economic situation, it risked starving the world economy of monetary liquidity; if, on the other hand, it accommodated the world's dollar needs, it invited domestic inflation and gradually undermined international confidence that the dollar would retain its value. That in turn created an irresistible pressure to convert dollars to gold and a crisis for the whole gold exchange system. [Thus,] the more the economies of other nations grew, the more this became a problem for the United States.*[13]

By the late 1950s, the United States was running a budget deficit of as much as $4 billion annually, although this was offset by its enormous trade surplus from its exports to Europe. Still, because of the worrisome deficit, some fiscally conservative European governments felt safer trading in their dollars for gold. The rush to convert dollars to gold soon left Europe with $19 billion more in gold reserves than the United States. To add insult to injury, by the 1960s, Japanese and West German exports had taken a huge bite out of U.S. dominance in the export market, and before long the U.S. trade surplus dwindled. It seemed inevitable that, sooner or later, the United States would have to devalue the dollar. That day came in August 1971 when, with the additional inflationary costs of the Vietnam War, President Nixon devalued the dollar and departed from the gold standard.

U.S. Economic Policy and the Road to Globalization

With the pressure on the dollar removed, the United States was free to pursue its free trade policies and push other nations toward less government involvement in and control over trade and capital. Many, such as Japan and South Korea, rejected the American system and grew their economies based on their own cultural and historical models. Most of these models incorporated significant degrees of government intervention in key industries or areas of macroeconomic policy.

Although nearly all economists recognize and promote the benefits of free trade, the liberalized trade agenda pushed by American neoliberals was and is often viewed as extreme. Yet the United States was determined to give its industries and banks a leg-up in the global marketplace by becoming the leading proponent of liberalized free trade and globalization. The idea was simple: The more laissez-faire the global economy became, the more the U.S. economy would benefit. In a liberalized, laissez-faire global economic system, barriers to trade in both goods and services, as well as capital, would crumble. This would give powerful U.S. corporations and financial institutions greater access to overseas markets, and the profits they generated, while foreign governments would have to relinquish considerable control over their economies.

The United States and International Financial Institutions

The United States played a key role in the establishment of the WB, as well as in the Uruguay Round of talks that led to the birth of the WTO. Its influence on the IMF is so great, it is the only nation that has veto power over the activities and policies of that organization. As an economic powerhouse, the United States continues to have enormous influence over all of these organizations. Its financial institutions, too, became power players in the global economy.

After the oil crises of the 1970s, American banks became bloated with eurodollars. Money that just sits in a bank does the bank no good. The money must be lent out at interest for the bank to make a profit. America's large international banks turned to the U.S. government to create policies that would help them unload their mountains of cash. To this end, the U.S. government strove mightily to get the nations of the world to do two things: (1) open their financial markets to foreign banks and (2) borrow lots of money from U.S. banks for development projects.

There were several reasons given for pushing this policy. First, many economists believe that the United States equated a healthy international financial system with the profitability of its international banks. The U.S. Treasury used its enormous influence on the IMF to ensure that it implemented policies that benefited U.S. international lending institutions. Second, by imposing austerity measures on borrowers, the IMF ensured that debtor countries would have to keep returning, cup in hand, to seek more loans to cover previous defaults; U.S. international banks also imposed IMF-like conditionalities on the foreign borrowers. Third, U.S. banks were themselves in financial trouble. U.S. banks had been deregulated, blurring the line between banking and commerce and allowing them to engage in more risky financial ventures, some of which led to money-losing investments and left some banks on the brink of failure. Finally, the oil crises of the 1970s, along with the deficit spending resulting from the Vietnam War, had caused serious inflation and driven U.S. interest rates up to about 20 percent. Many U.S. banks had an uncomfortable share of their money lent out at interest rates far below this; for example, people who had gotten mortgages years earlier may have been paying only 7 percent on their loans. For this reason, banks were losing significant amounts of money on their outstanding, low-interest loans. They needed to find borrowers they could lend money to for 20 percent or more in interest. At the same time, developing and LDC countries were forced to borrow money due to the oil crises. They often turned to U.S. banks because the United States used its veto power in the IMF to prevent that organization from increasing its lending capabilities. Since developing countries had very limited SDRs in the IMF, there was little they could do.

As it became increasingly clear that developing and LDC nations would not be able to repay their loans, the value of these loans decreased. (For example, if it is clear that a borrower can only hope to repay 50 cents on each dollar borrowed, the value of the loan decreases to 50 cents per dollar.) Yet instead of devaluing the amount owed based on what developing countries could reasonably pay, U.S. banks retained the loans—and the interest due on them—at the full value. This is a major reason that debtor countries fell further behind economically and still cannot repay their outstanding debts.

By the late 1970s, U.S. banks realized more than 50 percent of their profits from loans given to developing nations. By 1982, nine of the largest U.S. banks had more than 200 percent of their total equity capital tied up in these loans.[14]

An Inevitable Comparison

After the East Asian financial crisis in 1997–98, the trade liberalization policies of the United States, particularly as carried out by the IMF, became highly suspect. Long-suffering debtor nations felt freer to speak openly about the effects these policies had on their economies. They also felt emboldened to criticize the double standard that underlay U.S. free trade policy.

In absolute value, the United States is the world's most indebted nation; it was the 35th most indebted nation in percentage of its GDP in 2005. The total U.S. national debt, as of February 16, 2006, was $8.25 trillion dollars, and rising.[15] Most of the national debt is held as Treasury notes by foreign nations, especially Japan, China, the United Kingdom, Taiwan, Germany, and the OPEC nations.[16] The United States also has a huge and growing trade deficit (a record $725.8 billion in 2005). By its own and IMF standards, the U.S. fiscal house is in serious disarray.

Yet the United States does not impose on itself the same austerity measures that a similar situation would call forth in a developing nation. The United States does not devote itself to increasing exports, as its huge trade deficit makes clear. It does not alter its tax policy to increase revenues. It does not cut spending but pays its way with yet more borrowing. Finally, it most certainly does not permit the IMF or any other external organization to dictate its economic policies. Instead, for decades its policy has been to try to increase the national GDP at a faster pace than the debt so that the national debt measured as a percentage of GDP decreases, even if the debt continues to increase. As Paul Krugman has said, "Policy makers in Washington and bankers in New York often seem to prescribe for other countries the kind of root-canal economics that we would never tolerate here in the U.S.A."[17]

THE UNITED STATES AND REGIONAL TRADE AGREEMENTS

There are many benefits to multilateral regional trade agreements, including economies of scale and a larger consumer market. Another reason nations may join in a regional trade bloc is to create a counterweight to the increasing economic power of other regional trade organizations. The growing dominance of the EU, for example, was one reason that the United States strove to create trade blocs in its hemisphere.

A major impetus to free trade in the United States was President Nixon's demand that he be given the authority to negotiate "fast-track" trade deals with other nations. *Fast track* refers to the executive's authority to negotiate trade pacts without consulting Congress and then presenting the finalized agreement for a speedy congressional up-or-down vote, with no amendments permitted. Fast track remained in force from 1973 until 1993.

On August 12, 1992, President George H. W. Bush signed the North American Free Trade Agreement (NAFTA). Throughout most of 1993, Congress was embroiled in a heated and often bitter debate about the creation of NAFTA, which would be the broadest and most liberalized trade bloc in the world. Despite intense opposition from many congresspeople concerned about labor, human rights, the environment, and its potential costs to the U.S. economy, in November 1993 Congress ratified the treaty. With strong support from President Bill Clinton, the measure passed 234-200 in the U.S. House of Representatives and 61-38 in the U.S. Senate. NAFTA entered into force on January 1, 1994.

The North American Free Trade Agreement

NAFTA established a free-trade zone encompassing Canada, the United States, and Mexico. It set out a schedule for the reduction and eventual elimination of all tariffs on goods moving among these nations. Before NAFTA, the U.S. tariff on imports from Mexico averaged 4 percent, while Mexico imposed a 10 percent tariff on U.S. imports. Over the course of 15 years, NAFTA would completely eliminate tariffs on more than 10,000 goods traded among the three member countries. Under NAFTA, each member country was required to treat the investments from member nations in the same way as domestic investments, to establish rules regarding the movement of people across the borders of member nations, and to protect the intellectual property of member nations. The original agreement contained no provisions for minimum labor standards or environmental protection. To make NAFTA more palatable to the American public, President Clinton approved "side agreements" to NAFTA that dealt with these issues. The side agreements said just enough to aid NAFTA's passage in Congress, but because they did not address enforcement, they were essentially meaningless.

WHAT NAFTA PROMISED

The congressional debate over NAFTA was notable for being the most highly lobbied up to that time. Lobbyists representing industries of every type and interest put intense pressure on congresspeople to pass NAFTA. They, and other NAFTA supporters, promised that the trade agreement would yield unprecedented prosperity for all of the nations involved. Some NAFTA proponents admitted that some American jobs might be lost in the short term, but in the long term, they believed that the U.S. job gains would be enormous, in the range of hundreds of thousands. Pro-NAFTA economists and politicians projected an equally rosy economic future for Mexico and Canada.

WHAT NAFTA DELIVERED

Jobs

Before NAFTA, Mexico was the only nation with whom the United States had a trade surplus; proponents of NAFTA predicted that, as a direct result of the treaty, this surplus would grow to more than $1 billion, with the creation of at least 20,000 high-paying U.S. industrial jobs. A study conducted by the U.S. Department of Labor revealed that between 1994 and 2002, NAFTA cost the United States more than 525,000 jobs. A more detailed study done by the Economic Policy Institute, a nonpartisan economic think tank and research organization in Washington, D.C., showed that the number of American industrial jobs lost due to NAFTA in this period was closer to 880,000. Though these job losses were partially masked by the U.S. economic boom of the 1990s, by 2003, it became clear that about 2.4 million American jobs had been lost due to NAFTA. Most of these jobs had been in the U.S. manufacturing sector. Nearly every state in the nation was affected, with California, Ohio, Michigan, Illinois, Texas, and Pennsylvania among the states suffering the greatest industrial job losses.[18] By 2004, at least 3,600 U.S. firms had relocated all or part of their manufacturing facilities to Mexico. All the U.S. employees in these factories were replaced with cheaper Mexican labor.[19]

Most U.S. firms built factories in areas near the Mexican border with the United States that had been set aside for this purpose even before NAFTA. These industrial areas are called maquiladoras, which comes from the Spanish phrase *maquilas de oro,* or "mills of gold." The "gold" produced by the maquiladoras goes directly to the corporate bottom line; certainly, precious little of it is given to workers as wages. Although the productivity of Mexican workers in the maquiladoras is higher now than it was 20 years ago, their average wages have declined by about 40 percent in the same period and today are about one-tenth of U.S. wages (down from one-third in 1980).[20] In 1981, 49 percent of Mexicans lived in poverty; by 2000, after NAFTA had been in force for nearly six years, that number jumped to 75 percent.[21]

Living conditions in the maquiladoras are atrocious. Most workers live in shacks without plumbing or electricity. Sewage treatment is almost unknown in maquiladoras, and community improvements are never made because the U.S. owners of the nearby factories pay no taxes to help provide services to citizens.

One benefit that industry chief executive officers (CEOs) see in relocating to Mexico is its lax enforcement of its own labor laws. Theoretically, Mexican workers have the right to organize, but in maquiladoras, strong-arm tactics and/or threat of dismissal are used to thwart all attempts at unionizing. Many of the industries that have moved to Mexico, such as the auto industry, had union labor in the United States. These companies saved vast amounts of money on wages and benefits when they hired nonunionized Mexican workers, yet it is uncertain that American consumers have noticeably benefited from the lower wages in significantly reduced retail prices. It can be argued that manufacturing in Mexico has limited what might otherwise have been steep price hikes. In fact, most new car prices have increased between 1994 and 2005. However, it is difficult to predict what the retail price of consumer goods might have been had NAFTA not been in force. What is known is the toll NAFTA has taken on industrial workers in the United States.

One of the primary arguments made in favor of NAFTA stated that Mexican workers would realize great economic benefits from the treaty, leading to an expansion of the middle class. That has not happened; in fact, most Mexicans have seen their standard of living decline since NAFTA. As a result, another promise of NAFTA has also gone unfulfilled: U.S. exports of consumer goods did not skyrocket because the demand for these products did not increase in Mexico. With poverty and income inequality increasing in Mexico, it is no wonder that the promised U.S. export gains from NAFTA never materialized.

U.S. Balance of Payments

NAFTA supporters, and free traders in general, claim that NAFTA has led to a better balance of payments for the United States. Proponents have stated that NAFTA has produced an increase in trade between Mexico and the United States of about $120 billion, with most of that being American exports that increase the plus side of the U.S. balance of trade.

Representative (now senator) Sherrod Brown of Ohio, on the other hand, states that U.S. exports to Canada and Mexico have increased by 41 percent and 95 percent, respectively, while the United States has increased its imports from Canada by 61 percent and from Mexico by 195 percent. According to Brown, what had been a $30 billion trade deficit with these countries in 1993 had ballooned to an $85 billion deficit in 2002, resulting in an increase in the U.S. net export deficit of 281 percent.[22]

The discrepancy between the two sets of data is due to the fact that the lion's share of U.S. exports to Mexico are in the form of components sent from the United States to assembly plants in Mexico. Once they are incorporated into the product, these same components (now part of a car, for example) are shipped back into the United States for sale to American consumers. Supporters of NAFTA list the components shipped to Mexico as genuine exports, as if they were products made in America and sold to Mexican consumers. Economists call this type of exports "industrial tourists" because they spend such a short time in Mexico before they are shipped back to their home country. As Brown reveals, "These 'revolving door' exports accounted for the entire [reported] export increase for the United States." In pre-NAFTA 1993, about 60 percent of U.S exports to Mexico consisted of real, or final, goods; by 1996, only 38 percent of exports were in this category.[23]

According to the Economic Policy Institute, the U.S. balance of trade with Mexico, which showed a surplus of $1.7 billion in 1993, turned into a "real" trade deficit of $54.4 billion in 2003.[24] The trade deficit means that the United States is not creating jobs and exporting its goods to Mexico but rather that the United States has hemorrhaged jobs to Mexico, where companies exploit cheap labor, and is importing goods from south of the border.

Chapter 11

NAFTA's Chapter 11 gives unprecedented power to corporations acting under the agreement. Chapter 11 provides special protections for investors engaged in FDI, specifically prohibiting certain requirements regarding the operation of corporations in any of the three NAFTA nations. Chapter 11 forbids governments from (1) requiring that a certain percentage of FDI-produced manufactures be exported (thus improving the nation's balance of payments), (2) requiring a minimum amount of domestic content in manufactured products, (3) requiring that technology used in FDI facilities be transferred to the host nation, and (4) implementing any other limitations that might negatively affect FDI. Chapter 11 also contains an "investor state" clause that guarantees that corporations will be compensated for any lost profits they may incur due to acts that may be considered "expropriation." Under Chapter 11, private corporations can sue the host government for perceived loss of profits for almost any reason. The threat of corporate lawsuits has intimidated governments so much that they have admittedly refrained from passing environmental regulations, as such regulations necessarily affect corporate profits. For example, the U.S. firm Metalclad sued the Mexican government after it passed a law nixing the company's plan to construct a toxic waste dump. Metalclad won its suit (the toxic dump law was ruled a trade barrier) and was paid $16.5 million in compensation by the Mexican government. In another case, a Canadian company sued the United States for $970 million because of California's law banning the toxic gasoline additive MTBE, which had contaminated many wells and aquifers in the state.[25]

The Central American Free Trade Agreement

The American experience with NAFTA and skepticism of trade liberalization in general made the passage of a similar treaty with the nations of Central America very controversial. Nevertheless, the Central American Free Trade Agreement, or CAFTA, was passed by the U.S. House of Representatives on July 27, 2005, after ratification by the Senate a month earlier. The NAFTA experience in some ways made CAFTA less onerous, particularly in terms of labor rights and in the agricultural and textile manufacturing sectors. However, it is still too early to document the effects of this treaty.

If ratified by all member countries, CAFTA would eliminate most trade barriers on most goods traded among the United States, Honduras, Costa Rica, Nicaragua, El Salvador, and the Dominican Republic. Honduras and El Salvador have passed CAFTA in hopes that it will bring needed FDI and jobs to their impoverished nations. CAFTA has not yet been ratified by Nicaragua, Costa Rica, or the Dominican Republic, where opposition to it remains high. Although many tariffs on imports from these countries had been eliminated under a prior treaty (the Caribbean Basin Initiative), CAFTA would eliminate high tariffs on U.S. exports to Central America. As with NAFTA, supporters insist that it will improve the U.S. trade balance, guarantee higher wages in Central America, and be a boon to American agriculture, as it would permit greater U.S. agricultural exports.

CAFTA does provide for punitive action against nations that do not enforce agreed-upon labor standards, and Central American farmers are cautiously optimistic that it will boost their exports to the United States. U.S. sugar growers, however, are seething at the prospect of cheap imports of Central American sugar. In response to this powerful interest, the U.S. Department of Agriculture (USDA) has already violated the treaty by promising to limit sugar imports—at 20 percent, up from 15 percent—only to the extent needed to maintain prices for U.S. producers. Further, the USDA has promised to purchase sufficient amounts of U.S. sugar to keep domestic prices high; the sugar would be used to make ethanol.[26]

Other provisions in CAFTA convinced lawmakers from textile-industry states that cooperation with Central America in textile and clothing manufacture would improve U.S. competitiveness with China in this area. A CAFTA provision stipulates a minimum amount of U.S.-produced fabric in all textiles and clothing imported to the United States from Central America.

In addition, CAFTA opened Central American signatories to privatization in their service sectors. The United States used its power to force GATS-like provisions on the Central American countries, while specifically exempting itself from opening its service industries to ownership by a foreign company.

The Free Trade Area of the Americas

The United States has also been pushing for the creation of the Free Trade Area of the Americas (FTAA) for some years now. It is an ambitious project that would unify all of the Americas (with the exception of Cuba) in a single trade bloc. The impetus behind the FTAA was to unite the already existing trade blocs (Latin American Free Trade Association, Central American Common Market, Caribbean Free Trade Association, and the Andean Pact) into a single, overarching organization that included the United States, Canada, and Mexico.

The United States waited until after NAFTA was in force before it began FTAA talks in earnest with the nations of Latin America. The first round of negotiations took place in Miami, Florida, in December 1994. Although the talks did address the elimination of tariffs and other trade barriers (most of which had been lowered through the earlier trade agreements listed above), the United States was adamant that the FTAA must greatly expand trade in services and increase protection for intellectual property. Most other nations were more concerned with a U.S. reduction in agricultural subsidies and U.S. acceptance of more agricultural imports. Little was accomplished at this meeting.

The nations convened again in Quebec City in 2001, where they were met by huge antiglobalization demonstrations. Similar protests occurred at the 2004 meeting in Miami. No agreements could be reached at either of these meetings.

Since then, many South American nations have elected left-wing or left-of-center governments that, to some extent, have promised to rein in corporatization and globalization. Hugo Chávez, the president of Venezuela, is the most vocal critic of the FTAA, painting it as a U.S. imperialist move to expand its corporate exploitation throughout the Western Hemisphere. (Chávez has proposed instead that the nations of South America form a union similar to the EU.) Evo Morales, the president of Bolivia, opposes the FTAA for similar reasons. Other leftist leaders, such as presidents Luiz Inácio Lula da Silva of Brazil, Néstor Kirchner of Argentina, and Tabaré Vázquez of Uruguay, might consider signing the FTAA as long as it had strong provisions about government control of the economy and a drastic reduction in U.S. farm subsidies.

The most recent meeting of the 34 potential FTAA nations took place at the Mar del Plata resort in Argentina in November 2005. Though 29 nations wanted to continue negotiations on the treaty, five major actors (Brazil, Venezuela, Argentina, Uruguay, and Paraguay) insisted that further negotiations await the outcome of the WTO talks in Hong Kong in December 2005, which were to discuss further the issue of U.S. and EU agricultural subsidies.

The meeting in Argentina was besieged by thousands of antiglobalization and anti-Bush (U.S. president George W. Bush) protesters, and, indeed, the U.S. president had a tough time trying to convince other delegates that the FTAA was in their economic interest. As reported in the *New York Times*, "[T]he feeling among many Latin Americans is that the United States is coming with little to offer other than the usual nostrums about free trade, open markets, privatization, and fiscal austerity, the same recipe that has vastly increased social inequality throughout Latin America during the past decade. . . . 'We've all of us been down that road, and it didn't work,' said [one South American diplomat] . . . 'The United States continues to see things one way, but most of the rest of the hemisphere has moved and is heading in another direction.'"[27]

Hope is dwindling in Washington, D.C., that a trade agreement will be finalized, as a "growing number of Latin American nations . . . appear to be turning away from neoliberal economics to forge a path of their own." In Bolivia, President Morales has promised to "nationalize all of Bolivia's natural resources."[28] Similar promises have been made to electorates by other recently elected left-of-center South American leaders.

Meanwhile, for those leaders who awaited a positive outcome of the WTO talks in Hong Kong, they waited in vain. So divisive was the issue of U.S. and EU agricultural subsidies that the Hong Kong meeting very nearly resulted in the total collapse of the WTO itself. In 2003, the G-90 group of developing and LDC nations walked out of the WTO meeting in Cancún, Mexico, to protest the one-sided, pro-West provisions that were being foisted on them. In Hong Kong, too, these nations refused to be taken to the cleaners by the developed world; they were particularly angered by its refusal to do anything to reduce agricultural subsidies. As often happens, the WTO was saved by a resolution among members to meet again.

OUTLOOK FOR THE U.S. ECONOMY

> *The most visible aspect of the global imbalances problem is a very large deficit in the current account of the balance of payments of the United States—amounting to about 6¼ percent of GDP and a correspondingly large surplus in the external accounts of other countries, including oil exporters . . . and China. . . . [I]n the United States, repeated current account deficits have resulted in growing external indebtedness . . . The main problem is that in the United States savings are too low. . .Meanwhile the fiscal deficit remains high. . . . It is . . . increasingly urgent that the United States tackle its current account deficit.*[29]

This rather critical appraisal of the current state of the U.S. economy did not come from a rant by some antiglobalization fanatic. It is from a 2006 speech by Rodrigo de Rato, the managing director of the IMF. For far too long, the United States has believed itself to be so economically invincible that it has ignored, and continues to ignore, warnings that it mend its fiscal ways.

The United States owes more money to more countries than any other nation on earth. It pays back both principal and interest on its debt by incurring yet more debt. In this sense, the U.S. economy is run like a Ponzi scheme, a term coined to describe a type of financial sleight of hand in which new liabilities are used to finance existing liabilities.

The United States must borrow to remain solvent because its balance of payments is so skewed: The value of its imports exceeds the value of its exports by nearly $800 billion, so the Treasury is not nourished from this source. It also borrows excessively because it does not balance its budget. U.S. government expenditures far outstrip its revenues. Rather than raise taxes—an unpopular move—the federal government continues to borrow to cover its expenses.

De Rato challenges Americans to save more. It is true that for many Americans, consumption is far more important than savings, even if consumption means the accumulation of dangerous levels of personal debt. Yet there is another side to this equation. Since NAFTA came into effect, the United States has lost millions of well-paying jobs to Mexico. NAFTA is not the only destroyer of American jobs. The explosion of U.S. FDI throughout the developing world has led to huge job losses through "outsourcing." Outsourcing is hiring workers in foreign countries to do the work that American workers once did. Supporters postulate that outsourcing has "multiple strains of competitive advantage for U.S. companies."[30] Among the benefits cited are cost savings, using highly qualified workers who produce high-quality goods, and taking advantage of different time zones to enable rapid responses in production processes. In this view, outsourcing is not the export of jobs, but the "import [of] competitiveness."[31] Supporters also cite the need for U.S. companies to tap foreign talent to compensate for the lack of trained personnel in the United States and the increased managerial efficiencies that come from coordinating with a foreign workforce. A 2004 report indicates that outsourcing of jobs—some of them high-paying, white-collar jobs—is skyrocketing. The report documents that 48,417 jobs were outsourced from the United States in the first quarter of 2004 alone. Taking into account those corporations that underestimated the number of jobs outsourced, the researchers believe that at least 406,000 jobs were moved overseas in 2004, up from 204,000 in 2001.[32]

What these figures show is that it is becoming increasingly difficult for Americans to save money because well-paid employment is being shipped overseas. Today, most families must have two wage earners to make ends meet, and even then they often have difficulty paying the bills, let alone saving money for their children's college education or a health emergency. After adjustment for inflation, the median income for an American household increased only $1,260 between 1973 and 1997.[33] With most new jobs being created in the low-wage service industries, it is no wonder that the U.S. savings rate is so low.

IMF managing director de Rato states:

> *There are two obvious ways in which global imbalances could unwind quickly and in a very disruptive way. One would be an abrupt fall in the rate of consumption growth in the United States, which has been holding up the world economy ... [I]f [consumption] slows abruptly, it will take away a major support from world demand before other supports are in place.... Another possibility is that... investors become unwilling to hold increasing amounts of U.S. financial assets, and demand higher interest rates and a depreciation of the U.S. dollar, which in turn forces U.S. domestic demand to contract... as well as financial market disruptions.*"[34]

Though many Americans may think that they were "born to shop," if the downward pressure on wages continues and personal debt continues to increase, U.S. consumption may well decline. This would have a drastic effect on U.S. creditors, as these nations buy American debt (U.S. Treasury bills) mainly because American consumers buy their exports and so help keep their economies humming. If Americans stop buying, other nations may deem it too risky to continue investing in such a highly indebted nation. If these nations start selling or simply stop buying their Treasury bills, the United States will be in a lot of trouble. It could raise interest rates, as de Rato suggests, to make Treasury bills more enticing, but high interest rates would cause the U.S. economy to contract, resulting in recession. Most Americans, whether in debt from overconsumption or underpayment, would suffer immensely if interest rates rose. So would indebted corporations.

The U.S. government's creditors have so far been sanguine about the overvalued dollar because it helps them export goods to the United States. But if both personal and federal debt continue to spiral out of control, and if U.S. consumption declines, these nations would likely look for somewhere else to invest their money. With demand for the dollar falling, the dollar would lose value; an official devaluation of the dollar would be inevitable.

For decades, the dollar has been the world's reserve currency because, simply, it has been the "only game in town." That may no longer be the case. Recently there have been reports that Iran, and possibly some OPEC nations, are considering pegging the price of oil to the euro, not the dollar. This is a terrifying prospect for the U.S. government and its citizens alike. If the dollar loses its dominance as the currency not only of reserves but of international trade, it is less likely that investors will prop it up. Then the whole house of cards might tumble.

Such is the might of the United States in world economic affairs that a faltering U.S. economy could well bring down the world economy. A serious setback in the American economy would inevitably have repercussions not only for other economies but for the nature of globalization and trade. If it happens that the United States experiences a serious economic meltdown, the fiercely neoliberal policies that dominate the global marketplace today may be modified. Though the EU is certainly procorporate, it is also more responsive to its citizens, the majority of whom oppose corporate-run globalization. Combine this opposition with the newfound assertiveness of developing and LDC countries, and the globalization model as it exists presently may undergo radical reform.

---

[1] Sherrod Brown. *Myths of Free Trade.* New York: New Press, 2004, p. 183.

[2] Brown. *Myths of Free Trade,* p. 186.

[3] Robert L. Pennington. *Economics.* Austin, Tex.: Holt, Rinehart, and Winston, 1999, pp. 130–131.

[4] Pennington. *Economics,* p. 440.

[5] Thomas D. Schoonover. *Uncle Sam's War of 1898 and the Origins of Globalization.* Lexington: University of Kentucky Press, 2003, p. 77.

[6] Schoonover. *Uncle Sam's War,* p.79.

[7] Schoonover. *Uncle Sam's War,* p. 83.

[8] Schoonover. *Uncle Sam's War,* p. 91.

[9] Schoonover. *Uncle Sam's War,* p. 99.

[10] Of the many books written about the New Deal, a good introductory volume is William E. Leuchtenburg's *Franklin Delano Roosevelt and the New Deal* (New York: Harper Perennial, 1963).

[11] Robert Kuttner. *The End of Laissez-Faire.* New York: Knopf, 1991, p. 47.

[12] Kuttner. *The End of Laissez-Faire,* pp. 57–58.

[13] Kuttner. *The End of Laissez-Faire,* pp. 59–60.

[14] Kuttner. *The End of Laissez-Faire,* pp. 240–243.

[15] Bureau of the Public Debt. U.S. Treasury "The Debt to the Penny and Who Holds It." Available online. URL: http://www.publicdebt.treas.gov/opd/opddodt.htm. Accessed on February 27, 2006.

[16] U.S. Department of the Treasury. Available online. URL: http://www.budget.senate.gov. Accessed on February 21, 2006.

[17] Quoted in Brown. *Myths of Free Trade,* p. 185.

[18] Economic Policy Institute. "New Report Shows U.S. Job Losses from NAFTA-Style Trade." Available online. URL: http://www.epinet.org/content/cfm/briefingpapers_b0p147. Accessed on March 2, 2006.

[19] Brown. *Myths of Free Trade,* p. 151.

[20] Brown. *Myths of Free Trade,* pp. 142, 155.

[21] Brown. *Myths of Free Trade,* p. 154.

22 Economic Policy Institute. "New Report Shows U.S. Job Losses."

23 Brown. *Myths of Free Trade,* p. 151.

24 Economic Policy Institute. "New Report Shows U.S. Job Losses."

25 Economic Policy Institute. "New Report Shows U.S. Job Losses."

26 Globalization101.org. "U.S. Lawmakers Approve CAFTA." August 8, 2005. Available online. URL: http://www.globalization101.org/news.asp?NEWS_ID=90. Accessed March 2, 2006.

27 Larry Rohter. "Bush Faces Tough Time in South America." The New York Times on the Web, November 2, 2005. Available online. URL: http://www.nytimes.com/2005/11/02/international/americas/. Accessed on March 3, 2006.

28 Daphne Eviator. "Evo's Challenge in Bolivia." *The Nation* (January 23, 2006), p. 11.

29 Rodrigo de Rato. "Shared Responsibilities: Solving the Problem of Global Imbalance." February 3, 2006. Available online. URL: http://www.imf.org/external/np/speeches/2006/020306.html. Accessed on February 28, 2006.

30 C. K. Prahalad. "The Art of Outsourcing" (Commentary). *The Wall Street Journal,* June 8, 2005, p. A14.

31 Prahalad. "The Art of Outsourcing," p. A14

32 Cornell University. "Bureau of Labor Statistics Grossly Underestimate U.S. Jobs Lost to Outsourcing." Press release, October 15, 2004. Available online. URL: http://www.news.cornell.edu/releases/Oct04/Bronf.outsourcing.rpt.1m.html. Accessed on March 3, 2006.

33 John Micklethwaite and Adrian Wooldridge. *A Future Perfect.* New York: Random House, 2003, p. 246.

34 De Rato. "Shared Responsibilities."

3

Global Perspectives

EAST ASIA: MARKET LIBERALIZATION AND A CRISIS OF CONFIDENCE

Background

In 1993, a WB report hailed the economies of the nations of East Asia as "remarkably successful in creating and sustaining macroeconomic stability."[1] A year later, the WB delightedly reported that "Thailand provides an excellent example of the dividends to be obtained through outward orientation, reciprocity to foreign investment and a market-friendly philosophy backed up by conservative macroeconomic management and cautious external borrowing policies."[2] The nations of East Asia had been so wildly successful at liberalizing their rapidly expanding economies that their economic growth was referred to as the "East Asia miracle." Yet by the summer of 1997, East Asia would experience the worst economic depression the world had known since the 1930s.

Decades of Growth

For the three decades prior to 1997, the nations of East Asia not only experienced astounding rates of growth; they experienced no serious economic downturns. Government policies included extensive government investment in education, facilitating domestic investment in key industries, and encouraging a high savings rate among citizens. The result of these policies was an unprecedented growth rate and a rising standard of living for all citizens. To a great extent, the nations of East Asia followed the dicta of the Washington Consensus and largely liberalized their economies. The main way in which they diverged from orthodox liberalization policies was in their insistence on a gradual and well-sequenced, rather than an abrupt and immediate, adoption of liberal policies. For example, as these countries liberalized, most waited until they had in place the institutions needed to control FDI and liberalization. They also implemented policies to more equitably distribute the gains from economic growth, thus greatly decreasing levels of poverty.

In the wake of the collapse of the Thai currency (the *baht*, on July 2, 1997, neoliberals pointed to intrusive government as the cause of the economic collapse. According to Joseph Stiglitz, however, it was precisely these government policies that had grown the East Asian economies in the first place and created the "miracle" the neoliberals had lauded.[3]

Capital Liberalization and Speculation

One of the greatest changes that has occurred as part of globalization since the early 1970s is the liberalization of capital markets, or the buying and selling of currencies, and investments in foreign stock markets and in foreign-currency projects. Perhaps in no other realm of macroeconomics is the need for strong domestic controls more urgent because of the damage currency speculation can do to an economy. In countries with little available capital, it can be argued that the liberalization of capital markets may attract badly needed investment, but this was not the case in East Asia, where high savings rates and thriving economies provided sufficient capital. One thing the East Asian nations did not have was a mature and functional financial infrastructure created and run by the government and its central bank to help control or head off the havoc that "runs" on their currency might create. Despite their unease about capital liberalization, and in the face of international pressure, many East Asian nations liberalized their capital markets before they had the requisite safety net in place. Because neoliberal orthodoxy frowns on such controls, East Asian nations were discouraged from taking the time to implement needed regulations in this area.

Financial market speculation involves taking advantage of short-term volatility in world currencies. The primary goal of traders in capital markets is making quick profits through short-term speculation on tiny variations in a currency's value. When the value of a currency dips even slightly, speculators buy. When the currency's value goes up, the traders sell and pocket the profits. Today, the big players in capital market speculation are mainly managers of huge pension funds, mutual funds, hedge funds, or any other financial entity with millions of dollars at its disposal that can be zipped around the world, into and out of markets, via computer. Fund managers look to invest in strong currencies, whose variations are small and which are fairly certain to regain their value after a dip. Highly volatile currencies, which may dip and then crash—never to rise again—are very risky and generally avoided. When their computers show the tiniest downtick in a strong currency, fund managers buy. When the value of the currency ticks up again, they sell. Because they trade in millions or billions of dollars, the profits realized are enormous.

Today, global financial transactions far outstrip "real" investments. FDI, for example, usually involves long-term investments in "real" assets, such as factories, that produce goods and employ people. In contrast, financial trading does nothing to increase the productivity of the nation affected. Yet global financial speculation dwarfs FDI by more than nine to one. In 1980, daily foreign exchange (currency) trading was only $80 billion; by 2002, more than $1.5 trillion in currency was traded each day.[4]

One type of short-term capital market speculation is called foreign portfolio investment (FPI). In FPI, foreigners buy shares of stock on a foreign stock exchange, wait a short time for the stock price to go up, and then sell to turn a quick profit. Frequently, FPI speculators buy a large volume of shares of a particular foreign stock in order to artificially boost the stock price. Other investors, attracted by what appears to be the appreciating value of the company's stock, plow in their money, thinking that the stock price will continue to rise. Once the speculators have inflated the stock price, they sell short (quickly) and realize a handsome profit. After selling their huge number of shares, the stock price falls, and small investors are left to absorb the losses. A 1998 UNCTAD report on investment stated that, worldwide, the ratio of FPI to FDI was three to one. In some countries—most pertinently the nations of East Asia—FPI actually outstripped FDI by an even greater margin. In the early to mid-1990s, East Asia was considered ideal for FPI because its economies were strong, and its currencies therefore posed less risk than more volatile currencies.[5]

Like all speculative investments, capital speculation is subject to a "herd mentality," in which even a rumor or hint of a downturn can result in panic selling that is devastating to the currency or the company whose stock is in play. Herd behavior underscores the contradictory nature of capital market liberalization as a policy. When a nation has a strong currency and healthy economy, it is least in need of capital inflows, yet that is precisely when speculators descend on it en masse. When that same nation is experiencing economic difficulty and may be in dire need of an influx of capital, the herd abandons it, and no capital comes its way.

The Immediate Causes of the East Asia Crisis

THAILAND

In the year and a half prior to the East Asia crisis, more speculative capital had entered the region than in the previous 10 years combined.[6] Only a few years prior to the crisis and at the urging of the IMF, which had hoped to stimulate foreign investment in the region, the East Asian nations of Thailand, Malaysia, Indonesia, South Korea, and the Philippines had liberalized their capital markets.

Thailand, particularly, was a magnet for foreign speculative investment. Hot money poured into the country, mainly into the real estate market. Before the 1990s, Thailand had strict controls on how much money banks could lend for real estate investment. Beginning in the 1990s, Thailand gave in to the demands of the IMF and rescinded the regulations. Because business was booming, by the mid-1990s many billions of dollars were flowing into Thailand to buy baht, which were used to construct a virtual forest of skyscrapers and office buildings. The IMF encouraged this, even though speculative real estate invcstment is known to be highly destabilizing, as it is prone to "bubbles," which inevitably burst. A real estate bubble arises when investors predict that real estate prices will continue to go up, so they invest heavily, pushing prices up still further. The rising prices entice more people to invest in real estate in hopes of reaping profits. In Bangkok, as real estate prices rose, Thai banks lent increasing amounts of money to both foreign and domestic investors who clamored for a way into the booming real estate market. Office buildings sprouted like mushrooms after a monsoon rain. It did not take long before capacity was reached, and there was no one left to rent or buy all the office space that had been built. The builders could not rent their new offices, so they defaulted on their bank loans. The housing bubble burst. To this day, these "bubble" buildings remain untenanted.

By 1996, it is estimated that $24 billion in hot money had flooded into Bangkok real estate alone. Many more millions were invested in the Thai stock market. This huge influx of foreign investment artificially raised the value of the baht. But when foreign investors realized in 1997 that they had invested in real estate no one wanted and that the Thai banks that had extended credit for the building spree now had billions in unpaid loans, they panicked and withdrew their funds from Thailand. The value of the baht plummeted. The Thai stock market crashed. Thai banks were in danger of bankruptcy. Though economic growth had been strong in Thailand, many of its manufacturing firms carried significant debt and needed recapitalization to continue operating. With Thai banks on the brink of failure, Thai companies could not get the capital they needed to stay in business. The Thai economy collapsed.

SOUTH KOREA

South Korea had grown its economy essentially without foreign investment because it had used the vast savings of its citizens to finance its growth. Savings were kept in banks, and the banks lent this money to manufacturing companies to increase production. This policy of mostly domestic capitalization worked wonders for the South Korean economy, which grew at an astounding rate and became a contender in global markets. Since the end of the Korean War in 1953, South Korea's economic policies had increased per capita income more than eightfold, and poverty was nearly eradicated. So successful was South Korea's economic progress that early in the 1990s it was invited to join other highly industrialized nations as a member of the OECD. If the South Korean economy had an Achilles heel, it was the indebtedness of its industry. Most South Korean firms borrowed extensively to finance production and expansion; however, they were fiscally sound and had not defaulted on their debts.

As in the case of Thailand, the IMF and the U.S. Treasury put pressure on South Korea to open and deregulate its financial sector to permit foreign investment. By the mid-1990s, South Korea finally gave in and liberalized its financial sector. South Korean firms began to borrow heavily from U.S. banks. Then, in late 1997, something strange happened.

Though all debt payments were made and no foreign bank had suffered any losses, ominous rumors began to circulate. The word on Wall Street was that South Korea was in financial trouble. The rumors of a South Korean default—though entirely unfounded—sent Wall Street into a panic. The U.S. banks that had just months before been overjoyed at extending credit to South Korea now refused to roll over its loans. They also immediately called in balances due on outstanding loans. Now it was South Korea's turn to go into panic mode. The rumor mill had begun a process that became a self-fulfilling prophecy. Capital flew out of Korea. South Korean industries and firms, which relied heavily on borrowing for capital investment, could find no one to lend them the money they needed to continue production. Many businesses folded. Unemployment soared. With its main source of capital withdrawn, the South Korean economy, which prior to the pernicious rumors had been robust, now was in real trouble.

CONTAGION

Financial contagion refers to the spreading of an economic downturn, or crisis, from one nation to another. In East Asia, the infection began to spread as soon as foreign banks cut off credit to South Korea and foreign investors pulled out of their Thai investments.

When investors stampeded from Thai markets and sold their baht-backed investments, the value of the baht took a nosedive. The Thai government attempted to bolster the value of its currency by selling its dollar reserves to buy baht. So precipitous was the decline of the baht, however, that it did not take long before the Thai government used up its reserves and could no longer purchase its own currency to bolster its value. The only course open at this point was to devalue the baht.

The contagion spread from Thailand and throughout East Asia in several ways. Other East Asian nations had investments in Thailand and, thus, in baht. When the baht was devalued, these investments lost much of their value, and this hurt other East Asian economies. Thai businesses had outstanding loans with banks in East Asian nations. With the devaluation of the baht, they had to pay far more in their local currency because of the skewed foreign exchange rate. Many of the Thai companies defaulted on their loans, threatening the banks in other East Asian nations with failure and bankruptcy; this further weakened East Asian economies. Other East Asian nations were also important trading partners with Thailand. As Thailand's economy sank along with its currency, it had to limit its imports significantly. The devalued baht could no longer buy as many imported goods. Thailand greatly reduced imports from its East Asian neighbors, and reduced exports were another blow that contracted their economies. All in all, losses from investments, defaults, and contracting trade brought Thailand's neighbors down along with it.

The contagion spread throughout the region. It did not take long before the world's international financial powers began selling off the currencies of other East Asian nations, in addition to the baht. The panic selling by capital investors in developed countries greatly exacerbated the depth and extent of the crisis in East Asia.

As East Asian economies contracted, their demand for oil and other globally traded commodities declined significantly. This led to a steep drop in global commodity prices. Nations that depended on commodity exports as their primary source of revenue experienced a significant loss of income, so the economies of these nations contracted as well. In fairly short order, the contagion from the East Asia crisis spread to countries around the world, leading to recession in many of them.

The IMF Response to the Crisis

In response to the East Asia crisis, the IMF put together a bailout loan of about $95 billion, most of it coming from the G-7 (industrialized) countries. The reasoning behind this move was simple: It would inspire confidence in foreign investors to know that the Thai currency was backed by sufficient dollar reserves, and it would stabilize the exchange rate. However, most of the loan was used to service Thai debt to foreign banks. The tens of billions did not, in fact, bail out the Thai currency and economy but instead bailed out Western banks that were owed money by Thailand.

The loans also came with conditionalities, including raising interest rates (by as much as 25 percentage points), forcing draconian cutbacks in government spending and regulation, and increasing taxes. According to Stiglitz, these measures were imposed because they had worked reasonably well to reverse economic downturns in Latin America, but "East Asia was vastly different from Latin America; [in East Asia] governments had surpluses and the economy enjoyed low inflation."[7] High interest rates were intended to attract investment and restore confidence in East Asian economies. Generally, economists recommend raising interest rates to limit borrowing and to contract an economy with a serious macroeconomic inflation problem, yet East Asian economies were not experiencing inflation (debt was held by businesses not the national treasury), and what they needed was not contraction (they were in deep recession) but expansion. Because East Asian firms, particularly in South Korea, were highly in debt, raising interest rates only made it more difficult, if not impossible, for them to raise capital to get production going again. Raising interest rates made climbing out of the crisis nearly impossible; in fact, many East Asian companies went bankrupt when interest rates were hiked. The IMF's hoped-for foreign investments in East Asia never materialized because its policy of high interest rates made the economic situation worse, scaring investors away.

As businesses failed, the unemployment rate skyrocketed. Ever since the Great Depression of the 1930s, it has generally been acknowledged that if no other form of capital is available, government spending to get people working again is the best way to put an economy back on its feet. Any economy on the skids needs stimulation, and if businesses cannot provide it, then the government should. Yet the IMF insisted that East Asian nations implement the directives of the Washington Consensus, which require government nonintervention in the economy, raising interest rates to curb inflation and reduce the deficit, and creating a positive balance of payments. The IMF instructed the East Asian governments to balance their budgets and avoid deficit spending. Thus, the governments were unable to jump-start the economy by putting people back to work. With so many businesses closed and so many people out of work, the nations of East Asia saw a severe curtailment of import and tax revenue. Lack of revenue meant that any steps governments took to increase employment would necessarily entail deficit spending, but this was forbidden.

The IMF also demanded that the nations of East Asia work toward improving their balance of payments, or creating a trade surplus. This injunction proved difficult for several reasons. For one thing, building a trade surplus means that a nation must export more than it imports, but because so many East Asian businesses had gone belly-up, production was too low to permit expanding exports. And the currency collapse meant that foreign credit was unavailable to rebuild industry (and government investment in industry was prohibited). Increasing exports was therefore out of the question.

Another way to create a trade surplus is to drastically cut back on imports. Since they could not increase exports, East Asian nations tried to balance their payments this way. Of course, one nation's reduction of imports is another country's lack of exports. As they all cut back on imports, trade among East Asian nations dwindled. Overall, this severe cutback in trade reduced revenues among all East Asian trading partners, spreading and deepening the contagion of depression and intensifying the economic downturn.

By 1998, the East Asian contagion had spread globally. IMF policies did not create a net under falling currencies. They did not increase investor confidence in East Asian economies because these policies had made the economic situation in these nations worse, not better. And the forced reduction in trade spread the infection beyond East Asia to the rest of the world. In October 1998, the New York Stock Exchange crashed, falling more than 500 points, as did exchanges in Europe and other parts of the world.

The Results of Collapse

All economic indicators in the region turned negative in the wake of the crisis. Unemployment rose tenfold in Indonesia, fourfold in South Korea, and threefold in Thailand. Urban poverty doubled or tripled in these nations. In Indonesia, 75 percent of all businesses closed or contracted; in Thailand, about 50 percent of all bank loans were in arrears or default. GDP fell, too, by 13.1 percent in Indonesia, 6.7 percent in South Korea, and 10.8 percent in Thailand. Even three years after the crisis, GDP remained depressed throughout East Asia.[8] As Stiglitz notes, "Probably no country could have withstood the sudden change in investor sentiment, a sentiment that reversed [a] huge inflow to a huge outflow as investors, both foreign and domestic, put their funds elsewhere. . . . [the downturn] would be equivalent to a reversal in capital flows for the United States of an average of $765 billion per year between 1997 and 1999."[9]

The IMF's policies went a long way toward helping Western banks recoup the money they were owed on East Asian loans, yet little money was dedicated to help alleviate the suffering of people plunged into poverty by the crisis. Only after riots erupted in Indonesia did the IMF's managing director, Michel Camdessus, allocate money for food and lift his organization's ban on government-subsidized help to the poor.

The IMF's policies both initiated the East Asian crisis (by forcing capital market liberalization) and exacerbated it (by enforcing contractionary policies that only worsened the situation). In each case, its intent to boost confidence in East Asian economies and currencies backfired and led to an even greater exodus of needed capital.

The East Asian financial crisis also led to a significant loss of confidence in the IMF itself. The East Asia meltdown was front page news the world over, and its effects were felt around the globe. IMF policies in East Asia were seen to be so counterproductive and devastating that its economic advice and its reputation have since lost much of their luster. The crisis in East Asia also showed that markets can behave extremely irrationally. In this case, they exhibited "irrational mania" both in the initial enthusiasm for investment and in the subsequent panicked flight from the market.[10] The East Asian financial crisis is important in that it "made more credible to many people the charge that economic globalization has significantly increased international economic instability and has been harmful to domestic societies. It is certainly undeniable that the economic plight of East Asia attests to the ability of international financial markets to wreak havoc on domestic economies."[11]

PRIVATIZATION IN COCHABAMBA: WHO OWNS THE RAIN?

Background

"There's huge growth potential. There will be world wars fought over water in the future. It's a limited, precious resource, so the growth market is always going to be there." So said a water privatization firm's senior executive, who also refers to water as "the petroleum of the 21st century."[12] Increasingly, globalization is opening up markets for "commodities" such as water that many believe are the birthright of every living being. Yet the WB and the EU, as well as corporations in the United States and elsewhere, are attempting to cash in on the commodification of the resources on which life depends.

One study shows that between 1996 and 2002, 84 water-project loans awarded by the WB had privatization as a condition. That is triple the number requiring privatization that were awarded between 1990 and 1995. Whereas in 1990, only about 15 percent of the WB's structural adjustment loans required some type of water privatization, by 2002 that number climbed to more than 80 percent.[13]

In a 2003 investigative report, it was found that officials of the European Commission (EC) were requesting and receiving from water privatization firms the language and guidelines the companies wanted inserted into the GATS agreement of the WTO. E-mails clearly show that "[The EC] is using GATS to pursue the market expansion interests of large EU-based water corporations."[14] If water privatization becomes an integral part of the WTO, nations that do not want to privatize their water systems could find themselves on the losing end of DSB litigation and thus face potentially ruinous fines and trade sanctions. In this way, water privatization could be forced on countries that cannot afford to be cut out of global trade.

Bechtel Corporation, and others like it, insist that privatization is necessary in order to prevent wasteful usage of water. If people are forced to pay for the water they use, the argument goes, people will have a greater incentive not to waste it but to conserve it. Without privatization, they claim, the growing human population would be so profligate in its use of water that we would soon run out, or at least run in to extremely serious shortages.

There is no question that the people of the world are going to have to learn to use water resources more wisely. Presently, one-third of the human population lives in a water-stressed region; by 2025, two-thirds of humanity will struggle to find adequate water supplies. By 2020, human water use is expected to rise 40 percent over current usage. If wastage is not curtailed, humanity surely will be in trouble.[15] However, privatization is not necessarily the answer. The following example shows that the effects of privatization of water can be devastating.

Bolivia's Economy

Bolivia in the 1970s was suffering through both dictatorship and hyperinflation. Inflation, which rose at an annual rate of 25,000 percent, was beggaring the Bolivian economy. Supported by the right-wing government, the IMF and the WB took control of the Bolivian economy. The IMF imposed its rigid anti-inflationary policies, which, in this case, were exactly what the Bolivian economy needed. Government spending was cut drastically, the currency was devalued, wage and price controls were abolished, and government-run industries were privatized. This "shock therapy" successfully conquered the nation's hyperinflation; however, it left many ordinary Bolivians impoverished.

In the mid-1990s, the Bolivian president had committed his government to building a large dam project, the Misicuni Dam, ostensibly to provide needed water to nearby Andean communities, including Cochabamba, the third largest city in Bolivia with about 800,000 residents. The WB opposed the dam project as unnecessary and wasteful, but the government was keen on seeing it built. (It has been reported that one top government official had a financial interest in the dam project.) The government plan was to use some of the profits from the sale of Cochabamba's water system to help finance the dam. The privatization of the water system was, however, also a part of the WB's strategy for the Bolivian economy. At meetings with the Bolivian president in 1997, the WB is reported to have stated that "privatization of the Cochabamba water system was . . . a precondition [for Bolivia] receiving international debt relief from the World Bank, IMF, and others."[16] In a 1999 report on Bolivia, WB officials wrote: "No public subsidies should be given to ameliorate the increases in water tariffs in Cochabamba."[17]

Privatizing the Water

Cochabamba has always had a water problem. Most of the city's water flows down to it from lakes in Andean highlands, but a good deal of this lake water is traditionally used for irrigation by farmers.

In early 1999, the Bolivian government decided that it was time to privatize Cochabamba's water, and the water system was put up for auction. The auction drew only a single bidder: a company called Aguas del Tunari. Aguas del Tunari is partly owned by the San Francisco–based Bechtel Corporation. The contract negotiations with Aguas were conducted in secret, but local newspapers published what they could find out. Reports indicated that Aguas had paid only $20,000 up front for a 40-year lease on a water system worth millions of dollars. It was also discovered that Aguas was required to pay no taxes and was guaranteed a 16–18 percent profit on its investment.

Aguas took over the water system in November 1999, and it immediately raised the rates the citizens of Cochabamba had to pay for water. The first rate increase came with the December 1999 water bills. Though Aguas had promised that its rate increase would not exceed 35 percent, when the water bills arrived, they reflected a 200–400 percent increase in the charge for water. Most citizens of Cochabamba are poor, with minimum or near-minimum wage earnings ranging from $60 to $100 per month per household. In most of these households, the water bill increased from about $5 per month to between $20 and $25 per month. That is 20–25 percent of a family's entire monthly income. Many poor Cochabambinos were forced to choose between having water to drink or buying food to feed their families. Even the more well-to-do residents of a condominium complex in Cochabamba saw their water bill jump from $50 for the whole building to $120. Everyone was furious.

Though the exact contents of Aguas's contract were kept secret as "intellectual property," it soon became known that the company was allowed to raise its already exorbitant rates no matter how poorly it performed its function. For many citizens, water availability was reduced to two hours a day; some days they had no water at all. Water pressure was dismal, so people "showered" out of buckets. And, to add insult to injury, Aguas claimed ownership of more traditional uses of water. For example, it became illegal to dig your own well for drinking water. People who dug their own well had to pay monthly fees to the company, or Aguas would cap it. It was also against the law to collect rain in a rain barrel. The outraged citizens of Cochabamba refused, en masse, to pay their water bills.

The Power of Protest

In December 1999, an alliance was formed among farmers, trade unionists, factory workers, environmentalists, and just about anybody else exercised enough to do something to return control of Cochabamba's water to its citizens. The organization formed was called La Coordinadora de Defensa del Agua y la Vida (The Coordinator for the Defense of Water and Life), or simply the Coordinator.

The first organized protests began on December 28, 1999, when about 20,000 people blockaded the streets and marched against Aguas. A general strike was called, and the city of Cochabamba was shut down for four days. For the first time in 18 years, the Bolivian government used tear gas on its own citizens. Still, the protesters did not disperse. Government officials met with representatives of the Coordinator but refused to cancel the contract with Aguas. On January 14, 2000, the government did agree to revise the Aguas contract and the laws, such as the rain-collecting prohibition, that supported it. However, the government refused out of hand any attempt at rolling back the price increases.

For nearly two months, the people of Cochabamba did not pay their water bills and maintained roadblocks in different parts of the city. On February 4, tired of waiting for word from the government, the Coordinator organized another demonstration. This was to be a peaceful march to the main plaza in Cochabamba. The Coordinator wanted to unite the citizenry in a massive and peaceful demonstration of solidarity.

The protest began on February 4 as a festive affair. Bands played, people danced and handed out flowers. The crowd of about 30,000 people was motley, with the very young to the very old, the well-off to the poorest peasant marching and mingling together and enjoying the upbeat mood. After a few hours at the plaza, the crowd began to disperse, with most people walking toward their homes. A few minutes after leaving the plaza, gunshots rang out. A thousand or more police appeared, some called to Cochabamba from as far away as the capital, La Paz. The people of Cochabamba fought the police for two days. "It was like a war," one of the leaders, Oscar Olivera, said. At least 175 protesters were injured and two people were blinded.[18]

New negotiations with the government yielded limited results. In March, an informal poll was taken of 60,000 people living in and around Cochabamba who were affected by the Aguas privatization. More than 90 percent responded that the government should cancel its contract with Aguas. The leaders of the Coordinator decided to tap into this overwhelming support to confront the government once again.

Mass demonstrations started again on April 4. Meetings with the government, the Coordinator, and local businesspeople were again convened.

That night the police arrived, and some pitched battles ensued. By the next day, even more protesters showed up. As a bishop arrived to say mass, the government imposed martial law.

The violence in the streets got worse. On Saturday, April 8, a 17-year-old boy was shot in the face by a policeman and killed. "The whole city was fighting," Olivera said.[19] On Sunday, the government announced that the Aguas representatives had volunteered to leave Cochabamba, but it refused to negotiate further with the Coordinator because it claimed they were "drug traffickers," an accusation that bewildered the little old ladies tending the barricades in the streets.

By Monday, April 10, the crowd of protesters had swelled to more than 80,000. People were angry and swore they would take over the government if the Aguas contract was not canceled. The government capitulated and signed a memo prepared by the Coordinator. On April 11, the legislature passed a law nullifying the Aguas contract and returning the water system to local control. The mood of the crowd turned from anger to jubilation. The people of Cochabamba were the first and only group of citizens to have successfully beaten water privatization.

In 2001, Olivera was awarded the Goldman Environmental Prize for Sustainable Development. In his acceptance speech, he said: "After 15 years of structural adjustment, when we thought that the most important human values had been wrested from us, when we thought we were incapable of overcoming fear, of having the ability to organize and unite, when we no longer believed we could make our voices heard, then our humble, simple, and hard-working people—men, women, children, and the elderly—demonstrated to the country and to the world that all this is still possible."[20]

In the case of Cochabamba, privatization overwhelmingly hurt the poor more than the rich, who are far more likely to be water wasters (for example, tending their lawns). It wrested control of a vital resource from citizens and put its control in the hands of those whose goal is to make a profit from its sale.

Something must be done to help save water and all the other resources people, and all living things, depend on. But as the experience in Cochabamba makes clear, commodifying these resources and placing the responsibility for managing them into the hands of profit-seeking corporations is not necessarily the best way to do it.

TRANSITIONAL ECONOMY IN RUSSIA: KLEPTO-CAPITALISM

A transitional economy is one that is moving from a command economy, as under communism, to a more open, free market, or capitalist economy. A command economy is one in which production is owned and controlled by the state. The transition from a communist to a capitalist economy can be wrenching under the best of circumstances, as entirely new institutions must be created to underpin and regulate the new economic structure. If proper guidance is absent and the sequence of transitional steps is disordered, the experience can be seriously destabilizing and cause immense suffering. This is what happened in Russia.

Background

Russia, once ruled by a czar, became a communist state after the Bolshevik Revolution in 1917, then becoming part of the Soviet Union. The Bolshevik Revolution was, in a sense, an experiment, an attempt to create a communist utopia in Russia (and its satellite nations). As Orlando Figes, a noted expert in Russian history and professor of history at Cambridge University and Birkbeck College, London, has pointed out, "The ultimate aim of the Communist system was the transformation of human nature."[21] Further, "The core of the Soviet system was always the certainty that human beings must be reshaped to fit the needs of a new 'rational' economy. The thought that the economy exists to serve the needs of human beings was dismissed.... Bolshevik doctrine required human beings to function as resources of the economy."[22]

The revolutionary reconfiguring of the Russian economy was disastrous. Industrial productivity dropped by 70 percent; peasant culture and traditional agriculture were destroyed in favor of industrialized farming methods, and millions died in "government-sponsored" famines. For 70 years, Russians managed as best they could to survive in their totalitarian state. As the decades passed, Russians became inured to the innate corruption of their society and their economic system.

To quote John Gray (1948–), a professor of European political philosophy at the London School of Economics:

> *A symbiosis of the state with organized crime has a long history in Russia. It has always been at the heart of Soviet institutions. The Soviet state was lawless; it contained nothing akin to an independent judiciary; the legal code permitted the state practically unlimited discretionary power. For ordinary citizens to keep within the bounds of law was an impossibility—if only because the law itself could mean anything that the authorities decided. Economic life functioned in a climate of continuous disregard of regulations.... In the Soviet Union corruption was not a problem; it was a solution in an otherwise unworkable economic system.*[23]

In the Soviet Union, the economy was ruled by state-run oligarchies, whose managers had close ties to the Kremlin. Managers often got their posts through kickbacks to government officials. A type of mafia arose in Russia to organize and profit from the control of nominally state-run industry. Thus, organized crime and government became intimately connected. "Inevitably, any kind of enterprise acquired criminal associations in ordinary people's perceptions. Often, such associations were real."[24]

During the presidency of Leonid Brezhnev, the Russian economy seemed to function, partly because the corruption and criminalization of industry had become institutionalized and so worked reasonably well. It is hardly surprising then that the political openness (*glasnost*) and economic reforms (*perestroika*) that President Mikhail Gorbachev introduced in the later 1980s were viewed with alarm and ultimately rejected by the Russian people. Gorbachev's anticorruption policies served only to reveal the depth of the corruption in the economy and the Soviet government. By 1991, the illegitimacy of the Soviet economic structure was so blatantly obvious that the communist system collapsed entirely.

In 1989, the breakup of the Soviet Union and its communist stranglehold on its Eastern European satellite nations were finalized with the fall of the Berlin Wall. Eastern European nations shed the burden of communist rule and themselves became transitional economies. With the downfall of Gorbachev and the rise of Boris Yeltsin to the Russian presidency, the demise of communism was complete. President Yeltsin, with help and encouragement from the IMF, WB, and the U.S. Treasury, attempted to transform the Russian economy into a modern-day capitalist system. Yet, the deep-seated and pervasive corruption of the Russian economy made this transition from an economy that had not known markets (or known only the black market) to a market economy especially challenging. In fact, an economic transition of this magnitude had never before been attempted, and no one really knew what would happen.

Shock Therapy

President Yeltsin's economic advisers were of two minds about the speed of reform. Some thought the requisite changes should be made gradually, to build up institutions and avoid failure; others believed they should be be made rapidly, to prevent backsliding into command-economy mode. The latter group, supported by the IMF and the U.S. government, worried that unless a well-heeled capitalist class was created quickly, there would be no one to promote and maintain the new order. The neoliberal faction was also concerned about the poor state of the Russian economy and felt that decisive action was needed. The former group, favored by Keynsian-type economists, put more emphasis on sequencing and moderating the effects on the Russian people of the inevitable economic shocks that result from transition. The policies supported by the IMF and the United States won out and shock therapy, or a very rapid liberalization and transition to a market economy, was initiated.

In 1991, the prevailing conditions in Russia were as follows:

- There were no legal institutions in place that could enforce contracts, settle commercial disputes, or handle bankruptcies in an orderly way.
- There were no institutions in place that could formulate and enforce regulations for businesses to follow.
- There were no institutions in place to oversee the formation of a securities market (stock exchange) or to set out regulations and laws about business management, the rights of shareholders, etc.
- Russian banks existed, but they had never made their own decisions about who was creditworthy and should get a loan, nor did they know how to ensure that a loan is repaid. The government had always simply told them whom to fund.
- Businesses did exist, but, like the banks, they had never made their own decisions about what to produce and how much to produce. These instructions came from the Kremlin. Businesses had never had to procure materials because they had always been provided by the state. Businesses were clueless about how to operate in a free market.
- Many businesses were corrupt, with managers (sometimes connected to organized crime) skimming off the top. Breaking the law was commonplace and was an integral part of doing business.
- Businesses had no idea how to set prices because there had never been a real market. Prices had been established by the state and often kept artificially low to keep the poorest citizens from sinking into poverty.
- Under Soviet rule, there was no unemployment and therefore no unemployment insurance. With guaranteed employment, such insurance had been unnecessary.
- People employed for life at one firm did not have to move. The housing market was controlled by the state. (With privatization, a housing market would be crucial, as the unemployed sought work where jobs were being created.)

Such was the situation in which a more or less instantaneous overhaul of the economy was to take place. By late 1991, when shock therapy was initiated, the

Russian economy had been so seriously weakened by Gorbachev's anticorruption reforms that many sectors of the economy had essentially disintegrated. This was especially true of the black market, one of the most vital sectors of the Soviet economy and one on which the Russian people may have depended the most. Further, the partial undermining of the party elite, who controlled or at least profited from corrupt business practices, left the economy in chaos, as established patterns of kickbacks and other perks undermined production of goods. The close ties between business managers and the government meant that the Russian government was itself in the process of collapse.

Price Liberalization and Emergency Stabilization

Allowing prices to find their natural level in the free market is crucial to a capitalist economy, and thus, one of the first steps in the transition process was to undo the system of fixed prices that had prevailed under the Soviet system.

On January 2, 1992, price controls on at least 90 percent of goods were lifted, though some staples, such as bread, were excluded. By January 3, prices on these goods had risen by 250 percent. Between 1992 and 1996, the inflation rate increased to nearly 1,700 percent.[25] Prices seemed to rise by alarming amounts almost daily or weekly. Russia was falling victim to hyperinflation. The exorbitant price increases wiped out the savings of many Russians. Most Russians lived on the fixed wages paid to them through the government-owned businesses where they worked. Though some wages were raised, to a maximum of about 50 percent, this increase could in no way compensate for triple-digit inflation. (The massive price increases did, however, yield windfall profits for industrial managers and for their government backers and organized crime syndicates.)

The dislocation and inflation brought about by this first foray into a market economy were so severe that the IMF stepped in to curb inflation. This was done by raising interest rates to stabilize the *ruble* (the Russian currency) and Russia's balance of payments. In addition to controlling inflation, the IMF required the Russian government to liberalize its capital markets to encourage foreign investment in Russia.

Not all prices were liberalized. The Russian government continued to keep prices low for certain vital goods, such as bread and milk, as well as its natural resources products, particularly oil, in order to keep energy prices low for its citizens. However, by keeping the price of domestic oil lower than its sale price on the global market, the controllers of this industry could buy domestic oil cheaply and then sell it at a much higher price on the global market. In this way, they lined their pockets with millions, if not billions, of dollars. Wary of the future of the shaky Russian economy, these newly minted millionaires sent their money to safe havens in overseas banks, instead of investing it domestically. This risk-averse behavior by the nouveau riche in Russia was understandable, given the rampant corruption in the Russian economy, yet it hobbled Russia in its efforts to invest in and build new businesses capable of competing in the capitalist market.

Privatization

The privatization of government-owned and -run businesses was intended to completely restructure the Russian economy. Privatization of a command economy necessarily entails a complete overhaul of business structure and practice. The first step is to transfer ownership of enterprises from the state to the private sector. Businesses also have to be oriented toward providing goods that consumers want instead of fulfilling quotas set by the government; businesses have to learn to be responsive to the demand for products. They also have to learn how, when, and where to get the materials they need for production. Perhaps most important, they have to learn how to operate efficiently. Under the Soviet system of guaranteed employment and wages, efficiency was not important. Why be efficient if you are going to be paid whether you work hard or not? The efficiency requirement of privatized industry terrified many Russian workers, and they were right to fear it. As industries privatize and efficiency increases, job loss is inevitable. In Russia, which had no unemployment insurance, little or nothing was done to help those who had lost jobs find new ones.

Russia was under pressure from the IMF to privatize quickly and to the greatest extent possible. The privatization segment of the shock therapy program began in July 1992. By the end of 1994, more than three-quarters of Russia's mid- to large-sized industries had been privatized.

Russian privatization was more like a fire sale than a well-thought-out policy of controlled transfer of industry to the private sector. Industrial plants and other businesses were sold for far less than they were worth. Reportedly, many sales involved significant kickbacks to government officials, and concomitantly, government officials were most likely to sell to those who would kick back the most money—sometimes those engaged in organized crime. Ownership of many industrial plants was, in fact, frequently turned over to the factory's longtime manager. Understanding how precarious the Russian economy was, these insiders often absconded with what they could get before any real functioning market or laws were put in place that might make their pilfering more difficult. In an effort to emulate Western markets, "shares" in a company were issued and were supposed to be offered for sale to the public, which had been given vouchers to help them buy the shares. Usually, it was the business managers and well-connected Kremlin bigwigs who bought up these vouchers and, thus, the company's shares. As majority stockholders, the managers could strip the company's assets at will. Their newfound wealth was usually sent overseas. Thus, many privatized firms did not promote efficiency, did not expand production (some abandoned production altogether), and did not create wealth for the economy.

Privatization was also supposed to eliminate government interference in business and the economy, and in some ways it did—at least in terms of the central government. Yet corrupt officials in the Russian provinces, or *oblasts,* took over the central government's role. With the Russian economy on a steep downward slide, provincial governments were starved of revenue (and many provincial officials wanted their piece of the privatized pie). Many extorted money from newly privatized enterprises.

The way privatization was undertaken in Russia severely undermined the populace's confidence in both Western-style free enterprise and in their government. Having all but given away state-run industries, the Kremlin was in dire need of money. The government therefore instituted a "natural resources tax," which, though doing little to fill the treasury, did make many of Yeltsin's closest associates billionaires. Aside from enriching the president's friends, the tax put an enormous burden on the legions of impoverished Russians, especially pensioners who somehow had to pay the tax (to keep from freezing in the winter) out of their $15 per month pensions.[26]

THE LOANS-FOR-SHARE PROGRAM

In an extreme example of privatization gone awry, the Russian government began its "loans-for-share" program in 1995. The loans-for-share program arose from the Kremlin's reliance on private banks, instead of its central bank, for the money it needed to keep functioning. These private banks were run by insiders, who had received the ownership of the banks as "gifts" from their Kremlin pals. The banks were unregulated because no structure existed for the regulation of privately owned financial institutions. In effect, bank ownership became a "license to print money." Bank managers approved loans to themselves, their family and friends, and to their government benefactors. The collateral offered to back the loans given to the government were shares in some remaining government-owned enterprises. In almost all cases, the government deliberately defaulted on its loans. When the government defaulted, the ownership of the enterprise was taken over by the bank—actually the bank manager. Almost overnight, bank managers stripped the assets of their newly acquired enterprises and became billionaires. These "oligarchs," as they were known because of their great wealth, moved their funds into banks in Europe and the United States.

Most of this largesse arose from the corrupt policies of Yeltsin. In exchange for enriching the oligarchs, Yeltsin received financial and media support (the media were also gifted to the oligarchs) for his reelection. It is estimated that, at most, 1.5 million Russian insiders benefited (enormously) from Russia's privatization schemes. At one point, the oligarchs claimed to control 50 percent of the nation's wealth.[27] Russia's oligarchs have been compared, unfavorably, with the Robber Barons of the U.S. Gilded Age. But although the Robber Barons of the American "Wild West," such as the Rockefellers, made fortunes building railroads or an oil industry, they also established viable industries that employed real people and created wealth for the country. In contrast, the oligarchs of Russia's "Wild East" created nothing except their own vast fortunes. Whereas American industrialists had made their nation richer, the Russian klepto-capitalists stripped their nation's assets, leaving it in dire poverty.[28]

Collapse

Between 1990 and 1997, industrial output in Russia fell by 40 percent.[29] For a short while in 1997, Russia saw its economic conditions improve slightly due to an uptick in oil prices. The recovery was short lived. By 1998, the contagion from the economic crisis in East Asia reached Russia. After the collapse of the East Asian economies, foreign investors were wary of sinking their money into shaky developing economies. Russia was an especially risky prospect. After having unloaded most of its assets for a song and privatized before a workable tax system was in place, the Kremlin resorted to borrowing heavily to make ends meet. Interest rates were raised, yet more Russians sent more money to overseas banks. By June 1998, the Russian government was paying 60 percent in interest rates on its domestic loans in rubles; several weeks later, that figure rose to 150 percent.[30] It seemed that nothing the government did could regain the confidence of the people in its currency. Despite the vertiginous Russian interest rates, an understandably skeptical oligarchy continued to ship its ill-gotten money to overseas banks.

When the East Asian economies collapsed, their demand for oil fell dramatically. This led to a decline in demand (and thus an increase in supply), and the price of oil plummeted by more than 40 percent.[31] Oil is one of Russia's main exports, and the lower price had a devastating effect on its economy. By early 1998, the price of oil on the global market was threatening to dip below Russia's cost of extraction and transport. In order to make Russian oil competitive on the global market, devaluation of the ruble seemed inevitable.

The signs that the ruble was overvalued were ubiquitous. Imported products were everywhere, and domestic products had a hard time competing with them. For ordinary people, many of whom were now unemployed, barter or the black market afforded their only access to goods. For them, the overvalued ruble was a nightmare. For the oligarchs, the story was quite different. A millionaire with overvalued rubles could frequent the upscale boutiques and car dealerships selling top-quality imported goods. For the newly rich, an overvalued ruble could buy more dollars and permit the purchase of the many expensive German cars and designer clothes that began to be seen on the streets of Moscow.

The IMF did whatever it could to forestall a devaluation of the ruble, fearing that a devalued ruble would rekindle hyperinflation. The IMF approved a loan for $22.6 billion, to be paid in installments, to bolster the Russian currency. The WB, which had identified Russia as one of the most corrupt countries in the world, at first refused to be party to the bailout. The WB viewed the loan as throwing good money after bad, and it believed that Russia should figure out a way to generate revenue legally from its wealth of natural resources, rather than continuing to rely on handouts.

Despite the obvious signs of collapse, U.S. banks continued to pour money into Russia. The impetus for this action had less to do with saving the Russian economy than it did with padding the banks' bottom line. In situations such as this, "moral hazard" arises. Moral hazard is the lender's incentive to make ill-conceived loans to a debtor nation based on the understanding that, no matter how dire the country's economic conditions get, the IMF will bail the lender out. Thus, the assurance that the IMF will always come to the rescue with millions or billions in loans if the borrowing country defaults encourages foreign banks to make loans they would otherwise not even consider.

Three weeks after the IMF loan began to be paid, Russia announced that it would cease payments on its debt and that it would devalue the ruble. The value of the ruble declined, and by January 1999, it had lost 75 percent of its value.[32] The Russian announcement resulted in a worldwide financial crisis. Interest rates on loans to LDCs soared; even growing developing nations had trouble attracting investment. Meanwhile, within only a few weeks, the Russian oligarchs had appropriated the billions in IMF money and stashed it safely in their personal bank accounts abroad. It was not only Russian klepto-capitalists who benefited from the IMF's actions; Western banks made out handsomely from IMF bailout money.

The Social Costs of Shock Therapy

Poverty had been a part of the Soviet system, yet it had been ameliorated by modest pensions and other financial assistance from the state. The abject impoverishment of most Russians after shock therapy occurred on a scale and a depth unknown in that country's peacetime modern history.

With almost all the nation's wealth siphoned off to a few million oligarchs, managers, and government officials who benefited from privatization, income inequality became extremely pronounced. Among the 3–5 percent of the population who were New Russians (the rich), monthly income was as high as $100,000, while one-fourth of the population lived on less than $70 a month, or below the poverty line.[33] In 1989, only 2 percent of the Russian population lived in poverty; by late 1998, that figure had risen to 23 percent, based on a $2 per day standard. On a $4 per day standard, the number in poverty had increased to 40 percent.[34]

Between 1990 and 1998, industrial production in Russia fell by 42.9 percent; its GDP dropped by 45 percent.[35] Spending on what had been an enormous sector in the Soviet economy, the military industry, was cut by two-thirds, throwing one-eighth of the Russian workforce out of their jobs.[36] (Significantly, none of tne savings realized from these shutdowns was used to create new jobs or to help the jobless.) Unemployment was rampant, though precise figures are hard to come by. Many "officially" unemployed people eked out a living through barter, on the black market, or through "informal" employment, such as plumbing, painting, and general contracting. Experts estimate that at least 50 percent of Russia's economic activity during this period came from barter. Some of the unemployed joined organized crime syndicates to feed their families. Many of the elderly who depended on government pensions were left totally without income. Western television reports showed them, ragged and impoverished, begging on the streets or sifting through Dumpsters for scraps of food.

The collapse of the Russian economy became evident in many other ways. Life expectancy declined across the board. In the Soviet Union, health care had been universal and free. When the Russian middle class saw its savings wiped out by inflation, it could no longer afford to pay for privatized health care. By 1998, the life expectancy of Russian women had fallen from 74 to 72 years; for men, it had fallen from 62 years to 58 years. Suicide among Russian men increased 53 percent, and alcohol-related deaths more than tripled. Owing to Russians' impoverishment and pessimism about the future, the birth rate declined by nearly 50 percent.[37]

Crime also exploded. In 1994, Russia's 30,000 murders were three times the per capita murder rate in the United States.[38] In 1995, kidnappings rose 100 percent, and armed assaults increased by more than 600 percent. Contract killing became commonplace; property crime soared. Much of the economy of Russia today consists of "criminalized markets" run by organized crime syndicates. In a state with few laws and little or no enforcement, kleptocracy, or rule by thieves, naturally arises. Reportedly, privatized companies and banks routinely pay 10–20 percent of their profits to organized crime for "protection." There are purportedly about 150 organized crime syndicates in present-day Russia, controlling between 35,000 and 40,000 businesses and about 400 banks.[39]

As Stephen Cohen, professor of Russian studies at New York University, wrote, "For the great majority of families, Russia has not been in transition, but in an endless collapse of everything essential for a decent existence—from real wages, welfare provisions, and health care to birthrates and life expectancy; from industrial and agricultural production to higher education, science, and traditional culture; from safety in the streets to prosecution of organized crime and thieving bureaucrats."[40]

Prospects

Many economists believe that the shock therapy of rapid liberalization exacerbated Russia's already deep-seated problems, and attempts at economic restructuring brought them to the fore. Russia's GDP is presently growing at about 4 percent per year. At that rate, it will take Russia another decade to regain the economic strength it had in 1989. Foreign investors are still very wary of Russia, and FDI is only 10 percent of what it was in 1990.[41] Russia today is growing, albeit slowly, but its economy is still run by the kleptos and oligarchs. Ordinary Russians still suffer inordinately.

Perhaps, with honest and prudent management, Russia will be able to harness the recent rise in oil prices to haul itself out of its economic black hole. That will only happen if the kleptocrats are unseated as the rulers of the economy. And that can be done only by establishing and rigorously enforcing laws that govern corporate practice.

According to Gray, Russia, in many ways, has been the subject of two experiments in utopianism during the 20th century. The first utopian experiment had been communism. The second, neoliberal capitalism, has many parallels with the first: "Like the Utopia envisaged by Lenin, the global free market aims to bring into being a state of affairs that has never hitherto existed in human society ... This is Utopia divorced from history, hostile to vital human needs, and finally [is] as self-destroying as any that has been attempted in our century."[42]

CHINA: CONTROLLED TRANSITION

Modern China has the world's fastest growing economy. Unlike Russia, China's central government is not generally corrupt. Because the central communist government tightly controls the economy, it is able to carefully plan and gradually implement market reforms in a way that makes them far less traumatic for Chinese citizens than they have been for Russians. The enormous power wielded by China, due in no small measure to its immense size and vast population, has enabled the Chinese government to ignore the orthodoxies of the Washington Consensus and craft its own economic policies based on its unique history and culture. By turning its back on the practitioners of neoliberalism and developing its economy in its own way, China has become an exemplar of carefully considered, homegrown economics.

Background

In the early years of the 20th century, China was ruled by a corrupt emperor, and its people suffered intense poverty. A revolutionary uprising overthrew the Manchu dynasty in 1911, and Sun Yat-sen became leader of the new republic. On the death of Sun Yat-sen's son, competing warlords vied for power; they were overthrown only after a protracted civil war led by Chiang Kai-shek, whose Nationalist forces were assisted by the Chinese Communists. In 1927, Chiang began another civil war to rid China of the Communists, forcing them to retreat, but also enabling them to regroup. In 1931, Japan invaded and occupied Manchuria, and by 1937, it had successfully launched a full-scale invasion of China. The Chinese suffered horribly under Japanese rule, but the occupation ended when Japan was defeated in World War II (1945).

The Nationalists and Communists had fought uneasily side by side to defeat the Japanese, but when this conflict ended, they began fighting each other, and another civil war erupted. In 1949, the Communists, led by Mao Zedong, defeated the Nationalists, who retreated to Taiwan. Mao and the Communists took over the country, renaming it the People's Republic of China.

Mao instituted strict communist policies and a command economy, collectivizing agriculture and essentially closing China to external trade. All private property was abolished, most landlords and landowners were executed, and farmland was distributed to poor peasants. Both foreign-owned and privately owned property and businesses were seized and nationalized. All industries were state run, and as in all command economies, production quotas were set by the central government for both agricultural and industrial products. Under Mao's Great Leap Forward program, Chinese production targets were raised to phenomenal heights. In an excess of ideological zeal, in the late 1950s, China's farmers over-reported crop production figures. The Communist government used much of this (nonexistent) surplus to pay back a loan to the Soviet Union. About 30 million Chinese died of starvation.

Reform from Within

Mao's death in 1976 was followed by a power struggle between Maoists and moderates, with moderate Deng Xiaoping winning out as leader of the Communist government. One of Deng's first proposals was to reform China's agricultural sector by slowly instituting market reforms. Deng was a practical man, and one of his favorite phrases was "seek truth from facts, not from ideology."[43] Deng initiated experimental market reforms in China's agricultural sector. The first test of his reforms occurred in a single province. Farmers there were still required to meet government-set quotas for crop yields, but the farmers in this province were also permitted to sell on the open (local) market any crops they produced in excess of the quota and to keep the profits from the sale. The experiment was a huge success, and agricultural production increased notably. Furthermore, the reform had the overwhelming support of the farmers. Over the next two years, this experimental program in partial privatization was gradually extended to other provinces. In every case, the result was positive. Within three years, agricultural market reform was in effect throughout China.

China's initial foray into an economic system based on private property, profits, and the market bears all the hallmarks of its future reforms. First, the reform was initially implemented on a small, experimental scale. Only if the test case succeeded was the reform expanded. Second, the reform's success was measured not only by output but by the support of the workers involved. Reform was not forced on the people from on high, but had to be enthusiastically embraced by the people for it to be deemed successful. Only when it was established that the program was popular and caused little or no economic or social dislocation was it expanded. Third, reform was a natural outgrowth of the existing economic system. For example, the collectivized agricultural system was not eradicated in one fell swoop and replaced with something totally different and alien. The old system was allowed to continue functioning, while the reform grew out of that existing system. This avoided any economic disturbances reform might cause. Fourth, the reform was done gradually so that over time, people could become used to it, recognize its success, support it, and even improve on it. This was as far from shock therapy as one can get and still move an economy toward a market-oriented system.

In the early 1980s, with the agricultural reforms performing excellently, China turned to reforming its industries. It used the same approach as it had in agriculture. The existing system of government-set quotas, industrial management, and output was retained, but gradually, step by step, industries were given some autonomy that allowed them increasing control over production and distribution of the goods they produced. Industry still had to meet its production quotas, but some of the excess goods produced could be traded on the local market. Because of the personal incentive (profit) that was an integral part of the program, industrial output increased significantly; industries became more efficient and more productive.

The Problem of Prices

In a command economy, the government not only owns all production but also sets all prices. Frequently, prices are set artificially low to make goods affordable to the poor. The Chinese government wanted to expand its market reform successes but was uncertain about what to do about pricing. How does one make a smooth transition from fixed prices set by the government to prices set by the market? How does one determine what the market price for any particular good should be?

The Chinese government began by instituting a program of two-tiered pricing. The original, fixed prices were retained on goods produced under the old quota system. All the goods produced in excess of the quota—that is, all the privately marketable goods—were allowed to find their price on the free market. As with its other reforms, the two-tiered pricing system was allowed to expand very gradually once it had been shown to work well. Slowly, the state-subsidized prices were phased out as the market developed, prices stabilized, and no undue economic hardship resulted. By about 1986, the two-tiered price system had done its job, and the two price systems were melded into a single market price. This most difficult of transitions had been accomplished with little or no economic upheaval—and no inflation. There were no sudden price hikes from privatization that wiped out the savings of ordinary people, as had happened in Russia. The smooth and gradual transition led to the creation of a market economy that not only increased production but raised the standard of living of both Chinese consumers and producers.

Contract Responsibility

Once market prices were established and working well, the "contract responsibility" system was introduced. This reform permitted managers to lease the company that they ran. Under the terms of the lease, management ran the company and was responsible for its productivity. The Chinese government imposed a fixed tax on the company, but once the tax was paid, management could market its products and keep the resulting profits to do with as it pleased. As intended, many managers used their profits to reinvest in the business, expanding or diversifying its production and making it more efficient and competitive. The gradually implemented program worked well and production increased.

Promoting Local Initiative and Innovation

One of China's most successful reform programs provided incentives to townships and villages to create their own businesses. With the free market boom in agriculture, many people in rural townships and villages could expend their energy elsewhere. Rural residents were encouraged to invest their savings and agricultural profits in creating new enterprises that they could run for a profit. The townspeople oversaw the running of the enterprise and controlled how its funds were used and its profits distributed. As the program expanded, townships and villages vied with one another to come up with the most innovative and efficient businesses. The competition among localities led to the creation of profitable businesses throughout China, and these created wealth and jobs for millions of rural Chinese.

The village incentives program was, curiously for China, an exercise in democracy as well as the free market. Local people controlled the governance of their businesses. Business managers were accountable to the villagers for the production methods they used, the workers they hired, and the profits they generated. Significantly for overpopulated China, the program's success tended to discourage rural residents from abandoning their villages for work in overcrowded cities, a phenomenon that too often accompanies industrialization in many countries. The village incentives program was, perhaps, the most dynamic engine of economic growth in China in the 1980s and 1990s.

So successful were the contract responsibility program and the village incentives program that by 1996, only 29 percent of gross industrial output came from state-owned enterprises (SOEs). Collectively owned, individually owned, and other types of privately owned enterprises were, by that time, generating 39 percent, 16 percent, and 17 percent of China's gross output, respectively.[44]

Thrift is a tradition among the Chinese people. With the additional income they were realizing through market reforms, the savings rate in China soared. In 1979, the amount of money in domestic savings accounts was equivalent to 32 percent of China's GDP. By 2004, that percentage soared to 49 percent of GDP, giving China one of the highest savings rates in the world. These savings provide a huge pool of available capital for further investment in economic development in China.[45]

Trade Zones

In 1977, even before the above reforms had been carried out, the Chinese government had established EPZs (export processing zones) in several of its most important coastal cities. These Special Economic Zones, or SEZs, were established to encourage FDI in China. The Chinese government offered tax and trade incentives to attract businesses to these areas. In exchange, foreign investors brought revenue and the latest production technology to China. This "open door" policy drew investors in droves. China undertook huge construction projects to create its free zones and the housing and other amenities needed by workers. Many thousands of workers were lured to the SEZs by the prospect of employment. Chinese foreign trade exploded, accounting for 20 percent of GDP by 1985.[46] FDI, which amounted to $1.8 billion in 1984, increased to a whopping $41.7 billion in 1996, by which time more than 60 percent of China's exports came from SEZs.[47] China's SEZs have some of the same problems as EPZs elsewhere. Wages are often relatively low, and workers are often tied to their jobs because the government refuses them "passes" to move elsewhere. But the Chinese government exerts enough control over the SEZs to ensure that, for the most part, workers have better living and working conditions than laborers in EPZs in other developing countries and, especially, in LDCs.

China and the East Asia Crisis

China's economy was in a far stronger position than the economies of other East Asian nations when the 1997 crisis struck. In 1997, China had no inflation, its currency was not overvalued, and it had a huge and enviable trade surplus, which meant that it had enormous currency reserves. Further, FDI in China consisted of long-term investments; China had almost no short-term debt, so it was not vulnerable to the collapse that panic selling by investors or withdrawal of funds by creditors can cause.

Chinese economists had recognized the danger of short-term foreign investment prior to the Asian financial crisis. To prevent such a crisis in China, the government implemented a plan of two-tiered investments in two of the country's stock exchanges. The plan divided stocks into two groups. Shares of Group A stocks were for sale only to Chinese nationals. Foreign investors could buy only shares of Group B stocks. Thus, drastic fluctuations in Group B stocks affected only foreign investors. Steps could then be taken to shield the stocks in Group A should foreign investors panic and divest themselves of their Group B shares.

The primary effect of the East Asia crisis for China was a notable reduction in its exports. The nations of East Asia were (and are) important trading partners with China. With their economies in shambles, these countries had to restrict greatly the quantity of goods they imported from China. In 1998, for the first time in two decades, the value of China's exports decreased.

Because it was not dependent on foreign investment, and thus foreign pressure, when the crisis hit, the Chinese government was able to spend heavily on infrastructure in order to employ Chinese workers laid off because of lower exports. Over three years, the government poured $1.2 trillion into building railroads and highways and into construction of water and municipal facilities of every type. Thus, the Chinese people did not suffer the same effects of unemployment as those in other East Asian economies, and the Chinese economy did not dip into recession. While other East Asian economies contracted dramatically, in 1998 China's GDP increased 7.8 percent. This rate of growth was, admittedly, lower than its more usual 9 percent or more annual growth rate, yet it is remarkable when compared with the negative growth experienced at that time by many other countries. By 1999, China's GDP was again up to 8.9 percent, and it has not looked back since.[48]

Economic Giant: The Effects of Reform

China is on track to become the world's largest and most successful economy. It is certainly the fastest growing. Between 1979 and 2005, China's economy has grown an average of 9.6 percent per year. In 2005, the growth rate topped 10 percent. China's GDP has grown at a rate of 10 percent or more annually in eight of the last 16 years. In 1992 and 1993, its GDP grew at more than 14 percent per annum.[49]

Most of China's wealth comes largely from its exports, which increased 28.4 percent in 2005, to $762 billion. Between 1979 and 2005, China's exports exploded from $14 billion to $762 billion. In just three years, from 2002 to 2005, China's global trade more than doubled. In 2005, it imported $660 billion worth of goods (an increase of 17.6 percent), giving it a trade surplus for 2005 of $102 billion. China today has the world's third-largest trade economy (after the United States and Germany), but many believe it is well on its way to number one.[50]

China's exports to the United States have increased from 15.3 percent of total Chinese exports in 1986 to 33.1 percent in 2004. Its abundance of low-wage labor is certain to keep China's share of production and exports growing. Significantly, China has the world's second-largest foreign exchange, with reserves totaling more than $769 billion in September 2005, up nearly 50 percent over the same period just one year earlier.[51] China's remarkable economic growth has many U.S. economists and government officials worried. China's economy affords a stark contrast to the U.S. economy in many ways. Whereas the United States has a huge deficit, China has vast currency reserves; whereas the United States has an enormous trade deficit, China has a gargantuan trade surplus. The United States believes that most government interference in the economy is anathema and that the laissez-faire free market will self-correct and is the best solution for economic problems; the Chinese government is proactive in guiding and growing the world's most dynamic economy.

The United States has brought pressure to bear on China to adjust its currency to make its imports less attractive to Americans. On July 21, 2005, the Chinese government appreciated its currency, yielding an exchange rate of 8.11 yuan to the U.S. dollar (from 8.28 yuan to the dollar). Whether this will curb Chinese imports to the United States and improve the U.S. trade balance as is hoped remain to be seen.[52]

Challenges Ahead

There are aspects of the Chinese economy and the Chinese nation that may slow or even reverse the remarkable economic progress it has made.[53] For one thing, state-owned industrial production still makes up about one-third of all industrial production in China. These SOEs are as inefficient as ever and are a definite drag on the Chinese economy. If China wants to maintain its spectacular growth rate, it will probably have to accelerate the privatization of these SOEs.

Chinese workers are also suffering a degree of unemployment, something totally unknown in the command economy. Unemployment reached a high of 4.0 percent in 1997 (during the East Asia crisis) but fell back to 3.2 percent a year later. Still, Chinese workers are unused to unemployment and are resentful of it. Yet the Chinese government has extensive programs to help the unemployed, including a financial safety net and a comprehensive program of job training, in addition to its ongoing government-funded infrastructural projects, which provide many unemployed Chinese workers with jobs.[54]

Corruption remains a problem in China, especially in the provinces and rural areas. In some cases, corruption is a carryover from the command economy, when local officials and industrial managers faked production numbers to impress the central government. These practices continue today, as do bribes to overseers to cut corners and save money on construction or other projects. And because the central government remains so powerful, it often happens that those who have close ties to government officials get the perks and the profitable projects, not the ordinary people.

Perhaps the greatest threat China faces at present is environmental degradation. Chinese cities have some of the worst air pollution in the world. Of 338 Chinese cities monitored, two-thirds had air quality below globally accepted health standards. Toxic and particulate emissions pose a significant threat to the health of many Chinese people.

Poor land-use policies have led to expanding desertification, especially in northern China. Dust storms periodically blow into Beijing, forcing residents to wear face masks in order to breathe. It is estimated that one-third of China's land, approximately 818 million acres (331 million hectares), is acutely vulnerable to desertification. Of this, about 647 million acres (262 million hectares) are actually undergoing desertification or have become desert. The rate of China's desertification seems to correlate with its rate of economic growth, as land degradation has noticeably increased in the last two decades. Desertification in China is due largely to overgrazing by livestock; as Chinese have become more affluent, the demand for meat has increased dramatically. Yet the desertification of China's vital northern agricultural lands seriously imperils its food supply. Prior to the years of reform, China pursued a policy of food self-sufficiency. That goal, though still dreamed of, now seems impossible. Too much land has been given over to industry and other types of development—including housing a population in excess of 1.3 billion people.

By the late 1990s, about 12 million acres (4.8 million hectares) of farmland were lost to other uses.[55] Deforestation is also a huge problem in China. With hillsides denuded of trees, the annual floods that occur in China have become increasingly deadly. In 1998, the Chinese government issued a ban on logging in many areas and initiated a program of tree planting. Though a final assessment is premature, these programs seem to be having some positive effect.

Of all the environmental problems China faces, perhaps none has more potential for damaging both lives and the economy than a lack of water resources. Both a burgeoning population and a booming economy are making demands on water resources far beyond what the resources can provide. Between 1980 and 1993, urban water consumption increased 350 percent; industrial demand for water doubled in the same period. The World Bank asserts that, in many areas in China, water problems are reaching "crisis proportions."[56]

This crisis also includes the quality of water. Industries in northern China spew effluent into rivers that carry them south. In its haste to develop economically, China has overlooked the need for pollution controls, and in many places untreated industrial effluent and municipal raw sewage enter rivers and streams. Many Chinese cities obtain drinking water from nearby rivers, so many Chinese citizens are forced to drink highly polluted, untreated water. Both municipal and industrial withdrawals from rivers have also seriously restricted the flow of many of China's once mighty waterways. Increasingly, China's major waterways, such as the Yangtze and Yellow rivers, dry up before reaching the sea. In the highly industrialized coastal region, sewage and industrial contamination of coastal waters has led to an eightfold increase in the incidence of toxic red tides.[57]

In its race for growth, China's demand for water has far outstripped its natural supply. Not only are the rivers of the relatively arid (and increasingly desertifying) north drying up; groundwater under many northern provinces is disappearing as well. Chinese research has confirmed that the water table beneath the North China Plain—the region that produces 40 percent of China's grain—has been dropping an average of 1.5 meters (5 feet) per year since the mid-1990s. At least 70 percent of the agricultural output of this region depends on irrigation, yet the sources of irrigation water are disappearing.[58]

China's human population continues to grow (though more slowly than before), and as the standard of living increases, so does residential water demand. Chinese studies estimate that as China's growing population enjoys a higher standard of living, residential water use will increase fourfold, from 31 billion tons in 1995 to 134 billion tons in 2030. Already, 300 of China's more than 600 cities are facing water shortages. Meanwhile, agriculture presently uses 85 percent of surface and groundwater for irrigation. As the population rises and the demand for food increases, even more water will be needed for irrigation.

Finally, as China's industrialization advances even more rapidly than its population, industry's demand for water is expected to more than quadruple. One study indicates that if GDP grows at 5 percent per year, industry's demand for water will increase from 52 billion tons to 269 billion tons per year. However, for years, China's GDP has been growing at twice that rate, which means that industrial demand for water will likely increase eightfold.[59] Obviously, there are just too many sectors of Chinese society that are demanding increasing access to China's finite water resources. It is unknown which sector will win in the inevitable struggle that will arise over access to dwindling water supplies.[60]

It is obvious that all sectors in China cannot demand a larger slice of a constantly shrinking pie. If China does not somehow address its lack of water, shortages may be the factor that puts the brakes on what otherwise seems to be an unstoppable economic expansion. Under current circumstances, it is difficult to predict what China will do. Its people need water to survive, but they also need the jobs that expanding industries provide. If demands from these sectors are granted, then China faces a serious shortfall in food production. China then would be forced to import food in a world where food scarcity (due to increasing population and environmental degradation) may be widespread. It will be interesting to see how China's leaders, so astute in their economic reforms, grapple with and resolve these problems.

---

1 Robert Gilpin. *Global Political Economy.* Princeton, N.J.: Princeton University Press, 2001, p. 267.

2 Wayne Ellwood. *A No-Nonsense Guide to Globalization.* Oxford (UK): Verso, p. 78.

3 Joseph Stiglitz. *Globalization and Its Discontents.* New York: W. W. Norton, 2003, p. 90.

4 Ellwood. *A No-Nonsense Guide to Globalization,* p. 72.

5 Ellwood. *A No-Nonsense Guide to Globalization,* pp. 75–76.

6 Ellwood. *A No-Nonsense Guide to Globalization,* p. 77.

7 Stiglitz. *Globalization and Its Discontents,* p. 104.

8 Stiglitz. *Globalization and Its Discontents,* p. 97.

9 Stiglitz. *Globalization and Its Discontents,* p. 99.

10 Gilpin. *Global Political Economy,* p. 268.

11 Gilpin. *Global Political Economy,* p. 267.

12 Bob Carty. "The Water Barons: A Look at the World's Top Water Companies." CBC News, February 3, 2003. Available online. URL: http://www.cbc.ca/news/features/water/business.html. Accessed on March 7, 2006.

[13] Center for Public Integrity. "Promoting Privatization." February 3, 2003. Available online. URL: http://www.icij.org/water/report.aspx?aid=45. Accessed on March 7, 2006.

[14] Daniel Politi. "Privatizing Water: What the European Commission Doesn't Want You to Know." April 7, 2003. Center for Public Integrity. Available online. URL: http://www.icij.org/report.aspx?aid=173. Accessed on March 8, 2006.

[15] CBC News Online. "Water: By the Numbers." August 25, 2004. Available online. URL: http://www.cbc.ca/news/background/water/bynumbers.html. Accessed on March 10, 2006.

[16] Jim Shultz. "Bolivia's War over Water." The Democracy Center. Available online. URL: http://www.democracyctr.org/waterwar. Accessed on March 9, 2006.

[17] Shultz. "Bolivia's War over Water."

[18] International Monitor. "The Fight for Water and Democracy: Interview with Oscar Olivera." Available online. URL: http://internationalmonitor.org/mm2000/00june/interview.html. Accessed on March 9, 2006.

[19] International Monitor. "The Fight for Water and Democracy."

[20] Goldman Environmental Prize. "Oscar Olivera." Available online. URL: http://www.goldmanprize.org/node/150. Accessed on March 13, 2006.

[21] Orlando Figes. *A People's Tragedy.* Quoted in John Gray. *False Dawn.* New York: New Press, 1997, p. 135.

[22] Gray. *False Dawn,* p. 136.

[23] Gray. *False Dawn,* pp. 153–154.

[24] Gray. *False Dawn,* p. 154.

[25] Gray. *False Dawn,* p. 145.

[26] Stiglitz. *Globalization and Its Discontents,* p. 159.

[27] Stiglitz. *Globalization and Its Discontents,* pp. 159–160.

[28] Stiglitz. *Globalization and Its Discontents,* pp. 159–160.

[29] Stiglitz. *Globalization and Its Discontents,* p. 144.

[30] Stiglitz. *Globalization and Its Discontents,* p. 146.

[31] Stiglitz. *Globalization and Its Discontents,* p. 144.

[32] Stiglitz. *Globalization and Its Discontents,* p. 149.

[33] Gray. *False Dawn,* p. 147.

[34] Stiglitz. *Globalization and Its Discontents,* p. 153.

[35] Gray. *False Dawn,* p. 156.

[36] Gray. *False Dawn,* p. 156.

[37] Gray. *False Dawn,* pp. 148, 150.

[38] Gray. *False Dawn,* p. 148.

[39] Gray. *False Dawn,* p. 155.

[40] Quoted in Gray. *False Dawn,* p. 151.

[41] Joseph Stiglitz. "The Ruin of Russia." *The Guardian,* April 9, 2002. Available online. URL: http://www.globalpolicy.org/socecon/bwi-wto/imf/2003/0409ruin.htm. Accessed on March 16, 2006.

[42] Gray. *False Dawn,* p. 140.

[43] Gregory C. Chow. "China's Economy: Reform and Perspectives." April 15, 1999. Available online. URL: http://www.princeton.edu/~gchow/China.html. Accessed on March 22, 2006.

[44] Chow. "China's Economy."

[45] Congressional Research Service. "China's Economic Conditions." January 12, 2006. Available online. URL: http://www.fas.org/crs/row/IB98014.pdf. Accessed on March 24, 2006.

[46] PBS. "Commanding Heights: China, Economic." Available online. URL: http://www.pbs.org/wgbh/commandingheights/lo/countries/cn/cn_economic.html. Accessed on March 17, 2006.

[47] Chow. "China's Economy."

[48] Chow. "China's Economy."

[49] Congressional Research Service. "China's Economic Conditions."

[50] Congressional Research Service. "China's Economic Conditions."

[51] Congressional Research Service. "China's Economic Conditions."

[52] Congressional Research Service. "China's Economic Conditions."

[53] It must be stated that China's lack of democracy and its appalling human rights record are not being included in this discussion of its economic prospects.

[54] Chow. "China's Economy."

[55] World Bank. *China: Air, Land, and Water.* 2000, pp. 17–20. Available online. URL: http://lnweb18.worldbank.org/eap/eap.nsf/Attachments/China+Env+Report/$File/China+Env+Report.pdf. Accessed on March 28, 2006.

[56] World Bank. *China: Air, Land, and Water,* p. 47.

[57] World Bank. *China: Air, Land, and Water,* pp. 49–50.

[58] Worldwatch Institute. "China's Water Shortage." World Water Conservation.com. Available online. URL: http://worldwaterconservation.com/chinawater1.html. Accessed on March 28, 2006.

[59] Worldwatch Institute. "China's Water Shortage."

[60] Worldwatch Institute. "China's Water Shortage."

PART II

Primary Sources

4

United States Documents

The primary sources in this chapter are divided into three sections:

Historic Documents

Testimonies and Speeches on the Effects of Globalization

NAFTA

HISTORIC DOCUMENTS

Fireside Chat, President Franklin Delano Roosevelt (October 22, 1933)

During the Great Depression, President Franklin D. Roosevelt spoke directly to the nation via his frequent radio broadcasts, called Fireside Chats, which were enormously popular among Americans at that time. In these "chats," the president used his considerable charm, sense of humor, and friendly, down-home conversational style to inform the nation about the actions he was taking to improve the economy and explain why these actions were necessary and how they would help lift the pall of the depression. This particular transcript, which deals with the currency situation at that time, was broadcast on October 22, 1933.

On the Currency Situation

Franklin D. Roosevelt

Sunday, October 22, 1933

1. It is three months since I have talked with the people of this country about our national problems; but during this period many things have happened, and I am glad to say that the major part of them have greatly helped the well-being of the average citizens. Because, in every step which your

Government is taking we are thinking in terms of the average of you—in the old words, "the greatest good to the greatest number"—we, as reasonable people, cannot expect to bring definite benefits to every person or to every occupation or business, or industry or agriculture. In the same way, no reasonable person can expect that in this short space of time, during which new machinery had to be not only put to work, but first set up, that every locality in every one of the 48 states of the country could share equally and simultaneously in the trend to better times.

2. The whole picture, however—the average of the whole territory from coast to coast—the average of the whole population of 120,000,000 people—shows to any person willing to look, facts and action of which you and I can be proud.

3. In the early spring of this year there were actually and proportionately more people out of work in this country than in any other nation in the world. Fair estimates showed 12 or 13 millions unemployed last March. Among those there were, of course, several millions who could be classed as normally unemployed—people who worked occasionally when they felt like it, and others who preferred not to work at all. It seems, therefore, fair to say that there were about 10 millions of our citizens who earnestly, and in many cases hungrily, were seeking work and could not get it. Of these, in the short space of a few months, I am convinced that at least 4 millions have been given employment—or, saying it another way, 40% of those seeking work have found it.

4. That does not mean, my friends, that I am satisfied, or that you are satisfied that our work is ended. We have a long way to go but we are on the way.

5. How are we constructing the edifice of recovery—the temple which, when completed, will no longer be a temple of money-changers or of beggars, but rather a temple dedicated to and maintained for a greater social justice, a greater welfare for America—the habitation of a sound economic life? We are building, stone by stone, the columns which will support that habitation. Those columns are many in number and though, for a moment the progress of one column may disturb the progress on the pillar next to it, the work on all of them must proceed without let or hindrance.

6. We all know that immediate relief for the unemployed was the first essential of such a structure and that is why I speak first of the fact that three hundred thousand young men have been given employment and are being given employment all through this winter in the Civilian Conservation Corps Camps in almost every part of the Nation.

7. So, too, we have, as you know, expended greater sums in cooperation with states and localities for work relief and home relief than ever before—sums which during the coming winter cannot be lessened for the very simple reason that though several million people have gone back to work, the necessities of those who have not yet obtained work is more severe than at this time last year.

8. Then we come to the relief that is being given to those who are in danger of losing their farms or their homes. New machinery had to be set up for farm credit and for home credit in every one of the thirty-one hundred counties of the United States, and every day that passes is saving homes and farms to hundreds of families. I have publicly asked that foreclosures on farms and chattels and on homes be delayed until every mortgagor in the country shall have had full opportunity to take advantage of Federal credit. I make the further request which many of you know has already been made through the great Federal credit organizations that if there is any family in the United States about to lose its home or about to lose its chattels, that family should telegraph at once either to the Farm Credit Administration or the Home Owners Loan Corporation in Washington requesting their help.

9. Two other great agencies are in full swing. The Reconstruction Finance Corporation continues to lend large sums to industry and finance with the definite objective of making easy the extending of credit to industry, commerce and finance.

10. The program of public works in three months has advanced to this point: Out of a total appropriated for public works of three billion three hundred million, one billion eight hundred million has already been allocated to Federal projects of all kinds and literally in every part of the United States and work on these is starting forward. In addition, three hundred millions have been allocated to public works to be carried out by states, municipalities and private organizations, such as those undertaking slum clearance. The balance of the public works money, nearly all of it intended for state or local projects, waits only on the presentation of proper projects by the states and localities themselves. Washington has the money and is waiting for the proper projects to which to allot it. Another pillar in the making is the Agricultural Adjustment Administration [AAA]. I have been amazed by the extraordinary degree of cooperation given to the Government by the cotton farmers in the South, the wheat farmers of the West, the tobacco farmers of the Southeast, and I am confident that the corn-hog farmers of the Middle West will come through in the same magnificent fashion. The problem we seek to solve had been steadily getting worse for twenty years, but during the last six months we have made more rapid progress than any nation has

ever made in a like period of time. It is true that in July farm commodity prices had been pushed up higher than they are today, but that push came in part from pure speculation by people who could not tell you the difference between wheat and rye, by people who had never seen cotton growing, by people who did not know that hogs were fed on corn—people who have no real interest in the farmer and his problems.

11. In spite, however, of the speculative reaction from the speculative advance, it seems to be well established that during the course of the year 1933 the farmers of the United States will receive 33% more dollars for what they have produced than they received in the year 1932. Put in another way, they will receive $400 in 1933, where they received $300 the year before. That, remember, is for the average of the country, for I have reports that some sections are not any better off than they were a year ago. This applies among the major products, especially to cattle raising and the dairy industry. We are going after those problems as fast as we can.

12. I do not hesitate to say, in the simplest, clearest language of which I am capable, that although the prices of many products of the farm have gone up and although many farm families are better off than they were last year, I am not satisfied either with the amount or the extent of the rise, and that it is definitely a part of our policy to increase the rise and to extend it to those products which have as yet felt no benefit. If we cannot do this one way we will do it another. Do it, we will.

13. Standing beside the pillar of the farm—the A.A.A.—is the pillar of industry—the N.R.A. [National Recovery Administration]. Its object is to put industry and business workers into employment and to increase their purchasing power through increased wages.

14. It has abolished child labor. It has eliminated the sweat shop. It has ended sixty cents a week paid in some mills and eighty cents a week paid in some mines. The measure of the growth of this pillar lies in the total figures of reemployment which I have already given you and in the fact that reemployment is continuing and not stopping. The secret of N.R.A. is cooperation. That cooperation has been voluntarily given through the signing of the blanket codes and through the signing of specific codes which already include all of the greater industries of the Nation.

15. In the vast majority of cases, in the vast majority of localities—the N.R.A. has been given support in unstinted measure. We know that there are chisellers. At the bottom of every case of criticism and obstruction we have found some selfish interest, some private axe to grind.

16. Ninety per cent of complaints come from misconception. For example, it has been said that N.R.A. has failed to raise the price of wheat and corn and hogs; that N.R.A. has not loaned enough money for local public works. Of course, N.R.A. has nothing whatsoever to do with the price of farm products, nor with public works. It has to do only with industrial organization for economic planning to wipe out unfair practices and to create reemployment. Even in the field of business and industry, N.R.A. does not apply to the rural communities or to towns of under twenty-five hundred population, except in so far as those towns contain factories or chain stores which come under a specific code.

17. It is also true that among the chisellers to whom I have referred, there are not only the big chisellers but also petty chisellers who seek to make undue profit on untrue statements.

18. Let me cite to you the example of the salesman in a store in a large Eastern city who tried to justify the increase in the price of a cotton shirt from one dollar and a half to two dollars and a half by saying to the customer that it was due to the cotton processing tax. Actually in that shirt there was about one pound of cotton and the processing tax amounted to four and a quarter cents on that pound of cotton.

19. At this point it is only fair that I should give credit to the sixty or seventy million people who live in the cities and larger towns of the Nation for their understanding and their willingness to go along with the payment of even these small processing taxes, though they know full well that the proportion of the processing taxes on cotton goods and on food products paid for by city dwellers goes one hundred per cent towards increasing the agricultural income of the farm dwellers of the land.

20. The last pillar of which I speak is that of the money of the country in the banks of the country. There are two simple facts.

21. First, the Federal Government is about to spend one billion dollars as an immediate loan on the frozen or non-liquid assets of all banks closed since January 1, 1933, giving a liberal appraisal to those assets. This money will be in the hands of the depositors as quickly as it is humanly possible to get it out.

22. Secondly, the Government Bank Deposit Insurance on all accounts up to $2500 goes into effect on January first. We are now engaged in seeing to it that on or before that date the banking capital structure will be built up by the Government to the point that the banks will be in sound condition when the insurance goes into effect.

23. Finally, I repeat what I have said on many occasions, that ever since last March the definite policy of the Government has been to restore commodity price levels. The object has been the attainment of such a level as will enable agriculture and industry once more to give work to the unemployed. It has been to make possible the payment of public and private debts more nearly at the price level at which they were incurred. It has been gradually to restore a balance in the price structure so that farmers may exchange their products for the products of industry on a fairer exchange basis. It has been and is also the purpose to prevent prices from rising beyond the point necessary to attain these ends. The permanent welfare and security of every class of our people ultimately depends on our attainment of these purposes.

24. Obviously, and because hundreds of different kinds of crops and industrial occupations in the huge territory that makes up this Nation are involved, we cannot reach the goal in only a few months. We may take one year or two years or three years. No one who considers the plain facts of our situation believes that commodity prices, especially agricultural prices, are high enough yet.

25. Some people are putting the cart before the horse. They want a permanent revaluation of the dollar first. It is the Government's policy to restore the price level first. I would not know, and no one else could tell, just what the permanent valuation of the dollar will be. To guess at a permanent gold valuation now would certainly require later changes caused by later facts.

26. When we have restored the price level, we shall seek to establish and maintain a dollar which will not change its purchasing and debt paying power during the succeeding generation. I said that in my message to the American delegation in London last July. And I say it now once more.

27. Because of conditions in this country and because of events beyond our control in other parts of the world, it becomes increasingly important to develop and apply the further measures which may be necessary from time to time to control the gold value of our own dollar at home.

28. Our dollar is now altogether too greatly influenced by the accidents of international trade, by the internal policies of other nations and by political disturbance in other continents. Therefore the United States must take firmly in its own hands the control of the gold value of our dollar. This is necessary in order to prevent dollar disturbances from swinging us away from our ultimate goal, namely, the continued recovery of our commodity prices.

29. As a further effective means to this end, I am going to establish a Government market for gold in the United States. Therefore, under the clearly defined authority of existing law, I am authorizing the Reconstruction

Finance Corporation to buy gold newly mined in the United States at prices to be determined from time to time after consultation with the Secretary of the Treasury and the President. Whenever necessary to the end in view, we shall also buy or sell gold in the world market.

30. My aim in taking this step is to establish and maintain continuous control.

31. This is a policy and not an expedient.

32. It is not to be used merely to offset a temporary fall in prices. We are thus continuing to move towards a managed currency.

33. You will recall the dire predictions made last spring by those who did not agree with our common policies of raising prices by direct means. What actually happened stood out in sharp contrast with those predictions. Government credit is high, prices have risen in part. Doubtless prophets of evil still exist in our midst. But Government credit will be maintained and a sound currency will accompany a rise in the American commodity price level.

34. I have told you tonight the story of our steady but sure work in building our common recovery. In my promises to you both before and after March 4th, I made two things plain: First, that I pledged no miracles and, second, that I would do my best.

35. I thank you for your patience and your faith. Our troubles will not be over tomorrow, but we are on our way and we are headed in the right direction.

Source: New Deal Network. "On the Currency Situation." Available online. URL: http://newdeal.feri.org/chat/chat04.htm. Accessed August 25, 2006.

Abstract of a Conversation with John Maynard Keynes (May 8, 1936)

This document contains the views of economist John Maynard Keynes as expressed in an interview conducted and recorded by A. P. Chew on May 8, 1936. The transcript of the recorded interview, from which this document was taken, was sent to President Franklin D. Roosevelt at his request.

DEPARTMENT OF AGRICULTURE
WASHINGTON
May 8, 1936.
The President,
The White House.

Dear Mr. President:

In conformance with our conversation at Cabinet yesterday, I am sending you herewith the abstract of the conversation of A. P. Chew, Assistant to the Director of Information of this Department, with John Maynard Keynes.

I am also sending you abstract of the conversation Mr. Chew had with John A. Hobson and H. N. Brailsford.

Respectfully yours,
[Henry Wallace]
Secretary.

Enclosure.
WASHINGTON
Abstract of conversation with Mr. John Maynard Keynes.

1. The problem of foreign trade, while important, is not the primary economic problem. It is necessary first to increase the domestic demand. With that accomplished, foreign trade will increase in actual volume, while declining in relative importance. If the industrial nations all set to work to increase their domestic demand, they would soon have a revival in their foreign trade without having to worry about it.

2. Demand can increase through investment—through the creation of new capital goods. It is not necessary to depend either on price declines, or on wage-advances. Ultimately, of course, an increase in capital goods means an increase in consumers goods, and consumption per capita must go up if the balance between production and consumption is to be maintained. But the advantage, particularly in periods of recovery from depression, in raising demand through investment rather than mainly through direct increases in individual consumption is that the operation enlists the cooperation rather than the hostility of the investing groups.

3. Low interest rates make this procedure possible. American attention should be turned to housing. Comparatively little has been done as yet in the United States, despite the passage of much housing legislation. It should be remembered that interest rates, though low on short-time loans, are not yet low on long investments. It is not yet cheap to finance housing.

4. Britain appears to be about 18 months ahead of the United States in recovery. I think there is no doubt the United States will follow; but how long the recovery will endure cannot be foretold. I should think not very long. It is vitally important not to relinquish the social services and economic controls that have been developed during the depression, for they will be more necessary than ever in the next one. It is problematical if capi-

talism can stand another shock like the last one. Certainly, it cannot stand a succession of shocks without social means of alleviating the effects.

5. Wall Street and the bankers will probably say, when the brief recovery comes, that it came of itself, and would have come more quickly had the government not interfered. They will use that argument as an excuse for going back to complete anarchy. But it is a false argument. The recovery in very large measure is a result of what the administration has done, and further government action is desirable to keep in existence the instrumentalities that have demonstrated their value. . . .

8. As a means of developing the trade of the United States on a sound basis, I should recommend domestic in preference to foreign investment. Fighting for a reopened door in the Orient would be idle. You might as well dig a hole and bury your surplus capital. I believe that, as yet, the United States lacks the experience, the facilities, and the required investment psychology, for doing a large and successful business in foreign lending. This is largely an affair of experience, judgment and in fact tradition. You have lost enormously in foreign investments; in investments which you might have better studied, as well as in those that have to be written off as war losses. France has lost immense sums which she had placed in Russia, Mexico, the Balkans and South America. By contrast the British loss in commercial foreign investment, as distinguished from war loans, is small. It has lost a lot in Turkey; and for the time being the worst risk is the investment in China. But, in the main, its foreign investments have been extremely successful. I do not attach as much importance to British imperial power as a factor in achieving this result as many persons do.

9. As interest rates fall in the United States, and capital accumulates, investors will be tempted to try the foreign field again. I should expect them to lose heavily. It would be much better to invest at home, even at low rates of interest; and the effect of that course is to increase the domestic demand and decrease the relative importance of foreign trade. I do not think the United States need fear a flight from the dollar for budgetary reasons. Your debt is nothing like ours, your resources and your margin are immense. There is little danger of inflation. It will not be a shock to the national credit that will cause a heavy exportation of capital, if any such movement occurs, but rather a desire to earn higher returns than can be obtained at home. I should consider unfortunate any considerable yielding to that temptation. The old effort to balance consumption with demand by means of favorable balances of trade does not work out in the long run. That is a lesson we have all to learn.

10. The main defects in our present society are its failure to provide full employment, and its inequitable distribution of wealth and incomes. Perhaps these two defects may be considered dual aspects of a single basic trouble; for economists have long recognized a connection between unemployment and the maldistribution of purchasing power. In Great Britain, especially since the end of the nineteenth century, something has been done to correct very great disparities of wealth and income. Income taxes, death duties and public expenditure for social services have contributed to this result. Further progress in the same direction may be checked by two considerations: (1) the fear of putting an excessive premium on tax evasion; and (2) the belief that the growth of capital depends on the strength of the motive for individual saving. As to the first point, it has no doubt some weight; but with regard to the second, it appears that the growth of capital depends not on a low consumption, or in other words on a distribution of income that gives a minority a huge surplus for saving, but on the contrary that measures for the redistribution of incomes in a way likely to raise the propensity to consume may actually favor the growth of capital. (In Mr. Keynes latest book he develops this argument in detail.) Only when employment is full is the further growth of capital dependent on "A low propensity to consume."

11. In the conditions that now exist the "abstinence" of the rich impedes the growth of wealth, and action to remove great inequalities increases it. There is social and psychological justification for significant inequalities of incomes and wealth, but not for such large disparities as exist today. The stakes need not be so high. What is still more important is the rate of interest. Hitherto economists have justified a moderately high rate of interest as a means of providing an inducement to save, but it appears that effective saving depends on the scale of investment, which varies inversely with the rate of interest. Thus it is socially advantageous to reduce the rate of interest. This criterion, should it be well founded and be generally adopted, will lead to a much lower rate of interest than has ruled heretofore. It would be possible to increase the stock of capital to a point at which the use of capital goods would cost little more than enough to cover wastage and obsolescence. This state of affairs, though it would leave scope for individual enterprise, would tend to eliminate the rentier, and to weaken the power of the capitalist to exploit the scarcity value of capital. The rentier aspect of capitalism would disappear when its work is done, and the functionless investor would have no place in the economy. This would simply be the prolonged continuance of what we have seen recently in Great Britain and would need no revolution.

12. That these ideas have a significant bearing on the problem of international trade is obvious. As the question arises within the framework of our

conventional views, the inquiry as to what the effect of Europe's economic nationalism will be on America's farm exports seems to admit of only one answer. It seems to indicate that economic nationalism and international trade are natural opposites. But that assumes a more or less unchanging level of production and consumption. Assuming a rising level, we can see the possibility of making various countries relatively more self-sufficient than they used to be, and at the same time more eager to trade with the outside world. With consumption raised domestically, the export surpluses would become relatively less burdensome, without necessarily being reduced in their absolute amount. They would move into world-trade channels more easily because purchasing power would be well enough diffused throughout the world to absorb them. From the standpoint of international advantage in consumption, we have not nearly exhausted the possibilities of international trade. The stumbling block is not a general lack of desire for foreign goods, but a distribution system that reduces the power to consume. . . .

Source: New Deal Network. "Abstract of conversation with Mr. John Maynard Keynes." Available online. URL: http://newdeal.feri.org/misc/keynes1.htm. Accessed July 27, 2006.

TESTIMONIES AND SPEECHES ON THE EFFECTS OF GLOBALIZATION

"The International Monetary Fund and the National Interests of the United States" by C. Fred Bergsten (February 24, 1998)

This document is a transcript of testimony that economist C. Fred Bergsten gave before the U.S. Congress's Joint Economic Committee on February 24, 1998. In his testimony, Bergsten explains how the International Monetary Fund promotes U.S. national interests, particularly its economic interests around the world. He also describes the criticisms levied against the IMF, concluding that, although some reforms are needed, most criticisms are unfounded.

The International Monetary Fund and the National Interests of the United States
C. Fred Bergsten
Institute for International Economics
Testimony before the Joint Economic Committee
United States Congress
Washington, DC

February 24, 1998

The national interests of the United States are strongly supported by the International Monetary Fund, as we saw in the Mexican crisis in 1995 and are seeing again in the current Asian crisis. The IMF is in fact one of the best possible deals we could ever imagine: its programs cost us nothing yet it provides enormous benefits for our economy and our foreign policy. Hence I strongly support prompt Congressional approval of both the proposed $3.5 contribution to the New Arrangements to Borrow and $14.5 billion for our share of the internationally agreed increase in Fund quotes.

The Cost of the IMF

It is essential at the outset to clarify the cost side of the equation. *Our contributions to the IMF have zero—repeat, zero—cost to the American taxpayer and economy.* Every dollar we contribute produces an equal amount of US claims to draw yen, DM [deutsche mark] or other currencies from the Fund ourselves. Hence these contributions amount to an "exchange of assets," with no budget cost or requirement for appropriated funds (an arrangement which, incidentally, I worked out with the Congress in conformity with the new Budget Act of 1974 when serving as Assistant Secretary of the Treasury for International Affairs in 1977–81.

The ability of the United States to draw on the Fund itself is not a theoretical proposition. The United States has borrowed foreign currencies from the IMF on 28 different occasions, more than any other country. We drew about $3 billion of DM and yen in 1978 to help defend the dollar in the exchange markets. The IMF has always been a two-way street for the United States and the Administration's analogy with a credit union is apt.

In addition, the IMF enables the United States to effectively leverage its funding to induce other countries to support internationally agreed programs. *Our share in the Fund is less than 20 percent so every $1 we contribute is matched by more than $4 from others.* The IMF is thus an extremely useful tool to achieve our perennial goal of sharing the burden of international efforts with countries around the world.

Hence it would be impossible to oppose the proposed IMF contributions on budgetary or cost grounds. The meaningful debate is over whether the Fund effectively promotes US economic and foreign policy interests.

Does the IMF Need More Money?

A second point to clarify at the outset is that the IMF clearly needs more money. The Fund now has about $45 billion in "uncommitted loanable resources.' However, $30–35 billion of that total is unconditionally available to member countries and thus could be withdrawn on demand. Only $10–15 billion is clearly available for additional country programs. . . .

It is quite possible that another major country, such as Brazil or Argentina or Turkey, could run into a payments crisis at literally any time—especially if the Asian crisis were to erupt again into an additional round of sharp currency declines, which is quite possible. It would then be impossible for the Fund to become involved and the risks of contagion to the rest of the world, and costs to the world economy including the United States, could be multiplied many times.

It is thus clear that the Fund needs additional resources. . . . Hence we again come solely to the central question: does the Fund effectively promote US economic and foreign policy interests?

US Interests in the World Economy

The United States has two central interests in the world economy. The first is the maintenance of maximum rates of economic growth and employment that are consistent with reasonable price stability. The second is the most widespread possible application of market-oriented policies rather than governmental controls and directives. These goals, incidentally, demonstrably serve our broader national security and foreign policy interests as well as our economic interests.

The IMF plays a crucial role in supporting both fundamental US objectives. When a member country asks the IMF for help to respond to a crisis, the Fund produces two things: financial assistance and policy requirements. Both are central to inducing and enabling the country to (1) adjust gradually to its crisis rather than precipitously and (2) adopt constructive, market-oriented policy measures rather than draconian *dirigiste* controls.

A country, whether Mexico in 1994–95 or Korea in 1997–98 (or, for that matter, the United Kingdom and Italy in 1992), experiences a financial crisis because it can no longer pay its foreign bills and/or faces a sharp fall in its exchange rate. It must enact new policies to put its house in order. But there are also two crucial choices:

1. Must it enact measures, however draconian, that take effect immediately or can it phase in the adjustment over a period of time?

2. Closely related, must it clamp on trade and capital controls or can it alter the market environment in a way that will produce adjustment of a much more economically sound, and thus sustainable, nature?

The IMF plays a critical role in the answers to both questions. An IMF program brings external financing that tides the crisis country over an intermediate period that permits gradual rather than abrupt phasein of the adjustment measures. The conditions attached to that program require the country to employ sound, market-oriented measures rather than "quick fix" controls. In essence, the IMF is an international lender of last resort in the same way that the Federal Reserve is a lender of last resort in our domestic financial crises.

The United States has a huge interest in these IMF contributions. It is far better for us that a crisis country adjusts gradually and constantly—via sound budget and monetary policies, trade and investment liberalization, and needed structural reforms as are required now in Asian financial and corporate governance systems—rather than by instituting import controls, even sharper depreciations of currencies, and even deeper economic turndowns. Our economic and foreign policy interests would be imperiled if major countries, such as Mexico and Korea, were forced to go the latter route because there was no IMF to point them in constructive directions.

One might of course suggest that the United States itself, or somebody else, could provide the needed external funding and policy advice instead of the IMF. We would hardly want to pick up the entire financial costs of significant support programs, however. Moreover, it is likely that any unilateral US attempt to impose adjustment conditions would either fail and/or worsen rather than improve our relations with the crisis country. A multilateral institution, of which the crisis country itself is a member, is the optimal—indeed, probably the only effective—means for carrying out such programs at this point in history. It is literally true that we would have to create the IMF it did not exist.

Some observers who share my assessment of US goals nevertheless oppose the IMF because they believe that, contrary to my arguments, it does not promote those goals effectively. Some even believe that the IMF has counterproductive efforts. We must therefore turn to those critiques.

Criticisms of the IMF

First, some believe the world would be better off without the IMF or any similar institution. They would let the market take care of all crises on its own.

As noted, the IMF promotes market-oriented solutions and the United States strongly supports that approach. The problem, however, is that markets occasionally go haywire and far overshoot the rational bounds of underlying economic conditions. The results can be catastrophic for both the countries involved and the world economy as a whole.

For example, huge amounts of private capital continued to pour into Mexico and the Asian countries until literally the eve of their crises—despite impending signs of trouble and frequent warnings from many quarters. Then the private capital flow totally reversed and drove the countries' currencies down much further than can be justified by any objective analysis. This "roller coaster effect" of the private capital markets was already seen in the runup to, and aftermath of, the Third World debt crisis of the 1970s. It demonstrates why we cannot rely wholly and solely on market forces.

The United States knows about these problems from direct experience. As recently as early 1995, the foreign exchange markets drove the dollar to its all-time lows against the yen and most European currencies despite the stellar performance of our economy and relative stagnation in Japan and Europe. Our own Treasury, despite its strong preference for market solutions, felt compelled to intervene to drive the dollar back up. Since that time, the dollar has risen by 60 percent against the yen and 40 percent against the DM—demonstrating again the "roller coaster" or "bandwagon" effect, and revealing clearly that the dollar had fallen much too far only three years ago.

It would be enormously risky to rely solely on market forces to resolve currency and other financial crises.

As noted above, crisis countries would then be wholly on their own and would inevitably have to accept much sharper recessions, much sharper declines in their currencies, and/or draconian trade and capital controls. Such alternative adjustment paths would hardly support US economic or broader interests. The archtypical example was of course the competitive depreciations and trade warfare of the 1930s that helped bring on the Great Depression—and that induced the world to create the IMF after World War II in an effort to avoid ever repeating such a disaster.

A second criticism is that the IMF "doesn't work." Proponents of this view note the continued shakiness of Asian currencies and stock markets, and conclude that the IMF program has failed. No institution is perfect. Crisis management and recovery are extremely difficult. We should not expect a miraculous recovery in every IMF program country.

But patience is required. It took about six months for the markets to stabilize in Mexico in 1995, which is a dramatic success story whose economy has grown by an average of 7 percent in 1996–97 after suffering only one year of adjustment. Stabilization in Asia will almost certainly take longer because of the regional spread of the crisis and the structural nature of the needed reforms. Moreover, one can only expect success if countries faithfully implement the IMF programs. Both Thailand and Korea had to navigate political successions before they were able to start applying the needed remedies. Indonesia has not yet begun to do so. Once can hardly charge the IMF with failure until its prescriptions have been in place long enough to be fairly tested.

A third and more nuanced criticism is that IMF remedies are "too extreme" and/or "not tailored to the differing situations in different countries." These complaints are voiced particularly in the current Asian context, where the problems are mainly structural and financial rather than presenting the traditional problems of excessive budget deficits and monetary expansions.

The unique nature of the Asian problem has indeed meant that the IMF has had to "learn while doing." As it moved from Thailand to Indonesia to Korea and now back to Indonesia, and as time has passed, it has been modifying its programs and especially their priorities. Some of the earlier fiscal targets turned out to be too tight, in light of subsequent circumstances, and have been modified with little or no harm done. The overwhelming emphasis of the programs is now on financial restructuring and corporate governance, which is correct.

The most difficult dilemma resides with monetary policy. On the one hand, moderate interest rates are highly desirable to facilitate financial restructuring and to avoid unnecessary economic slowdown. On the other hand, high interest rates help defend the currency and avoid even further depreciations. The IMF strategy is to insist on sufficiently tight money to achieve the latter goal but to approve relaxation as soon as circumstances permit, as they are starting to do in Korea. Judgment calls have to be made on the spot but the basic strategy appears sound.

The most understandable criticism is that the IMF creates "moral hazard" by assuring private investors that they will be bailed out and hence encourages the destructive "roller coaster" effects described above. Policymakers, including at the IMF, do indeed face an acute dilemma when confronting a country in crisis. Their immediate imperative is to stop capital outflow and restore capital inflows, to finance the (usually sizable) external deficit until it can be corrected, and then to permit gradual and constructive adjustment. This counsels avoidance of hits to existing investors that could scare them off and undermine the whole strategy. At the same time, however, this approach may create the "moral hazard." . . .

A final criticism relates to the transparency of IMF operations. The IMF insists that its borrowers increase the transparency and accountability of their policies and processes. Hence it is eminently logical to ask whether the IMF is sufficiently transparent itself.

The IMF is in fact more transparent than most observers realize. Almost every IMF program is available in full detail, including on the internet. But the process of disclosure is random and unstructured, and much more order could be brought to it. The United States has in fact been pushing for more IMF openness for at least twenty years.

The greatest need, in my view, is publication of the analyses of country outlooks by the IMF staff. The data portions of the Fund's country consultations are already published. But the markets need to know when country problems are foreseen, both to limit or avert the continued influx of unsound loans and to help induce the country to take preventative policy steps.

It must be recognized, however, that the Fund faces a genuine dilemma in this area as well. Full public disclosure of Fund materials would deter some countries from providing full data to the institution. Sovereign nations, including our own and certainly many industrial as well as developing countries, will always want to preserve a degree of confidentiality for some of their most sensitive financial and economic data. The Fund would thus probably lose access to some of its most important inputs if it mandated full disclosure. I would still support increased disclosure, as noted above, but a judicious balance must be struck in answering this question.

Conclusion

I thus conclude that the various criticisms of the IMF are either unfounded or can be answered through readily available changes in Fund policy and programs. The Congress should certainly urge the Administration to pursue such changes. . . .

The United States has an enormous interest in an effective and fully funded IMF. The Asian crisis reinforces and underlines that interest. I urge the Committee, and the Congress, to approve the Administration's proposals fully and promptly.

Source: Institute for International Economics. "The International Monetary Fund and the National Interests of the United States." Available online. URL: http://www.iie.com/publications/papers/paper.cfm?ResearchID=307. Accessed July 27, 2006.

". . . After Seattle?" by David C. Korten (December 3, 1999)

This document contains excerpts of a speech given by antiglobalization activist David C. Korten at a protest meeting in Seattle, Washington, on December 3, 1999, during the WTO meeting in that city that generated widespread and massive protests against the World Trade Organization and globalization.

Korten describes the "Battle in Seattle," its causes, and the goals of the protesters. He appeals for greater corporate responsibility and responsiveness, and he sets out a list of suggested reforms for the WTO and its corporate supporters.

. . . After Seattle?
by David C. Korten
Speech given December 3, 1999 at WTO event

Taking on the Corporate and Financial Rulers: Our Goal is Political and Economic Democracy

. . . Despite the scattered violence that has captured so much media attention, for the majority of people in the streets, this week has been one of the most remarkably inclusive and hopefully significant acts of . . . solidarity in human history. The new union forged between working people and environmentalists is surely of historic significance.

I have great admiration for the courage of the young people who acted here with well-informed commitment, putting their lives and liberty on the line in deeply meaningful and effective acts of nonviolent civil disobedience to assure that our message would finally be heard by those who have closed their eyes, their ears, and their minds to the reality of a world in deep pain. My heart goes out to all of you who have made it happen. We now have a critical opening in the long struggle to create a world that works for all. And we must use it wisely. . . .

Of all the many important issues discussed in Seattle this week, in my mind the most fundamental is democracy. Who will make the rules by which we will live? Will it be people—through the exercise of their birth rights as persons and citizens? Or will it be the institutions of the global economy—global financial markets and corporations?

In very practical terms, will we adapt ourselves to the system of global financial and corporate rule even as we seek to reform it—sitting at its tables and seeking to use its power to achieve human and planetary ends? Or will we make a commitment similar to the one made by those some 200 years ago who decided the time had come to replace the institutions of monarchy with the institutions of democracy? It is a critical choice central to how we move ahead beyond the historic events of which we have been a part this week.

The Publicly Traded Corporations, Limited Liability as an Institutional Pathology

We must come to terms with the basic nature of the limited liability, publicly traded corporation—the institution that dominates both the WTO and the global economy. It's a legal instrument designed to concentrate economic power without accountability—which means it is both anti-democratic and anti-market.... Contrary to corporate propaganda, the corporation was invented not to create wealth, as to extract and concentrate it—and that is what all too many of them are still in the business of doing....

Paul Hawken has compiled data suggesting that corporations in the United States now receive more in direct public subsidies than they pay in total taxes. That's only a small part of the story as it doesn't include the costs to society of unsafe products, practices, and workplaces or from outright corporate crime. In the United States we have over billing by defense contractors of $26 billion. Over billing by medicaid insurance contractors of $23 billion. $54 billion a year in health costs from cigarette smoking. $136 billion for the consequences of unsafe vehicles. $275 billion for deaths from work place cancer. Pretty soon it starts adding up to some real money.

It is sobering to note that the corporation is one of the most authoritarian of human institutions. No matter what authority a corporate CEO may delegate, he can with draw it with a snap of his fingers. In the U.S. system, which is rapidly infecting Europe and the rest of the world, the corporate CEO can virtually hire and fire any worker, open and close any plant, change transfer prices, create and drop product lines almost at will—with no meaningful recourse by the persons or communities affected. Given that our largest corporations command economies larger than those of most states, this represents an extraordinary anomaly in supposedly democratic societies.

With these characteristics in mind, let's review some frequently suggested responses to corporate rule.

• *Appeal to the corporate conscience to act more responsibly.* This buys into the fiction that the corporation has the qualities and moral sensibilities of a human being. A legal contract has no conscience and no loyalty to people or place. The people who work for corporations are merely employees subject to dismissal if they bring to bear any interests other than the short-term profits of shareholders.

• *Let the dynamics of the global market place take their course and trust that market forces will correct the dysfunctions by rewarding the responsible corporations over the irresponsible.* This suggestion is based on the false premise that market forces work naturally in the direction of rewarding corporations that internalize their full costs. It is a logical contradiction, since cost externalization is clearly an enormous source of profit.

• *Let the market decide as consumers and investors express their economic choices. People who want high labor and environmental standards will make their purchasing and investment choices accordingly—paying higher prices and accepting lower investment returns where necessary.* This presumes that corporations have a right to externalize their costs onto the community and that if people want it otherwise they must pay. It also requires that consumers and investors resist corporate wrong doing corporation by corporation, deed by deed, through consumer and investment boycotts. It strips us of our rights as citizens and reduces us to expressing our preferences only in our economic roles as consumers and investors.

- *Regulate corporations through governmental action.* While regulation is essential in any market economy, relying on governmental regulation to reliably curb the excesses of corporations that command more resources than most states is a weak and temporary solution because of the inherent instability of the resulting balance of powers. Historically such balances have always broken down as corporation's have chosen to reassert their power.

- *Realign economic structures in ways that bring economic relationships into a more natural alignment with the public interest.* This requires replacing the present system of unaccountable rule by a corporate and financial elite with a system of political and economic democracy—a project comparable to the human project of eliminating monarchy. It involves the elimination of the publicly traded, limited liability corporation as an institutional form. I submit that this is the only option consistent with the goal of creating just, sustainable, and compassionate societies that work for all.

It leads to an ambitious agenda, but one I believe to be within our means given how much is at stake and the evidence of a remarkable human awakening revealed by the events of the past week. Let me lay out some of its elements to illustrate the possibilities I believe we should be giving serious consideration.

- Radical campaign finance reform

    Public financing of elections.

    Free air time for candidates.

- Eliminate Special Corporate Rights and Exemptions

    Legislation or constitutional amendment to strip away the legal fiction of corporate personhood.

    Legislation to remove the corporation's limited liability provisions. Corporate shareholders should bear the same responsibility and liability for the care and use of the corporate property as does any property owner.

- Eliminate Corporate Welfare

Withdraw corporate subsidies and tax breaks.

Implement cost recovery fees to offset otherwise externalized costs.

- From Absentee to Stakeholder Ownership

Incentives for stakeholder buyouts.

Education on economic democracy and ownership participation.

Restructure worker pension funds to exercise rights of workers as non-financial stakeholders.

- Give Preference to Human-Scale Enterprises

Strong enforcement of anti-trust provisions.

Prohibitions on mergers and acquisitions.

Graduated corporate income and asset taxes.

- Restore the Integrity of Money

Eliminate dependence on debt based money by imposing a 100% reserve requirement on demand deposits.

Prohibit all lending for financial speculation—eliminate the buying of stocks on margin and prohibit lending to hedge funds.

Restore unitary community banking.

- Reform international financial markets and economic management.

Currency exchange only on presentation of an invoice or airline ticket.

Restore national ownership and control of productive assets in low income countries—a kind of international land reform initiative.

Eliminate Third World debts and the mechanisms by which they are created.

Assign responsibility for matters relating to the international regulation of trade, finance, and corporations to an upgraded United Nations.

Close the WTO and the World Bank.

Reform and restaff the IMF with a new mission: to help countries balance international accounts and finance temporary short-falls in current accounts. Make it strictly accountable to the United Nations.

I suggest we be clear that our goal is not to reform global corporate and financial rule—it is to end it. The publicly traded, limited liability corporation is a pathological institutional form and financial speculation is inherently predatory. As a first step both must be regulated. The appropriate longer term goal is to rid our economic affairs of these institutional pathologies—much as our ancestors eliminated the institution of monarchy.

Source: Yes! "... After Seattle?" Available online. URL: http://www.yesmagazine.org/other/pop_print_article.asp?ID=1105. Accessed August 25, 2006.

"Globalization" by Alan Greenspan (October 24, 2001)

This speech, by longtime chairman of the U.S. Federal Reserve Alan Greenspan, was given at a meeting of the Institute for International Economics on October 24, 2001. In his speech, Greenspan explains globalization, delineates the arguments against it, and, ultimately, provides cogent reasons for supporting it. His argument and examples focus primarily on the United States.

Globalization
Alan Greenspan
Chairman of the Federal Reserve Board
Speech at the Institute for International Economics' First Annual Stavros S. Niarchos Lecture
October 24, 2001

I am pleased to be with you tonight. . . . I am also pleased to note that you are celebrating your twentieth year in the business of thinking critically about vital international economic issues. It hardly seems that long.

Before the tragic events of September 11, [2001,] discussions of the international economy had increasingly come to be centered on issues related to the growing integration of our economies. The strife we had witnessed over economic globalization was the twenty-first century's version of debates over societal organization that go back at least to the dawn of the industrial revolution, and many of the intellectual roots of those debates go back far longer.

There has been a simmering down of the more vociferous protests against globalization since September 11. But the debate surrounding the increasing cross-border integration of markets inevitably will be rejoined. The issue elicits such strong reaction because it centers on the important question of how economies are organized and, specifically, how individuals deal with one another.

Globalization as generally understood involves the increasing interaction of the world's peoples through their national economic systems. Of necessity, these economic systems are reasonably compatible and, in at least some important respects, market oriented.

During the past half-century, barriers to trade and to financial flows have generally come down, resulting in a significant broadening of world markets. Expanding markets, in turn, have enhanced competition and nurtured what Joseph Schumpeter called "creative destruction," the continuous scrapping of old technologies to make way for the new. Standards of living rise because the depreciation and other cash flows of industries employing older, increasingly obsolescent, technologies are marshaled, along with new savings, to finance the production of capital assets that almost always embody cutting-edge technologies. This is the process by which wealth is created incremental step by incremental step. It presupposes a continuous churning of an economy in which the new displaces the old.

The process is particularly evident among those nations that have opened their borders to increased competition. Through its effect on economic growth, globalization has been a powerful force acting to raise standards of living. More open economies have recorded the best growth performance; in contrast, countries with inward-oriented policies have done less well. Importantly, as real incomes have risen on average, the incidence of poverty has declined.

Nevertheless technological advance and globalization distress those who once thrived in industries that were at the forefront of technology but which have since become increasingly noncompetitive.

In each step of incremental advance, the distance between gainers and losers is necessarily narrow. So it is understandable that our exceptionally complex system for the international distribution of goods, services, and finance is not universally recognized as successful at enhancing standards of living and promoting civil values worldwide. Indeed, those who perceived the need to protect economies from open trade have endeavored since its inception to slow or even reverse the forces supporting global expansion. It would be most unfortunate if the wheels of progress were stopped because of an incapacity or unwillingness to assist those disadvantaged by these broader gains, an issue I will address later.

In recent years, protectionism has also manifested itself in a somewhat different guise by challenging the moral roots of capitalism and globalization. At the risk of oversimplification, I would separate the differing parties in that debate into three groups. First, there are those who believe that relatively unfettered capitalism is the only economic organization consistent with individual and political freedom. In a second group are those who accept capitalism as the only practical means to achieve higher standards of living but who are disturbed by the seeming incivility of many market practices and outcomes. In very broad brush terms, the prevalence with which one encounters allegations of incivility defines an important difference in economic views that distinguishes the United States from continental Europe—two peoples having deeply similar roots in political freedom and democracy.

A more pronounced distinction separates both of these groups from a third group, which views societal organization based on the profit motive and corporate culture as fundamentally immoral.

This group questions in particular whether the distribution of wealth that results from greater economic interactions among countries is, in some sense, "fair." Here terms such as "exploitation," "subversion of democratic choice," and other value-charged notions dominate the debate. These terms too often substitute for a rigorous discussion of the difficult tradeoffs we confront in advancing the economic welfare of our nations. Such an antipathy to "corporate culture" has sent tens of thousands into the streets to protest what they see as "exploitive capitalism" in its most visible form—the increased globalization of our economies.

Though presumably driven by a desire to foster a better global society, most protestors hold misperceptions about how markets work and how to interpret market outcomes. To be sure, those outcomes can sometimes appear perverse to the casual observer. In today's marketplace, for example, baseball players earn much more than tenured professors. But that discrepancy expresses the market fact that more people are willing to pay to see a ball game than to attend a college lecture. I may not personally hold the same relative valuation of those activities as others, but that is what free markets are about. They reflect and give weight to the values of the whole of society, not just those of any one segment.

Market doubters sometimes respond that consumers' values are manipulated by corporate advertising that induces people to purchase goods and services they do not really want. Most corporate advertising directors would wish that were true. Instead, they will argue that the evidence suggests that only the best products in the marketplace win over time. Consumers are not foolish; indeed, it would be an act of considerable hubris to argue otherwise.

What are the dissidents' solutions to the alleged failures of globalization? They are, in fact, seemingly quite diverse. Frequently, they appear to favor politically imposed systems, employing the power of the state to override the outcomes arrived at through voluntary exchange. The historical record of such approaches does not offer much encouragement. One would be hard pressed to cite examples of free and prosperous societies that shunned the marketplace.

Contrary to much current opinion, developing countries need more globalization, not less. Such a course would likely bring with it greater economic stability and political freedom. Indeed, probably the single most effective action that the industrial countries could implement to alleviate the terrible problem of poverty in many developing countries would be to open, unilaterally, markets to imports from those countries.

Setting aside the arguments of the protestors, even among those committed to market-oriented economies, important differences remain about the view of capitalism and the role of globalization. These differences are captured most clearly for me in a soliloquy attributed to a prominent European leader several years ago. He asked, "What is the market? It is the law of the jungle, the law of nature. And what is civilization? It is the struggle against nature."

While acknowledging the ability of competition to promote growth, many such observers, nonetheless, remain concerned that economic actors, to achieve that growth, are required to behave in a manner governed by the law of the jungle.

In contrast to these skeptical views, the ethical merits of market-driven outcomes are argued with increasing vigor by many others, especially in the United States: The crux of the argument is that because unencumbered markets reflect the value preferences of consumers, the resulting price signals direct a nation's savings into those capital assets that maximize the production of goods and services most valued by consumers. Largely unfettered markets create a consumer-led society. In such an economy, the value of reputation, capitalized as good will in the market value of companies, competitively encourages perseverance in pursuing the objectives of quality and excellence. Moreover, the limited role for government in these arrangements is conducive to greater political freedom.

Such a paradigm, however, is viewed by many at the other end of the philosophical spectrum as obsessively materialistic and largely lacking in meaningful cultural values.

But is there a simple tradeoff between civil conduct, as defined by those who find raw competitive behavior demeaning, and the quality of material life they, nonetheless, seek? It is not obvious that such a tradeoff exists in any meaningful sense when viewed from a longer-term perspective.

Clearly not all activities undertaken in markets are civil. Many, though legal, are decidedly unsavory. Violation of law and breaches of trust do undermine the efficiency of markets. But solid legal foundations and the discipline of the marketplace limit these aberrations. On net, vigorous competition over the years has produced a significant rise in the quality of life for the vast majority of the population in market-oriented economies, including those at the bottom of the income distribution.

GLOBALIZATION AND FREE TRADE

During the past century, economic growth created resources far in excess of those required to maintain subsistence. That surplus in democratic capitalist societies has, in large measure, been employed to improve the quality of life along many dimensions. To cite a short list: (1) greater longevity, owing first to the widespread development of clean, potable water, and later to rapid advances in medical technology, (2) a universal system of education that enabled greatly increased social mobility, (3) vastly improved conditions of work, and (4) the ability to enhance our environment by setting aside natural resources rather than employing them to sustain a minimum level of subsistence. At a fundamental level, we have used the substantial increases in wealth generated by our market-driven economy to purchase what many would view as greater civility.

If the issue of a tradeoff between growth and civility were not in dispute, much of the debate that surrounds globalization today would have long since been silenced in its favor.

But even if open and free global markets are consonant with political freedom and have in the past contributed greatly to raising world standards of living, there still remains the important practical issue: Can globalization continue to work? Is it as viable a model for world economic growth now as it has been in the past? Despite globalization's patent capacity to elevate standards of living over time, we have been challenged by periodic disruptions in the system's functioning. The financial crises of 1997–98 and the stresses apparent in some emerging-market economies over the past year underscore evident structural weaknesses in our global system.

It can readily be argued that certain conditions of stress increase the probability of emerging-market country default and potential contagion. For example, extensive short-term foreign currency liabilities of financial intermediaries that are used to fund unhedged long-term lending in a domestic currency are tinder awaiting conflagration. This is especially the case if foreign currency reserves are inadequate and exchange rates are fixed.

But why has this phenomenon in different garb reappeared so frequently in the postwar era? No nation deliberately seeks to expose itself to financial distress and bankruptcy. But political pressures can lead to actions that increase these risks. In all economies, political constituencies seek to employ the powers of the state to increase their share of limited government resources. While the record of developed economies is far from unblemished, they have had greater success in fending off such demands. One indication of that success is that exchange rate regimes have not often been upended by domestic political pressures in these economies.

Although the range of outcomes has been wide, many emerging-market nations have had less success in insulating their international financial positions from domestic political pressures. Those pressures, at times, have become exceptionally difficult to deal with. To close the gap between the financial demands of political constituencies and the limited real resources available to their governments, many countries too often have bridged the difference by borrowing from foreign investors. In effect, the path of least resistance has been external borrowing rather than confronting politically difficult tradeoffs.

Periodically, as an economy borrows its way to the edge of insolvency with debt denominated in foreign currency, government debt-raising capacity appears to vanish virtually overnight. It is this vanishing capacity that characterizes almost all financial crises. Lending institutions will provide funds beyond the immediate visible short-term cash flow of a borrower only if they perceive that maturing debt will be capable of being rolled over. The first whiff of inadequacy in debt-raising capacity induces a run to the exits—not unlike a bank run. Thus, an economy's necessary condition for solvency, indeed, a necessary condition for the stability of global finance, is the maintenance of significant unused financing capacity.

A developed nation's financial status is largely defined by an unquestioned capacity to roll over its debt seemingly without limit into the future. Developed nations, of course, have on occasion run into refunding difficulties and found international lending markets closed. But those occasions have been rare.

What then is an adequate buffer? What level of foreign currency reserves and tradable real assets does an emerging-market economy need to obtain and sustain debt-capacity credibility? That level, of course, can be known only in retrospect. One measure of the probability that the current or prospective level of reserves will be adequate can be gleaned from the yield spread of dollar-denominated government debt over U.S. Treasuries. That spread reflects not only the risk of dollar credit default but also the underlying strength of the domestic currency. Exchange-market pressures on the latter obviously reduce dollar debt-raising capacity.

Debt capacity, by this model, is reached before rising nominal interest rates and, hence, payments on government debt threaten a vicious fiscal cycle of ever-growing deficits and debt. Unless debt capacity is continuously confirmed in the marketplace by modest spreads, "bank run" crises seem inevitable in such a leveraged system.

How then does an emerging-market nation obtain and sustain debt-capacity credibility? First, it needs to create a much larger relative reserve buffer than that of a developed nation—which has a larger capacity to draw on real resources, through taxation if necessary, to make good on its obligations. Nations that have met the market test no longer need to put up "collateral" to certify their financial prudence. Of course, even adequate or outsized reserves may not be perceived as sufficient for some, if the political system is judged unstable.

In this regard, there are two critical criteria that all lenders require for government debt issuance: (1) a legal system that is presumed to protect property rights of the lender through the maturity of the debt instrument and (2) if the debt is denominated in a foreign currency, a fiscal and monetary regime that is presumed to be sufficiently responsible to ensure repayment in equivalent real resources.

To be sure, one can borrow with these conditions less than fully satisfied, but only at interest rates that price the risk. Too often these rates are at levels inconsistent with fiscal stability or ongoing debt-raising capacity.

At root, debt-raising capacity is not a technical issue; it is a profoundly political one, which means that it is driven by the values and culture of the society. Unless consensus exists within a society as to resource limits to which all must adhere, an adequate debt-capacity buffer will be difficult to achieve and maintain.

The United States has benefited enormously from the opening up of international markets in the postwar period. We have access to a wide range of goods and services for consumption; our industries produce and employ cutting-edge technologies; and the opportunities created by these technologies have attracted capital inflows from abroad. These capital inflows, in turn, have reduced the costs of building our country's capital stock and added to the productivity of our workers. It would be a great tragedy if progress toward greater openness were stopped or reversed.

Rather than inhibiting international competition to assist those displaced by "creative destruction," we should be directing our efforts at enhancing job skills and retraining workers—a process in which the private market is already engaged. If necessary, selected income maintenance programs can be employed for those over a certain age, where retraining is problematic. Protectionism will only slow the inevitable transition of our workforce to more productive endeavors. To be sure, an added few years on the job may enable some workers to reach retirement with reasonable security and dignity, but if we hinder competitive progress, we will almost certainly slow overall economic growth and keep frozen in place younger workers whose opportunities to secure jobs with better long-run prospects diminish with time. . . .

I trust that we will go forward expeditiously with the pending new trade round. The differences to be resolved in such talks are small relative to the larger issue of maintaining our freedoms to travel and trade on a global scale.

Globalization admittedly is an exceptionally abstract concept to convey to the general public. Economists can document the analytic ties of trade to growth and standards of living. A far greater challenge for us has been, and will continue to be, making clear that globalization is an endeavor that can spread worldwide the values of freedom and civil contact. . . .

Globalization, in addition to its myriad material benefits, needs to be seen as a reflection of human freedom in economic terms by a vast majority of its participants. It needs to be seen as offering opportunities to raise the standards of living of all participants in the world trading system. If we fail to make that case, renewed barriers to commerce could fill the void, and the advances associated with globalization could be slowed or even reversed. Should that occur, a few might be better off. Surely, the world will not.

Source: Institute for International Economics. "Globalization." Available online. URL: http://www.iie.com/publications/papers/paper.cfm?ResearchID=425. Accessed August 25, 2006.

"America's Win-Win-Win Trade Relations with China" by Daniel T. Griswold (October 31, 2003)

This document contains excerpts of Daniel T. Griswold's written testimony submitted to the U.S. House Ways and Means Committee on October 31, 2003. Griswold, associate director of the Cato Institute, argues that China's spectacular economic growth affords important opportunities for economic expansion in the United States. He makes a case that job losses in the United States are not related to the rise of industry in China and emphasizes that maintaining close economic ties to China will only benefit the U.S. economy.

WRITTEN TESTIMONY OF
Daniel T. Griswold
Associate Director, Center for Trade Policy Studies
The Cato Institute
submitted to the
House Ways and Means Committee
Washington, DC
"America's Win-Win-Win Trade Relations With China"
October 31, 2003

There is no minimizing the fact that the last three years have been brutal for U.S. manufacturing. Output is only now slowly recovering from its plunge in 2001, and 2.7 million fewer Americans work in factories today than three years ago. The real debate is about why we've suffered this slump in manufacturing output and employment, whether the cause is trade with China or other factors closer to home, and what if anything Congress can and should do about it.

First, some perspective: American manufacturing is not about to disappear. We are not "deindustrializing" or "losing our manufacturing base." Our nation remains a global manufacturing power. Despite the recent slump, manufacturing output is still up 40 percent from a decade ago, according to the Federal Reserve Board's monthly index of manufacturing activity. Manufacturing output today is double what it was in the early 1970s and triple what it was in the 1960s. . . . [and] manufacturing output actually accelerated after implementation of NAFTA and the Uruguay Round Agreements in the mid-1990s. In fact, U.S. industry added a net half million manufacturing jobs in the five years after NAFTA. American companies are world leaders in hundreds of sophisticated products, and they run neck and neck with German companies as the world's leading exporters of manufactured goods. This is not the profile of a nation losing its industrial base.

Second, trade with China or the rest of the world is not to blame for the manufacturing recession and loss of jobs. The problem is not too much trade but not enough domestic demand and growth, especially investment and business spending. What put the kibosh on U.S. manufacturing was the dot-com meltdown, slumping business investment, lingering uncertainty from the war on terrorism, corporate scandals, and slow growth abroad. Critics of trade are quick to blame imports, but the real story is that import growth has been negative or sluggish during the last three years. Only now are monthly import numbers finally recovering to their previous levels of pre-recession 2000.

Conventional wisdom would tell us that more imports mean less domestic output. Every widget we import means one less widget made and fewer widget workers employed, or so we are told. But for manufacturing as a whole, the reality is quite the opposite. . . . Manufacturing imports to the United States and U.S. domestic manufacturing output for each year since 1988 [have increased]. . . . In those years where manufacturing imports grew the fastest, so did domestic manufacturing output. In the booming 1990s, when manufacturing output was growing the fastest, manufacturing imports were surging by double digits. In 2001, when manufacturing output fell, so did manufacturing imports. We seem to either enjoy years of strong growth in imports and output or endure years of weak growth in imports and output.

The reason is straightforward. Imports and output both rise and fall with domestic growth and demand. An expanding economy creates demand for both domestic production and imports. And as U.S. companies expand production, they import more intermediate goods for assembly and capital machinery to make their plants more efficient. The positive connection between imports and output exposes the protectionist mirage that raising new barriers to imports will somehow promote domestic output. That mirage rests on the false assumption that if we can just reduce imports, through tariffs and currency adjustments, we can make those widgets ourselves and employ more workers. But a combination of falling imports and rising domestic production does not appear to be a realistic option. In our economy today, trade and prosperity are a package deal. When we prosper, we trade; when we trade, we prosper.

Why have so many manufacturing jobs been lost in the past three years? Two reasons stand out: A cyclical downturn in the economy reduced demand for manufactured goods, and amazing advances in worker productivity have allowed American companies to produce more goods with fewer workers. American factories are using the Internet, just-in-time inventory, and new technologies—all spurred by international competition—to raise worker productivity. American factories are producing three times the volume of manufactured goods they did in the mid-1960s with fewer workers because today's workers are three times more productive. And we all know that productivity growth is the only long-term foundation for rising prosperity.

Despite those underlying realities, China has become the focus of economic anxiety, just as Japan was 15 years ago. Imports from China do compete with products made by certain U.S. factories and they do displace a relatively small number of U.S. workers. Along with the dislocation it causes, trade with China delivers huge benefits to the U.S. economy. First and most important, American families benefit as consumers. China is a leading supplier of imported clothing, shoes, furniture, toys, sporting goods, and consumer electronics. Those are products poor and middle-class families commonly buy at a discount store, where Chinese imports keep prices down and raise the real wages of American workers. American producers also benefit from the lower-cost inputs from China, such as machine parts, office machines, and plastic moldings. Those inputs allow American-based manufacturers to retain their competitive edge in global markets.

Imports from China have indeed grown rapidly in recent years, but they are nothing like a flood. In 2002, Americans bought $125 billion worth of goods made in China—10 percent of our total imports and a small fraction of our $10.4 trillion economy. There is nothing alarming about Americans spending about one penny of every dollar of our income on products made by the one-fifth of mankind that lives in Mainland China.

There has been no wholesale movement of U.S. factories and investment moving across the Pacific to China. If the critics were right, U.S. multinationals would be falling over themselves to relocate capacity to China to take advantage of its low wages. In reality, U.S. investment in China has been stable and modest. According to figures compiled by the Bureau of Economic Analysis at the U.S. Commerce Department, from 1999 through 2002, American manufacturers directly invested an annual average of $1.2 billion in Mainland China, and that figure has not been going up. In fact, it went down last year to about $500 million.

That modest investment in China compares to an annual average of $16 billion in outward U.S. direct manufacturing investment in the European Union during that same period, $3.8 billion of that in the Netherlands alone. In other words, American companies invest three times more each year in manufacturing in the tiny Netherlands, population 16 million, than they invest in all of China. Our manufacturing investment in China is less than 1 percent of the $200 billion invested each year in America's domestic manufacturing capacity. And it is overwhelmed by the average net inflow of $20 billion in foreign direct manufacturing investment to the United States each year.

If low wages drive U.S. manufacturing investment to go abroad, then why does the large majority of outward investment go to other high-wage, high-standard countries? Most of our outward FDI flows to other rich countries because wages account for a relatively small share of the cost of production. Other considerations for investing are the size of local markets, skills and education levels of workers, political and economic stability, the rule of law, and the reliability of the infrastructure. As many American companies can attest, investing profitably in China and other developing countries remains a challenge—because of their underdeveloped infrastructure and legal systems, undereducated workforces, remaining trade barriers, and limited consumer markets.

That leads to my final point: How can we hope to see hundreds of millions of people in China and India become middle-class consumers of U.S. products if we do not allow them to participate in the global economy?

Critics of trade with China ignore the country's growing appetite for consumption and imports. While China is the world's fourth leading exporter, it is also the world's sixth leading importer. It has become the engine of demand growth in East Asia. It is rapidly becoming one of the world's top markets for automobiles. And China has now displaced the United States as the world's top importer of steel. In fact, by soaking up global steel supplies and lifting global steel prices, China has become the U.S. steel industry's best friend. While America's total exports to the rest of the world were falling in 2002, our exports to China rose 14 percent.

And what do the people and government of China do with all those dollars they earn from exports to the United States but do not spend buying our goods and services—the infamous bilateral trade deficit? They invest those dollars in the United States, typically in U.S. Treasury notes. That investment helps finance the U.S. federal budget deficit, keeping domestic interest rates lower than they would be otherwise and freeing private U.S. savings for investment in the private sector. So our trade with China is blessing us three times over, through low-cost imports, through rising demand for our exports, and through capital inflows that keep our domestic interest rates low. It is truly a win-win-win relationship for the United States.

If Congress and the Bush administration want to help U.S. manufacturing, they should focus their efforts on promoting a more robust economy and renewed confidence in the business sector. Declaring war on imports will only hurt American families, producers, and the overall economy at the expense, not the salvation, of manufacturing and jobs.

Source: Center for Trade Policy Studies. "America's Win-Win-Win Trade Relations with China." Available online. URL: http://www.freetrade.org/pubs/speeches/ct-dg103103.html. Accessed August 25, 2006.

NAFTA

Remarks by President Bill Clinton upon the Signing of the NAFTA Side Agreements (September 14, 1993)

President Bill Clinton gave this speech in the East Room of the White House at the signing of the NAFTA side agreements on September 14, 1993. In it, the president argues strongly in favor of NAFTA, and of free trade agreements in general, and predicts the positive effects the side agreements on environment and labor will have on the treaty's member nations.

REMARKS BY PRESIDENT CLINTON, PRESIDENT BUSH, PRESIDENT CARTER, PRESIDENT FORD, AND VICE PRESIDENT GORE IN SIGNING OF NAFTA SIDE AGREEMENTS

The East Room
10:39 A.M. EDT

THE PRESIDENT: Thank you very much. . . .

It's an honor for me today to be joined by my predecessor, President [George H. W.] Bush, who took the major steps in negotiating this North American Free Trade Agreement; President Jimmy Carter, whose vision of hemispherical development gives great energy to our efforts and has been a consistent theme of his for many, many years now; and President [Gerald] Ford who has argued as fiercely for expanded trade and for this agreement as any American citizen and whose counsel I continue to value.

These men, differing in party and outlook, join us today because we all recognize the important stakes for our nation in this issue. Yesterday we saw the sight of an old world dying, a new one being born in hope and a spirit of peace. Peoples who for a decade were caught in the cycle of war and frustration chose hope over fear and took a great risk to make the future better.

Today we turn to face the challenge of our own hemisphere, our own country, our own economic fortunes. In a few moments, I will sign three agreements that will complete our negotiations with Mexico and Canada to create a North American Free Trade Agreement. In the coming months I will submit this pack to Congress for approval. It will be a hard fight, and I expect to be there with all of you every step of the way.

We will make our case as hard and as well as we can. And, though the fight will be difficult, I deeply believe we will win. And I'd like to tell you why. First of all, because NAFTA means jobs. American jobs, and good-paying American jobs. If I didn't believe that, I wouldn't support this agreement.

As President, it is my duty to speak frankly to the American people about the world in which we now live. Fifty years [ago,] at the end of World War II, an unchallenged America was protected by the oceans and by our technological superiority; and, very frankly, by the economic devastation of the people who could otherwise have been our competitors. We chose, then, to try to help rebuild our former enemies and to create a world of free trade supported by institutions which would facilitate it.

As a result of that effort, global trade grew from $200 billion in 1950 to $800 billion in 1980. As a result, jobs were created and opportunity thrived all across the world. But make no mistake about it: Our decision at the end of World War II to create a system of global, expanded, freer trade and the supporting institutions played a major role in creating the prosperity of the American middle class.

Ours is now an era in which commerce is global and in which money, management, technology are highly mobile. For the last 20 years in all the wealthy countries of the world, because of changes in the global environment, because of the growth of technology, because of increasing competition, the middle class that was created and enlarged by the wise policies of expanding trade at the end of World War II has been under severe stress. Most Americans are working harder for less. They are vulnerable to the fear tactics and the adverseness to change that is behind much of the opposition to NAFTA.

But I want to say to my fellow Americans, when you live in a time of change the only way to recover your security and to broaden your horizons is to adapt to the change, to embrace, to move forward. Nothing we do—nothing we do in this great capital can change the fact that factories or information can flash across the world; that people can move money around in the blink of an eye. Nothing can change the fact that technology can be adopted once created by people all across the world, and then rapidly adapted in new and different ways by people who have a little different take on the way the technology works.

For two decades, the winds of global competition have made these things clear to any American with eyes to see. The only way we can recover the fortunes of the middle class in this country so that people who work harder and smarter can at least prosper more, the only way we can pass on the American Dream of the last 40 years to our children and their children for the next 40 is to adapt to the changes which are occurring.

In a fundamental sense, this debate about NAFTA is a debate about whether we will embrace these changes and create the jobs of tomorrow, or try to resist these changes, hoping we can preserve the economic structures of yesterday.

I tell you, my fellow Americans, that if we learn anything from the collapse of the Berlin Wall and the fall of the governments in Eastern Europe, even a totally controlled society cannot resist the winds of change that economics and technology and information flow have imposed in this world of ours. That is not an option. Our only realistic option is to embrace these changes and create the jobs of tomorrow.

I believe that NAFTA will create 200,000 American jobs in the first two years of its effect. I believe if you look at the trends . . . starting about [1988], over one-third of our economic growth, and in some years over one-half of our net new jobs came directly from exports. And on average, those export-related jobs paid much higher [wages] than jobs that had no connection to exports.

I believe that NAFTA will create a million jobs in the first five years of its impact. And I believe that that is many more jobs than will be lost, as inevitably some will be as always happens when you open up the mix to a new range of competition.

NAFTA will generate these jobs by fostering an export boom to Mexico; by tearing down tariff walls which have been lowered quite a bit by the present administration of President [Carlos] Salinas [of Mexico] . . .

Already Mexican consumers buy more per capita from the United States than other consumers in other nations. Most Americans don't know this, but the average Mexican citizen—even though wages are much lower in Mexico, the average Mexican citizen is now spending $450 per year per person to buy American goods. That is more than the average Japanese, the average German, or the average Canadian buys; more than the average German, Swiss and Italian citizens put together.

So when people say that this trade agreement is just about how to move jobs to Mexico so nobody can make a living, how do they explain the fact that Mexicans keep buying more products made in America every year? Go out and tell the American people that. Mexican citizens with lower incomes spend more money—real dollars, not percentage of their income—more money on American products than Germans, Japanese, Canadians. That is a fact. And there will be more if they have more money to spend. That is what expanding trade is all about.

In 1987, Mexico exported $5.7 billion more of products to the United States than they purchased from us. We had a trade deficit. Because of the free market, tariff-lowering policies of the Salinas government in Mexico, and because our people are becoming more export-oriented, that $5.7-billion trade deficit has been turned into a $5.4-billion trade surplus for the United States. It has created hundreds of thousands of jobs.

Even when you subtract the jobs that have moved into the Maquilladora areas, America is a net job winner in what has happened in trade in the last six years. When Mexico boosts its consumption of petroleum products in Louisiana, where we're going tomorrow to talk about NAFTA, as it did by about 200 percent in that period, Louisiana refinery workers gained job security. When Mexico purchased industrial machinery and computer equipment made in Illinois, that means more jobs. And guess what? In this same period, Mexico increased those purchases out of Illinois by 300 percent.

Forty-eight out of the 50 states have boosted exports to Mexico since 1987. That's one reason why 41 of our nation's 50 governors, some of them who are here today . . . support this trade pact. I can tell you, if you're a governor, people won't leave you in office unless they think you get up every day trying to create more jobs. They think that's what your jobs is if you're a governor. And the people who have the job of creating jobs for their state and working with their business community, working with their labor community, 41 out of the 50 have already embraced the NAFTA pact.

Many Americans are still worried that this agreement will move jobs south of the border because they've seen jobs move south of the border and because they know that there are still great differences in the wage rates. There have been 19 serious economic studies of NAFTA by liberals and conservatives alike; 18 of them have concluded that there will be no job loss.

Businesses do not choose to locate based solely on wages. If they did, Haiti and Bangladesh would have the largest number of manufacturing jobs in the world. Businesses do choose to locate based on the skills and productivity of the work force, the attitude of the government, the roads and railroads to deliver products, the availability of a market close enough to make the transportation costs meaningful, the communications networks necessary to support the enterprise. That is our strength, and it will continue to be our strength. As it becomes Mexico's strength and they generate more jobs, they will have higher incomes and they will buy more American products.

We can win this. This is not a time for defeatism. It is a time to look at an opportunity that is enormous.

Moreover, there are specific provisions in this agreement that remove some of the current incentives for people to move their jobs just across our border. For example, today Mexican law requires United States automakers who want to sell cars to Mexicans to build them in Mexico. This year we will export only 1,000 cars to Mexico.

Under NAFTA, the Big Three automakers expect to ship 60,000 cars to Mexico in the first year alone, and that is one reason why one of the automakers recently announced moving 1,000 jobs from Mexico back to Michigan.

In a few moments, I will sign side agreements to NAFTA that will make it harder than it is today for businesses to relocate solely because of very low wages or lax environmental rules. These side agreements will make a difference. The environmental agreement will, for the first time ever, apply trade sanctions against any of the countries that fails to enforce its own environmental laws. I might say to those who say that's giving up of our sovereignty, for people who have been asking us to ask that of Mexico, how do we have the right to ask that of Mexico if we don't demand it of ourselves? It's nothing but fair.

This is the first time that there have ever been trade sanctions in the environmental law area. This ground-breaking agreement is one of the reasons why major environmental groups, ranging from the Audubon Society to the Natural Resources Defense Council, are supporting NAFTA.

The second agreement ensures the Mexico enforces its laws in areas that include worker health and safety, child labor and the minimum wage. And

I might say, this is the first time in the history of world trade agreements when any nation has ever been willing to tie its minimum wage to the growth in its own economy.

What does that mean? It means that there will be an even more rapid closing of the gap between our two wage rates. And as the benefits of economic growth are spread in Mexico to working people, what will happen? They'll have more disposable income to buy more American products and there will be less illegal immigration because more Mexicans will be able to support their children by staying home. . . .

The third agreement answers one of the primary attacks on NAFTA that I heard for a year, which is, well, you can say all this, but something might happen that you can't foresee. . . .

Now, the third agreement protects our industries against unforseen surges in exports from either one of our trading partners. And the flip side is also true. Economic change, as I said before, has often been cruel to the middle class, but we have to make change their friend. NAFTA will help to do that.

This imposes also a new obligation on our government . . . We do have some obligations here. We have to make sure that our workers are the best prepared, the best trained in the world.

Without regard to NAFTA, we know now that the average 18-year-old American will change jobs eight times in a lifetime. The Secretary of Labor has told us, without regard to NAFTA, that over the last 10 years, for the first time, when people lose their jobs most of them do not go back to their old job, they go back to a different job; so that we no longer need an unemployment system, we need a reemployment system. And we have to create that.

And that's our job. We have to tell American workers who will be dislocated because of this agreement or because of things that will happen regardless of this agreement, that we are going to have a reemployment program for training in America, and we intend to do that.

Together, the efforts of two administrations now have created a trade agreement that moves beyond the traditional notions of free trade, seeking to ensure trade that pulls everybody up instead of dragging some down while others go up. We have put the environment at the center of this in future agreements. We have sought to avoid a debilitating contest for business where countries seek to lure them only by slashing wages or despoiling the environment.

This agreement will create jobs, thanks to trade with our neighbors. That's reason enough to support it. But I must close with a couple of other points.

NAFTA is essential to our long-term ability to compete with Asia and Europe. Across the globe our competitors are consolidating, creating huge trading blocks. This pact will create a free trade zone stretching from the Arctic to the tropics, the largest in the world—a $6.5 billion market, with 370 million people. It will help our businesses to be both more efficient and to better compete with our rivals in other parts of the world.

This is also essential to our leadership in this hemisphere and the world. Having won the Cold War, we face the more subtle challenge of consolidating the victory of democracy and opportunity and freedom.

For decades, we have preached and preached and preached greater democracy, greater respect for human rights, and more open markets to Latin America. NAFTA finally offers them the opportunity to reap the benefits of this. Secretary [of Health and Human Services Donna] Shalala represented me recently at the installation of the President of Paraguay. And she talked to presidents from Colombia, from Chile, from Venezuela, from Uruguay, from Argentina, from Brazil. They all wanted to know, tell me if NAFTA is going to pass so we can become part of this great new market. More, hundreds of millions more of American consumers for our products.

It's no secret that there is division within both the Democratic and Republican parties on this issue. . . . But if you strip away the differences, it is clear that most of the people that oppose this pact are rooted in the fears and insecurities that are legitimately gripping the great American middle class. It is no use to deny that these fears and insecurities exist. It is no use denying that many of our people have lost in the battle for change. But it is a great mistake to think that NAFTA will make it worse. Every single solitary thing you hear people talk about that they're worried about can happen whether this trade agreement passes or not, and most of them will be made worse if it fails. And I can tell you it will be better if it passes.

So I say this to you: Are we going to compete and win, or are we going to withdraw? Are we going to face the future with confidence that we can create tomorrow's jobs, or are we going to try against all the evidence of the last 20 years to hold on to yesterday's? Are we going to take the plain evidence of the good faith of Mexico in opening their own markets and buying more of our products and creating more of our jobs, or are we going to give in to the fears of the worst-case scenario? Are we going to pretend that we don't have the first trade agreement in history dealing seriously with labor standards, environmental standards and cleverly and clearly taking account of unforeseen consequences, or are we going to say this is the best you can do and then some?

In an imperfect world, we have something which will enable us to go forward together and to create a future that is worthy of our children and grandchildren, worthy of the legacy of America, and consistent with what we did at the end of World War II. We have to do that again. We have to create a new world economy. And if we don't do it, we cannot then point the finger at Europe and Japan or anybody else and say, why don't you pass the GATT agreement; why don't you help to create a world economy. If we walk away from this, we have no right to say to other countries in the world, you're not fulfilling your world leadership, you're not being fair with us. This is our opportunity to provide an impetus to freedom and democracy in Latin America and create new jobs for America as well. It's a good deal and we ought to take it.

Thank you.

Source: HistoryCentral.com. "Remarks by President Clinton . . . in Signing of NAFTA Side Agreements." Available online. URL: http://www.multieducator.com/Documents/Clinton/SigningNAFTA.html. Accessed July 27, 2006.

"Measuring the Costs of Trade-Related Job Loss" by Lori G. Kletzer (July 20, 2001)

This document contains excerpts of the testimony given by economist and professor Lori G. Kletzer before the U.S. Senate Committee on Finance, on July 20, 2001. In it, Kletzer describes how U.S. workers have lost jobs (both industrial and high-tech) due to trade agreements such as the North American and Central American Free Trade Agreements and to outsourcing. She describes the usually permanent decline in the standard of living of individuals and families affected by free trade–related job loss, and she recommends the establishment of a "reemployment industry" to help workers obtain well-paying jobs.

Measuring the Costs of Trade-Related Job Loss
Lori G. Kletzer
Institute for International Economics
Testimony prepared for the Committee on Finance
United States Senate
Washington, DC
July 20, 2001

My testimony addresses what we know about the costs of job displacement, specifically trade-related job displacement. My focus is on workers: who gets displaced and the consequences of that job loss.

Summary

For most displaced workers, what matters is the kind of job lost and the kind of job regained. Why the job was lost does not matter much at all. If workers and consequences are alike, across differing causes of job loss such as increasing foreign competition, technological change, downsizing, then policymakers should consider adjustment policy for all displaced workers, and broaden program eligibility beyond "trade-displaced workers."

Trade and Jobs: Asking the Right Questions

I will offer one general comment before I turn to the specifics. Lost in the debate over the number of jobs created or destroyed by increased economic integration is the really important question: what kind of work will Americans do, as the dynamic American economy continues to change, with more trade and technological advancement? In a dynamic economy, jobs are lost and created and workers are displaced and reemployed continuously. Rather than focus on how many jobs will be affected, we need to understand workers, who they are and how they will be affected. Specifically, who are the workers displaced from import-competing industries? What are their basic individual characteristics? Are they different from other workers who lose their jobs? What happens to them after displacement? How do workers adjust to economic change? What can we learn from the pattern of reemployment and earnings that will aid in the (re)design of government programs to assist workers?

Defining Import-Competing Job Loss

Studies reveal that there is a set of industries facing sustained import competition, those with both high levels of import share and increasing import share, where the rate of job loss is high. Beyond these industries, the rising import share-high rate of job loss relationship is considerably weaker. This means that increasing imports play a small role in aggregate economy job loss, but a larger role in traditional import-competing industries.

From this base . . . I define high import-competition industries as those in the top 25 percent in a ranking by changes in import share over the period 1979–94. . . . [or] industries with an increase in import share exceeding 13 percentage points. Applying this definition to a nationally representative sample of displaced workers drawn from the Displaced Worker Surveys yields a sample of import-competing displaced workers.

The set of high import-competing industries includes: apparel, footwear, motor vehicles, knitting mills, leather products, textiles, blast furnaces, other primary metals, tires and inner tubes, cycles and miscellaneous transport, radio and television, toys and sporting goods. These are the traditional import-competing industries. Import-competing job loss is concentrated in a few large employment industries: electrical machinery, apparel, motor vehicles, nonelectrical machinery, blast furnaces.

Over the 21-year period from 1979–99:

- 6.4 million workers were displaced from an import-competing industry; these workers represented about 38 percent of manufacturing displacement. These industries accounted for just under 30 percent of manufacturing employment.

- 17 million workers [were] displaced from the manufacturing sector; these workers accounted for about 37 percent of total nonagricultural displacement, when manufacturing's average share of total nonagricultural employment was about 18 percent.

These numbers reveal that manufacturing workers are overrepresented among displaced workers, as compared to their employment share and high import-competing workers are overrepresented among manufacturing displacement, relative to their employment share.

Basic Worker Characteristics

Compared to workers displaced from other sectors of the economy, such as wholesale and retail trade, utilities, or services, manufacturing workers are slightly older, notably less educated, with longer job tenures, somewhat more likely to be minority, and far more likely to be production oriented (just less than one-half of manufacturing displaced are lower-skilled blue collar workers—fabricators, laborers, etc.). Twenty-one percent of manufacturing displaced are high school dropouts, compared to 11.9 percent of nonmanufacturing displaced. This difference widened in the 1990s as compared to the 1980s: the high school dropout share fell throughout the economy, but more so outside of manufacturing. Manufacturing workers are less likely to be college graduates: over 1979–99, workers with a college degree or higher comprised about 14 percent of manufacturing displaced and 22 percent of nonmanufacturing displaced.

Import-competing workers are similar to other displaced manufacturing workers, with respect to age, educational attainment, and job tenure. The most striking difference between import-competing displaced workers and other displaced manufacturing workers is the degree to which import-competing industries employ and displace women. Women account for 45 percent of import-sensitive displaced workers, compared to 37 percent of overall manufacturing displaced. Some industries stand out: women account for 80 percent of the displaced from apparel, 66 percent of the footwear displaced, 76 percent of the displaced from knitting mills (part of the textiles industry). Women dominate the group of displaced workers from these import-competing industries as a result of their high representation in employment.

What Happens to Workers after Job Displacement?

The first outcome is reemployment. About 65 percent of manufacturing displaced workers were reemployed at their survey date, as compared to 69 percent of nonmanufacturing displaced workers. This difference, 4.3 percentage points, is not large, but it is statistically significant. The likelihood of reemployment was markedly higher in the 1990s than in the 1980s. Import-competing displaced workers are a little less likely to be reemployed (63.4 percent were reemployed at their survey date) than other displaced manufacturing workers (65.8 percent reemployed). Particularly for the high import-competing group, reemployment was more difficult in the 1980s with a lower rate of 62.3 percent, than it was in the 1990s when 65.4 percent of workers were reemployed on average.

To understand what kinds of workers face difficult labor market adjustments following job loss, we need to estimate statistical models. The first is a model of the likelihood of reemployment. Estimation of this model can tell us what characteristics of workers and industries explain the lower reemployment likelihood for high import-competing workers relative to other manufacturing displaced workers and similarly for manufacturing workers relative to nonmanufacturing workers.

Consider some comparisons. A "representative" worker in our sample, a displaced worker who is 38 years old, with 5.3 years job tenure, a high school graduate with less than one year of post-secondary schooling, male, married, nonminority, who lost a full-time job in wholesale and retail trade and services in 1989, has a 68.1 percent chance of being reemployed. Our representative worker, if displaced from nondurable goods manufacturing, faces a 62 percent chance of reemployment, if displaced from durable goods manufacturing, a 65.2 percent chance of reemployment. These differences are statistically significant.

When age at displacement, job tenure, educational attainment, racial and ethnic minority status, and full-time status before displacement are accounted for, these sectoral differences narrow. The narrowing of what we might call "the industry effect" is important; it means that individual demographic and labor market characteristics are importantly and systematically related to reemployment. If these factors are truly explaining differences in reemployment, then policy design, when looking for potential signals of labor market adjustment difficulties, should turn first to these worker characteristics.

Certain characteristics stand out:

- Younger workers are more likely to be reemployed. Workers who are 25–34 years of age or 35–44 years of age are about 11 percentage points more likely to be reemployed than workers who were 45 years of age or older at the time of displacement.

- Education matters too. Compared to high school dropouts, workers with a college degree (or higher) are 25 percentage points more likely to be reemployed, high school graduates 9.4 percentage points more likely and workers with some college experience 11 percentage points more likely to be reemployed.

- The overall health of the economy and the labor market matters a great deal. A worker displaced from nondurable goods manufacturing in the strong economy of the mid-to-late 1990s (1993 to 1999), 45 years of age or older, a high school dropout, more than 10 years tenure on the old job, full-time at the time of displacement, nonminority and married has a predicted chance of reemployment of 53.7 percent. The same worker, displaced during the deep 1980s recession (1981–83), had a 34.5 percent chance of reemployment, more than one-third (35.7 percent) lower.

While it may not be enough (particularly for older, less educated and more tenured workers), a strong labor market clearly provides the necessary setting for displaced workers to find the next job.

I offer one final illustration of the strength of these effects. We can consider the worker to whom I just referred (displaced from nondurable goods manufacturing in the mid-to-late 1990s, 45 years of age or older, a high school dropout, more than 10 years tenure on the old job, full-time at the time of displacement, nonminority and married) a representative trade-displaced worker. Again, this worker has a predicted likelihood of reemployment of 54 percent. If that worker was younger, say 25 to 44 years old instead of 45 years or older, the chance of reemployment rises to nearly 66 percent. As a high school dropout, the chance of reemployment is about 65 percent. For a college graduate, reemployment jumps to 78.5 percent. These differences are a striking illustration of the importance of education (which can be changed) and age (which cannot) in getting the next job. And the effect of more formal schooling is stronger for younger workers than for older workers.

One clear interpretation of this analysis is that import competition is associated with low reemployment rates because the workers vulnerable to rising import job loss experience difficulty gaining reemployment, based on their individual characteristics. It is not import competition per se; it is who gets displaced from (and is employed by) industries with rising import competition. What limits the reemployment of import-competing displaced workers? The same characteristics that limit the reemployment of all displaced workers: low educational attainment; advancing age, high tenure, minority status; marital status. Married women, even those displaced from full-time jobs, are much less likely to be reemployed.

Earnings Losses Upon Reemployment

Earnings are measured in the Displaced Worker Surveys as weekly earnings, and the available comparison is between weekly earnings at the time of displacement and, if reemployed, weekly earnings at the time of the survey. Earnings losses can be measured by comparing earnings on the old job to those on the new job. This measure will "miss" earnings growth that would have occurred on the old job, in the absence of displacement. Manufacturing displaced workers experience large earnings losses on average, 12 percent at the mean, compared to a loss of just under 4 percent for non-manufacturing displaced workers.

Among the reemployed, import-competing displaced workers experience sizeable average weekly earnings losses of about 13 percent. This large average loss masks considerable variation: one-third of import-competing displaced workers report earning the same or more on their new job as they earned on the old job, and one-quarter reported earnings losses of 30 percent or more. This average and distribution is very similar to what I find for manufacturing workers as a group. Older, less educated, lower-skilled production workers, with established tenures on the old job, are more likely to experience earnings losses in excess of 30 percent. . . .

For most high import-competing workers, the time needed to find a new job is within the usual 26-week period of eligibility for unemployment compensation. Half of these workers had unemployment spells of 8 weeks or less. Yet a full quarter of workers were unemployed for more than 26 weeks (six months), the normal length of unemployment insurance benefits.

The Importance of Reemployment Industry

The industry where workers are reemployed matters a great deal for understanding the variation in earnings losses. There are a few clear observations. Overall one-tenth of reemployed manufacturing workers are in Retail trade, and this percentage is similar for import-competing displaced workers. In contrast, 21 percent of nonmanufacturing displaced workers are reemployed in retail trade.

Second, there is considerable reemployment within manufacturing. Among the reemployed, about one-half of workers displaced from high import competing industries are reemployed in manufacturing. Incorporating their 63 percent chance of reemployment, note that about one-third (32.9 percent) of all high import-competing displaced workers return to manufacturing after their job loss. Another one-third are reemployed in the nonmanufacturing sectors and the remaining one-third are not reemployed.

For manufacturing workers, regaining employment in manufacturing greatly reduces earnings losses. Mean earnings losses are smallest for workers reemployed in durable goods (at 4.5 percent), and next smallest in nondurable goods (5.8 percent). Earnings losses are largest for manufacturing workers reemployed in retail trade (about 10 percent of the reemployed).

Displaced manufacturing workers who gain reemployment in manufacturing also experience the shortest median weeks of joblessness (6–8 weeks), as compared to workers reemployed elsewhere. This may be a result of searching first in familiar labor markets in manufacturing, and turning to less familiar markets and networks only after some period of unsuccessful search. These spells of joblessness are well within the standard period of eligibility for unemployment compensation (26 weeks).

Regaining employment in the same detailed industry is associated with small or no earnings losses, on average. For the import-competing displaced group, half of the workers who return to the same industry report no earnings losses or a gain. Mean earnings losses are around 2 percent, about \$8/week for the average import-competing displaced worker compared to predisplacement earnings. Reemployment in the same detailed industry does not guarantee that earnings will not be reduced, but it greatly reduces the average loss (from nearly 20 percent to 2 percent) and it greatly reduces the percent of workers with very large earnings losses (from 34 percent to 15 percent).

The experience of workers who change detailed industry is very different. For the import-competing displaced group, half of all workers who change industry have earnings losses greater than 10 percent, with the mean change a loss of 20 percent. Judged against old earnings, the loss is around \$81/week, or \$4200 per year. Thirty-four percent of these workers experience an earnings loss greater than 30 percent.

Policy Implications

The patterns of reemployment and labor market adjustment have implications for addressing some of the holes in the existing safety net for displaced workers. We can understand more clearly that the consequences of job loss vary and how some discernible transitions are better than others. Age, education and job tenure emerge as strong predictors of difficult readjustment. Middle-aged (or older), significantly tenured, less educated worker may be ill-prepared to enter a changed labor market. While highly skilled for production work, in many cases they may be less equipped to adapt to new production techniques or lack the educational background to transfer to well-paid service economy jobs.

The strong association between advanced age, less formal education, long tenure, and difficult labor market adjustment can be used to target assistance at certain groups of workers, rather than providing the same services, up front, to all program participants. This approach is in the spirit of the worker profiling used by states for the provision of reemployment services.

We know that job search assistance can be offered at a low cost. Enhanced, industry-specific job search assistance could aid (some) workers in becoming reemployed in manufacturing, where their earnings losses will likely be minimized. This type of job search assistance, focused on reemployment in the old industry, might make sense for the current generation of established workers in import-competing industries. For these workers, reemployment outside of manufacturing produces large and persistent earnings losses and (yet) the costs of retraining are high. The cost-effective approach may be to encourage reemployment where and for as long as the job opportunities exist.

At the same time, reallocation to growing sectors of the economy can be costly for manufacturing workers. With society benefitting overall from the reallocation, these private costs deserve close consideration. These costs can be addressed directly by wage insurance, a program of financial assistance upon reemployment, for workers who lose jobs, for any reason, through no fault of their own. The goal of a wage insurance program is to get workers back to work as soon as possible, while minimizing longer-term earnings losses. A key aspect of the program, and the difference between it and other adjustment assistance programs, is the employment incentive created by making benefits conditional on reemployment. . . .

In brief, the program would be open to all workers who could provide documentation that they were "displaced" according to criteria similar to the operational definition of displacement used by the Bureau of Labor Statistics in its Displaced Worker Surveys (plant closing or relocation, elimination of position or shift, and insufficient work). Eligibility can be limited to a minimum period of service on the old job.... Workers reemployed in a new job that pays less than the old job ... would have a substantial portion of their lost earnings replaced, for up to two years following the date of initial job loss. For example, a displaced worker who once earned $40,000 per year, reemployed in a new job paying $30,000 per year would receive $5,000 per year, for a period from the time of reemployment to two years after initial job loss. Annual payments could be capped, perhaps at $10,000.

Wage insurance addresses some of the criticisms leveled at TAA and NAFTA-TAA. First, the structure of the program, with benefits available only upon reemployment, presents an incentive for workers to find new jobs quickly. Second, workers' job search efforts may be broader, as entry-level jobs become more attractive to workers when the earnings gap is reduced. Third and relatedly, the program effectively subsidizes retraining on the job, where it is likely to be far more useful than in a training program where reemployment prospects are uncertain. Fourth, the program directly addresses the critical problem in evidence here: earnings losses upon reemployment.

Many American workers fear job loss and its consequences. There is a narrow, but significant band of workers for whom import-competing job loss is very costly. For other workers, realized costs are smaller. Wage insurance focuses precisely on these costs. It gets workers back to work and offers assistance to meet workers' real needs.

Source: Institute for International Economics. "Measuring the Costs of Trade-Related Job Loss." Available online. URL: http://www.iie.com/publications/papers/paper.cfm?ResearchID=418. Accessed July 27, 2006.

5

International Documents

The primary sources in this chapter are divided into six sections:

Bretton Woods
The International Monetary Fund
The World Trade Organization
Effects of Globalization
East Asian Financial Crisis
China

BRETTON WOODS

The Bretton Woods Agreement (1944)

This document was signed by the delegates to the Bretton Woods conference on July 22, 1944. Its rather formal and legalistic language is typical of international treaties and documents of this type. The agreement is complete, except for minor, technical details, such as the locations of future meetings, that are not relevant to the understanding of the document.

(a) Articles of Agreement of the International Bank for Reconstruction and Development, July 22, 1944

The Governments on whose behalf the present Agreement is signed agree as follows:

INTRODUCTORY ARTICLE

The International Bank for Reconstruction and Development is established and shall operate in accordance with the following provisions:

ARTICLE I. PURPOSES

The purposes of the Bank are:

i. To assist in the reconstruction and development of territories of members by facilitating the investment of capital for productive purposes, including the restoration of economies destroyed or disrupted by war, the reconversion of productive facilities to peacetime needs and the encouragement of the development of productive facilities and resources in less developed countries.

ii. To promote private foreign investment by means of guarantees or participations in loans and other investments made by private investors; and when private capital is not available on reasonable terms, to supplement private investment by providing, on suitable conditions, finance for productive purposes out of its own capital, funds raised by it and its other resources.

iii. To promote the long-range balanced growth of international trade and the maintenance of equilibrium in balances of payments by encouraging international investment for the development of the productive resources of members, thereby assisting in raising productivity, the standard of living and conditions of labor in their territories.

iv. To arrange the loans made or guaranteed by it in relation to international loans through other channels so that the more useful and urgent projects, large and small alike, will be dealt with first.

v. To conduct its operations with due regard to the effect of international investment on business conditions in the territories of members and, in the immediate post-war years, to assist in bringing about a smooth transition from a wartime to a peacetime economy.

The Bank shall be guided in all its decisions by the purposes set forth above.

ARTICLE II. MEMBERSHIP IN AND CAPITAL OF THE BANK

SECTION 1. MEMBERSHIP

a. The original members of the Bank shall be those members of the International Monetary Fund which accept membership in the Bank before the date specified in Article XI, Section 2 (e).

b. Membership shall be open to other members of the Fund, at such times and in accordance with such terms as may be prescribed by the Bank. . . .

ARTICLE III. GENERAL PROVISIONS RELATING TO LOANS AND GUARANTEES

SECTION 1. USE OF RESOURCES

a. The resources and the facilities of the Bank shall be used exclusively for the benefit of members with equitable consideration to projects for development and projects for reconstruction alike.

b. For the purpose of facilitating the restoration and reconstruction of the economy of members whose metropolitan territories have suffered great devastation from enemy occupation or hostilities, the Bank, in determining the conditions and terms of loans made to such members, shall pay special regard to lightening the financial burden and expediting the completion of such restoration and reconstruction.

SECTION 2. DEALINGS BETWEEN MEMBERS AND THE BANK

Each member shall deal with the Bank only through its Treasury, central bank, stabilization fund or other similar fiscal agency, and the Bank shall deal with members only by or through the same agencies.

SECTION 3. LIMITATIONS ON GUARANTEES AND BORROWINGS OF THE BANK

The total amount outstanding of guarantees, participations in loans and direct loans made by the Bank shall not be increased at any time, if by such increase the total would exceed one hundred percent of the unimpaired subscribed capital, reserves and surplus of the Bank.

SECTION 4. CONDITIONS ON WHICH THE BANK MAY GUARANTEE OR MAKE LOANS

The Bank may guarantee, participate in, or make loans to any member or any political sub-division thereof and any business, industrial, and agricultural enterprise in the territories of a member, subject to the following conditions:

i. When the member in whose territories the project is located is not itself the borrower, the member or the central bank or some comparable agency of the member which is acceptable to the Bank, fully guarantees the repayment of the principal and the payment of interest and other charges on the loan.

ii. The Bank is satisfied that in the prevailing market conditions the borrower would be unable otherwise to obtain the loan under conditions which in the opinion of the Bank are reasonable for the borrower.

iii. A competent committee, as provided for in Article V, Section 7, has submitted a written report recommending the project after a careful study of the merits of the proposal.

iv. In the opinion of the Bank the rate of interest and other charges are reasonable and such rate, charges and the schedule for repayment of principal are appropriate to the project.

v. In making or guaranteeing a loan, the Bank shall pay due regard to the prospects that the borrower, and, if the borrower is not a member, that the guarantor, will be in position to meet its obligations under the loan; and the Bank shall act prudently in the interests both of the particular member in whose territories the project is located and of the members as a whole.

vi. In guaranteeing a loan made by other investors, the Bank receives suitable compensation for its risk.

vii. Loans made or guaranteed by the Bank shall, except in special circumstances, be for the purpose of specific projects of reconstruction or development.

SECTION 5. USE OF LOANS GUARANTEED, PARTICIPATED IN OR MADE BY THE BANK

a. The Bank shall impose no conditions that the proceeds of a loan shall be spent in the territories of any particular member or members.

b. The Bank shall make arrangements to ensure that the proceeds of any loan are used only for the purposes for which the loan was granted, with due attention to considerations of economy and efficiency and without regard to political or other non-economic influences or considerations.

c. In the case of loans made by the Bank, it shall open an account in the name of the borrower and the amount of the loan shall be credited to this account in the currency or currencies in which the loan is made. The borrower shall be permitted by the Bank to draw on this account only to meet expenses in connection with the project as they are actually incurred. . . .

ARTICLE V. ORGANIZATION AND MANAGEMENT

SECTION 1. STRUCTURE OF THE BANK

The Bank shall have a Board of Governors, Executive Directors, a President and such other officers and staff to perform such duties as the Bank may determine.

SECTION 2. BOARD OF GOVERNORS

a. All the powers of the Bank shall be vested in the Board of Governors consisting of one governor and one alternate appointed by each member in such manner as it may determine. Each governor and each alternate shall serve for five years, subject to the pleasure of the member appointing him, and may be reappointed. No alternate may vote except in the absence of his principal. The Board shall select one of the governors as Chairman.

b. The Board of Governors may delegate to the Executive Directors authority to exercise any powers of the Board, except the power to:

i. Admit new members and determine the conditions of their admission;

ii. Increase or decrease the capital stock;

iii. Suspend a member;

iv. Decide appeals from interpretations of this Agreement given by the Executive Directors;

v. Make arrangements to cooperate with other international organizations (other than informal arrangements of a temporary and administrative character);

vi. Decide to suspend permanently the operations of the Bank and to distribute its assets;

vii. Determine the distribution of the net income of the Bank. . . .

SECTION 3. VOTING

a. Each member shall have two hundred fifty votes plus one additional vote for each share of stock held.

b. Except as otherwise specifically provided, all matters before the Bank shall be decided by a majority of the votes cast.

SECTION 4. EXECUTIVE DIRECTORS

a. The Executive Directors shall be responsible for the conduct of the general operations of the Bank, and for this purpose, shall exercise all the powers delegated to them by the Board of Governors.

b. There shall be twelve Executive Directors, who need not be governors, and of whom:

i. five shall be appointed, one by each of the five members having the largest number of shares;

ii. seven shall be elected according to Schedule B by all the Governors other than those appointed by the five members referred to in (i) above.

For the purpose of this paragraph, "members" means governments of countries whose names are set forth in Schedule A, whether they are original members or become members in accordance with Article II, Section I (b). When governments of other countries become members, the Board of Governors may, by a four-fifths majority of the total voting power, increase the total number of directors by increasing the number of directors to be elected.

Executive directors shall be appointed or elected every two years. . . .

SECTION 5. PRESIDENT AND STAFF

a. The Executive Directors shall select a President who shall not be a governor or an executive director or an alternate for either. The President shall be Chairman of the Executive Directors, but shall have no vote except a deciding vote in case of an equal division. He may participate in meetings of the Board of Governors, but shall not vote at such meetings. The President shall cease to hold office when the Executive Directors so decide.

b. The President shall be chief of the operating staff of the Bank and shall conduct, under the direction of the Executive Directors, the ordinary business of the Bank. Subject to the general control of the Executive Directors, he shall be responsible for the organization, appointment and dismissal of the officers and staff.

c. The President, officers and staff of the Bank, in the discharge of their offices, owe their duty entirely to the Bank and to no other authority. Each member of the Bank shall respect the international character of this duty and shall refrain from all attempts to influence any of them in the discharge of their duties.

d. In appointing the officers and staff the President shall, subject to the paramount importance of securing the highest standards of efficiency and of technical competence, pay due regard to the importance of recruiting personnel on as wide a geographical basis as possible.

SECTION 6. ADVISORY COUNCIL

a. There shall be an Advisory Council of not less than seven persons selected by the Board of Governors including representatives of banking, commercial, industrial, labor, and agricultural interests, and with as wide a national representation as possible. In those fields where specialized international organizations exist, the members of the Council representative of those fields shall be selected in agreement with such organizations. The Council shall advise the Bank on matters of general policy. The Council shall meet annually and on such other occasions as the Bank may request.

b. Councillors shall serve for two years and may be reappointed. They shall be paid their reasonable expenses incurred on behalf of the Bank.

SECTION 7. LOAN COMMITTEES

The committees required to report on loans under Article III, Section 4, shall be appointed by the Bank. Each such committee shall include an expert selected by the governor representing the member in whose territories the project is located and one or more members of the technical staff of the Bank.

SECTION 8. RELATIONSHIP TO OTHER INTERNATIONAL ORGANIZATIONS

a. The Bank, within the terms of this Agreement, shall cooperate with any general international organization and with public international organizations having specialized responsibilities in related fields. Any arrangements for such cooperation which would involve a modification of any provision of this Agreement may be effected only after amendment to this Agreement under Article VIII.

b. In making decisions on applications for loans or guarantees relating to matters directly within the competence of any international organization of the types specified in the preceding paragraph and participated in primarily by members of the Bank, the Bank shall give consideration to the views and recommendations of such organization. . . .

SECTION 11. DEPOSITORIES

a. Each member shall designate its central bank as a depository for all the Bank's holdings of its currency or, if it has no central bank, it shall designate such other institution as may be acceptable to the Bank.

b. The Bank may hold other assets, including gold, in depositories designated by the five members having the largest number of shares and in such other designated depositories as the Bank may select. Initially, at least one-half of the gold holdings of the Bank shall be held in the depository designated by the member in whose territory the Bank has its principal office, and at least forty percent shall be held in the depositories designated by the remaining four members referred to above, each of such depositories to hold, initially, not less than the amount of gold paid on the shares of the member designating it. However, all transfers of gold by the Bank shall be made with due regard to the costs of transport and anticipated requirements of the Bank.

In an emergency the Executive Directors may transfer all or any part of the Bank's gold holdings to any place where they can be adequately protected.

SECTION 12. FORM OF HOLDINGS OF CURRENCY

The Bank shall accept from any member, in place of any part of the member's currency, paid in to the Bank under Article II, Section 7 (i), or to meet amortization payments on loans made with such currency and not needed by the Bank in its operations, notes or similar obligations issued by the Government of the member or the depository designated by such member, which shall be non-negotiable, non-interest-bearing and payable at their par value on demand by credit to the account of the Bank in the designated depository . . .

ARTICLE VI. WITHDRAWAL AND SUSPENSION OF MEMBERSHIP: SUSPENSION OF OPERATIONS

SECTION 1. RIGHT OF MEMBERS TO WITHDRAW

Any member may withdraw from the Bank at any time by transmitting a notice in writing to the Bank at its principal office. Withdrawal shall become effective on the date such notice is received.

SECTION 2. SUSPENSION OF MEMBERSHIP

If a member fails to fulfill any of its obligations to the Bank, the Bank may suspend its membership by decision of a majority of the Governors, exercising a majority of the total voting power. The member so suspended shall automatically cease to be a member one year from the date of its suspension unless a decision is taken by the same majority to restore the member to good standing.

While under suspension, a member shall not be entitled to exercise any rights under this Agreement, except the right of withdrawal, but shall remain subject to all obligations.

SECTION 3. CESSATION OF MEMBERSHIP IN INTERNATIONAL MONETARY FUND

Any member which ceases to be a member of the International Monetary Fund shall automatically cease after three months to be a member of the Bank unless the Bank by three-fourths of the total voting power has agreed to allow it to remain a member.

SECTION 4. SETTLEMENT OF ACCOUNTS WITH GOVERNMENTS CEASING TO BE MEMBERS

a. When a government ceases to be a member, it shall remain liable for its direct obligations to the Bank and for its contingent liabilities to the Bank so long as any part of the loans or guarantees contracted before it ceased to be a member are outstanding; but it shall cease to incur liabilities with respect to loans and guarantees entered into thereafter by the Bank and to share either in the income or the expenses of the Bank.

b. At the time a government ceases to be a member, the Bank shall arrange for the repurchase of its shares as a part of the settlement of accounts with such government in accordance with the provisions of (c) and (d) below. For this purpose the repurchase price of the shares shall be the value shown by the books of the Bank on the day the government ceases to be a member.

c. The payment for shares repurchased by the Bank under this section shall be governed by the following conditions:

i. Any amount due to the government for its shares shall be withheld so long as the government, its central bank or any of its agencies remains liable, as borrower or guarantor, to the Bank and such amount may, at the option of the Bank, be applied on any such liability as it matures. No amount shall be withheld on account of the liability of the government resulting from its subscription for share under Article II, Section 5 (ii). In any event, no amount due to a member for its shares shall be paid until six months after the date upon which the government ceases to be a member.

ii. Payments for shares may be made from time to time, upon their surrender by the government, to the extent by which the amount due as the repurchase price in (b) above exceeds the aggregate of liabilities on loans and guarantees in (c) (i) above until the former member has received the full repurchase price.

iii. Payments shall be made in the currency of the country receiving payment or at the option of the Bank in gold.

iv. If losses are sustained by the Bank on any guarantees, participations in loans, or loans which were outstanding on the date when the government ceased to be a member, and the amount of such losses exceeds the amount of the reserve provided against losses on the date when the government ceased to be a member, such government shall be obligated to repay upon demand the amount by which the repurchase price of its shares would have been reduced, if the losses had been taken into account when the repurchase price was determined. In addition, the former member government shall remain liable on any call for unpaid subscriptions under Article II, Section 5 (ii), to the extent that it would have been required to respond if the impairment of capital had occurred and the call had been made at the time the repurchase price of its shares was determined.

d. If the Bank suspends permanently its operations under Section 5 (b) of this Article, within six months of the date upon which any government ceases to be a member, all rights of such government shall be determined by the provisions of Section 5 of this Article.

SECTION 5. SUSPENSION OF OPERATIONS AND SETTLEMENT OF OBLIGATIONS

a. In an emergency the Executive Directors may suspend temporarily operations in respect of new loans and guarantees pending an opportunity for further consideration and action by the Board of Governors.

b. The Bank may suspend permanently its operations in respect of new loans and guarantees by vote of a majority of the Governors, exercising a majority of the total voting power. After such suspension of operations the Bank shall forthwith cease all activities, except those incident to the orderly realization, conservation, and preservation of its assets and settlement of its obligations.

c. The liability of all members for uncalled subscriptions to the capital stock of the Bank and in respect of the depreciation of their own currencies shall continue until all claims of creditors, including all contingent claims, shall have been discharged.

d. All creditors holding direct claims shall be paid out of the assets of the Bank, and then out of payments to the Bank on calls on unpaid subscriptions. Before making any payments to creditors holding direct claims, the Executive Directors shall make such arrangements as are necessary, in their judgment, to insure a distribution to holders of contingent claims ratably with creditors holding direct claims.

e. No distribution shall be made to members on account of their subscriptions to the capital stock of the Bank until

i. all liabilities to creditors have been discharged or provided for, and

ii. a majority of the Governors, exercising a majority of the total voting power, have decided to make a distribution.

f. After a decision to make a distribution has been taken under (e) above, the Executive Directors may by a two-thirds majority vote make successive distributions of the assets of the Bank to members until all of the assets have been distributed. This distribution shall be subject to the prior settlement of all outstanding claims of the Bank against each member.

g. Before any distribution of assets is made, the Executive Directors shall fix the proportionate share of each member according to the ratio of its shareholding to the total outstanding shares of the Bank.

h. The Executive Directors shall value the assets to be distributed as at the date of distribution and then proceed to distribute in the following manner:

i. There shall be paid to each member in its own obligations or those of its official agencies or legal entities within its territories, insofar as they are available for distribution, an amount equivalent in value to its proportionate share of the total amount to be distributed.

ii. Any balance due to a member after payment has been made under (i) above shall be paid, in its own currency, insofar as it is held by the Bank, up to an amount equivalent in value to such balance.

iii. Any balance due to a member after payment has been made under (i) and (ii) above shall be paid in gold or currency acceptable to the member, insofar as they are held by the Bank, up to an amount equivalent in value to such balance.

iv. Any remaining assets held by the Bank after payments have been made to members under (i), (ii), and (iii) above shall be distributed pro rata among the members.

i. Any member receiving assets distributed by the Bank in accordance with (h) above, shall enjoy the same rights with respect to such assets as the Bank enjoyed prior to their distribution. . . .

Source: Pearson Prentice Hall. "The Bretton Woods Agreements." Available online. URL: http://phschool.com/atschool/primary_sources/bretton_woods_agreements.html. Accessed August 25, 2006.

Excerpts from the International Monetary Fund Agreement (1944)

This document contains excerpts of the original agreement, signed at the Bretton Woods conference, that established the International Monetary Fund. Several different sections, or parts of the IMF charter, are included to provide a sense of the treaty and its original mission.

Articles of Agreement of the International Monetary Fund

Introductory Article

The Governments on whose behalf the present Agreement is signed agree as follows:

(i) The International Monetary Fund is established and shall operate in accordance with the provisions of this Agreement as originally adopted and subsequently amended.

(ii) To enable the Fund to conduct its operations and transactions, the Fund shall maintain a General Department and a Special Drawing Rights Department. Membership in the Fund shall give the right to participation in the Special Drawing Rights Department.

(iii) Operations and transactions authorized by this Agreement shall be conducted through the General Department, consisting in accordance with the provisions of this Agreement of the General Resources Account, the Special Disbursement Account, and the Investment Account; except that operations and transactions involving special drawing rights shall be conducted through the Special Drawing Rights Department. . . .

Article IV—Obligations Regarding Exchange Arrangements

Section 1. General obligations of members

Recognizing that the essential purpose of the international monetary system is to provide a framework that facilitates the exchange of goods, services, and capital among countries, and that sustains sound economic growth, and that a principal objective is the continuing development of the orderly underlying conditions that are necessary for financial and economic stability, each member undertakes to collaborate with the Fund and other members to assure orderly exchange arrangements and to promote a stable system of exchange rates. In particular, each member shall:

(i) endeavor to direct its economic and financial policies toward the objective of fostering orderly economic growth with reasonable price stability, with due regard to its circumstances;

(ii) seek to promote stability by fostering orderly underlying economic and financial conditions and a monetary system that does not tend to produce erratic disruptions;

(iii) avoid manipulating exchange rates or the international monetary system in order to prevent effective balance of payments adjustment or to gain an unfair competitive advantage over other members; and

(iv) follow exchange policies compatible with the undertakings under this Section.

Section 2. General exchange arrangements

(*a*) Each member shall notify the Fund, within thirty days after the date of the second amendment of this Agreement, of the exchange arrangements it intends to apply in fulfillment of its obligations under Section 1 of this Article, and shall notify the Fund promptly of any changes in its exchange arrangements.

(*b*) Under an international monetary system of the kind prevailing on January 1, 1976, exchange arrangements may include (i) the maintenance by a member of a value for its currency in terms of the special drawing right or another denominator, other than gold, selected by the member, or (ii) cooperative arrangements by which members maintain the value of their currencies in relation to the value of the currency or currencies of other members, or (iii) other exchange arrangements of a member's choice.

(*c*) To accord with the development of the international monetary system, the Fund, by an eighty-five percent majority of the total voting power, may make provision for general exchange arrangements without limiting the right of members to have exchange arrangements of their choice consistent with the purposes of the Fund and the obligations under Section 1 of this Article.

Section 3. Surveillance over exchange arrangements

(*a*) The Fund shall oversee the international monetary system in order to ensure its effective operation, and shall oversee the compliance of each member with its obligations under Section 1 of this Article.

(*b*) In order to fulfill its functions under (*a*) above, the Fund shall exercise firm surveillance over the exchange rate policies of members, and shall adopt specific principles for the guidance of all members with respect to those policies. Each member shall provide the Fund with the information necessary for such surveillance, and, when requested by the Fund, shall consult with it on the member's exchange rate policies. The principles adopted by the Fund shall be consistent with cooperative arrangements by which members maintain the value of their currencies in relation to the value of the currency or currencies of other members, as well as with other exchange arrangements of a member's choice consistent with the purposes of the Fund and Section 1 of this Article. These principles shall respect the domestic social and political policies of members, and in applying these principles the Fund shall pay due regard to the circumstances of members.

Section 4. Par values

The Fund may determine, by an eighty-five percent majority of the total voting power, that international economic conditions permit the introduction of a widespread system of exchange arrangements based on stable but adjustable par values. The Fund shall make the determination on the basis of the underlying stability of the world economy, and for this purpose shall take into account price movements and rates of expansion in the economies of members. The determination shall be made in light of the evolution of the international monetary system, with particular reference to sources of liquidity, and, in order to ensure the effective operation of a system of par values, to arrangements under which both members in surplus and members in deficit in their balances of payments take prompt, effective, and symmetrical action to achieve adjustment, as well as to arrangements for intervention and the treatment of imbalances. Upon making such determination, the Fund shall notify members that the provisions of Schedule C apply.

Section 5. Separate currencies within a member's territories

(*a*) Action by a member with respect to its currency under this Article shall be deemed to apply to the separate currencies of all territories in respect of which the member has accepted this Agreement under Article XXXI, Section 2(*g*) unless the member declares that its action relates either to the metropolitan currency alone, or only to one or more specified separate currencies, or to the metropolitan currency and one or more specified separate currencies.

(*b*) Action by the Fund under this Article shall be deemed to relate to all currencies of a member referred to in (*a*) above unless the Fund declares otherwise. . . .

Source: International Monetary Fund. "Articles of Agreement of the International Monetary Fund." Available online. URL: http://www.imf.org/external/pubs/ft/aa/aa00.htm. Accessed August 25, 2006.

"The G-20 Statement on Reforming the Bretton Woods Institutions (October 2005)

The G-20 is a group of developing and LDC nations that have openly criticized some of the negative effects neoliberal globalization has had on poor nations. In this 2005 position statement, financial officers from the G-20 nations contrast the original intent of the Bretton Woods institutions with what they have become today. They conclude with suggestions about how these institutions may become more responsive to the needs of poor nations.

The G-20 Statement on Reforming the Bretton Woods Institutions

1. We, the Finance Ministers and Central Bank Governors of the G-20, highlight the vital role the Bretton Woods Institutions (BWIs) should play in promoting macroeconomic and financial stability, economic growth, and poverty reduction. We recognize the need for the BWIs to be effective in delivering these objectives and believe that high standards of governance and internal management are critical. We welcome the IMF Managing Director's Strategic Review. More work is needed to develop a "roadmap"

for the future strategic reform of the BWIs, and we look forward to the work underway at the IMF to develop further details of the Strategic Review.

2. It is our shared view that more innovative approaches and renewed commitments are needed to cope with dynamic issues, such as growing international interdependence and interactions through trade and financial integration, uneven progress toward alleviating poverty and achieving the development goals of UN Millennium Declaration, prevention and resolution of international financial crises, and external shocks. Within this context, we agree upon the strategic importance for the BWIs to reinvigorate their fundamental missions and roles in meeting new challenges in a globalized world economy.

Mission of BWIs

3. We reaffirm the complementary roles that the BWIs are called to play, and recognize that promoting macroeconomic and financial stability and development continue to be of critical importance. Likewise, we believe there is a need to ensure effective pursuit of, and tangible progress towards, these objectives to further strengthen efficient cooperation between the two institutions. The IMF should primarily focus on national and international macroeconomic and financial stability, exercising enhanced surveillance of the global economy, international capital markets and strengthening crisis prevention and resolution. The World Bank should keep its focus on development, sharpening its financial and technical assistance roles for both least-developed countries and emerging markets. We welcome the review of the division of responsibilities launched by the two managements, taking into account external expertise, as part of the strategic review and look forward to their report to the International Monetary and Financial Committee (IMFC) and the Development Committee (DC) at the Spring Meetings in 2006.

Governance of the BWIs

4. The world economy has evolved considerably since the founding of the BWIs, with fast growth in many emerging markets and deepened integration in industrialized countries. We reaffirm the principle that the governance structure of the BWIs—both quotas and representation—should reflect such changes in economic weight. The G-20 underscores the critical importance of achieving concrete progress on quota reform by the next International Monetary Fund (IMF) and World Bank Annual Meetings in Singapore. The G-20 will seek to identify principles for quota reform which could be an important input into the IMF's Thirteenth General Review of Quotas, scheduled to be completed by January 2008.

Management and Operational Strategies of the BWIs

5. We believe the IMF and the World Bank should work to enhance their institutional effectiveness, and that the strategic review needs to consider how to improve internal governance. The selection of senior management should be based on merit and ensure broad representation of all member countries.

6. We believe the BWIs should adjust their operations in a timely manner so as to meet the changing needs of their members, while maintaining their high quality standards and results-orientation. The BWIs should continue improving their lending frameworks, and consider ways to best meet their members' needs for financial assistance, while ensuring continued financial strength and minimizing moral hazard.

7. All G-20 members are committed to ensuring the continued role of the BWIs and will focus their efforts on strategic reform measures in the coming years. We will revisit these issues at our next meeting in Australia in 2006.

Source: Group of 20. "The G-20 Statement on Reforming the Bretton Woods Institutions." Available online. URL: http://www.g20.org/Public/Publications/Pdf/2005_statement_on_reforming_bwis.pdf. Accessed August 25, 2006.

THE INTERNATIONAL MONETARY FUND

What Should the Bank Think about the Washington Consensus?" by John Williamson (July 1999)

This paper was prepared by the "author" of the Washington Consensus as a background to the World Bank's World Development Report 2000. In it, John Williamson explains his original intent in explicating the Washington Consensus and describes how it has, at times, been misinterpreted and misapplied, particularly regarding its effects on poverty in the developing world.

What Should the Bank Think about the Washington Consensus?
John Williamson
Institute for International Economics
Paper prepared as a background to the World Bank's
World Development Report 2000
July 1999

Ten years ago I invented the term "Washington Consensus". While it is jolly to become famous by inventing a term that reverberates around the world, I have long been doubtful as to whether the phrase that I coined served to advance the cause of rational economic policymaking. My initial source of concern was that the phrase invited the interpretation that the liberalizing economic reforms of the past two decades were imposed by Washington-based institutions like the World Bank, rather than having resulted from the process of intellectual convergence that I believe underlies them. From this standpoint, much better terms would have been Richard Feinberg's "universal convergence" . . . or Jean Waelbroeck's "one-world consensus." . . .

However, I have gradually developed a second and more significant concern. I have realized that the term is often being used in a sense significantly different to that which I had intended, as a synonym for what is often called "neoliberalism" in Latin America, or what George Soros (1998) has called "market fundamentalism". When I first came across this usage, I asserted that it was erroneous since that was not what I had intended by the term. Luiz Carlos Bresser Pereira patiently explained to me that I was being naïve in imagining that just because I had invented the expression gave me some sort of intellectual property rights that entitled me to dictate its meaning: the concept had become the property of mankind. To judge by the increasing frequency with which this alternative concept is being employed by highly reputable economists . . . , I fear that Bresser had a point.

The battle of economic ideas is . . . fought to a significant extent in terms of rhetoric. This means that the dual use of a term with strong ideological overtones can pose serious dangers, not only of misunderstanding, but also of inadvertently prejudicing policy stances. Specifically, there is a real danger that many of the economic reforms that the Bank tends to favor—notably macroeconomic discipline, trade openness, and market-friendly microeconomic policies—will be discredited in the eyes of many, simply because the Bank is inevitably implicated in views that command a consensus in Washington and the term "Washington Consensus" has come to be used to describe an extreme and dogmatic commitment to the belief that markets can handle everything. . . .

The objective of this paper is to consider what should be done to minimize the damage to the cause of intellectual understanding, and therefore of rational economic reform, that is being wrought by the current widespread use of the term "Washington Consensus" in a sense quite different to that originally employed. Should one, for example, try to insist that the original usage is the "correct" one? Or should one simply refuse to debate in these terms? Or could one escape by declaring fidelity to some "post-Washington Consensus"? The paper is based on the presumption that the first stage in adopting an appropriate stance is a careful examination of the semantic issues involved. . . .

The paper therefore starts by reviewing my original version of the Washington Consensus. It goes on to cite a considerable number of alternative "definitions" that have been offered in the past couple of years, to establish the thesis that the term has come to be used as a caricature of my original definition. It then proceeds to discuss whether "Washington Consensus policies" promote or prejudice the cause of poverty reduction. Finally, it considers alternative possible reactions to the semantic dilemma that has been created by the appropriation of the term to mean something different to what was originally intended.

The Original Version

My original paper . . . argued that the set of policy reforms which most of official Washington thought would be good for Latin American countries could be summarized in ten propositions:

- Fiscal discipline.
- A redirection of public expenditure priorities toward fields offering both high economic returns and the potential to improve income distribution, such as primary health care, primary education, and infrastructure.
- Tax reform (to lower marginal rates and broaden the tax base).
- Interest rate liberalization.
- A competitive exchange rate.
- Trade liberalization.
- Liberalization of FDI inflows.
- Privatization.
- Deregulation (in the sense of abolishing barriers to entry and exit).
- Secure property rights.

The first three reforms are, so far as I am aware, widely accepted among economists. . . . All the others have stimulated a measure of controversy, and therefore merit comment. I note in particular reactions to them within the Bank and in East Asia.

In my original paper, I specified the fourth reform as "interest rate liberalization". I am well aware that there are people in the Bank, starting with the Bank's Chief Economist, Joseph Stiglitz, who would have reservations about that formulation. As a matter of fact, I have such reservations myself: in a recent paper with Molly Mahar . . . , we identified interest rate liberalization as merely one of six dimensions of financial liberalization. Moreover, Stiglitz . . . has argued that interest rate liberalization should often come toward the end of the process of financial liberalization, inasmuch as a ceiling on the deposit interest rate (equal to the Treasury Bill rate, he suggests) might provide a constraint on gambling for redemption. I find this argument persuasive, and long ago changed my description of the fourth element of the Washington Consensus to "financial liberalization". More recently Stiglitz . . . has expressed a much more basic objection than this, and argued (citing the World Bank's *East Asian Miracle* study in support) that one important element of the success of some East Asian countries stems from their policy of directing credit to particular industries rather than allowing the market to determine the allocation of credit. . . . That argument is highly contentious, specially in the aftermath of the East Asian crisis.

My fifth reform area, a competitive exchange rate, is one where I long since concluded I was a bad reporter of the Washington scene. By 1989, I suspect that a majority of economists, in Washington as elsewhere, were already in favor of either firmly fixed or freely floating exchange rates, and hostile to the sort of intermediate regime that in my judgment gives the best promise of maintaining the exchange rate competitive in the medium term. . . . But the East Asian countries, in contrast, did by and large achieve and maintain competitive exchange rates, at least prior to about 1996 (and even then it is not obvious that the failure was wider than Thailand).

My sixth reform was trade liberalization. Here I see little reason to doubt that I reported accurately on opinion in the Washington of the international financial institutions and the central economic agencies of the US government (although parts of Congress and the Department of Commerce are not noted for their dedication to liberal trade). But this is another area where critics can rightly claim that the policies that nurtured the East Asian miracle were, at least in some countries, at odds with what was endorsed in the Washington Consensus. Much the same is true of FDI, except that in that dimension there was less hostility to a policy of openness in East Asia, with only Korea having kept itself largely closed to FDI during the years of the miracle.

Privatization commanded a lot of support in Washington, from where it had been put on the international agenda by James Baker when he was Secretary of the U.S. Treasury, in his speech to the Bank/Fund Annual Meetings in Seoul in 1985. It was controversial in much of the rest of the world, where one's attitude to public versus private ownership had long provided the litmus test as to whether someone would qualify as left-wing or right-wing. Deregulation was rather less politically polarizing: it had been initiated by the centrist Carter administration, rather than the right-wing Thatcher government which pioneered privatization. Again, however, this was not a policy that had reverberated in East Asia, where the industrial policies pursued in some (though not all) countries ran very much in the opposite direction. The notion of the importance of secure property rights had come both from the law and economics school in Chicago and the work of Hernando de Soto in Peru. The concept was presumably offensive to those who resisted the advance of the market economy, but this was an extinct breed in Washington by 1989 (if, indeed, it had ever existed). My impression is that the institution of private property was somewhat more securely entrenched in East Asia than in most of the rest of the developing world.

So much for the content of my version of the Washington Consensus. From where did it come? In an immediate sense, it originated from my attempt to answer a question posed to me . . . , namely, what were these "sensible" policies that were now being pursued in most of Latin America, and which I was arguing merited approval . . . for debt relief? In a more profound sense, it was an attempt to distill which of the policy initiatives that had emanated from Washington during the years of conservative ideology had won inclusion in the intellectual mainstream, rather than being cast aside once Ronald Reagan was no longer on the political scene. Standing back even more, one can view it as an attempt to summarize the policies that were widely viewed as supportive of development at the end of the two decades when economists had become convinced that the key to rapid economic development lay not in a country's natural resources, or even its physical or human capital, but rather in the set of economic policies that it pursued.

Let me emphasize that the Washington Consensus as I conceived it was in principle geographically and historically specific, a lowest common denominator of the reforms that I judged "Washington" could agree were needed in Latin America as of 1989. But in practice there would probably not have been a lot of difference if I had undertaken a similar exercise for Africa or Asia rather than Latin America, and there was still a lot of overlap when I revisited the topic (with regard to Latin America) in 1996 . . . This doubtless made it easier for some to interpret the Washington Consensus as a policy manifesto that its adherents supposedly believed to be valid for all places and at all times—which takes us on to consider the alternative interpretation of the concept that has become so popular in recent years.

Current Usage

Let me offer a selection of recent definitions of the Washington Consensus that I have happened to stumble across. . . .

"A die-hard liberalization advocate (or a Washington-consensus believer) . . ." Takatoshi Ito, "The Role of IMF Advice", a paper presented to an IMF conference on Key Issues in Reform of the International Monetary and Financial System in Washington on 29 May 1999.

". . . the self-confident advice of the 'Washington consensus'—free-up trade, practice sound money, and go home early . . ." David Vines, in an obituary for Susan Strange, the Newsletter of the ESRC Programme on Global Economic Institutions, no. 9, 1999.

". . . the Washington Consensus: policy prescriptions based on free market principles and monetary discipline." Koichi Hamada, in Nikko's *Capital Trends,* September 1998.

"The Washington Consensus had the following message: 'Liberalize as much as you can, privatize as fast as you can, and be tough in monetary and fiscal matters.'" Gregorz Kolodko in *Transition,* June 1998.

"The bashing of the state that characterized the policy thrust of the Washington Consensus . . ." Annual Report of the United Nations University, 1998.

"This new imperialism, codified in the 'Washington Consensus . . .'" M. Shahid Alam "Does Sovereignty Matter for Economic Growth?", in J. Adams and F. Pigliaru, eds., *Economic Growth and Change* (Cheltenham: Edward Elgar, 1999).

"The Brazilian crisis has reignited the debate over the so-called Washington Consensus on the creation of a laissez-faire global economy." Ramkishen S. Rajan in a Claremont Policy Brief on "The Brazilian and other Currency Crises of the 1990s", May 1999.

These examples suggest that, in the minds of many economists, the term has become a synonym for "neoliberalism" or what George Soros (1998) has called "market fundamentalism" (which is far and away my favorite term for this set of beliefs). Now anyone who read the preceding section of this paper will recognize that this was hardly the sense in which I originally used the term. On the contrary, I thought of the Washington Consensus as the lowest common denominator of policy advice being addressed by the Washington institutions to Latin American countries as of 1989. . . .

Do Washington Consensus Policies Promote Poverty Reduction?

The answer, quite obviously, depends on which interpretation of the Washington Consensus one is referring to.

Let me take first the popular, or populist, interpretation of the Washington Consensus as meaning market fundamentalism or neo-liberalism: laissez-faire, Reganomics, let's bash the state, the markets will resolve everything... It will presumably come as no surprise that I would not subscribe to the view that such policies would be good for poverty reduction. We know that poverty reduction demands efforts to build the human capital of the poor, but on the populist interpretation the Washington Consensus signally fails to address that issue. We know that an active policy to supervise financial institutions is needed if financial liberalization is not to lead to financial collapse, which invariably ends up by using tax revenues to write off bank loans that were made to the relatively rich. And some measure of income redistribution would be recommended by any policy that was primarily directed at reducing poverty rather than simply maximizing growth, but all income redistribution is ruled out as plunder by market fundamentalists. For these three reasons, at least, I would agree that the populist interpretation of the Washington Consensus is inconsistent with the Bank's emphasis on poverty reduction....

A plausible alternative concept of the Washington Consensus would be that it consists of the set of policies endorsed by the principal economic institutions located in Washington: the US Treasury, the Federal Reserve Board, the IMF, and the World Bank. There is at least one respect in which I would argue that the policies they advocated in the 1990s were inimical to the cause of poverty reduction in emerging markets: namely, their advocacy of capital account liberalization. This was in my view the main cause of the contagion that caused the East Asian crisis to spread beyond Thailand ..., and the crisis has caused a tragic interruption to the poverty reduction those countries had achieved in the preceding years.

Consider finally my version of the Washington Consensus, which, I have suggested, may also be the interpretation used by some Bank staff. The inflation caused by fiscal indiscipline is bad for income distribution, so I see no reason to apologize on that score. The second reform specifically involved redirecting public expenditure inter alia toward primary health and education, i.e. toward building the human capital of the poor. Tax reform can be distributionally neutral or even progressive. A competitive exchange rate is key to nurturing export-led and crisis-free growth, hence in the general interest, including that of the poor. Trade liberalization, certainly in low-income, resource-poor countries, increases the demand for unskilled labor and decreases the subsidies going to import-competing industries that use large volumes of capital and employ small numbers of workers, many of them highly skilled, and therefore tends to be pro-poor. FDI helps to raise growth and to spread technology, provided, at least, that import protection is not excessive . . . The impact of privatization depends, in my view, very much on how it is done: the sort of insider/voucher privatization that happened in Russia allows the plunder of state assets for the benefit of an elite, but a well-conducted privatization with competitive bidding can raise efficiency and improve the public finances, with benefits to all, including the poor. Deregulation will in general involve the dismantling of barriers that protect privileged elites . . . , and hence there is a strong presumption that it will be pro-poor. Private property rights are certainly a defense primarily for those who have private property, but the improvement of such rights is nonetheless very likely to be pro-poor, because the people who find themselves especially unable to defend their property when property rights are ill-defined are principally the poor. . . .

Note that I have omitted one of the ten reforms from the preceding list, namely financial/interest rate liberalization. This is the primary focus of Stiglitz's criticisms when he talks of something that I can recognize as akin to my version of the Washington Consensus. I have recognized for some time . . . that my first formulation was flawed, in that it neglected financial supervision, without which financial liberalization seems all too likely to lead to improper lending and eventually a crisis that requires the taxpayers to pick up the losses that result from making loans that turn bad to the relatively rich. . . . But should we therefore endorse the view that directed lending as happened in some (not all) of the East Asian countries is pro-growth and thus ultimately pro-poor? On this issue, at least, I would have thought that the East Asian crisis, especially what happened in Korea, should have tempered enthusiasm for East Asian practice. The high debt/equity ratios that resulted from the directed lending were certainly among the causes of the financial fragility that so deepened the impact of the crisis.

I conclude that, for most of the reforms embodied in my version of the Washington Consensus, the presumption is very much that they will be pro-poor. In a few cases this conclusion is sensitive to the way in which reform is implemented: this is certainly true of tax reform, of privatization, and above all of financial liberalization. But I see no reason for backing away from endorsement of my version of the Washington Consensus by a Bank that has reaffirmed poverty reduction as its overarching mission. That is not at all to claim that the Washington Consensus, in any version, constituted a policy manifesto adequate for addressing poverty. My version quite consciously eschewed redistributive policies, on the view that George [H. W.] Bush's Washington had not reached a consensus on their desirability. In broad terms, with the qualifications that have been noted above, I would subscribe to the view that the policies embodied in my version of the Washington Consensus are pro-poor but need to be supplemented in a world that takes the objective of poverty reduction seriously. . . .

Source: Institute for International Economics. "What Should the Bank Think about the Washington Consensus?" Available online. URL: http://www.iie.com/publications/papers/paper.cfm?ResearchID=351. Accessed August 25, 2006.

"The IMF View on IMF Reform" by Rodrigo de Rato (September 2005)

In this speech, presented at the Conference on IMF Reform held in Washington, D.C., on September 23, 2005, Rodrigo de Rato, director general of the IMF, explains his views about some of the IMF's failures and suggests ways that the IMF can be reformed to be more responsive to the needs of the nations it assists.

The IMF View on IMF Reform
Rodrigo de Rato
International Monetary Fund
Speech presented at the Conference on IMF Reform
Institute for International Economics
Washington, DC
September 23, 2005

Thank you for inviting me to this conference. After browsing some of the papers for the conference, and especially Ted Truman's masterly overview of the issues on IMF reform, I will begin by paraphrasing Mark Twain and assuring you that reports of the IMF's death have been greatly exaggerated. In fact, I think that the level of interest in the Fund's activities, including this conference, suggests that the Fund is still recognized for what it is—the central institution of global monetary cooperation. To continue fulfilling this responsibility as effectively as possible, we do need to make some changes in the way we work. I have some ideas on this, and I would like to share them with you today. . . .

I want to talk mostly about the agenda for reform of the IMF that I am presenting to our governors for their discussion tomorrow. But first I want to share something about my perspective from inside the Fund and explain why I find some of the suggestions made today unrealistic, especially the suggestion that the Fund "enforce the rules" of the international monetary system.

Let me lead into this with a story from a great scholar of the American presidency, the late Richard Neustadt. In his book, *Presidential Power,* Neustadt quotes President Harry Truman as speculating about how unhappy Eisenhower will be when he becomes president. "He'll sit here," Truman would remark (tapping his desk for emphasis), "and he'll say, 'Do this! Do that!' And nothing will happen. Poor Ike—it won't be a bit like the army. He'll find it very frustrating." Truman's broader point was that even the president of the United States needs to persuade others if he is to exercise power effectively. In the same way, the influence of the Fund in the world comes almost entirely from its ability to persuade its members that they should follow its advice—advice that is based on the consensus of the membership. If we want the US Congress to enact budgets to reduce the deficit, then we have to make recommendations that are convincing and communicate them in a way that will resonate with US authorities, Congress, and the broader public. If we want China to adopt more exchange rate flexibility, then we need to be sensitive to the Chinese authorities' concerns, too. I am a strong advocate of transparency, but if you're in a room with a friend, you don't need to talk through a megaphone. I think quiet diplomacy, as some have characterized it, has produced good results, and not just in the area of exchange rates. For example, I am very pleased that China has announced, during the most recent Article IV Consultation discussion, its intention to participate in the Financial Sector Assessment Program.

We also need to persuade--rather than dictate to—members on the issue of IMF reform. I view the next two days as an important opportunity to make progress on some of the ideas that I have proposed in my report on the IMF's objectives and its medium-term strategy. Let me tell you more about these.

First, I believe that the Fund must intensify its focus on helping countries come to grips with globalization. This is the most important force at work in the world economy today. We have seen huge changes in real sector conditions—the global transfer of goods, services, technology, and jobs—and in recent decades we have been experiencing financial globalization, the creation of a global savings pool. This has allowed world savings to be allocated into more productive and diversified investments, but it has also allowed countries to build up much larger current account imbalances, with correspondingly greater risks. A couple of the papers for this seminar mention the case of Long-Term Capital Management (LTCM). The problems of LTCM, and the damage that could have been done to the US financial system by its fall, stemmed from both increasing interlinkages in global capital markets and a discontinuity in the markets: the Russian default of 1998. I hope that defaults will not become a regular feature of 21st century crises, but we can bet that discontinuities of one kind or another will recur. Given the integration of capital as well as goods markets, these will affect advanced economies as well as emerging-market economies. The challenges that advanced economies will face—in macroeconomic policy, in financial-sector policy, and of international economic integration—are too little recognized and too often misjudged by decision makers.

This has important implications for the Fund. We need to be able to give all of our members—in our country, regional, and global surveillance—concrete advice on the consequences of increasing integration. Here are some of the things we need to do.

We need to understand the issues more deeply ourselves, and especially the benefits, imbalances, and fragilities caused by cross-border flows of goods, capital, and people. One possibility is that staff from all the departments in the Fund that currently work on these issues separately will work together intensively on selected topics and distill their work into an annual report on the macroeconomics of globalization.

We need to improve multilateral dialogue. I note with interest but respectfully dissent from Fred Bergsten's proposals for a new steering committee for the world economy. I don't think we need a new committee. We have vigorous discussion of issues in the IMF Executive Board, and where we need to raise issues at the level of Ministers, I would prefer that this take place through an equally vigorous discussion in the International Monetary and Financial Committee. Indeed, I hope we have such a discussion tomorrow.

We need better surveillance of financial markets. Understanding capital flows has become much more difficult in an increasingly globalized capital market, but it has also become much more important. I don't want to get into the organizational mechanics of this at the moment, especially as the Fund's work on the financial sector is still being reviewed by the McDonough Group. But one thing that is already clear is that we need to have better integration of financial expertise into area department country work.

Our country surveillance work needs to be more focused and more pointed to anticipate upcoming problems and give candid advice on them. Specifically, area department teams should be given greater flexibility to streamline the coverage of reports and to focus on the most pressing macroeconomic issues from the point of view of stability and the challenges of globalization. I would hope that there is also scope for streamlining some of our other country work, including in the area of standards and codes. In this area, great progress has been made, and in most cases the need is for follow-up.

Emerging-market economies are the countries most at risk from volatile capital flows. The Fund has made significant improvements in its work on crisis prevention over the past few years. I am thinking in particular of our internal work on vulnerability assessments and the development of the balance sheet approach to financial crises. We have also, of course, stepped up and provided support for our members when they have needed it, from Thailand, Korea, and Indonesia through Turkey, Brazil, and Argentina. But this is not an area on which one can ever declare victory and withdraw. Much remains to be done.

On crisis prevention, I would like to see more work in the Fund both on the underlying vulnerabilities in emerging-market countries and on the risks from supply-side disturbances in advanced-country financial markets. On crisis resolution, we need to continuously review the effectiveness of the Fund's instruments, including the lending into arrears policy. I have said in the past that we need to have a Fund that can say no. I still believe that.

We also need to consider further the possible ways in which the Fund's instruments can provide insurance to its members against crises, such as through high access precautionary arrangements or a successor to the Contingent Credit Lines. The problem with the latter was trying to balance the member's need for assurances that it can draw on the Fund's resources quickly if needed and the institution's need for assurances that the Fund's support will be part of a package of financing and measures that works—one that enables the member to both get out of trouble and eventually repay the Fund. We need to keep looking for a solution that achieves this balance.

Another issue very relevant to the situation of emerging-market economies is capital account liberalization. The Fund has been heavily criticized on this issue in the past, and I think much of that criticism is unfair. In the face of that criticism, it is tempting to withdraw and let the advocates and enemies of capital account liberalization just fight it out. But I don't think we can do that. Countries are choosing to liberalize their capital accounts because they want to take advantage of the huge and growing pool of global savings. And this liberalization brings macroeconomic challenges that require careful management, including of the sequencing of liberalization with financial-sector reforms. The Fund must have a view on this area. So I think it is important that the Fund deepen its knowledge of the issues surrounding capital market liberalization. And we will do so in the months ahead.

We also need to deepen our work on low-income countries. There is a body of opinion that thinks that the Fund ought to get out of the business of supporting low-income countries and turn over its responsibilities to the World Bank. I completely disagree with this view. The low-income countries need macroeconomic advice from the Fund, and they often need financial support from us, which we provide through the Poverty Reduction and Growth Facility. Moreover, we are at a critical juncture in trying to help countries achieve the Millennium Development Goals, and we have an opportunity arising from the growing consensus in wealthy countries that aid must be increased and debt must be reduced. Now is the time when we have the best opportunity to make a difference in the lives of billions of people.

I do think we need to improve the focus of the Fund's work on low-income countries. This will probably involve doing less in some areas. Over the coming months, we will have a discussion with our colleagues at the World Bank on what the right allocation of work between the two institutions is. I think there may be scope for changes. I'm also concerned that the Fund's work on low-income countries is overloaded with procedures that absorb substantial resources but yield questionable gains. Our work must be streamlined.

But there are also areas where we need to do more. We need to deepen the Fund's involvement in advising countries on how to deal with the macroeconomic effects of higher aid flows. The impact of large aid flows on macroeconomic management takes many forms. Fiscal management can be complicated by large aid flows, and the quality of spending can suffer. So there is a need to improve public expenditure management to ensure that additional aid does not lead to wasteful and inefficient spending. In addition, large aid financing can also weaken longer-run incentives to develop an adequate domestic revenue base and strengthen the tax system. The Fund has an important role to play in improving fiscal management, which is often key to raising aid effectiveness. Higher aid flows can also cause real exchange rate appreciation, leading to weaker external competitiveness and slower growth. The Fund has a crucial role here too, advising on the potential for macroeconomic problems and coming up with solutions to them. For example, real exchange rate appreciation can be countered by enacting structural reforms and using aid resources to improve productivity in the domestic economy. All of these are areas where the Fund has a comparative advantage and where our support will be very important.

One issue on which I agree strongly with views expressed by many of the participants in this conference is the need for a change in IMF voting shares and representation. The Fund's ability to persuade our members to adopt wise policies depends not only on the quality of our analysis but also on the Fund's perceived legitimacy. And our legitimacy suffers if we do not adequately represent countries of growing economic importance. This means, in particular, increases in voting power for some of the emerging-market economies, especially in Asia. We must also ensure that our members in Africa, where so many people are profoundly affected by the Fund's decisions, are adequately represented. It's usually taken as axiomatic that if some countries "win" from a reallocation of quotas, others must "lose." I don't agree. This is not a zero-sum game. If there is broad acceptance of the IMF's legitimacy, the institution and all of its members will benefit.

I referred earlier to both the quality of the Fund's advice and the effectiveness of our communicating that advice as being important in determining the Fund's influence. Let me talk some more about the second part of this, the importance of communication, because this is another area where we may need to change our practices. As many have noted, there are countries where the Fund gives advice that is not followed. Sometimes this is because of disagreement on the analysis of the issue. These are cases where we obviously need a serious, engaged dialogue with the member on the nature of the problem and how to fix it. But there are also plenty of cases where there is agreement on the analysis but reluctance to act on that analysis for political reasons. In these cases, I would like the Fund to be more forthright in making the case for the policies we support, including to the public. In globalized democracies, public opinion can be changed by persuasive arguments, and changes in public opinion can change the positions of policymakers. We should certainly make sure that the Fund's position is not misunderstood or misstated—that our views are clear. In the best cases, where we help generate public support for good policies, we can go further and do a service to our member governments by making the case for reform in a clear and forthright way.

Finally, I would like to share with you a point that was made by an executive director when we discussed this issue of communication in the Board. He said it was important that the Fund listen as well as talk. I agree with that completely. We want to engage in dialogue, not adversarial politics. In that spirit, I would once again like to thank the Institute for International Economics and the organizers of this conference, and especially Ted Truman, for their work in promoting dialogue on reform of the IMF.

Source: Institute for International Economics. "The IMF View on IMF Reform." Available online. URL: http://www.iie.com/publications/papers/paper.cfm?ResearchID=565. Accessed August 25, 2006.

THE WORLD TRADE ORGANIZATION

Excerpts from the Marrakesh Agreement Establishing the World Trade Organization (April 1994)

This document contains excerpts of articles that pertain primarily to WTO policy on the environment. Among these are excerpts from Article XX of the General Agreement on Tariffs and Trade (GATT), the Agreement on Technical Barriers to Trade (TBT), the Agreement on Sanitary and Phytosanitary Measures (SPS), the Agreement on Agriculture (AoA), the Agreement on Trade-Related Aspects of Intellectual Property Rights (TRIPS), and the General Agreement on Trade in Services (GATS). They are intended to reveal, at least in part, the scope of the World Trade Organization's mandate.

Marrakesh Agreement Establishing the World Trade Organization

Preamble

The *Parties* to this Agreement,

Recognizing that their relations in the field of trade and economic endeavour should be conducted with a view to raising standards of living, ensuring full employment and a large and steadily growing volume of real income and effective demand, and expanding the production of and trade in goods and services, while allowing for the optimal use of the world's resources in accordance with the objective of sustainable development, seeking both to protect and preserve the environment and to enhance the means for doing so in a manner consistent with their respective needs and concerns at different levels of economic development, . . .

Agree as follows:

GATT

Article XX

General exceptions

"Subject to the requirement that such measures are not applied in a manner which would constitute a means of arbitrary or unjustifiable discrimination between countries where the same conditions prevail, or a disguised restriction on international trade, nothing in this Agreement shall be construed to prevent the adoption or enforcement by any contracting party of measures: . . .

(b) necessary to protect human, animal or plant life or health; . . .

(d) necessary to secure compliance with laws or regulations which are not inconsistent with the provisions of this Agreement, including. . . ;

(g) relating to the conservation of exhaustible natural resources if such measures are made effective in conjunction with restrictions on domestic production or consumption;. . . ."

Agreement on Technical Barriers to Trade

Preamble

". . . *Recognizing* that no country should be prevented from taking measures necessary to ensure the quality of its exports, or for the protection of human, animal or plant life or health, of the environment, or for the prevention of deceptive practices, at the levels it considers appropriate, subject to the requirement that they are not applied in a manner which would constitute a means of arbitrary or unjustifiable discrimination between countries where the same conditions prevail or a disguised restriction on international trade. . . ."

Article 2

Preparation, Adoption and Application of Technical Regulations by Central Government Bodies

"With respect to their central government bodies:

2.1 Members shall ensure that in respect of technical regulations, products imported from the territory of any Member shall be accorded treatment no less favourable than that accorded to like products of national origin and to like products originating in any other country.

2.2 Members shall ensure that technical regulations are not prepared, adopted or applied with a view to or with the effect of creating unnecessary obstacles to international trade. For this purpose, technical regulations shall not be more trade-restrictive than necessary to fulfil a legitimate objective, taking account of the risks non-fulfilment would create. Such legitimate objectives are, *inter alia:* national security requirements; the prevention of deceptive practices; protection of human health or safety, animal or plant life or health, or the environment. In assessing such risks, relevant elements of consideration are, *inter alia:* available scientific and technical information, related processing technology or intended end-uses of products. . . .

2.4 Where technical regulations are required and relevant international standards exist or their completion is imminent, Members shall use them, or the relevant parts of them, as a basis for their technical regulations except when such international standards or relevant parts would be an ineffective or inappropriate means for the fulfilment of the legitimate objectives pursued, for instance because of fundamental climatic or geographical factors or fundamental technological problems.". . . .

Agreement on Sanitary and Phytosanitary Measures
Annex A
Definitions

"1. *Sanitary or phytosanitary measure*—Any measure applied:

(a) to protect animal or plant life or health within the territory of the Member from risks arising from the entry, establishment or spread of pests, diseases, disease-carrying organisms or disease-causing organisms;

(b) to protect human or animal life or health within the territory of the Member from risks arising from additives, contaminants, toxins or disease-causing organisms in foods, beverages or feedstuffs;

(c) to protect human life or health within the territory of the Member from risks arising from diseases carried by animals, plants or products thereof, or from the entry, establishment or spread of pests; or

(d) to prevent or limit other damage within the territory of the Member from the entry, establishment or spread of pests." . . .

Agreement on Agriculture

Annex 2

Domestic Support: the Basis for Exemption from the Reduction Commitments

". . . 12. Payments under environmental programmes

(a) Eligibility for such payments shall be determined as part of a clearly-defined government environmental or conservation programme and be dependent on the fulfilment of specific conditions under the government programme, including conditions related to production methods or inputs.

(b) The amount of payment shall be limited to the extra costs or loss of income involved in complying with the government programme." . . .

Agreement on Trade-Related Aspects of Intellectual Property Rights
Article 27
Patentable Subject Matter

". . . 2. Members may exclude from patentability inventions, the prevention within their territory of the commercial exploitation of which is necessary to protect *ordre public* or morality, including to protect human, animal or plant life or health or to avoid serious prejudice to the environment, provided that such exclusion is not made merely because the exploitation is prohibited by their law.

3. Members may also exclude from patentability:

(a) diagnostic, therapeutic and surgical methods for the treatment of humans or animals;

(b) plants and animals other than micro-organisms, and essentially biological processes for the production of plants or animal other than non-biological and microbiological processes. However, Members shall provide for the protection of plant varieties either by patents or by an effective *sui generis* system or by any combination thereof. The provisions of this subparagraph shall be reviewed four years after the date of entry into force of the WTO Agreement." . . .

General Agreement on Trade in Services
Article XIV
General Exceptions

"Subject to the requirement that such measures are not applied in a manner which would constitute a means of arbitrary or unjustifiable discrimination between countries where like conditions prevail, or a disguised restriction on trade in services, nothing in this Agreement shall be construed to prevent the adoption or enforcement by any Member of measures: . . .

(b) necessary to protect human, animal or plant life or health; . . .

Source: World Trade Organization. "Marrakesh Agreement Establishing the World Trade Organization." Available online. URL: http://www.wto.org/english/tratop_e/envir_e/issu4_e.htm. Accessed August 25, 2006.

"Understanding the World Trade Organization" by Marcus Noland (February 2000)

This paper is a summary of a speech given by economist Marcus Noland of the Institute for International Economics at a Washington, D.C., meeting of the League of Women Voters on February 16, 2000. It is a useful overview of the creation and operations of the World Trade Organization and its role in a globalizing economy. The speech's topics range from historical background to global trade and the future of the WTO.

Understanding the World Trade Organization
Marcus Noland
Institute for International Economics
Paper summarizing speech given on the WTO to the D.C. League of Women Voters
Washington, DC
February 16, 2000

We tend to assume that our world constantly progresses, that conditions are always improving or advancing. That is not necessarily the case. World economic integration in the 1890's, or globalization as we now label it, was surprisingly advanced, quite comparable to that of the 1990's. At the end of the 19th century, trade was very free. Goods moved freely across borders. There was tremendous population movement. Tens of millions of people left other parts of the world, mainly Europe but also to a certain extent Asia, to settle in North America and other so-called areas of new settlement. Financial markets were relatively well integrated. Millions of British pounds (the key currency of that era) moved across national borders. *The Economist* magazine published stock market indexes not only for London, but for New

York, Buenos Aires, and other key markets. That world was underpinned, in economic terms, by the gold standard and British hegemony. It would take nearly a century to re-attain that level of economic integration achieved by the end of the nineteenth century.

This "globalization" of a century ago began to fail at the beginning of the 20th century. It ended with the First World War. Attempts to revive it after the First World War were unsuccessful. As countries around the world came under economic pressure in the period after the First World War, they erected trade barriers.

In 1922, the United States passed the Fordney-McCumber tariff, the largest single increase in the US tariff rates. The US Constitution grants the Congress the prerogative to regulate international commerce. Thus, individual Congressmen were in a position to literally trade votes over individual tariff lines and they did. A Congressman from Texas might have approached a Congressman from New York offering to vote for a higher tariff on chemicals in return for his vote for a higher tariff on cotton. There was a horse-trading process by which individual Congressmen struck deals to get higher tariffs to protect workers and industries in their respective constituencies. The end result was the huge Fordney-McCumber tariff increase.

The situation worsened when the Great Depression struck. The United States and other countries began raising their tariffs in an attempt to divert national demand away from imports and toward domestically produced goods.

As the United States and other countries imposed these tariffs to try to keep national demand internal, the volume of world trade spiraled downward. To illustrate the resulting contraction of world trade volume, Mr. Noland referred to the Kindleberger spiral, a visual display of the contraction of trade over the months following January 1929. (It is the creation of Charles Kindleberger, a retired professor of economics at M.I.T. [Massachusetts Institute of Technology].) Using twelve spokes of a wheel for the months of the year, the volume of world trade in any given month is measured along that month's spoke. The higher the trade, the further out on the spoke it is displayed. The lower the trade volume, the closer it appears to the wheel's center. In January 1929, the volume of world trade was about 3 trillion dollars. As countries began imposing trade barriers, the volume of world trade spiraled downward toward the center. By March 1933, approximately the time Hitler came to power in Germany, the volume of world trade had fallen to less than $1 trillion. Along that downward spiral, the United States imposed the infamous 1930 Smoot-Hawley Tariff. Smoot-Hawley proved to be the last time individual Congressmen would trade votes over tariffs.

This collapse of world trade and the world economy at the onset of the Great Depression coincided with a rise in extremist movements all over the world. Given the disastrous subsequent history, we have come to view the maintenance of world trade and an integrated world economy as essential to the maintenance of world peace.

By the time Franklin Roosevelt was elected President of the United States, in 1932, world trade was sharply reduced and still declining. Seeking to reverse this process, Roosevelt sent Secretary of State Cordell Hull abroad to negotiate lower tariffs. The approaching war in Europe made it extremely difficult to reach agreements with European countries. Cordell Hull managed, however, to negotiate a few trade agreements mainly with Latin American countries, which remained largely outside the war.

Following World War II, the architects of the post-war world sought to create a new international trade system, a set of rules of the road, to prevent this kind of collapse from ever happening again. They devised a set of rules governing how nations would regulate their international commerce. An International Trade Organization (ITO) was designed to enforce the rules. However, when the US Congress rejected the ITO in 1950, the ITO was stillborn.

The General Agreement on Tariffs and Trade (GATT), negotiated in 1947, was a treaty containing reciprocal obligations to reduce tariffs following the pattern of US bilateral treaties negotiated by Cordell Hull. GATT was never intended to become an organization. It was supposed to depend on the ITO for its organizational context and secretariat services. Nevertheless, it managed to fill the void left by the failed ITO and emerged as the de facto international trade organization.

GATT is a set of bilateral agreements among countries around the world. It is basically a global generalization of what the United States started in the 1930's. A major weakness of the GATT as a world trade organization was that it had no real enforcement mechanism. If a country broke a bilateral agreement with another country, nothing could be done. There were some rules for enforcement but they were basically dysfunctional. Furthermore, the GATT system survived by taking sensitive areas of trade outside the rules. When member countries' internal political pressures or special-interest demands became overwhelming, the "rules" were ignored. Thus, both agriculture and the textile and apparel industries were taken outside the rules.

From the late 1940's through the mid 1980's, the imperfect GATT system was surprisingly successful due to ingenious and highly pragmatic leadership. The US Congress chose to shield itself from domestic special-interest demands for tariff protection by delegating its Constitutional prerogative over international trade to the President. Basically, Congress told the President to go out and make the trade deals and promised to pass them. There followed a series of international trade negotiations or "rounds," approximately one each decade, during which bilateral agreements were reached. Congress ratified them.

That system of coherent but weakly enforced rules on the global level and Congressional acquiescence to Executive Branch leadership on the national level began to come apart in the 1980's. The United States was running very large trade deficits as well as unprecedented budget deficits. A Republican President and a Democratic Congress were wrangling over economic restructuring while failing manufacturing industries, especially in the "rust belt" and the upper mid-West, sought protection from international competition. The Democratic Congress grew restless and began to reassert its Constitutional prerogative to regulate trade. There followed a series of Congressional initiatives that were basically protectionist.

The [Ronald] Reagan Administration sought to counter this protectionist trend by calling for a new round of global trade negotiations. The new round opened in Punta del Este, Uruguay in 1986, and is therefore known as the Uruguay Round. Negotiations dragged on from 1986 until 1993.

The Uruguay Round came to grips with a number of festering trade issues. Regional trade pacts, such as the US-Canada Free Trade Agreement, which would later be generalized as NAFTA, were on the rise. Agriculture and the textile and clothing industries remained outside the GATT system and needed to be addressed. Countries wanted some coherent regulation of the growing trade in services, an area that had never come under the GATT. Producers of high tech and innovative products in countries such as the United States wanted protection for intellectual property rights. They wanted rules to stop the pirating of their products, including books, records, movies, pharmaceuticals and electronics. Finally, there was a need for an improved system to settle trade disputes. Under the dysfunctional GATT dispute-settlement procedures, the loser in a case could simply block any kind of quasi-judicial GATT judgement finding it out of compliance with treaty obligations.

By 1993, compromises had been negotiated in all of these areas. Agriculture, politically sensitive in all countries, had been negotiated but the result was a political compromise, essentially between the United States and the EU, that allowed both parties to continue practices that were not consistent with GATT rules. Textiles and apparel were to be brought back under the GATT, although completion of liberalization in these industries was back-loaded. It was to be phased in over ten years. Most of the real liberalization has yet to occur. Trade in services became subject to a new General Agreement on Trade in Services (GATS), although GATS fell short of what the US wanted. Protection was provided for intellectual property rights. Some very mild protection for investment was introduced—not as much as the US wanted but as much as could be gotten in the context of the negotiations.

Finally, the dispute settlement system was vastly improved and the WTO was established to adjudicate claims of treaty violation. Thereafter, a country found to be in violation of its treaty obligations by the WTO would either have to bring its offending practices into compliance or face WTO-authorized retaliation by the injured country. Countries could no longer violate trade treaty obligations with impunity. The GATT continues to exist as a substantive agreement, establishing a set of disciplines on the trade policies of its members. The WTO itself does not embody substantive rules regarding government policies—it is simply a formal institutional structure under whose auspices members negotiate and implement their trade agreements.

Trade issues in agriculture and services were not satisfactorily resolved during the Uruguay Round. Having made little progress on trade in agriculture and remaining fundamentally in violation of GATT rules, the US and the EU agreed not to bring trade cases against each other over violations in agricultural trade for a period of ten years. This is known as the "peace clause." The "peace clause" is due to expire in 2003. Because of the "peace clause" and US dissatisfaction with the services agreement, the Uruguay Round ended with a "built-in agenda" for further negotiations. It was specified in the Uruguay Round agreement that the organization would reconvene to address agriculture and services issues.

The "built-in agenda" was the reason for convening the WTO trade Ministerial meeting in Seattle at the end of November. Seattle did not occur because of a ground swell of public support for further trade liberalization around the world. In fact, most developing countries felt that the Uruguay Round had saddled them with tremendous obligations that they were having trouble implementing. The last thing they needed was a new set of obligations to implement. Promised technical assistance to the developing countries had not been forthcoming. They found themselves to have undertaken obligations making them subject to punishment for noncompliance, yet they literally did not have the technical capacity or money to institute required changes. Nevertheless, the "built-in agenda" loomed. The approaching expiration of the "peace clause" and the risk of an EU-US agricultural trade war in the offing meant that new negotiations were urgently needed.

Once underway, new negotiations were not going to be limited to the "built-in agenda," i.e., agriculture and services. Anti-dumping laws, a Canadian innovation enthusiastically adopted by the US and more recently elsewhere around the world, have been a major irritant to many countries, especially the developing countries, which argue that they are too often used to protect domestic producers from legitimate import competition. (Economists point out that the way in which anti-dumping provisions are implemented produces economically irrational results.) The Europeans and the Japanese wanted to explore ways of dealing with this problem through competition policy or, to use US terminology, anti-trust measures. The US did not want to address this issue. Developing countries were unhappy about investment protections, limited though they were, permitted in the Uruguay Round agreement while the rich OECD countries were pushing for further investment protections after failing to reach an agreement among themselves at OECD-sponsored talks a couple of years ago. Regionalism-sorting out how regional trade agreements such as NAFTA are to fit fairly and legally into this global system-needed to be addressed. Finally, there were the new social policy issues, labor standards, human rights and protection of the environment-headline issues in the US but not necessarily elsewhere in the world. And not to be forgotten, there were the normal tariff-cutting deals that are always on the agenda in a trade round.

The Seattle Ministerial was a fiasco. Street protests, police tear gassing, fist fights and inability of foreign delegates to even enter the building where the meetings were held made headline news. Foreign delegates were outraged by the abuse to which they were subjected. Some negotiators from developing countries regarded their bad treatment as an intentional attempt by the US government to physically intimidate foreign delegations—a quite plausible tactic in many of their own countries. Foreign delegates got their backs up. Although little reported by the press, there was a substantive fiasco as well. The fundamental conflict between the EU and the US over agriculture could not be overcome.

Finally, President [Bill] Clinton arrived telling everyone that he thought it might be a good idea to use trade sanctions to enforce workers' rights in other countries. His comments sabotaged efforts underway to find a compromise. There had been a compromise proposed by the EU, accepted by labor according to sources in the AFL-CIO [American Federation of Labor–Congress of Industrial Organizations], and even by developing country delegations, such as the Indian delegation, that have traditionally been very skeptical regarding this issue. President Clinton's comments scared people off.

From an insider's perspective, Seattle marked the debut of the developing countries as highly organized assertive players pursuing their own trade interests. Believing that they had been taken to the cleaners in the Uruguay Round, the developing countries were determined not to let that happen again. Coalitions formed among developing country delegations. It is clear that the developing countries as a block have to be taken seriously in the future. OECD countries will no longer be able to strike a deal and expect the rest of the world to acquiesce to its terms.

The Seattle debacle leaves us with the prospect of an agricultural trade war in 2003 when the "peace clause" expires. Moreover, there is new recognition, based on Seattle, that if the US and, to a secondary extent, the EU want to pursue the linkage of environmental objectives and labor standards to trade, they will have to do something to woo the developing countries. Confidence-building measures or, in economic jargon, down payments will be needed to persuade the developing countries to enter into serious negotiations on these issues. Recognizing this, the EU and, secondarily, Japan have been trying to organize new low-key negotiations with a much narrower agenda. Such mini-negotiations would focus on down payments, to convince the developing countries of our good faith, and on the "built-in agenda," agriculture and services. Hopefully, once underway, such negotiations might also deal with competition policy, investment and the newer labor and environment issues.

While the EU and Japan have been trying to initiate new talks, the US has remained relatively passive for two reasons. First, President Clinton has been unable to win "fast-track" negotiating authority from Congress. Because the US Constitution gives the Congress the prerogative to regulate international commerce, when the President through his Office of the US Trade Representative (USTR) negotiates new trade agreements, Congress could normally amend those agreements. Obviously, other countries would not negotiate with the US knowing that very sensitive compromises worked out at the WTO might be altered by the US Congress. Therefore, to make US negotiations credible, Congress has for the past twenty-five years committed itself for specified periods of time to vote on trade agreements in a simple yes/no manner without any possibility of amendment. This is called "fast-track" negotiating authority. President Clinton's last two attempts to win "fast-track" negotiating authority from Congress have failed. The President is unlikely to win "fast-track" authority during an election year and the next administration will not complete the appointment of new officials and gear up for serious trade negotiations before May or June of 2001. The US is simply not ready to play.

The second reason for US passivity concerning new trade talks is that the President's immediate trade priority is to win permanent "normal trade" status for China. China is the battle in which he will spend his political capital. He will not use his political capital on "fast-track." Nor will he use it to repair the damage inflicted on the WTO in Seattle.

China is not a member of the WTO and does not enjoy permanent "normal trading" status. To become a member of the WTO, China must, of course, apply. To succeed in gaining membership, it must then negotiate bilaterally with the countries that are already members to reach agreements on tariffs, agriculture, services, etc. When negotiations are completed, the WTO Secretariat will compile them into a document called a "protocol" embodying the best possible deal that any WTO member got. This is the origin of the phrase "most-favored nation." For example, if China agreed to a 10% tariff on watches with country A and a 5% tariff on watches with country B, both country A and country B would get the better deal, the 5%. Moreover, so would all of the other member countries. They would get the best deal that any member was able to negotiate. The US has reached a bilateral agreement with China though neither the US nor the Chinese government has released the contents of that agreement. The EU is the last major player that must negotiate with China. Those negotiations are going on now.

China is, of course, a "specified" Communist or non-market economy subject to the Jackson-Vanik Amendment, an artifact of the Cold War, passed in the 1970's to encourage the former Soviet Union to permit the emigration of Jews. Thus, it is among the countries which the President, if Congress so demands, must certify annually to be meeting certain obligations. Until the 1989 Tiananmen Square massacre this was a pro forma process. Since 1989, annual Presidential certification of China to grant it "most-favored nation" status or what is now called "normal trading relation" status has been politically rancorous. Yet, Congress has always certified China and, in the last several years, Congressional margins supporting the Administration have grown larger.

When China accedes to the WTO, the US must grant China permanent "normal trading status." Should the US fail to grant China "normal trading relation" status, we would violate our WTO obligations to another member country and China has made it clear that it would not accept a continuation of the annual renewal of certification—a dubious practice under WTO rules. China insists that its "normal trading" status be made permanent.

The upcoming Congressional vote for or against permanent "normal trading relation" status for China is not a vote to permit China to accede to the WTO. That decision was made by President Clinton when he signed the bilateral agreement with China late last year. The US has already signed off on China's entry into the WTO. China is going into the WTO as soon as it reaches an agreement with the Europeans.

The political priority accorded to the upcoming China vote is demonstrated by President Clinton's avowed commitment to seek Congressional approval of permanent "normal trading" status for China before the WTO protocol is drafted, i.e., before Chinese negotiations with the EU are completed and, therefore, before we know what the final deal will be. There is, of course, no risk in going ahead with an early vote, treating this as a bilateral deal with China, because the worst terms would be those that we have already gotten from the Chinese. If the EU were to win better terms from the Chinese, we would get whatever terms the Europeans had managed to negotiate. Although the Congressional leadership seemed unenthusiastic when, in his State of the Union message, President Clinton proposed such early action, it is possible that the US will vote on permanent "normal trade relations" for China this year.

Source: Institute of International Economics. "Understanding the World Trade Organization." Available online. URL: http://www.iie.com/publications/papers/paper.cfm?ResearchID=369. Accessed August 25, 2006.

EFFECTS OF GLOBALIZATION

International Labour Organization Declaration on Fundamental Principles and Rights at Work (June 1998)

This declaration was prepared by the International Labour Organization at its 86th Session, held in Geneva, Switzerland, in June 1998. It is a formal document that sets out the ILO's vision of fundamental workers' rights and the labor standards that should be adopted by all nations and companies.

Declaration
ILO Declaration on Fundamental Principles and Rights at Work
86th Session, Geneva, June 1998

Whereas the ILO was founded in the conviction that social justice is essential to universal and lasting peace;

Whereas economic growth is essential but not sufficient to ensure equity, social progress and the eradication of poverty, confirming the need for the ILO to promote strong social policies, justice and democratic institutions;

Whereas the ILO should, now more than ever, draw upon all its standard-setting, technical cooperation and research resources in all its areas of competence, in particular employment, vocational training and working conditions, to ensure that, in the context of a global strategy for economic and social development, economic and social policies are mutually reinforcing components in order to create broad-based sustainable development;

Whereas the ILO should give special attention to the problems of persons with special social needs, particularly the unemployed and migrant workers, and mobilize and encourage international, regional and national efforts aimed at resolving their problems, and promote effective policies aimed at job creation;

Whereas, in seeking to maintain the link between social progress and economic growth, the guarantee of fundamental principles and rights at work is of particular significance in that it enables the persons concerned, to claim freely and on the basis of equality of opportunity, their fair share of the wealth which they have helped to generate, and to achieve fully their human potential;

Whereas the ILO is the constitutionally mandated international organization and the competent body to set and deal with international labour standards, and enjoys universal support and acknowledgement in promoting Fundamental Rights at Work as the expression of its constitutional principles;

Whereas it is urgent, in a situation of growing economic interdependence, to reaffirm the immutable nature of the fundamental principles and rights embodied in the Constitution of the Organization and to promote their universal application;

The International Labour Conference

1. Recalls:

(a) that in freely joining the ILO, all Members have endorsed the principles and rights set out in its Constitution and in the Declaration of Philadelphia, and have undertaken to work towards attaining the overall objectives of the Organization to the best of their resources and fully in line with their specific circumstances;

(b) that these principles and rights have been expressed and developed in the form of specific rights and obligations in Conventions recognized as fundamental both inside and outside the Organization.

2. Declares that all Members, even if they have not ratified the Conventions in question, have an obligation arising from the very fact of membership in the Organization to respect, to promote and to realize, in good faith and in accordance with the Constitution, the principles concerning the fundamental rights which are the subject of those Conventions, namely:

(a) freedom of association and the effective recognition of the right to collective bargaining;

(b) the elimination of all forms of forced or compulsory labour;

(c) the effective abolition of child labour; and

(d) the elimination of discrimination in respect of employment and occupation.

3. Recognizes the obligation on the Organization to assist its Members, in response to their established and expressed needs, in order to attain these objectives by making full use of its constitutional, operational and budgetary resources, including, by the mobilization of external resources and support, as well as by encouraging other international organizations with which the ILO has established relations, pursuant to article 12 of its Constitution, to support these efforts:

(a) by offering technical cooperation and advisory services to promote the ratification and implementation of the fundamental Conventions;

(b) by assisting those Members not yet in a position to ratify some or all of these Conventions in their efforts to respect, to promote and to realize the principles concerning fundamental rights which are the subject of these Conventions; and

(c) by helping the Members in their efforts to create a climate for economic and social development.

4. Decides that, to give full effect to this Declaration, a promotional follow-up, which is meaningful and effective, shall be implemented in accordance with the measures specified in the annex hereto, which shall be considered as an integral part of this Declaration.

5. Stresses that labour standards should not be used for protectionist trade purposes, and that nothing in this Declaration and its follow-up shall be invoked or otherwise used for such purposes; in addition, the comparative advantage of any country should in no way be called into question by this Declaration and its follow-up.

Source: International Labour Organization. "ILO Declaration on Fundamental Principles and Rights at Work." Available online. URL: http://www.ilo.org/dyn/declaris/DECLARATIONWEB.static_jump?var_pagename=DECLARATIONTEXT. Accessed August 25, 2006.

"Sweatshop Blues: Companies Love Misery" by Charles Kernaghan (October 1998)

This document offers excerpts of a speech given in October 1998 at a forum sponsored by the Harvard Trade Union Program. The forum addressed "Global Standards and the Apparel Industry." Charles Kernaghan, a leader of the National Labor Committee, spotlights the terrible working conditions and poverty-level wages paid to garment workers in Central America and the Caribbean.

Sweatshop Blues: Companies Love Misery by Charles Kernaghan

Recently we [at the National Labor Committee] went to El Salvador with a group of college students. We dashed to the hotel, threw our stuff down, and went right to our first meeting. In came thirty or forty workers, who told us, "We just got off from work. We've been working seven days a week, sometimes up to 15 hours a day." They would get there at 6:45 in the morning and they'd go right through till 11:00 at night. On Saturdays they'd work until 5 PM, although sometimes they'd work 22 hours straight till 6 AM the next morning. If they didn't work 22 hours, they'd work till 4 PM on Sunday.

They told us about the piece rate, the pressure, the humiliation, the yelling at the workers. If a thread was hanging out of a garment, supervisors would throw the garments in the workers' faces, scream at them. They told us about the enormous pressure [to produce].

There was very limited access to the bathrooms—once in the morning, once in the afternoon. They told us about women who were tested for pregnancy—when they tested positive, workers were immediately fired. They told us the wages were 60 cents an hour. Those wages would meet about one-third of the Cost of living—real starvation wages.

They told us, "The week before you arrived, 18 workers were fired for protesting being forced to work on an important national holiday in El Salvador, Patron Saints' Day, and because of a rumor that the workers wanted to organize." This was the fifth time in this factory that workers had been illegally fired to break a union organizing drive.

In these factories companies pass around a sheet so you can "voluntarily" sign up for overtime. If you don't sign this sheet, you get suspended for three days without pay. The second time it happens, it's eight days' suspension without pay. The third time you're fired. So these workers were forced to work enormous overtime hours. They were not permitted sick days. If they took a sick day or a few hours off, they were docked two days' pay.

We said to them, "What label do you make?" They reached into their pockets and took out a label Liz Claiborne. The jacket cost $198 and the women in El Salvador were paid 84 cents to sew it. What's significant is that for the last two years the Liz Claiborne company has co-chaired the White House Task Force to eliminate sweatshop abuses. It says a lot about how far we have to move from the theory of ending sweatshops to the reality.

El Salvador is now the eighth-largest exporter worldwide of apparel to the United States. This year it will send us 288 million garments. There are 60,000 to 65,000 maquiladora workers, and not one union—they are not allowed.

As for the factory that the clothing was produced in, the cinder-block walls are ten feet high, topped by barbed wire, and there are locked metal gates. It's the same everywhere you go in Central America. There are teenagers going in to work. When the door opens, there are goons—armed guards—carrying pistols and sawed-off shotguns. They don't allow visitors. Many times Labor Ministry officials can't get into the factories. The workers are vulnerable and isolated.

BARELY SURVIVING

They were paid about $4.79 a day, and they told us how they lived on those wages. It costs 80 cents a day to go back and forth from work by bus, 91 cents for breakfast and $1.37 for a very small lunch—chili, tortillas, some rice. Just to survive and get back and forth to work cost them $3.08. When you make $4.79 that leaves you with $ 1.71. How do you feed your family, go to the doctor, buy clothing, send your children to school, pay rent and utilities? The women told us that the cheapest rent in the Progresso area of San Salvador would be $80 a month, for dilapidated living conditions—and $80 a month is $2.63 a day.

Obviously, if they pay their rent they have no money for food. The workers would work eleven hours a day making Liz Claiborne garments, and yet they would often go to bed hungry. They said to us, "We don't always go to bed hungry. If we can scrape together 28 cents, we have tortillas and eggs. That's our supper." They told us the cheapest child care you can get is about 68 cents a day, but no one would want to send their child into those sorts of conditions. We asked them if they could ever afford to buy new clothing, and they all laughed at us. Every single worker we know in Central America purchases secondhand goods from the United States. We give them to Goodwill, they sell them in El Salvador where the local entrepreneurs then sell them to the workers. Their children never had milk, meat or fish, juice, cereal, fruits, or vitamins.

To climb out of misery in El Salvador and just reach the poverty line, the wage would have to be about $1.18 an hour. Would that break the backs of Liz Claiborne and the other retailers? Sixty workers on a production line put out 600 jackets a day. At 60 cents an hour, there's 84 cents of labor in this jacket for the sewers. If they were to pay the stunning figure of $1.18 an hour, there would be $1.66 of labor in a jacket, which is only eight-tenths of 1% of the retail price of the garment.

WAL-MART'S LIES

It's startling to see the hypocrisy and the enormous lies of the companies. Take Wal-Mart, for example. If you go into Wal-Mart, you see flags flying everywhere and a statement saying, "Made right here in the United States. We support American manufacturers that support American jobs."

We thought this was very interesting. We're not a "Buy American" group, but if Wal-Mart was saying that they work with U.S. manufacturers and U.S. workers, it was another way for the largest retailer in the world to say that there are standards below which they won't go. So we called Wal-Mart and asked them how much of their clothing, handbags and shoes are produced in the United States. We got a funny response back: they said they didn't know. But of course they know what they're bringing into the stores!

So we decided to do something we wouldn't recommend to just anyone. We went into Wal-Mart and spent 100 hours counting clothing and handbags. We used hidden, voice-activated tape recorders, and I spent every Friday night, Saturday and Sunday in Wal-Mart. I went into 14 stores in 12 states.

We counted 105,000 items in Wal-Mart, and it took another 200 or 300 hours to transcribe the tapes. Of the 86,500 pieces of clothing we counted, only 17% were made in the United States, and 83% offshore. We counted 16,245 pairs of shoes, and only sixteen pairs—not 16%—were made in the United States; the rest were made in China. We counted 1,910 handbags and pocketbooks and stopped counting because zero were made in the United States. Of the famous Kathie Lee Gifford clothing line, only 11% was made in the United States and 89% was made offshore. The McKids brand of children's clothing from McDonald's had 4% made in the United States, with 96% offshore. Faded Glory men's clothing had 13% made in the United States, with 87% produced offshore. So Wal-Mart was flat-out lying to the American people.

We thought: Why don't we sue Wal-Mart for consumer fraud? But when we took a look at their small print we found out we couldn't sue them. Even though Wal-Mart declared its "unprecedented commitment to purchase American-made goods," in the small print it added, "whenever they meet the pricing available offshore." So Wal-Mart was completely covered. American workers were only going to get the job if they could compete with the nine-cent wages in Indonesia or the 50-cent wages in Mexico.

Wal-Mart produces private-label apparel in 48 countries around the world. The big producers for the Kathie Lee Gifford line right now are Mexico and Indonesia, where the currencies have fallen through the floor. Garment jobs are quickly going to these countries—in fact we lost 68,000 U.S. apparel jobs in the last 12 months. What Wal-Mart ultimately wants to do, of course, is to pit the American people against desperately poor people in the developing world in this race to the bottom. It comes down to who will accept the lowest wages, the least benefits and the most miserable living and working conditions.

THE BUCK STOPS HERE?

But after the exposure of Kathie Lee Gifford, The Gap, and Nike, the sweatshop issue is out of the bottle and the companies cannot get it back in again. The reason why the companies are even meeting to discuss codes of conduct and verification standards is because they realize the American people don't believe them anymore. If you picked up *The New York Times* in 1985, you would have read the retailers saying, "It's not our problem, it's the manufacturer." The manufacturer would point to the contractor. The contractor would blame the subcontractor. Each would rationalize that it was the government's problem to implement U.S. labor law, not theirs. They don't get away with that anymore.

So there has been a sea change. More people are aware of sweatshop conditions now than ever before. The American people are doing more to challenge the multinationals and to hold them accountable to respect human rights and to pay a living wage than anywhere else in the world. We shouldn't lose hope.

One of the most significant developments in the struggle to defend worker rights has been the involvement of students. Today there are student movements on 50 campuses demanding that their universities become sweat free. The companies are frightened about where this movement is going, frightened about the growing coalition of religious, labor and student groups. They realize that this is a struggle for the hearts and minds of the American people.

To shop with a conscience, we must have the "Right to Know" where, in which factories, under what conditions and for what wages the products we purchase are made. We need transparency in the global economy. We need to drag these factories out into the light of day, out from behind the barbed wire and armed guards, where it will be harder for the companies to use child labor or operate sweatshops. There are no easy answers, but one thing is sure: without a social movement pressuring the companies, they will quickly fly back to business as usual.

Source: Third World Traveler. "Sweatshop Blues: Companies Love Misery." Available online. URL: http://www.thirdworldtraveler.com/Labor/SweatshopBlues.html. Accessed August 25, 2006.

"Poverty and Globalisation" by Vandana Shiva (2000)

This document contains most of a speech given by the renowned globalization and agricultural expert and activist Vandana Shiva as part of the BBC Reith Lecture series in 2000. In the speech, Shiva describes in unsparing detail the plight of poor farmers and the effects globalization is having on them. Her focus is subsistence farmers in her native India, but her analysis and critique of globalization's effects on agriculture apply to poor farming communities in most, if not all, developing and LDC countries.

Poverty & Globalisation
Vandana Shiva

Recently, I was visiting Bhatinda in Punjab because of an epidemic of farmers suicides. Punjab used to be the most prosperous agricultural region in India. Today every farmer is in debt and despair. Vast stretches of land have become water-logged desert. And as an old farmer pointed out, even the trees have stopped bearing fruit because heavy use of pesticides have killed the pollinators—the bees and butterflies.

And Punjab is not alone in experiencing this ecological and social disaster. Last year I was in Warangal, Andhra Pradesh where farmers have also been committing suicide. Farmers who traditionally grew pulses and millets and paddy have been lured by seed companies to buy hybrid cotton seeds referred to by the seed merchants as "white gold," which were supposed to make them millionaires. Instead they became paupers.

Their native seeds have been displaced with new hybrids which cannot be saved and need to be purchased every year at high cost. Hybrids are also very vulnerable to pest attacks. Spending on pesticides in Warangal has shot up 2000 per cent from $2.5 million in the 1980s to $50 million in 1997. Now farmers are consuming the same pesticides as a way of killing themselves so that they can escape permanently from unpayable debt.

The corporations are now trying to introduce genetically engineered seed which will further increase costs and ecological risks. . . .

On March 27th, 25 year old Betavati Ratan took his life because he could not pay pack debts for drilling a deep tube well on his two-acre farm. The wells are now dry, as are the wells in Gujarat and Rajasthan where more than 50 million people face a water famine.

The drought is not a "natural disaster." It is "man-made." It is the result of mining of scarce ground water in arid regions to grow thirsty cash crops for exports instead of water prudent food crops for local needs.

It is experiences such as these which tell me that we are so wrong to be smug about the new global economy. I will argue in this lecture that it is time to stop and think about the impact of globalisation on the lives of ordinary people. This is vital to achieve sustainability.

Seattle and the World Trade Organisation protests last year have forced everyone to think again. Throughout this lecture series people have referred to different aspects of sustainable development taking globalisation for granted. For me it is now time radically to re-evaluate what we are doing. For what we are doing in the name of globalisation to the poor is brutal and unforgivable. This is specially evident in India as we witness the unfolding disasters of globalisation, especially in food and agriculture.

Who feeds the world? My answer is very different to that given by most people.

It is women and small farmers working with biodiversity who are the primary food providers in the Third World, and contrary to the dominant assumption, their biodiversity based small farms are more productive than industrial monocultures.

The rich diversity and sustainable systems of food production are being destroyed in the name of increasing food production. However, with the destruction of diversity, rich sources of nutrition disappear. When measured in terms of nutrition per acre, and from the perspective biodiversity, the so called "high yields" of industrial agriculture or industrial fisheries do not imply more production of food and nutrition.

Yields usually refers to production per unit area of a single crop. Output refers to the total production of diverse crops and products. Planting only one crop in the entire field as a monoculture will of course increase its individual yield. Planting multiple crops in a mixture will have low yields of individual crops, but will have high total output of food. Yields have been defined in such a way as to make the food production on small farms by small farmers disappear. This hides the production by millions of women farmers in the Third World—farmers like those in my native Himalaya who fought against logging in the Chipko movement, who in their terraced fields even today grow Jhangora (barnyard millet), Marsha (Amaranth), Tur (Pigeon Pea), Urad (Black gram), Gahat (horse gram), Soya Bean (Glycine Max), Bhat (Glycine Soya)—endless diversity in their fields. From the biodiversity perspective, biodiversity based productivity is higher than monoculture productivity. I call this blindness to the high productivity of diversity a "Monoculture of the Mind," which creates monocultures in our fields and in our world.

The Mayan peasants in the Chiapas are characterised as unproductive because they produce only 2 tons of corn per acre. However, the overall food output is 20 tons per acre when the diversity of their beans and squashes, their vegetables their fruit trees are taken into account.

In Java, small farmers cultivate 607 species in their home gardens. In sub-Saharan Africa, women cultivate 120 different plants. A single home garden in Thailand has 230 species, and African home gardens have more than 60 species of trees. . . .

Research done by FAO has shown that small biodiverse farms can produce thousands of times more food than large, industrial monocultures.

And diversity in addition to giving more food is the best strategy for preventing drought and desertification.

What the world needs to feed a growing population sustainably is biodiversity intensification, not the chemical intensification or the intensification of genetic engineering. While women and small peasants feed the world through biodiversity we are repeatedly told that without genetic engineering and globalisation of agriculture the world will starve. In spite of all empirical evidence showing that genetic engineering does not produce more food and in fact often leads to a yield decline, it is constantly promoted as the only alternative available for feeding the hungry.

That is why I ask, who feeds the world?

This deliberate blindness to diversity, the blindness to nature's production, production by women, production by Third World farmers allows destruction and appropriation to be projected as creation.

Take the case of the much flouted "golden rice" or genetically engineered Vitamin A rice as a cure for blindness. It is assumed that without genetic engineering we cannot remove Vitamin A deficiency. However, nature gives us abundant and diverse sources of vitamin A. If rice was not polished, rice itself would provide Vitamin A. If herbicides were not sprayed on our wheat fields, we would have bathua, amaranth, mustard leaves as delicious and nutritious greens that provide Vitamin A. . . .

But the myth of creation presents biotechnologists as the creators of Vitamin A, negating nature's diverse gifts and women's knowledge of how to use this diversity to feed their children and families.

The most efficient means of rendering the destruction of nature, local economies and small autonomous producers is by rendering their production invisible.

Women who produce for their families and communities are treated as "non-productive" and "economically" inactive. The devaluation of women's work, and of work done in sustainable economies, is the natural outcome of a system constructed by capitalist patriarchy. This is how globalisation destroys local economies and destruction itself is counted as growth.

And women themselves are devalued. Because many women in the rural and indigenous communities work co-operatively with nature's processes, their work is often contradictory to the dominant market driven "development" and trade policies. And because work that satisfies needs and ensures sustenance is devalued in general, there is less nurturing of life and life support systems.

The devaluation and invisibility of sustainable, regenerative production is most glaring in the area of food. While patriarchal division of labour has assigned women the role of feeding their families and communities, patriarchal economics and patriarchal views of science and technology magically make women's work in providing food disappear. "Feeding the World" becomes disassociated from the women who actually do it and is projected as dependent on global agribusiness and biotechnology corporations.

However, industrialisation and genetic engineering of food and globalisation of trade in agriculture are recipes for creating hunger, not for feeding the poor.

Everywhere, food production is becoming a negative economy, with farmers spending more to buy costly inputs for industrial production than the price they receive for their produce. The consequence is rising debts and epidemics of suicides in both poor and rich countries.

Economic globalisation is leading to a concentration of the seed industry, increased use of pesticides, and, finally, increased debt. Capital-intensive, corporate controlled agriculture is being spread into regions where peasants are poor but, until now, have been self-sufficient in food. In the regions where industrial agriculture has been introduced through globalisation, higher costs are making it virtually impossible for small farmers to survive.

The globalisation of non-sustainable industrial agriculture is literally evaporating the incomes of Third World farmers through a combination of devaluation of currencies, increase in costs of production and a collapse in commodity prices.

Farmers everywhere are being paid a fraction of what they received for the same commodity a decade ago. The Canadian National Farmers Union put it like this in a report to the senate this year:

"While the farmers growing cereal grains—wheat, oats, corn—earn negative returns and are pushed close to bankruptcy, the companies that make breakfast cereals reap huge profits. In 1998, cereal companies Kellogg's, Quaker Oats, and General Mills enjoyed return on equity rates of 56%, 165% and 222% respectively. While a bushel of corn sold for less than $4, a bushel of corn flakes sold for $133 . . . Maybe farmers are making too little because others are taking too much."

And a World Bank report has admitted that "behind the polarisation of domestic consumer prices and world prices is the presence of large trading companies in international commodity markets."

While farmers earn less, consumers pay more. In India, food prices have doubled between 1999 and 2000. The consumption of food grains in rural areas has dropped by 12%. Increased economic growth through global commerce is based on pseudo surpluses. More food is being traded while the poor are consuming less. When growth increases poverty, when real production becomes a negative economy, and speculators are defined as "wealth creators," something has gone wrong with the concepts and categories of wealth and wealth creation. Pushing the real production by nature and people into a negative economy implies that production of real goods and services is declining, creating deeper poverty for the millions who are not part of the dot.com route to instant wealth creation. . . .

Recently, the McKinsey corporation said: "American food giants recognise that Indian agro-business has lots of room tc grow, especially in food processing. India processes a minuscule 1 per cent of the food it grows compared with 70 per cent for the U.S. . . ."

It is not that we Indians eat our food raw. Global consultants fail to see the 99 per cent food processing done by women at household level, or by the small cottage industry because it is not controlled by global agribusiness. 99% of India's agroprocessing has been intentionally kept at the small level. Now, under the pressure of globalisation, things are changing. Pseudo hygiene laws are being uses to shut down local economies and small scale processing.

In August 1998, small scale local processing of edible oil was banned in India through a "packaging order" which made sale of open oil illegal and required all oil to be packaged in plastic or aluminium. This shut down tiny "ghanis" or cold pressed mills. It destroyed the market for our diverse oilseeds—mustard, linseed, sesame, groundnut, coconut.

And the take-over of the edible oil industry has affected 10 million livelihoods. The take over of flour or "atta" by packaged branded flour will cost

100 million livelihoods. And these millions are being pushed into new poverty.

The forced use of packaging will increase the environmental burden of millions of tonnes of waste.

The globalisation of the food system is destroying the diversity of local food cultures and local food economies. A global monoculture is being forced on people by defining everything that is fresh, local and handmade as a health hazard. Human hands are being defined as the worst contaminants, and work for human hands is being outlawed, to be replaced by machines and chemicals bought from global corporations. These are not recipes for feeding the world, but stealing livelihoods from the poor to create markets for the powerful.

People are being perceived as parasites, to be exterminated for the "health" of the global economy.

In the process new health and ecological hazards are being forced on Third World people through dumping of genetically engineered foods and other hazardous products.

Recently, because of a W.T.O. ruling, India has been forced to remove restrictions on all imports.

Among the unrestricted imports are carcasses and animal waste parts that create a threat to our culture and introduce public health hazards such as the Mad Cow Disease.

The US Centre for Disease Prevention in Atlanta has calculated that nearly 81 million cases of food borne illnesses occur in the US every year. Deaths from food poisoning have gone up more than four times due to deregulation. Most of these infections are caused by factory farmed meat. The US slaughters 93 million pigs, thirty seven million cattle, two million calves, six million horses, goats and sheep and eight billion chickens and turkeys each year.

Now the giant meat industry of US wants to dump contaminated meat produced through violent and cruel methods on Indian consumers.

The waste of the rich is being dumped on the poor. The wealth of the poor is being violently appropriated through new and clever means like patents on biodiversity and indigenous knowledge.

Patents and intellectual property rights are supposed to be granted for novel inventions. But patents are being claimed for rice varieties such as the basmati

Whereas the ILO should give special attention to the problems of persons with special social needs, particularly the unemployed and migrant workers, and mobilize and encourage international, regional and national efforts aimed at resolving their problems, and promote effective policies aimed at job creation;

Whereas, in seeking to maintain the link between social progress and economic growth, the guarantee of fundamental principles and rights at work is of particular significance in that it enables the persons concerned, to claim freely and on the basis of equality of opportunity, their fair share of the wealth which they have helped to generate, and to achieve fully their human potential;

Whereas the ILO is the constitutionally mandated international organization and the competent body to set and deal with international labour standards, and enjoys universal support and acknowledgement in promoting Fundamental Rights at Work as the expression of its constitutional principles;

Whereas it is urgent, in a situation of growing economic interdependence, to reaffirm the immutable nature of the fundamental principles and rights embodied in the Constitution of the Organization and to promote their universal application;

The International Labour Conference

1. Recalls:

(a) that in freely joining the ILO, all Members have endorsed the principles and rights set out in its Constitution and in the Declaration of Philadelphia, and have undertaken to work towards attaining the overall objectives of the Organization to the best of their resources and fully in line with their specific circumstances;

(b) that these principles and rights have been expressed and developed in the form of specific rights and obligations in Conventions recognized as fundamental both inside and outside the Organization.

2. Declares that all Members, even if they have not ratified the Conventions in question, have an obligation arising from the very fact of membership in the Organization to respect, to promote and to realize, in good faith and in accordance with the Constitution, the principles concerning the fundamental rights which are the subject of those Conventions, namely:

(a) freedom of association and the effective recognition of the right to collective bargaining;

(b) the elimination of all forms of forced or compulsory labour;

(c) the effective abolition of child labour; and

(d) the elimination of discrimination in respect of employment and occupation.

3. Recognizes the obligation on the Organization to assist its Members, in response to their established and expressed needs, in order to attain these objectives by making full use of its constitutional, operational and budgetary resources, including, by the mobilization of external resources and support, as well as by encouraging other international organizations with which the ILO has established relations, pursuant to article 12 of its Constitution, to support these efforts:

(a) by offering technical cooperation and advisory services to promote the ratification and implementation of the fundamental Conventions;

(b) by assisting those Members not yet in a position to ratify some or all of these Conventions in their efforts to respect, to promote and to realize the principles concerning fundamental rights which are the subject of these Conventions; and

(c) by helping the Members in their efforts to create a climate for economic and social development.

4. Decides that, to give full effect to this Declaration, a promotional follow-up, which is meaningful and effective, shall be implemented in accordance with the measures specified in the annex hereto, which shall be considered as an integral part of this Declaration.

5. Stresses that labour standards should not be used for protectionist trade purposes, and that nothing in this Declaration and its follow-up shall be invoked or otherwise used for such purposes; in addition, the comparative advantage of any country should in no way be called into question by this Declaration and its follow-up.

Source: International Labour Organization. "ILO Declaration on Fundamental Principles and Rights at Work." Available online. URL: http://www.ilo.org/dyn/declaris/DECLARATIONWEB.static_jump?var_pagename=DECLARATIONTEXT. Accessed August 25, 2006.

"Sweatshop Blues: Companies Love Misery" by Charles Kernaghan (October 1998)

This document offers excerpts of a speech given in October 1998 at a forum sponsored by the Harvard Trade Union Program. The forum addressed "Global Standards and the Apparel Industry." Charles Kernaghan, a leader

In giving food to other beings and species we maintain conditions for our own food security. In feeding earthworms we feed ourselves. In feeding cows, we feed the soil, and in providing food for the soil, we provide food for humans. This worldview of abundance is based on sharing and on a deep awareness of humans as members of the earth family. This awareness that in impoverishing other beings, we impoverish ourselves and in nourishing other beings, we nourish ourselves is the real basis of sustainability.

The sustainability challenge for the new millennium is whether global economic man can move out of the worldview based on fear and scarcity, monocultures and monopolies, appropriation and dispossession and shift to a view based on abundance and sharing, diversity and decentralisation, and respect and dignity for all beings.

Sustainability demands that we move out of the economic trap that is leaving no space for other species and other people. Economic Globalisation has become a war against nature and the poor. But the rules of globalisation are not god-given. They can be changed. They must be changed. We must bring this war to an end.

Since Seattle, a frequently used phrase has been the need for a rule based system. Globalisation is the rule of commerce and it has elevated Wall Street to be the only source of value. As a result things that should have high worth—nature, culture, the future—are being devalued and destroyed. The rules of globalisation are undermining the rules of justice and sustainability, of compassion and sharing. We have to move from market totalitarianism to an earth democracy.

We can survive as a species only if we live by the rules of the biosphere. The biosphere has enough for everyone's needs if the global economy respects the limits set by sustainability and justice.

As [Mohandas] Gandhi had reminded us: "The earth has enough for everyone's needs, but not for some people's greed."

[Answers to] QUESTIONS FROM THE FLOOR

. . . We were told we'd have a level playing field—we were told when the WTO rules come into place we would have a fair market for Indian farmers—that was the single most important reason why India justified signing on to the GATT treaty after the Uruguay round. It turns out we have a very unlevel playing field—the northern countries or OECD countries are giving 343 billion dollars of subsidies and these subsidies have actually doubled since the completion of the Uruguay round—meantime India's giving a negative subsidy of 25 billion. Now one could keep arguing about how the north is giving very high subsidies—I think the argument needs to shift to how can we ensure that small farmers in every country and the soil and water and biodiversity in every country be protected and how can we ensure that trade rules as they are written by totally fallible trade ministers and trade secretaries should be rewritten to ensure that this unequal playing field does not destroy the Earth and her producers.

... It's the WTO rules that are totally one sided because they really only protect the interest of one sector of the global community which is the global corporations, not in the local industry, not even local retail business, not small farmers anywhere, not in the north and not in the south. And those rules can be rewritten. That is the point I'm trying to make. Do not treat WTO rules in the Uruguay Round Treaty as the final word on how trade should be carried out. Those rules are being reviewed. What we have called for in Seattle is a more democratic input in what sustainable and just rules would look like for agriculture on intellectual property rights, in the area of services, in the area of investments, the four new areas which were brought in....

Source: BBC Online Network. "Poverty & Globalisation." Available online. URL: http://news.bbc.co.uk/hi/english/static/events/reith_2000/lecture5.stm. Accessed August 25, 2006.

"How Trade Liberalisation Impacts Employment" by Mike Moore (March 18, 2002)

The speech was given to a meeting of the International Labor Organization (ILO) by the director general of the World Trade Organization, Mike Moore. The ILO meeting was held in Geneva, Switzerland, on March 18, 2002. In the speech, Moore contends that globalization has improved the lot of working people around the world.

Geneva 18 March 2002

How Trade Liberalisation Impacts Employment

Speech to the International Labour Organization (ILO)

Thank you for this opportunity to address the ILO's Working Party on the Social Dimension of Globalization....

I welcome the fact that later in this session you will be looking at Trade Liberalization and Employment, as well as Investment in the Global innovation enthusiastically adopted by the US and more recently elsewhere around the world, have been a major irritant to many countries, especially the developing countries, which argue that they are too often used to protect domestic producers from legitimate import competition. (Economists point out that the way in which anti-dumping provisions are implemented produces economically irrational results.) The Europeans and the Japanese wanted to explore ways of dealing with this problem through competition policy or, to use US terminology, anti-trust measures. The US did not want to address this issue. Developing countries were unhappy about investment protections, limited though they were, permitted in the Uruguay Round agreement while the rich OECD countries were pushing for further investment protections after failing to reach an agreement among themselves at OECD-sponsored talks a couple of years ago. Regionalism-sorting out how regional trade agreements such as NAFTA are to fit fairly and legally into this global system-needed to be addressed. Finally, there were the new social policy issues, labor standards, human rights and protection of the environment-headline issues in the US but not necessarily elsewhere in the world. And not to be forgotten, there were the normal tariff-cutting deals that are always on the agenda in a trade round.

The Seattle Ministerial was a fiasco. Street protests, police tear gassing, fist fights and inability of foreign delegates to even enter the building where the meetings were held made headline news. Foreign delegates were outraged by the abuse to which they were subjected. Some negotiators from developing countries regarded their bad treatment as an intentional attempt by the US government to physically intimidate foreign delegations—a quite plausible tactic in many of their own countries. Foreign delegates got their backs up. Although little reported by the press, there was a substantive fiasco as well. The fundamental conflict between the EU and the US over agriculture could not be overcome.

Finally, President [Bill] Clinton arrived telling everyone that he thought it might be a good idea to use trade sanctions to enforce workers' rights in other countries. His comments sabotaged efforts underway to find a compromise. There had been a compromise proposed by the EU, accepted by labor according to sources in the AFL-CIO [American Federation of Labor–Congress of Industrial Organizations], and even by developing country delegations, such as the Indian delegation, that have traditionally been very skeptical regarding this issue. President Clinton's comments scared people off.

From an insider's perspective, Seattle marked the debut of the developing countries as highly organized assertive players pursuing their own trade interests. Believing that they had been taken to the cleaners in the Uruguay Round, the developing countries were determined not to let that happen again. Coalitions formed among developing country delegations. It is clear that the developing countries as a block have to be taken seriously in the future. OECD countries will no longer be able to strike a deal and expect the rest of the world to acquiesce to its terms.

The Seattle debacle leaves us with the prospect of an agricultural trade war in 2003 when the "peace clause" expires. Moreover, there is new recognition, based on Seattle, that if the US and, to a secondary extent, the EU want to pursue the linkage of environmental objectives and labor standards to trade, they will have to do something to woo the developing countries. Confidence-building measures or, in economic jargon, down payments will be needed to persuade the developing countries to enter into serious negotiations on these issues. Recognizing this, the EU and, secondarily, Japan have been trying to organize new low-key negotiations with a much narrower agenda. Such mini-negotiations would focus on down payments, to convince the developing countries of our good faith, and on the "built-in agenda," agriculture and services. Hopefully, once underway, such negotiations might also deal with competition policy, investment and the newer labor and environment issues.

While the EU and Japan have been trying to initiate new talks, the US has remained relatively passive for two reasons. First, President Clinton has been unable to win "fast-track" negotiating authority from Congress. Because the US Constitution gives the Congress the prerogative to regulate international commerce, when the President through his Office of the US Trade Representative (USTR) negotiates new trade agreements, Congress could normally amend those agreements. Obviously, other countries would not negotiate with the US knowing that very sensitive compromises worked out at the WTO might be altered by the US Congress. Therefore, to make US negotiations credible, Congress has for the past twenty-five years committed itself for specified periods of time to vote on trade agreements in a simple yes/no manner without any possibility of amendment. This is called "fast-track" negotiating authority. President Clinton's last two attempts to win "fast-track" negotiating authority from Congress have failed. The President is unlikely to win "fast-track" authority during an election year and the next administration will not complete the appointment of new officials and gear up for serious trade negotiations before May or June of 2001. The US is simply not ready to play.

The second reason for US passivity concerning new trade talks is that the President's immediate trade priority is to win permanent "normal trade" status for China. China is the battle in which he will spend his political capital. He will not use his political capital on "fast-track." Nor will he use it to repair the damage inflicted on the WTO in Seattle.

useful measurement of the human condition, we have seen the greatest advances in the history of our species during the last half century, according to data collected by the UNDP and other agencies.

- In 1900, average life expectancy was 30, today it is 67.
- On average, developing countries have increased their food intake from 2,463 to 2,663 calories per person over the past decade—an increase of 8%.
- In 1970, 35% of all people in developing countries were starving. In 1996, the figure had fallen to 18% and the UN expects the figure will have fallen to 12% by 2010.
- Between 1990–1999, adult illiteracy rates in low-income countries for males aged 15 and above decreased from 35%–29%; and for females aged 15 and above, the figure decreased from 56%–48%.
- While only 30% of people in the developing world had access to clean drinking water in 1970, today about 80% have.
- Wages and conditions have improved as economies grow.
- In the US, lead concentration in the air has dropped more than 97% since 1977. The US EPA [Environmental Protection Agency] estimates that about 22,000 deaths are avoided every year because of the dramatic decline in lead levels.
- Some of the Great Lakes were considered dead 30 years ago and rivers sometimes caught fire. Today, people can swim and fish in them.

None of this is to suggest that we should be happy with the current state of the world. There is still all too much injustice. But, as a recent IMF paper points out in trade-opening East Asian countries—the New Globalizers—the number of people in absolute poverty declined by over 120 million between 1993 and 1998. On the evidence to date, Globalisation has been good for an increasing number of people, including, of course, workers. . . .

We are making solid progress: according to the IMF, over the past two decades, the growth of world trade has averaged 6% annually, twice as fast as world output. My plea to you today is not to allow the negative forces fighting against Globalisation and market liberalisation to triumph.

Source: World Trade Organization. "How Trade Liberalisation Impacts Employment." Available online. URL: http://www.wto.org/english/news_e/spmm_e/spmm80_e.htm. Accessed August 25, 2006.

"The G-20 and the World Economy" by C. Fred Bergsten (March 4, 2004)

This document contains excerpts of a speech given by economist C. Fred Bergsten to the deputies of the G-20 (Group of Twenty developing and LDC nations) at a meeting in Leipzig, Germany, on March 4, 2004. The speech acknowledges some of the problems that globalization causes but elucidates the positive effects that globalization has on developing economies.

The G-20 and the World Economy
C. Fred Bergsten
Institute for International Economics
Speech to the Deputies of the G-20
Leipzig, Germany
March 4, 2004

I have been asked to address on this occasion your central agenda issues of macroeconomic stability and growth, the deeper sources of growth in both industrial and developing countries, and the relevance of the Washington Consensus in today's world economy. I am delighted to do so because I believe that the G-20 can play a major role in both developing a consensus on the underlying fundamentals of these issues and in directly addressing a number of the most important "stability and growth" questions facing the world economy at the present time. I will offer specific recommendations on the role of the G-20 after briefly surveying the state of thinking on growth strategies and especially the role that globalization plays in that context.

Globalization and Growth

Globalization is, of course, under attack throughout the world. Critics argue that some countries, and even entire regions, are affected adversely by the process. They argue that major groups within virtually all countries are losers and that the entire phenomenon should be rejected or, at a minimum, thoroughly revamped.

There is a very widespread intellectual consensus to the contrary, however, that demonstrates that globalization is an essential component of growth in rich and poor countries alike. The aggregate record is impressively positive, including for developing countries. It remains the case that no country has ever developed on a sustainable basis without participating actively in the global economy. The eminent economic historian Jeffrey Williamson of Harvard has succinctly summarized the analytical results: . . . Controlling for religion, culture, geography and institutions, openness is always correlated with faster growth. . . .

The Mayan peasants in the Chiapas are characterised as unproductive because they produce only 2 tons of corn per acre. However, the overall food output is 20 tons per acre when the diversity of their beans and squashes, their vegetables their fruit trees are taken into account.

In Java, small farmers cultivate 607 species in their home gardens. In sub-Saharan Africa, women cultivate 120 different plants. A single home garden in Thailand has 230 species, and African home gardens have more than 60 species of trees. . . .

Research done by FAO has shown that small biodiverse farms can produce thousands of times more food than large, industrial monocultures.

And diversity in addition to giving more food is the best strategy for preventing drought and desertification.

What the world needs to feed a growing population sustainably is biodiversity intensification, not the chemical intensification or the intensification of genetic engineering. While women and small peasants feed the world through biodiversity we are repeatedly told that without genetic engineering and globalisation of agriculture the world will starve. In spite of all empirical evidence showing that genetic engineering does not produce more food and in fact often leads to a yield decline, it is constantly promoted as the only alternative available for feeding the hungry.

That is why I ask, who feeds the world?

This deliberate blindness to diversity, the blindness to nature's production, production by women, production by Third World farmers allows destruction and appropriation to be projected as creation.

Take the case of the much flouted "golden rice" or genetically engineered Vitamin A rice as a cure for blindness. It is assumed that without genetic engineering we cannot remove Vitamin A deficiency. However, nature gives us abundant and diverse sources of vitamin A. If rice was not polished, rice itself would provide Vitamin A. If herbicides were not sprayed on our wheat fields, we would have bathua, amaranth, mustard leaves as delicious and nutritious greens that provide Vitamin A. . . .

But the myth of creation presents biotechnologists as the creators of Vitamin A, negating nature's diverse gifts and women's knowledge of how to use this diversity to feed their children and families.

The most efficient means of rendering the destruction of nature, local economies and small autonomous producers is by rendering their production invisible.

Women who produce for their families and communities are treated as "non-productive" and "economically" inactive. The devaluation of women's work, and of work done in sustainable economies, is the natural outcome of a system constructed by capitalist patriarchy. This is how globalisation destroys local economies and destruction itself is counted as growth.

And women themselves are devalued. Because many women in the rural and indigenous communities work co-operatively with nature's processes, their work is often contradictory to the dominant market driven "development" and trade policies. And because work that satisfies needs and ensures sustenance is devalued in general, there is less nurturing of life and life support systems.

The devaluation and invisibility of sustainable, regenerative production is most glaring in the area of food. While patriarchal division of labour has assigned women the role of feeding their families and communities, patriarchal economics and patriarchal views of science and technology magically make women's work in providing food disappear. "Feeding the World" becomes disassociated from the women who actually do it and is projected as dependent on global agribusiness and biotechnology corporations.

However, industrialisation and genetic engineering of food and globalisation of trade in agriculture are recipes for creating hunger, not for feeding the poor.

Everywhere, food production is becoming a negative economy, with farmers spending more to buy costly inputs for industrial production than the price they receive for their produce. The consequence is rising debts and epidemics of suicides in both poor and rich countries.

Economic globalisation is leading to a concentration of the seed industry, increased use of pesticides, and, finally, increased debt. Capital-intensive, corporate controlled agriculture is being spread into regions where peasants are poor but, until now, have been self-sufficient in food. In the regions where industrial agriculture has been introduced through globalisation, higher costs are making it virtually impossible for small farmers to survive.

The globalisation of non-sustainable industrial agriculture is literally evaporating the incomes of Third World farmers through a combination of devaluation of currencies, increase in costs of production and a collapse in commodity prices.

Farmers everywhere are being paid a fraction of what they received for the same commodity a decade ago. The Canadian National Farmers Union put it like this in a report to the senate this year:

A second key conclusion is that the political leadership in countries with some of the most remarkable development success stories has consciously used globalization, especially formal international economic integration, to overcome domestic resistance to effective reform strategies. Mexico sought NAFTA importantly to complete, and then lock in, the liberalization of its domestic as well as external economic policies. China joined the World Trade Organization largely so that it could employ the international rules to override opposition to its internal reforms. Egyptian reformers are now seeking a free trade agreement with the United States for precisely these reasons. The lesson is that sharp increases in openness, especially if they can be managed through major domestic initiatives that become national political priorities and thus enable a country's top officials to overcome entrenched resistance to change, can produce huge breakthroughs in development strategies and subsequent performance.

Globalization, however, while clearly a necessary condition for (rich or poor) countries to achieve sustainable growth, is equally clearly not a sufficient condition. Many studies show that countries must put additional supportive policies in place to enable them to take full advantage of globalization. Moreover, globalization generates costs and losers just like any other source of dynamic economic change. It thus becomes essential to elaborate sophisticated globalization-based development strategies, as the so-called Washington Consensus has attempted to do for the past decade or so.

The inventor of the term Washington Consensus and chronicler of its results to date, my colleague John Williamson, has recently offered a comprehensive update of that strategy. Addressed primarily to Latin America and conducted with a team of 14 top economists from that region, his new study concludes that the original consensus produced a disappointingly slow revival of growth mainly because its reforms "were not pushed far enough" and because a series of crises, reflecting the vulnerability of countries in the region, disrupted economic performance. The authors also acknowledge shortcomings in the strategy, however, notably an excessively narrow focus "on restoring growth [that] never really faced up to the need to expand employment in particular and opportunities in general so as to give poor people a chance to contribute their talents. . . ." Hence they propose a program of reforms "after the Washington Consensus" that emphasizes four areas:

- Crisis proofing. This can be furthered by anticyclical fiscal policies, hard budget constraints on subnational governments, stabilization funds, flexible exchange rates, inflation targeting, further strengthening of fiscal positions and completion of pension reform so as to reduce dependence on foreign savings, and regional peer monitoring of commitments to fiscal responsibility.

- Completion of first-generation reforms. It is important to liberalize the labor market so as to give those currently in the informal sector the opportunities that come only with formality; this should be sought by cooperation rather than confrontation. The labor market could also be made more flexible through comprehensive programs of labor retraining. Trade reforms need to focus primarily on improving market access to industrial countries, via the FTAA and WTO. There are still many enterprises, including state-owned banks, to be privatized.

- Aggressive second-generation (institutional) reforms. Needs differ by country and leading candidates include the political system, the civil service, the judiciary, and the financial sector.

- Income distribution and the social agenda. The fiscal system should be made more progressive, not by reverting to penal marginal tax rates but by imposing property taxes and by focusing expenditures on the universal provision of high-quality basic education and health care. Poor people need to be empowered by giving them access to the assets that will enable them to earn a decent living in a market economy: education, land, credit, and titling.

The G-20 could provide a benchmark for the entire globalization process, for the next decade or so, if it could reach agreement on significant portions of this very ambitious reform agenda. Such a consensus would add enormously to the luster and reputation of the G-20 if it decides to seek a leadership role in the evolution of the conceptual foundations, as well as operating modalities, of the world economy—as I believe it should.

There is, of course, a second set of requirements that must be present for globalization to succeed: a hospitable global economic environment. In particular, developing countries can only reap the expected benefits from globalization if the markets of the industrial countries are truly open to their most competitive products and their people. Here again is a major reason for the G-20 to focus on these issues, as it is the only possible steering committee for the world economy that comprises the leading countries from both sides of the per capita income divide.

Macroeconomic Stability and Growth

In the shorter run, and hopefully operating within the consensus on broader strategies just suggested, the G-20 could—as indicated in the list of purposes of

WAL-MART'S LIES

It's startling to see the hypocrisy and the enormous lies of the companies. Take Wal-Mart, for example. If you go into Wal-Mart, you see flags flying everywhere and a statement saying, "Made right here in the United States. We support American manufacturers that support American jobs."

We thought this was very interesting. We're not a "Buy American" group, but if Wal-Mart was saying that they work with U.S. manufacturers and U.S. workers, it was another way for the largest retailer in the world to say that there are standards below which they won't go. So we called Wal-Mart and asked them how much of their clothing, handbags and shoes are produced in the United States. We got a funny response back: they said they didn't know. But of course they know what they're bringing into the stores!

So we decided to do something we wouldn't recommend to just anyone. We went into Wal-Mart and spent 100 hours counting clothing and handbags. We used hidden, voice-activated tape recorders, and I spent every Friday night, Saturday and Sunday in Wal-Mart. I went into 14 stores in 12 states.

We counted 105,000 items in Wal-Mart, and it took another 200 or 300 hours to transcribe the tapes. Of the 86,500 pieces of clothing we counted, only 17% were made in the United States, and 83% offshore. We counted 16,245 pairs of shoes, and only sixteen pairs—not 16%—were made in the United States; the rest were made in China. We counted 1,910 handbags and pocketbooks and stopped counting because zero were made in the United States. Of the famous Kathie Lee Gifford clothing line, only 11% was made in the United States and 89% was made offshore. The McKids brand of children's clothing from McDonald's had 4% made in the United States, with 96% offshore. Faded Glory men's clothing had 13% made in the United States, with 87% produced offshore. So Wal-Mart was flat-out lying to the American people.

We thought: Why don't we sue Wal-Mart for consumer fraud? But when we took a look at their small print we found out we couldn't sue them. Even though Wal-Mart declared its "unprecedented commitment to purchase American-made goods," in the small print it added, "whenever they meet the pricing available offshore." So Wal-Mart was completely covered. American workers were only going to get the job if they could compete with the nine-cent wages in Indonesia or the 50-cent wages in Mexico.

Wal-Mart produces private-label apparel in 48 countries around the world. The big producers for the Kathie Lee Gifford line right now are Mexico and Indonesia, where the currencies have fallen through the floor. Garment jobs are quickly going to these countries—in fact we lost 68,000 U.S. apparel jobs in the last 12 months. What Wal-Mart ultimately wants to do, of course, is to pit the American people against desperately poor people in the developing world in this race to the bottom. It comes down to who will accept the lowest wages, the least benefits and the most miserable living and working conditions.

THE BUCK STOPS HERE?

But after the exposure of Kathie Lee Gifford, The Gap, and Nike, the sweatshop issue is out of the bottle and the companies cannot get it back in again. The reason why the companies are even meeting to discuss codes of conduct and verification standards is because they realize the American people don't believe them anymore. If you picked up *The New York Times* in 1985, you would have read the retailers saying, "It's not our problem, it's the manufacturer." The manufacturer would point to the contractor. The contractor would blame the subcontractor. Each would rationalize that it was the government's problem to implement U.S. labor law, not theirs. They don't get away with that anymore.

So there has been a sea change. More people are aware of sweatshop conditions now than ever before. The American people are doing more to challenge the multinationals and to hold them accountable to respect human rights and to pay a living wage than anywhere else in the world. We shouldn't lose hope.

One of the most significant developments in the struggle to defend worker rights has been the involvement of students. Today there are student movements on 50 campuses demanding that their universities become sweat free. The companies are frightened about where this movement is going, frightened about the growing coalition of religious, labor and student groups. They realize that this is a struggle for the hearts and minds of the American people.

To shop with a conscience, we must have the "Right to Know" where, in which factories, under what conditions and for what wages the products we purchase are made. We need transparency in the global economy. We need to drag these factories out into the light of day, out from behind the barbed wire and armed guards, where it will be harder for the companies to use child labor or operate sweatshops. There are no easy answers, but one thing is sure: without a social movement pressuring the companies, they will quickly fly back to business as usual.

Source: Third World Traveler. "Sweatshop Blues: Companies Love Misery." Available online. URL: http://www.thirdworldtraveler.com/Labor/SweatshopBlues.html. Accessed August 25, 2006.

International agreement on new rules, or even norms, for the exchange rate system would make it far easier to deal with the recurrent problem of global imbalances such as those we are seeing now. Such a regime would be of great help in answering the questions that must be faced today: How large must be the adjustments in the main countries' current account imbalances? How should those adjustments be achieved? Which countries should be responsible for corrective actions? Over what periods? These are very difficult questions, and it is understandable that officials shy away from addressing them. The alternative of leaving the outcome to a combination of market forces and wholly unilateral actions by national authorities, however, demonstrably produces results that are both unsustainable and manifestly unbalanced.

The current exchange rate regime is very weak, and even its minimal rules, such as the prohibition on "protracted large-scale intervention in one direction in the exchange market" to block currency adjustment, are being ignored by the IMF and the G-7 in important country cases today. Hence there is a need for fundamentally new understandings on the global exchange rate system. The G-20 should add this set of questions to its agenda.

Regional Economic Integration

One aspect of the backlash against globalization in its present form—and especially against its current lead institutions, including those located in Washington—has been the pursuit of regional alternatives, another item on the agenda for this meeting of the G-20. In particular, East Asian countries are actively negotiating a series of regional, subregional, and bilateral agreements in the areas of both money (i.e., the network of bilateral swap agreements under the Chiang Mai Initiative) and trade (e.g., China-ASEAN and Japan-Korea). Extensive subregional arrangements also exist in Latin America (Mercosur, Andean Pact) and elsewhere (South African Customs Union, Gulf Cooperation Council) with respect to trade but increasingly with an eye toward monetary and even macroeconomic cooperation as well.

Two implications of this trend are germane for the G-20 as it evolves toward becoming an important steering committee for the world economy. In the short run, it will be essential to assure that these new regional and subregional entities are compatible with the existing global rules and institutional arrangements—or that these rules and institutions are amended to encompass the regional newcomers in an agreed and harmonious manner.

The longer run significance for the G-20 could be even greater. Successful realization of these regional aspirations—especially in Asia, where until recently they have lagged far behind Europe and even the Western Hemisphere—could lead to the emergence of a tripolar world economic structure. Such a construct would encompass the European Union and its neighboring associates, a Free Trade Area of the Americas (or perhaps NAFTA and an expanded Mercosur in South America that were linked only loosely) and an East Asia Free Trade Area/Asian Monetary Fund. In such a world, a global steering committee that included the key players from each of the three regions—including China and Korea in East Asia, Brazil and Argentina in South America—would be of cardinal importance in managing relations among the regions, which would in turn be central for global harmony and stability.

The prospect of such a tripartite world, which is quite feasible over the next decade or even less, provides a powerful additional rationale for the proposition that the G-20 should gradually but steadily supersede the G-7 as the informal steering committee for the world economy. The G-7 would be even more inadequate for that task in a world where not only its share of the world economy continued to decline substantially but where leaders of key regional arrangements were outside the group.

In such a world, the G-7 could, of course, expand to include such countries. The far better course, however, especially in light of the other problems facing the G-7, as described throughout this paper, would be to anticipate such developments and start now to build the institutional framework that will be required to handle them. The creation of the G-20 five years ago already implied a judgment that the current institutional structure was inadequate, even outdated, for dealing with the main problems of the world economy. Recent events, notably the inability of the G-7 to resolve some of the most salient issues now facing the global system because its membership excludes countries whose participation is essential for doing so, underline the need for the G-20 to become an effective action organization. Achieving this role and addressing such problems forcefully should be the true agenda for the G-20 in 2004 and beyond.

Source: Institute for International Economics. "The G-20 and the World Economy." Available online. URL: http://www.iie.com/publication/papers/paper.cfm?ResearchID=196. Accessed August 25, 2006.

EAST ASIAN FINANCIAL CRISIS

"Learning from East Asia's Woes" by John Williamson (March 1998)

This paper was prepared by John Williamson while he was chief economist for the South Asia region at the World Bank. It was presented at a WB meeting held in Dhaka, Bangladesh, in March 1998. Williamson argues that the East Asia crisis could not have been predicted, that the East Asian economies were vulnerable to the vagaries of the international financial markets, and that the institutions of globalization were not to blame for the crisis.

Learning from East Asia's Woes
John Williamson
The World Bank
Paper presented in Dhaka, Bangladesh
March 1998

Introduction

For almost two decades East Asia was held up as a role model for developing countries, by economists in general and by those from the World Bank in particular. Since last July the region has been engulfed by a severe economic crisis, and innumerable sages have emerged from the woodwork to proclaim that the miracle was really a mirage, or that the region's problems are the penalty it has to pay for deviating from free market orthodoxy, or that the crisis is a deliberate act of sabotage of the region's progress by the West. The purpose of the present paper is to offer an interpretation of the crisis that will allow us to assess the validity of such claims, and then proceed to ask how other developing countries, particularly those of South Asia, should respond to the crisis.

A Crisis that Surprised

No one foresaw a crisis of the character and severity that has engulfed East Asia. True, some of us worried that Thailand was taking a risk in committing itself to the defence of a fixed exchange rate (defined in terms of a single currency, which resulted in large cycles in the effective exchange rate as the dollar went on its roller-coaster) given that a massive current account deficit had developed, but we never imagined that the ensuing crisis might result in a devaluation of almost 50 percent, or a fall in the stock market of over 40 percent, or that output would decline by 8 per cent. Still less did it occur to us that a Thai crisis would result in rapid and widespread contagion. And if we had asked ourselves who would be likely to suffer from any contagion that might occur, we surely would not have selected as the likely victims the other East Asian countries, who boasted just about the strongest "fundamentals" in the world, at least as we have been accustomed to thinking of the fundamentals (in terms of macroeconomic variables like the fiscal balance, inflation, savings, investment, and growth).

Common Features of Victims

For several months I think most of us were quite unable to detect a pattern in which countries fell victim to the crisis. We were relieved that no South Asian country succumbed in a serious way; we were also surprised because all the countries of South Asia are weaker than those of East Asia in terms of what we have been accustomed to thinking of as the fundamentals. But gradually a pattern emerged. With one partial exception, all the victims had three things in common:

- strong asset prices in the years preceding the crisis
- large exposure to the international markets, including a large stock of short- term debts denominated in foreign exchange
- a weak financial sector, notably banks of dubious solvency because of a large volume of non-performing loans.

It is not too difficult to understand why a country with those three features should suffer contagion from the Thai crisis (whose initiation, I have argued, can be understood as a conventional exchange rate crisis). The Thai crisis raised questions about the sustainability of asset prices in any country whose economic situation appeared to resemble that of Thailand. Similarly, the Thai demonstration that exchange rates could depreciate severely caused a rush for dollars on the part of those with uncovered positions in foreign exchange, especially if these were short-term, which rapidly precipitated the very depreciation that agents were trying to insure themselves against. This depreciation weakened the balance sheet position of most companies with foreign exchange exposure (the exception being firms heavily engaged in exporting), which reinforced the asset price declines, and thus further undermined the solvency of the financial sector. These crises have been dubbed "new-style crises", in contrast to old-style or conventional balance of payments/exchange rate crises.

Countries (such as those of South Asia) that exhibited only the last of the three features listed above, namely a weak banking system, were not vulnerable to a new-style crisis. But it would be a mistake to draw too much comfort from this; they remain vulnerable to old-style crises, and indeed their vulnerability to such a crisis may well have been increased by events in East Asia, notably the devaluations, which have reduced the competitiveness of South Asian exports.

Explaining East Asian Vulnerability

To say that the countries engulfed by the crisis were those with high asset prices, that had heavy exposure to the international financial markets, and that had weak banking systems immediately poses the question: how did countries get into this situation? It seems to me that there were at least three policy mistakes that contributed to creating the vulnerability in most or all of the victim countries.

The first, and the one highlighted in the most elegant piece of theorizing to have been spawned by the crisis so far, is the provision of explicit or implicit guarantees of the liabilities of financial intermediaries without the creation of a system of financial regulation and supervision adequate to restrain the moral hazard which such guarantees create. If the creditors of financial intermediaries believe they have no need to check the solvency of those to whom they are entrusting their assets, while the owners of the financial institutions believe that their losses will be socialized while they will reap the full benefits of the profits the institutions may make, they will have an incentive to undertake investments that are excessively risky from a social point of view. In the absence of a functioning system of regulation and supervision to restrain that moral hazard, the banks can be expected to acquire too many risky assets. That temptation may be expected to be particularly strong in the aftermath of financial liberalization, when bankers have been told it is their social duty to lend to those whom they judge it advantageous to lend to, and when they have not yet had the experience of a collapse to warn them against imprudent lending.

Guarantees without adequate regulation and supervision might go a long way toward explaining the weakness of the banking system, and they might go some way toward explaining how the prices of risky assets began to boom, but they certainly cannot explain how countries acquired a large exposure to the international financial market. To explain that, one needs also to recognize the second policy error, which was premature liberalization of the capital account of the balance of payments. It was this which allowed foreign as well as domestic wealth-holders to respond to the attractive (because presumed to be largely risk-free) returns offered by financial intermediaries, and thus provide the financial resources that in many cases powered asset price booms—booms that for a long time seemed to validate the excessively risky lending that was being undertaken. And in the process, of course, the countries acquired their large exposure to the international markets. I take the East Asian meltdown as decisive evidence showing the wisdom of the Tarrapore Committee (1997) in having argued that Indian capital account convertibility needs to be preceded by the establishment of a liberalized, well-supervised, domestic financial system. And I concede that a part of the blame for the East Asian crisis can legitimately be laid at the door of those in the West (including in the international organizations) who pushed for rapid, unconditional, and complete liberalization of capital account transactions.

While one can offer a complete explanation of the East Asian crisis in terms of those two policy errors, there is surely a third factor that contributed to the weakening of the banking systems in most or all of the victim countries. This is "crony capitalism", the favouring of particular enterprises controlled by the friends or relatives of the politically powerful. One of the ways in which the cronies received favors was in terms of access to credit, which weakened the banks when the cronies either were unable to repay or chose not to repay because they knew that their political patrons would defend them against the sanctions that are normally imposed on defaulters.

Interpreting the Crisis

If this is indeed how the East Asian meltdown developed, what does that imply for the sorts of claims mentioned at the beginning of this paper? Was the miracle a mirage? Was the disaster a consequence of deviating from the free market? Did the West sabotage the miracle?

Surely the miracle was no mirage. Per capita incomes rose faster in Korea and Thailand between 1970 and 1995 than in any other countries that started with a comparable level of income. According to one estimate, poverty in Indonesia fell from some 58 percent in 1971 to just 8 percent in the early 1990s, surely the only time in history that a country has lifted half of its population out of poverty in a couple of decades, and dramatically superior to South Asia's reduction of perhaps 20 percentage points (from a similar figure to that of Indonesia in 1971 to perhaps 35 percent in the early 1990s). Suppose that poverty doubles in Indonesia as a consequence of the crisis, which is surely an extreme assumption. It would still be less than half that in South Asia, even though poverty rates in the two regions were similar a quarter century ago. The miracle involved building productive assets and teaching people how to make good use of them, and those investments and skills are not going to evaporate because of a financial crisis, no matter how severe. The miracle was real, and the people of those countries will again benefit from the assets that were built up when the crisis passes, as it will.

Can one explain the collapse by governments forcing their populace to save or invest or export too much, or otherwise distorting the market? One can argue that there was some over-saving, especially in Singapore—but

Singapore is hardly at the eye of the storm. On the contrary, its over-saving has enabled it to build a financial position so strong that it was able to weather the storm with rather little damage. Advocates of the over-investment thesis seem unable to agree whether the problem was too much investment in nontradables (golf courses and shopping centres) that would not yield foreign exchange to service the debts that had been taken on, or too much investment in tradables so that they were satiating the world market. The latter version is quite implausible: most of the countries were importing more than they were exporting, and thus supporting rather than detracting from world demand. The former version is much more persuasive—but it amounts to saying the governments had let their former dedication to macroeconomic discipline, notably a competitive exchange rate, slip. And yes, crony capitalism had introduced distortions.

Did the West sabotage the miracle because it was jealous of the progress being made by a bunch of upstarts? The saboteurs were supposedly the speculators, who are presumed to have been responsible for causing the devaluations that initiated the crisis. No one can reasonably deny that the speculators were the proximate cause of the Thai devaluation (though it is not at all clear that they were responsible for the subsequent devaluations). The question is whether one believes that speculators act in response to a perception that prices (in this case exchange rates) are out of line with the fundamentals, thus presenting them with an opportunity to profit when the authorities are forced to face the facts, or whether they have the ability to make money by forcing a price away from its equilibrium level. This was the contention that Milton Friedman (1953) first challenged with his attempt to demonstrate that destabilizing speculation must be unprofitable (you make money by buying low and selling high, not vice versa). While I am among those who do not find this argument definitive in the context of a floating exchange rate, basically because of the possibility that stop-loss traders provide a source that can be milched almost systematically by traders who follow chartist rules, the equivalent argument in the context of a managed exchange rate system relies on governments being forced by the speculators to change their macro policies in a way that will validate the speculation. So far attempts to find instances where speculators have induced validating changes in government policies have failed. (I see not a shadow of evidence to support any wider charge that the West in general consciously set out to disrupt the economic progress being made in East Asia; on the contrary, most Western economists fell over themselves in trying to prove that the economic progress that they welcomed and admired was a consequence of the East Asian countries adopting their particular policy preferences.)

Is there any alternative interpretation at a similar level of generality that is suggested by the analysis in the preceding sections? I propose that we think of these countries as having been seduced by their own success into overconfidence and thence carelessness. They had lived so long without a macro crisis that they had forgotten the penalties of letting the exchange rate become uncompetitive, as well as the necessity of reacting with overwhelming force and determination when introducing a policy package designed to resolve a crisis. (Contrast Brazil's reaction to a speculative run last November with the initial dilly dallying in Thailand, Indonesia, and Korea.) They had enjoyed such a long boom that they mistook a speculative bubble in the asset markets for a natural market reward for success. They had profited by liberalizing their economies, and did not realise the lesson learned in South America in the early 1980s, that a necessary counterpart to financial liberalization has to be the institution of adequate regulation and supervision. The West told them that liberalizing international capital flows was a part of growing up, and they took the advice without questioning. Their poor had benefited spectacularly despite the favours bestowed on the cronies, so it did not seem particularly dangerous to allow the cronies ever bigger favours.

Policy Responses

I shall frame my lessons with a particular view to how the South Asian countries should respond, although most of the things that I say apply also to other developing, or even in some cases developed, countries.

Avoidance of an Old-style Crisis. Since the South Asian countries exhibit only one of the three factors that precipitated the new-style crises in East Asia, I do not see much reason to fear similar crises in South Asia. However, the danger of an old-style crisis, one in which a balance of payments deficit precipitates a run on the currency, has been increased by the troubles of East Asia. The major factor here is the increased competitive pressure from East Asian countries following their massive devaluations, reinforced by the fall in demand for South Asian exports caused by the recessions in East Asia but somewhat attenuated by the weakening in the prices of primary commodities (notably oil) which are imported by both East and South Asia. The appropriate policy response is a tightening of macro policy, notably a more austere fiscal policy (including a reduction in quasi-fiscal deficits) and, if not necessarily an immediate depreciation, then certainly a greater willingness to allow the exchange rate to respond promptly to signs of a deterioration in the external accounts.

Continue to Pursue a South Asian Miracle. Just about every country in South Asia has in recent years set itself the goal of a major acceleration in its growth rate, inspired by the example of East Asia and its demonstration that rapid economic progress is possible if the policy stance is appropriate. Perhaps the most tragic consequence of the East Asian crisis would be if it dissuaded other countries from learning from the truly impressive achievements of East Asia over the past 30 years or so. There is no reason to believe that the policies that most economists hold responsible for nurturing the miracle of high and sustained growth with a reasonably egalitarian distribution of its fruits—macroeconomic stability, until 1997; high savings rates (aided by an early demographic transition); investment in education, first at the primary level; providing the private sector with a reasonably level playing field; export orientation; neutrality on industry versus agriculture; or even industrial policy (if you believe that was a factor)—were those that induced the crisis. On the contrary, it was the recent departures from those policies—the risks with macro stability involved in borrowing too much abroad and stabilizing the exchange rate rather than making sure it remains competitive, the failure to follow through from the successes in primary education by equivalent attention to secondary education, the violations of neutrality involved in growing preferences to the cronies—plus the sudden embrace of capital account convertibility, that set the stage for the crisis. With the exception of the growth of crony capitalism (and the neglect of the environment, though that is another story), pre-1990 East Asia remains a role model to be emulated.

Preempt New-style Crises. While achieving a couple of decades of East Asian rates of growth should be the primary objective of economic policy in South Asia, it is obviously desirable to avoid that growth being interrupted at some point in the future by the emergence of a new-style crisis. This demands avoiding those mistakes bred of over-confidence that have laid East Asia low in recent months. First, while it is probably undesirable to avoid all guarantees of bank liabilities, it is quite essential that these be accompanied by good regulations (requiring transparent accounting, capital requirements at least up to the international norm, prohibitions on connected lending, a legal system that exacts sanctions if loans are not serviced conscientiously, etc.) which are enforced by a competent and motivated body of supervisors. Second, it suggests that countries should eschew dogmatic commitments to capital account convertibility, and retain some ability to require financial actors to maintain a reasonably balanced currency position, and to make it expensive for domestic agents to borrow abroad short-term (as Chile and Colombia do). Third, it argues the need to abandon crony capitalism once and for all.

Concluding Remarks

When this paper was written, in February 1998, I had started to hope that the countries of East Asia were beginning to emerge from the crisis. That hope proved premature, especially with regard to Indonesia, but as the paper is revised (in October 1998) the hope looks more secure, unless at least the crisis goes into a second round as it ripples further around the world. Even so, the costs of the crisis have been so massive that it is of obvious importance for other countries to learn how to avoid similar disasters in the future. South Asia certainly needs to learn that—but it needs even more to learn how to grow in the way that East Asia did for the preceding quarter century.

Source: Institute for International Economics. "Learning from East Asia's Woes." Available online. URL: http://www.iie.com/publications/papers/paper.cfm?ResearchID=309. Accessed August 25, 2006.

CHINA

"China: Just Say No to Monetary Protectionism" by Gerald P. O'Driscoll and Lee Hoskins (January 15, 2004)

This paper—written by Gerald P. O'Driscoll, a senior fellow at the Cato Institute, and Lee Hoskins, a senior fellow at the Pacific Research Institute and former president of the Federal Reserve Bank of Cleveland—argues against China's protectionist monetary policies. Though the authors criticize China's tight control of capital, they recognize that not antagonizing this economic giant better protects the economic interests of the United States in its relations with China. The paper was first published in the Free Trade Bulletin on January 15, 2004.

China: Just Say No to Monetary Protectionism
by Gerald P. O'Driscoll Jr., and Lee Hoskins

The [George W.] Bush administration is prone to wrapping protectionist policy in free-market rhetoric. Treasury Secretary John Snow recently urged China's leaders to adopt "a flexible, market-based, exchange rate" for its currency. China currently pegs its currency, the renminbi, at 8.28 to the U.S. dollar. A strong economic case can be made for countries' adopting freely floating exchange rates. The administration's goal, however, is the political one of increasing the value of the renminbi in order to make China's exports less competitive in the United States. In part, administration officials may be responding to congressional initiatives, such as the Senate bill cosponsored by Lindsay Graham (R-SC) and Charles Schumer (D-NY). That bill would impose a 27.5 percent across-the-board tariff on Chinese goods if China does not float its currency within six months of the bill's passage.

The constraints set by the World Trade Organization's rules on placing quotas or tariffs on Chinese imports—exemplified by the ill-fated experience with steel tariffs—leaves the administration the option of trying monetary protectionism to appease U.S. manufacturers. Monetary protectionism occurs when government officials try to obtain a trade or current account objective through monetary manipulation of nominal exchange rates.

The Bush administration wants China to break its long-held currency peg to the U.S. dollar, thereby causing the dollar to fall in nominal value relative to the renminbi and making U.S. goods more competitive with those of China. But such a policy will work only if a real depreciation of the dollar occurs. If Chinese manufacturers were to adjust their prices to reflect the new nominal exchange rate, any real depreciation of the dollar would be short-lived. Nevertheless, monetary protectionism gives the appearance that politicians are doing something for their manufacturing constituents.

The problem is not China's peg to the dollar. Many other countries peg to the dollar, or "dollarize" their economies, but they are not singled out as unfair competitors. Some economists favor floating exchange rates, while others prefer fixed exchange rates. Most agree, however, that either a pure fixed exchange rate system or a pure floating rate system is superior to a system of moving pegs and "dirty floats." A dirty float occurs when a central bank intervenes arbitrarily to alter the exchange rate in pursuit of monetary protectionism.

China has been and should be criticized for its system of capital controls, which impedes the free flow of capital. It is the capital controls that permit Chinese authorities to pursue monetary protectionism. The focus on fixed exchange rates is misplaced.

Hong Kong is a Special Administrative Region of China with its own legal system, customs policy, and currency. The Hong Kong dollar is also tightly linked to the U.S. currency. The Hong Kong Monetary Authority will not permit the Hong Kong dollar to fall below 7.8 to the greenback and, in practice, keeps the upper bound within 1 percent of that figure. No one in the Bush administration has hectored Hong Kong to float its currency.

In contrast to its mother country, Hong Kong has no capital controls. As do goods, money moves freely into and out of the city. Getting rid of capital controls would compel China's monetary authority to deal with market pressures on its currency. Either a new peg or a free float would be adopted.

U.S. protectionists could no longer claim that China's policy of undervaluing its currency provides its exporters with a competitive advantage. At the same time, China's central bank would no longer need to purchase U.S. Treasury obligations in voluminous quantities to maintain its currency peg. Economist David Hale estimates that the monetary authorities of China and Hong Kong purchased nearly $100 billion of U.S. Treasury securities (including mortgage-backed securities) in the last 18 months. That policy props up the value of the U.S. dollar.

Currently, China is in no position to eliminate capital controls. Four large state-owned banks in China have $300 billion to $400 billion of nonperforming loans. Cleaning up those loans would force state-owned enterprises (SOEs) to rationalize and downsize. SOEs, the major borrowers, still employ more than two-thirds of the labor force. The unemployment resulting from their sudden restructuring could lead to social upheaval and a political crisis.

China in crisis is not the Bush administration's goal, so it will not press on the real economic issue. Calling for China to float its currency is political rhetoric to salve U.S. domestic political wounds, not serious international economic policy. Under its WTO accession agreement, China committed to open its financial markets. Overall, China is living up to that agreement. Freer movement of capital will follow. Then China's leaders can decide whether to adopt a new peg or float the currency.

The monetary experience in Hong Kong confirms that a monetary authority can maintain a peg if it forgoes monetary sovereignty. With a peg, changes in the domestic money supply are triggered by change in international reserves. The monetary authority cannot guarantee domestic price stability with such a monetary system. Hong Kong has suffered price deflation for about five years. Because of the economy's flexibility, the dislocations caused by that deflation have been less severe than they would have been in many other countries.

It is doubtful, however, that Mainland China would choose such a system for the long run. Perhaps after one or more revaluations, China will float its currency. The question will then be whether to adopt a free or a dirty float.

An open trading and investment relationship between China and the United States would benefit the citizens of both countries. China's leaders need to move away from protectionism in all forms. President Bush should demonstrate leadership by not advocating further protectionism, including the monetary variety.

Source: Center for Trade Policy Studies. "China: Just Say No to Monetary Protectionism." Available online. URL: http://www.freetrade.org/pubs/FTBs/FTB-006.html. Accessed August 25, 2006.

PART III

Research Tools

6

How to Research Globalization and Free Trade

Globalization is an immensely complex subject. The following research guide is intended to help you begin your research on the topic.

USING THIS BOOK'S RESOURCES

There are a number of resources provided in this book that can help you begin researching globalization and free trade. You can start your research in any one of the categories of materials that are included in this part of the book.

You might want to begin by scanning the list of sources in the Annotated Bibliography. The bibliography lists books, magazine and newspaper articles, and reports and papers on various subjects relating to free trade and globalization. To make it easier for you to navigate this rather long list, the listings are separated into categories, such as poverty, agriculture, the IMF, and so on. If you are interested in a particular topic, find that listing in the Annotated Bibliography. The annotation that accompanies each listing gives you a brief overview of what the material contains and, occasionally, its point of view. If you do not yet know what particular area of globalization might interest you most, begin by looking at the books listed in the general globalization section of the Annotated Bibliography. Most of these books are general introductions to the topic.

Once you have chosen a book to read, you may find that it is an excellent resource for finding additional information. Most of the books contain their own bibliographies and notes that may point you to a source of additional information. So, getting started with just one introductory volume may launch your research into any subtopic related to globalization.

This book also contains a list of Key Players, who are people that have had a significant impact on or are in some way important to the globalization and free trade topics covered in this book. Perhaps one of the people you read about piqued your interest. You might read the short biography of that person in the Key Players section. Then, you can look for books or articles about that person. Before you read an entire book about a person, you might want to look the person up in a reliable reference book. Your library probably has an edition of *Who's Who* or a bibliographic encyclopedia, which are reference books that contain brief biographies of famous or important people.

You should also take a look at the list of Organizations and Agencies contained in this book. A brief description accompanies each organization or agency listed and tells you what type of work the agency does, what aspect of globalization the organization works on, or the organization's or agency's point of view about globalization and free trade. If you see an organization or agency description that interests you, visit its Web site if you have access to the Internet. Many of these organizations and agencies keep extensive archives of documents, studies, and/or news reports on their Web sites, so they are excellent sources of information.

FINDING INFORMATION ON YOUR OWN

How do you find the information you are looking for if your local library does not have the book you selected?

Your local or school library should have some materials on globalization and at least some of its subcategories. Use your library's card catalog or online catalog to find books on the topics you are interested in. In the following sections, you will find a review of how to find and use print as well as online sources of information.

PRINT SOURCES

Library Card Catalogs

If your library uses a card catalog to list the books it owns, you might begin by seeing if there are any books listed under the subject of "globalization." Write down the book's Dewey decimal number and find it on the library shelf. When you find the book, you might want to look at its title, its table of contents, its index, its date of publication, and any information it might give you about the author. This information will help you evaluate the book. It will give you a good idea of what is included in the book, how dated the information is, and the qualifications or background of the author (which might suggest to you any bias the author might have). If a book seems old, look more carefully at its contents and its index. Often, even an older book has solid background information on a topic. Be aware, though, of books that are too old to have the information you need. For example, if you are looking for a book about the WTO, you know that it has to have been written after the WTO was created, in 1995.

If you are looking for a book that is listed in the Annotated Bibliography, you may find the book by searching the card catalog under the book title (but omit *a, an, the,* etc. at the beginning of titles when you search). You can also look for the book under the author's name (last name, first name).

For magazine articles, you may ask your librarian if the library subscribes to the magazine you are looking for. Make sure to tell the librarian the issue date of the magazine to ensure that your library has the particular issue you need. Then find the issue in the library's magazine section.

Biographies are listed under the name of the subject of the biography. You can look up the name in the card catalog (for example, Nixon, Richard), or you can simply peruse the titles in your library's biography book section. The books in this section are organized alphabetically by the last name of the biography's subject. So, you would find a biography about Richard Nixon in the biography section under "N." The books should be labeled "B Nixon."

USING CORRECT KEYWORDS

There is a chance that you might not be able to find any listings in the card catalog under the subject word you searched. If that happens, ask the librarian for help. The librarian has a book that lists the "official" words used to classify different topics. Official keywords, or subject description words, are determined by the U.S. Library of Congress (LOC). Using a standard system of keywords helps librarians around the country categorize their books.

After you have explained to the librarian what you are looking for, he or she will help you find the correct subject words to look for in the card catalog. For example, you might have looked in the card catalog under "A" for "American economy." and found nothing listed. The librarian may then tell you that you can find books on this topic listed in the card catalog under "United States economy" If you could not find any books listed under "G" for "globalization," you might find out that the books you want are listed under "T" for "Trade, international." So, do ask the librarian if you are having trouble locating books on a particular subject.

If your library does not have the book you are interested in, ask the librarian if you can get a book through the library's interlibrary loan system. An interlibrary loan is a book that is sent to your local library from a different library, usually in your local or state library system.

Magazine Articles: Infotrac

Infotrac is a database that you can search to locate magazine and newspaper articles on a particular topic. Infotrac is likely available in your library. If your library has it in book form, ask your librarian how to use it. Other libraries have Infotrac on microfiche. Again, ask your librarian to show you how to use it. Like the card catalog, Infotrac may list articles by official subject names; however, you may also be able to find articles by words that occur in their titles. In this way, Infotrac is more user friendly and less rigid than the LOC system for books. For example, though you probably cannot find books by searching the term *antiglobalization* in the card catalog, you may be able to find articles listed on Infotrac that have this word in their title.

Your Library's Information Online

Many libraries have their own Web sites. If you have access to a computer that can log on to the Internet, type in the library's Web site address in the locator line and click on "Go" or simply press the "Enter" key on your keyboard. The library's Web page will open, and you should see a variety of buttons you can click to allow you to access the library's card catalog and/or its Infotrac database. Many library Web pages also give you access to other databases that provide information such as biographies, literature, and business data. Take time to explore your library's online content. You will probably find that it offers you a wealth of information that you can access easily from any computer.

INFOTRAC ONLINE

Most libraries with a Web page have Infotrac online. Once you have accessed the library Web page, find the link, for Infotrac. Click on the Infotrac link, and you will be taken to the Infotrac Web page (you may have to type in your library card ID number in order to access Infotrac). Once you are on the Infotrac Web page, you can type in a search word in the "Search" space. Infotrac searches its large database of magazines and newspapers to find articles that are related to your search word(s). Infotrac lists these articles by title, author, date, and source. In some cases, you can click on the article title, and a new Web page with the entire article appears. Then you can read the entire article online. Sometimes, though, Infotrac gives you only a citation or an abstract. A citation provides only the author, title, date, and publication of the article, without any text. An abstract provides all of the above plus a very brief description of what is in the complete article.

If the full article you are looking for is not available online, you should find out if your library has a collection of the magazine, journal, or newspaper you need. Then you should make sure that the library's collection includes the dates of the articles you want. For example, you may have found an interesting article listed on Infotrac about globalization and the environment that was published in the journal *Science* in April 2004. Ask the librarian if your library has a collection of the journal *Science.* Then find out if the library has the April 2004 issue of the journal. (Note that some specialty journals are not kept at most local libraries. Sometimes you can find these journals in a nearby college library.)

Most libraries keep older issues of magazines and newspapers on microfiche. Microfiche is a kind of film that has pictures of every page of a magazine or newspaper. You put the film in a special machine that allows you to find the article you are looking for and read it. Most microfiche machines are attached to a print copier. For a small fee, you can print out each page of the magazine or newspaper article you have read.

SEARCHING A LIBRARY'S ONLINE CATALOG

Your local library may no longer have its books listed in a card catalog. Instead, it may have all holdings listed on a computer. Sometimes you must go to the library to search on the computers there. Today, many libraries have a Web site, and you can search the library's holdings from any computer that has an Internet connection.

In many ways, online searching is similar to searching for a book in a card catalog. In the search space, you type in the subject word you are looking for. Here again, if you do not type in an "official" keyword search term, your search may yield no results. Keep trying by searching with other terms. It often helps to search by title if you cannot locate books by subject word. A title search may bring up a listing for a book that is just what you want. Or the Web page that shows the book may also list the subject keywords that the book is listed under. You can then type this subject keyword into the search space to find more books on your selected topic.

Except for persnickety problems with search terms, you use your library's online catalog in the same way as a card catalog. You can search for biographies by typing in the name of the person you want to read about. You can find books by typing in an author's name. You can also find books by typing in the book title, if you know it.

ONLINE SOURCES

This book provides you with an extensive list of Web sites in the Annotated Bibliography and Primary Sources sections, as well as in the section listing Organizations and Agencies. If you have access to the Internet, at home, at school, in the library, or elsewhere, these sites will introduce you to a vast amount of useful information. All the Web sites listed in this book are reputable; that is, the information that you find on them is considered accurate and trustworthy.

The organizations that are listed in this book are often treasure troves of good information about a specific topic, or about globalization in general. Many organizations provide up-to-the-minute news and information on a range of topics relating to globalization. The listings in this book provide you with links to the organization's or agency's Web site, where you can find more information.

If you have access to the Internet, type in the Web site address for one of the organizations or agencies listed in this book. You will be taken to the home page of that organization or agency. On the home page, you will find a description of what the organization or agency does. You may also find the latest news stories that deal with that organization's or agency's area of interest. Most Web sites have links that you can click that will take you to Web pages containing specific types of information. Make sure you read the lists of links on any Web site you visit. They may lead you to other organizations or sources of useful information.

The Web sites listed in the Annotated Bibliography and Primary Sources sections of this book also refer you to addresses on the Internet. The addresses take you to Web sites that contain important primary documents—such as speeches, reports, or text from treaties or agreements—having to do with globalization, free trade, and related topics. When you visit these Web sites, you will probably notice that they link to even more documents or to related sites on the Web that have more information. Read the links on these Web pages to find additional pages that may give you the information you are looking for.

Finding Reliable Information

You can feel confident that any of the Web sites listed in this book are reliable sources of information about globalization and free trade. But what if you want a different type of information or more information on a topic or person not listed? How can you be sure that the information you find on the Internet is reliable?

People use search engines when they are looking for information on the Internet. You use a search engine, such as Google, by typing in a word or phrase about which you are looking for information. Then you usually click a button that says "Find" or "Search." A new Web page opens with a list of Web sites that contain the words you searched for. The listings have titles, a brief description of what is on that Web page, and the Web page address. Read the title and description carefully to make sure that the Web page has the information you want. If it does, or seems to, click on the title or Web site address. That Web page will open. Skim the Web page to see if it contains useful information. If it does not, click on the "Back" button to go back to the search engine listings page. You almost always get several pages of search results, so if you do not find anything that looks promising on the first page of listings, click "Next" at the bottom of the page to see the following page of listed results.

HOW TO SEARCH WITH A SEARCH ENGINE

There are literally billions of Web sites on the Internet. Needless to say, you cannot possibly look at them all to see if they have the information you want. There are some techniques that you can use that will help you get the search results you want, while avoiding Web page listings that are inappropriate.

First, try to be as specific as you can in your search. For example, suppose you are looking for information about free trade and economic growth. If you type the single word *trade* in a search engine's search space, you will very likely get millions of results that you cannot use. You would likely get results that will take you to Web sites that deal with trade in baseball cards, or trade in stocks on Wall Street. This is not what you are looking for. To reduce the number of unwanted search results, your search should be more specific. Instead of typing *trade* in the search space, try typing in *free trade economic growth.* (Notice that you should leave out words like *the, a/an, and, if, with,* etc.) You should get some useful Web site addresses from this search. The more specific your search terms are the better the results. Still, you might get some Web sites that are irrelevant to your search. You might get a Web site that offers free trade in baseball cards for growth in your card collection. To make your search even more on target, you might try to use quotation marks to group words that you want to occur together in the Web site descriptions. So your best search option might be *"free trade" "economic growth."* If you type in these phrases with their quotations marks, you will probably get a good selection of Web sites that have the information you are looking for.

Sometimes, using quotation marks around search words limits too much the number of results you get. Use your best judgment and try searching with and without quotation marks to get the widest selection of results or to reduce the number of irrelevant results you get.

EVALUATING SEARCH RESULTS

Even if you are very specific in your search, you may still get lots of results that you are not sure about. How do you tell the difference between the good Web sites and the not-so-good Web sites?

All Web site addresses have what is called an "extension," which usually consists of three letters. For example, stores and sites that have things for sale have the extension *.com* (dot com). *Com* stands for "commercial," so you know that these Web sites are usually run by commercial enterprises. A typical Web address may be www.buyglobal.com. Sometimes, .com Web sites have useful information. For example, all magazines and newspapers have Web sites with a .com extension. Though they are commercial sites, they still contain useful and reliable information. Some reliable online encyclopedias also have a .com extension. Yet, sometimes .com sites do not have reliable information. It is often best to avoid .com Web sites that are not newspapers or reputable magazines when doing research. You may be fairly confident in using a .com Web site if you found it as a link on another well-known and respected Web site.

For the purposes of research, the most reliable Web sites have the extension *.edu,* which is the extension for educational institutions such as universities, or *.gov,* which is the extension for government agencies. Examples of such Web sites are www.harvard.edu or www.census.gov (the Web sites for Harvard University and the U.S. Bureau of the Census).

Sometimes a .org Web site has excellent information (for example, the many .org Web sites listed in this book under Organizations and Agencies); however, any organization can have a Web site with a *.org* extension. It is always advisable to double-check the information on a .org Web site you are not sure of. If you found the .org Web site via a link from a site you know is reliable, then it is likely that the .org Web site also has reliable information.

It is always recommended that you double-check any information you find online. Even a university Web site may contain an article that expresses the opinion of only one professor. A good way to check the facts you find on any Web site is to find the same facts on a different, reliable Web site, such as a .gov Web site. Another fact-checking strategy is to look up the facts in an encyclopedia, almanac, or other trusted reference book.

Many reliable Web sites that publish articles or data about globalization or free trade have notes attached to the end of the article. The notes are included in the article as superscript (raised) numbers. Notes, like the ones in this book, tell you where the information in the text came from. For example, an article may state that "The U.S. budget deficit has surpassed $8 trillion."[1] The superscript 1 tells you that the source of this information is listed at the end of the article under the number 1. If you look at the end of the article and it reads "1. U.S. Treasury Department Report, 2005," you know that the source of the economic information is reliable and correct.

A NOTE ABOUT STATISTICS

Statistics, numbers that are compiled from studies that purportedly tell you the truth about something, cannot always be trusted. The reason that statistics can be misleading is because they can be manipulated to make them appear to "prove" something they do not really prove. For example, a report may show a graph that indicates how much an economy grew due to its free trade policies. The report may then conclude that free trade is always a benefit to all countries. To accurately interpret the graph, you need to know what country's economic information was used to make the graph. China's economic growth from trade is *very* different from Sierra Leone's. Similarly, a chart that shows that free trade is universally bad should be viewed with skepticism. Always look for the source of statistics to determine if they really do "prove" what the author says they prove. For example, statistics derived from a government study are more reliable than statistics that are cited without any source. In this book, many statistics were taken from United Nations agencies, which have a reputation for not attempting to twist statistics to make them support one point of view or another. Statistics, in a word, are highly vulnerable to bias. Analyze any statistics you come across with a critical eye.

7

Facts and Figures

INTERNATIONAL TRADE

1.1 Multilateral Economic Organizations

GROUP	YEAR ESTABLISHED	MEMBERS, BY ORDER OF ENTRY
European Union (EU)	1957 (as the European Economic Community)	Belgium, France, West Germany, Italy, Luxembourg, Netherlands, Denmark, Ireland, United Kingdom, Greece, Portugal, Spain, reunified Germany, Austria, Finland, Sweden, Cyprus, Czech Republic, Estonia, Hungary, Latvia, Lithuania, Malta, Poland, Slovakia, Slovenia, Bulgaria, Romania
Central American Common Market	1958	El Salvador, Guatemala, Honduras, Nicaragua, Costa Rica
Latin American Free Trade Association	1960	Argentina, Brazil, Chile, Mexico, Paraguay, Peru, Uruguay, Bolivia, Colombia, Ecuador, Venezuela, Cuba
Arab Maghreb Union	1964	Algeria, Libya, Mauritania, Morocco, Tunisia
Association of Southeast Asian Nations (ASEAN)	1967	Indonesia, Malaysia, Philippines, Thailand, Singapore, Brunei, Vietnam, Laos, Myanmar (Burma), Cambodia, Papua New Guinea and East Timor (observer status)
Caribbean Community and Common Market (CARICOM)	1973	Barbados, Guyana, Jamaica, Trinidad and Tobago, Belize, Dominica, Grenada, Montserrat, St. Lucia, St. Vincent and the Grenadines, Antigua and Barbuda, St. Kitts and Nevis, the Bahamas, Suriname, Turks and Caicos, the British Virgin Islands, Anguilla, the Cayman Islands, Bermuda, Haiti

Economic Community of West African States (ECOWAS)	1975	Benin, Burkina Faso, Côte d'Ivoire, Gambia, Ghana, Guinea, Guinea-Bissau, Liberia, Mali, Mauritania (withdrew in 2002), Niger, Nigeria, Senegal, Sierra Leone, Togo, Cape Verde
Southern Common Market (MERCOSUR)	1991	Brazil, Argentina, Uruguay, Paraguay, Venezuela, Bolivia, Chile, Colombia, Ecuador, Peru
Common Market for Eastern and Southern Africa (COMESA)	1994	Angola, Burundi, Comoros, Democratic Republic of the Congo, Djibouti, Ethiopia, Kenya, Lesotho (withdrew in 1997), Madagascar, Malawi, Mauritius, Mozambique (withdrew in 1997), Namibia (withdrew in 2004), Rwanda, Sudan, Swaziland, Tanzania (withdrew in 2000), Uganda, Zambia, Zimbabwe, Eritrea, Egypt, Seychelles, Libya
Group of 20 (G-20)	2003 (WTO: Cancún, Mexico)	Argentina, Bolivia, Brazil, Chile, China, Cuba, Egypt, Guatemala, India, Indonesia, Mexico, Nigeria, Pakistan, Paraguay, Philippines, South Africa, Tanzania, Thailand, Uruguay, Venezuela, Zimbabwe

1.2 World Trade Organization Trade Rounds

ROUND	NUMBER OF PARTICIPANTS	KEY ISSUES/ ACCOMPLISHMENTS
1947	23	Tariff reduction
1949	13	Tariff reduction
1951	37	Tariff reduction
1956	26	Tariff reduction
1960–61: Dillon Round	26	Tariff reduction
1964–67: Kennedy Round	62	Tariff reduction; agreement on antidumping policies
1973–79: Tokyo Round	102	Tariff reduction; elimination of nontariff barriers to trade; framework agreements
1986–94: Uruguay Round	123	Tariff reduction; agreement to eliminate quotas in agriculture; TRIPS, DSB, integration of textiles into the agreements; creation of the WTO
2001–present: Doha Round	146	"Development Round"; agricultural issues, trade in services (GATS), TRIPS; market access; investment; competition; transparency in government; facilitation of trade; WTO rules. Most notable for insoluble conflict over agricultural subsidies by developed nations, an issue threatening to undermine the WTO. Last meeting in Hong Kong in December 2005; sole accomplishment: to agree to meet again.

1.3 Agricultural Subsidies

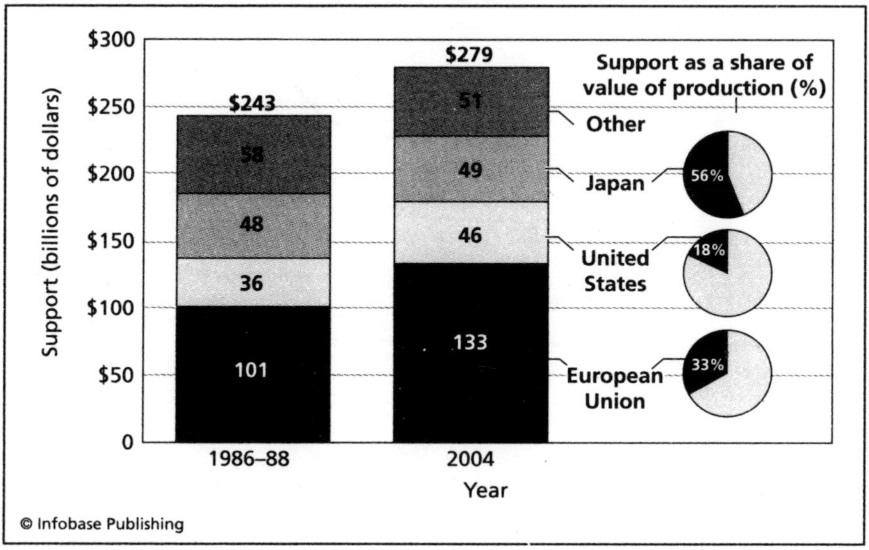

Source: UNCTAD. *Human Development Report 2005,* p. 129. Fig. 4.11, based on OECD, 2005.

1.4 World Exports as a Share of World Total

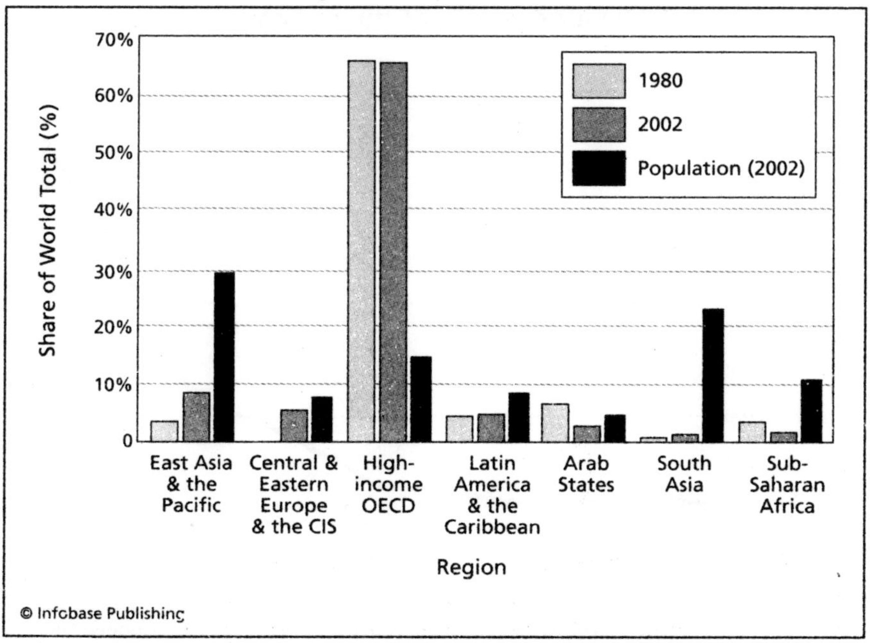

Source: UNCTAD. *Human Development Report 2005,* p. 118. Fig. 4.6. Calculated on the basis of data on exports and population from World Bank, 2005.

1.5 World Exports as a Share of Income

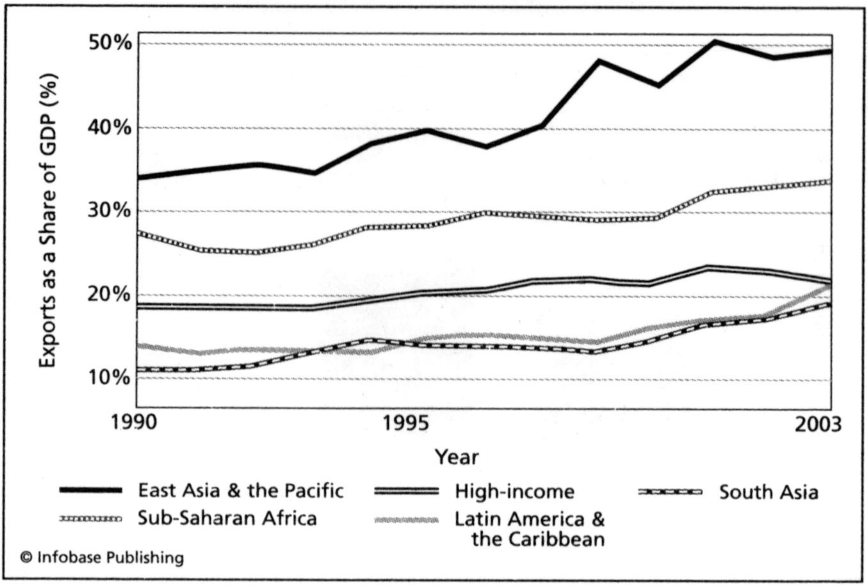

Source: UNCTAD. *Human Development Report 2005,* p. 115. Fig. 4.1. Based on World Bank, 2005.

1.6 Development of China's Economy

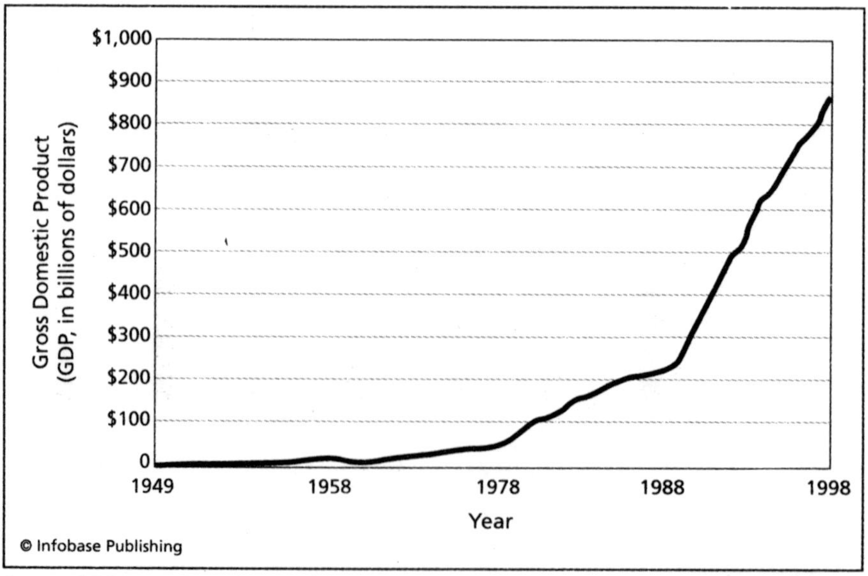

Source: BBC News. Based on World Bank and Carl Riskin, "China's Political Economy," URL: http://news.bbc.co.uk/olmedia/520000/images/_520874_china_gdp_300.gif. Accessed on July 25, 2006.

LEAST DEVELOPED COUNTRIES

2.1 Unsustainable External Debt for Selected Least Developed Countries as Percentage of Exports

COUNTRY	DEBT AS PERCENTAGE OF EXPORTS 1998–2000
Non-Oil Commodity Exporters	
Burundi	985%
Sierra Leone	800%
Democratic Republic of Congo	797%
Tanzania	395%
Ethiopia	343%
Mali	209%
Oil Exporters	
Angola	170%
Manufactures or Services Exporters	
Madagascar	333%
Myanmar	248%
Gambia	217%
Cambodia	158%
Senegal	151%

Source: [United Nations Conference on Trade and Development. *Least Developed Countries Report, 2004, p. 151; World Bank. Global Development Finance,* 2002. Available online. URL: www.unctad.org/Templates/WebFlyer.asp?intItemID=3074&lang=1. Accessed February 10, 2006.

2.2 Poverty in Least Developed Countries Based on Export Specialization: 1981–1983, 1997–1999

	COMMODITY EXPORTER		MANUFACTURE/ SERVICE EXPORTER		ALL LDCS	
	1981–83	*1997–99*	*1981–83*	*1997–99*	*1981–83*	*1997–99*
Number of people living on < $1/day	146,000,000	251,000,000	57,000,000	67,000,000	203,000,000	318,000,000
Number of people living on < $2/day	201,000,000	324,000,000	142,000,000	183,000,000	343,000,000	507,000,000
Percent of total population living on < $1/day	72	79	28	21	100	100
Percent of total population living on < $2/day	59	64	41	36	100	100

Source: United Nations Conference on Trade and Development. *The Least Developed Countries Report, 2004,* p. 125. Available online. URL: www.unctad.org/Templates/WebFlyer.asp?intItemID=3074&lang=1. Accessed February 10, 2006.

2.3 Top 20 Nations with Highest Inflation Rate, 2003

NATION	INFLATION RATE (PERCENT)
Angola	92
Venezuela	37
Gambia	31
Belarus	29
Ghana	29
Dominican Republic	27
Haiti	25
Uzbekistan	24
Romania	23
Nigeria	21
Turkey	21
Zambia	20
Paraguay	18
Uruguay	18
Laos	17
Iran	16
Eritrea	15
Tonga	15
Ethiopia	14
Russia	14

Source: World Bank. *World Development Indicators, 2005,* Section 4, Table 4d. Available online. URL: www.unctad.org/Templates/WebFlyer.asp?intItemID=3074&lang=1. Accessed February 10, 2006.

2.4 Foreign Direct Investment Inflows to Least Developed Countries, by Region, 1995–1999, 2000–2001, 2001–2002

	ANNUAL AVERAGE 1995–99	2000	2001	2002	1995–99	2000–01	2001–02
	(in millions of dollars)				(percentage change)		
Total LDCs	3,570.1	3,427.3	5,628.5	5,231.8	+63.5	+64.2	-7.0
African LDCs*	2,709.7	2,588.5	5,004.3	3,975.3	+83.0	+93.3	-20.6
Asian LDCs	786.0	689.9	612.1	339.7	+7.4	-11.3	-44.5
Pacific & Caribbean LDCs	32.2	20.8	7.7	10.3	-26.8	-63.1	+34.2

* = minus Chad

Source: United Nations Conference on Trade and Development. *The Least Developed Countries Report, 2004,* p. 17. Available online. URL: www.unctad.org/Templates/WebFlyer.asp?intItemID=3074&lang=1. Accessed February 10, 2006.

2.5 Key Economic Trends in Selected Least Developed Countries in the Pre- and Post-Liberalization Periods

COUNTRY	GDP GROWTH (ANNUAL %)		GDP GROWTH PER CAPITA (ANNUAL %)	
	Pre-liberalization	*Post-liberalization*	*Pre-liberalization*	*Post-liberalization*
Benin	0.4	5.1	-2.7	2.3
Gambia	4.3	3.3	1.2	-0.9
Haiti	0.3	1.3	-1.6	-0.8
Togo	3.3	0.2	-0.2	-2.7
Uganda	6.5	5.3	3.3	2.5
Zambia	0.8	1.5	-2.2	-0.8

COUNTRY	EXPORT GROWTH (ANNUAL %)		IMPORT GROWTH (ANNUAL %)	
	Pre-liberalization	*Post-liberalization*	*Pre-liberalization*	*Post-liberalization*
Benin	-11.9	6.8	-9.3	5.0
Gambia	15.6	4.9	-8.8	6.8
Haiti	-0.7	5.6	3.7	4.6
Togo	4.8	-1.1	11.6	-1.0
Uganda	3.6	6.1	5.6	15.4
Zambia	-2.9	3.4	-10.8	-1.7

COUNTRY	FOREIGN AID GROWTH PER CAPITA (ANNUAL %)	
	Pre-liberalization	*Post-liberalization*
Benin	21.3	-6.7
Gambia	-8.2	-6.1
Haiti	6.6	-19.9
Togo	2.8	-25.1
Uganda	29.7	-1.1
Zambia	12.3	3.3

Source: United Nations Conference on Trade and Development. *Least Developed Countries Report, 2004*, p. 196; World Bank. *World Bank Development Indicators, 2003*. Available online. URL: www.unctad.org/Templates/WebFlyer.asp?intItemID=3074&lang=1. Accessed February 10, 2006.

2.6 Imports of Food and Machinery in Selected Least Developed Countries Pre- and Post-Trade Liberalization

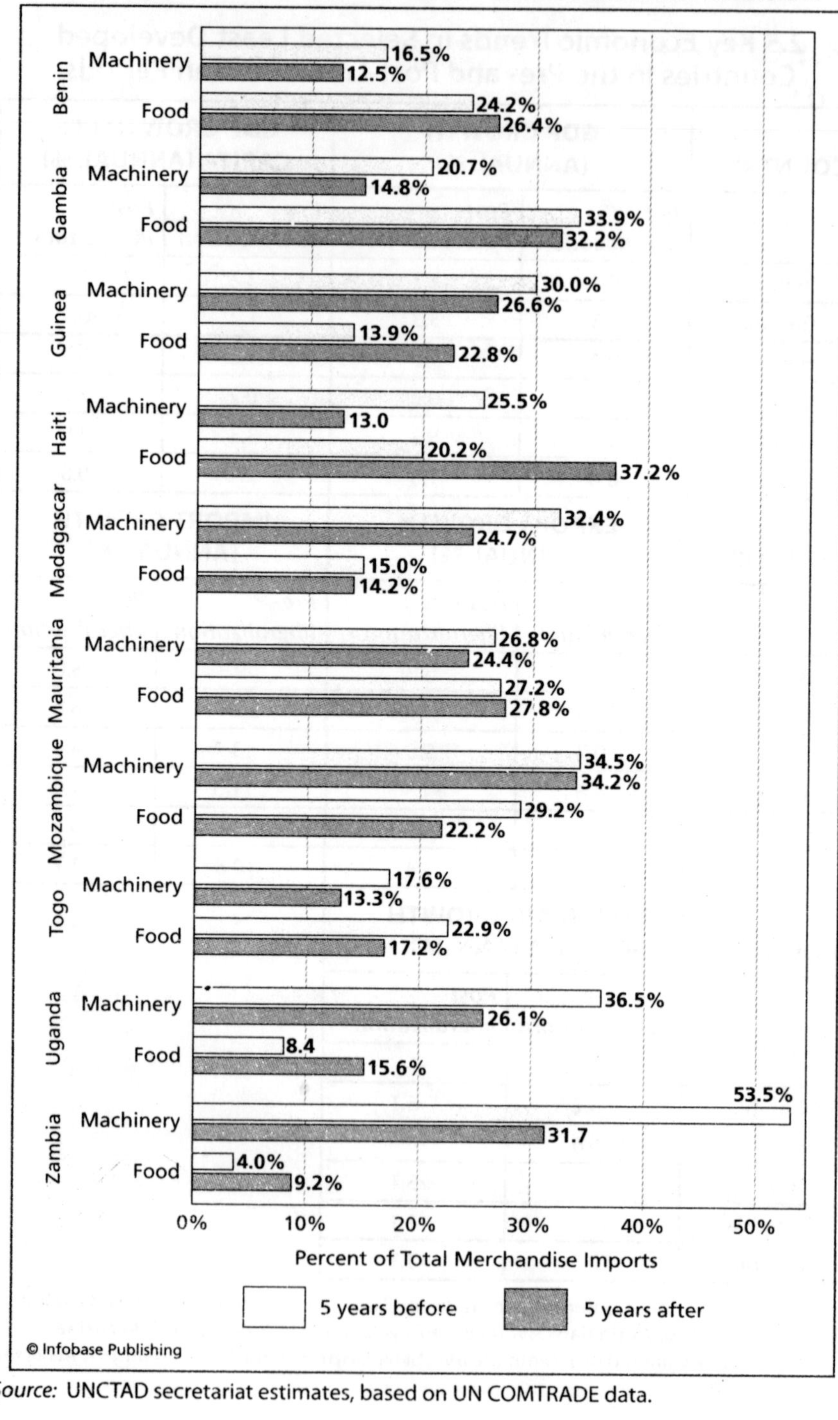

Source: UNCTAD secretariat estimates, based on UN COMTRADE data.

U.S. ECONOMY

3.1 U.S. Government Budget Surpluses and Deficits, 1970–2004 (in Billions of U.S. Dollars)

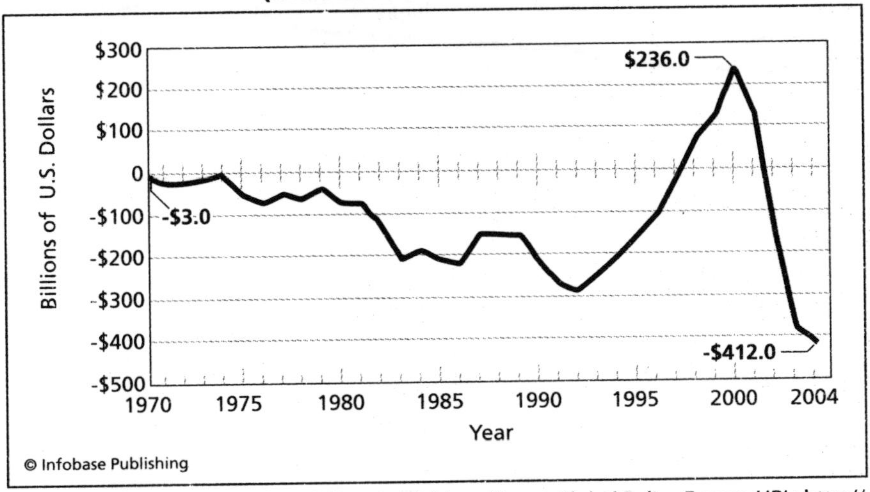

Source: Congresssional Budget Office. Available online at Global Policy Forum. URL: http://www.globalpolicy.org/socecon/crisis/tradedeficit/tables/budgetdeficit.htm. Accessed July 25, 2006.

3.2 U.S. National Debt from 1940 to 2004

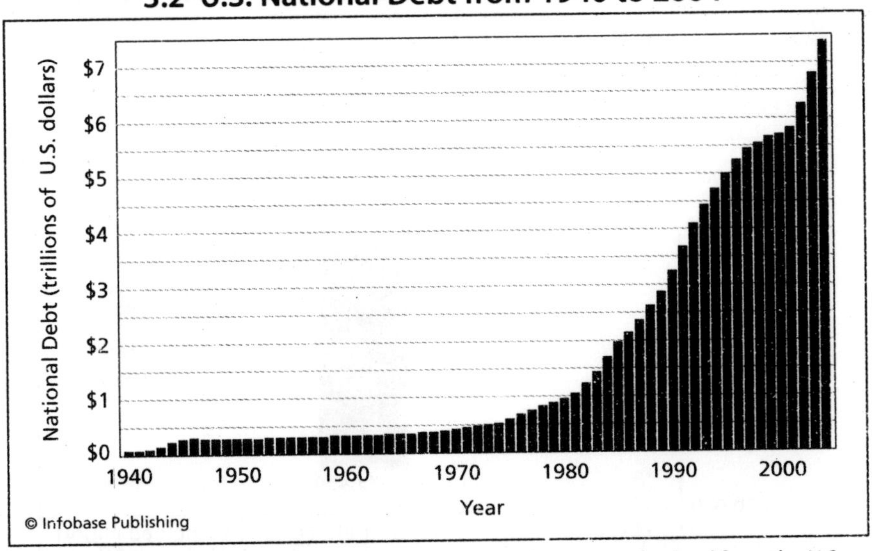

Source: Ed. Hall. "U.S. National Debt Clock." Based on information obtained from the U.S. Department of Treasury dated 21 July 2006. Available online. Chris H. Lewis, Ph.D. "America, the Environment, and the Global Economy." University of Colorado. URL: http://www.colorado.edu/AmStudies/lewis/ecology/history.gif. Accessed on July 25, 2006.

3.3 U.S. International Trade Goods and Services

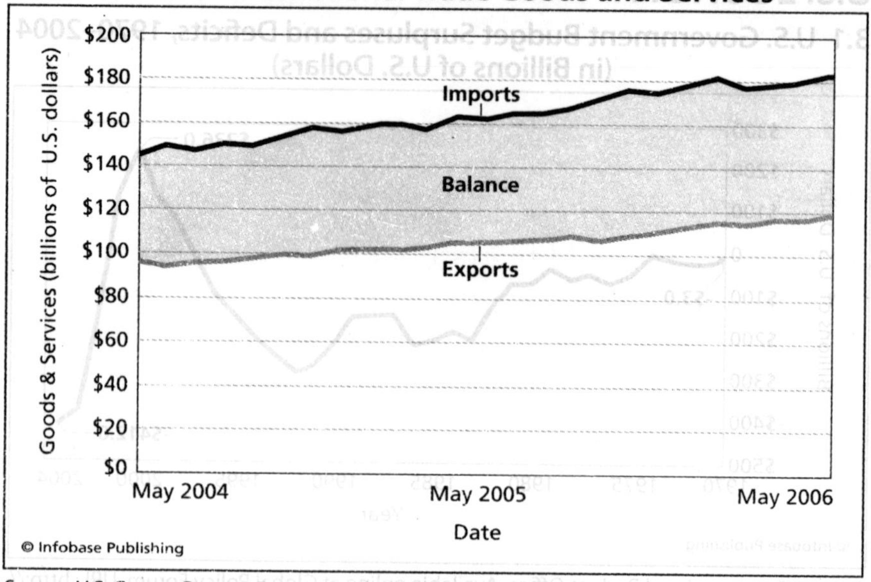

Source: U.S. Census Bureau. Foreign Trade Statistics. URL: http://www.census.gov/indicator/www/ustrade.html. Accessed on July 25, 2006.

3.4 Jobs Gained or Lost Due to U.S. NAFTA Trade, 1993–2002

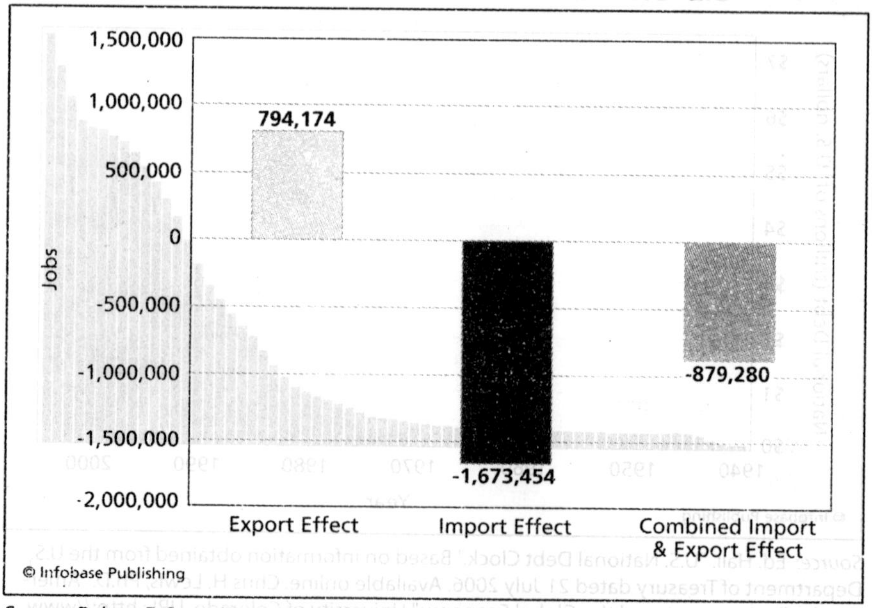

Source: Robert E. Scott. Economic Policy Institute. December 10, 2003. URL: http://www.epinet.org/content.cfm/webfeatures_snapshots_archive_12102003. Accessed on July 25, 2006.

8

Key Players A to Z

BAKER, JAMES A., III (1930–) Born to a wealthy Texas family in 1930, he pursued a long career in business and politics. Baker was secretary of the treasury under President Ronald Reagan and as such was a key proponent of conservative "trickle-down" economic policies. He was instrumental in fashioning the Baker Plan that instituted structural adjustment programs (SAPs), which became an integral part of the IMF's and WB's lending conditionalities. Baker had always had close personal and professional ties to the Bush family, and in 1988, he directed the successful presidential campaign of George H. W. Bush. He was subsequently rewarded for his service by being named secretary of state.

BHAGWATI, JAGDISH (1934–) This renowned economist and proponent of globalization and free markets was born in Bombay, India, in 1934. He is currently professor of economics at Columbia University. He is particularly interested in theories of international trade and has helped formulate GATT and other trade agreements. He is a prolific author, with *Protectionism, Lectures on International Trade,* and *In Defense of Globalization* among his many writings.

BUSH, GEORGE H. W. (1924–) The son of a wealthy and influential family in the Northeast, Bush was born in 1924. His background helped him become a businessman and multimillionaire. Bush was the director of the CIA from 1976 to 1977. He then became vice president under President Ronald Reagan and was elected to the presidency in 1988. Bush was considered to be primarily a foreign policy president, and his insensitivity to domestic issues is thought, by some, to have cost him his reelection. Economically, he was a conservative who publicly supported Reagan's trickle-down economics, though he was reported to have privately criticized these policies. He favored lowering taxes on the wealthy, a balanced U.S. budget, and free trade. Bush negotiated and signed NAFTA shortly before leaving office.

BUSH, GEORGE W. (1946–) The son of George H. W. Bush, he was born in 1946. Like his father, Bush became president of the United States (elected in 2000 and reelected in 2004) and benefited from the wealth and power of the family he was born into. Rich and powerful friends of his father's bankrolled several of his ventures in the oil business, but all his enterprises ultimately failed. However, as an investor in the Texas Rangers baseball club, Bush realized a considerable profit from the club's sale. He then ran for and became governor of Texas. Bush's economic policies are trickle down in the extreme, as he has repeatedly given tax cuts to the wealthiest Americans. His prosecution of the war in Iraq, which began in 2003, led to a national debt of more than $8 trillion. In 2006, Bush got Congress to raise the U.S. debt ceiling to nearly $9 trillion, while at the same time attempting to make the tax cuts for the wealthiest Americans permanent. Many conservative economists seriously question the 43rd president's economic policies, believing that the U.S. debt and trade deficit are spiraling dangerously out of control.

CAMDESSUS, MICHEL (1933–) Camdessus was managing director of the IMF from 1987 to 2000. Prior to that he had served in the French Ministry of Finance and Economic Policies, was a French delegate to the European Economic Community in Brussels, then returned to the Ministry of Finance in 1971. His interest in international finance involved him in the development of the European Monetary System. Between 1978 and 1984, Camdessus chaired the Paris Club, which is charged with rescheduling foreign debt. There he worked closely with the WB and the IMF. As IMF director, he sought to give debtor nations greater access to IMF credits, and he pushed for greater IMF surveillance over debtor nations. A longtime believer in economic liberalization, Camdessus's tenure at the IMF had its controversies, such as increasing the reserves of gold and currency a debtor nation must pledge against debts before loans are granted. Since the late 1990s, Camdessus made some efforts to "humanize" the IMF and international credit banks, asking them to consider the social consequences of the short-term adjustments they require of their debtors.

CHÁVEZ, HUGO (1954–) The son of schoolteachers in a poor community in Venezuela, Chávez entered the Venezuelan military and eventually earned a graduate degree in international relations from Simón Bolívar University. He worked within the system to end corruption in the military. In 1983, Chávez formed a military group called the Bolivarian Revolutionary Movement, which came to prominence in 1992, when Venezuela was riven by riots and strikes. His group attempted a coup, but it failed, and Chávez was jailed for two years. After his release, Chávez organized an alliance of 14 small political parties and, in March 1998, with wide popular support, launched his run for the Venezuelan presidency. He promised that he would create a government that would improve the lives of the millions of poor peasants and workers in his country. In December 1998, Chávez became Venezuela's youngest president, taking more than 56 percent of the vote. True to his word, Chávez implemented programs to channel some of Venezuela's considerable oil wealth to help the poor. He is a strong, vocal opponent of free trade agreements (especially the FTAA), seeing them as means to enrich the corporations of the developed world while exploiting the poor in developing nations. A decline in oil prices pushed Venezuela into recession in 1999, but subsequent increases in oil prices have boosted the nation's economy and helped Chávez implement more of his antipoverty programs.

CLAUSEN, ALDEN WINSHIP (1923–   ) Clausen was born in Illinois in 1923. After earning a law degree, he went to work for the Bank of America, where he became vice president in 1961 and president and CEO in 1970. He has been the chairman of the bank's Executive Committee since 1990. In 1981, Clausen was named president of the WB, where he enthusiastically implemented the policies of the Washington Consensus. He remained WB president until 1986, when he returned to the Bank of America.

CLINTON, WILLIAM (BILL) JEFFERSON (1946–   ) Born in 1946 in Arkansas, Clinton was a Rhodes scholar and earned a law degree, becoming Arkansas attorney general in 1976. He was governor of Arkansas from 1982 to 1992, when he ran for president and was elected. His campaign capitalized on the economic discontent in the country ("it's the economy, stupid") at that time to appeal to voters. Clinton served two terms as president. During his presidency, Clinton supported globalization policies, getting Congress to ratify NAFTA. Although the economy boomed during the 1990s and Clinton balanced the budget and actually turned the national debt into a national surplus, the U.S. trade deficit began to balloon during this time, due largely to increasing imports from China.

DENG XIAOPING (1904–1997) Deng was born in Sichuan, China, in 1937. He was a member of the Communist army, which fought with the Nationalists to oust Japan from China and then fought the Nationalists to wrest control of the country from them. Deng was a powerful force in the Chinese Communist government, becoming its finance minister in 1952. He continued to rise in the party and eventually became secretary general. Though early on he had been a supporter of Mao Zedong, after the disasters of the Great Leap Forward, Deng became disillusioned with official economic policies. During the upheavals of the Cultural Revolution (1962–65), Deng was denounced and spent two years working in a tractor factory. Later, the Cultural Revolution itself was denounced, and Deng regained his stature in the party. As China's leader, Deng implemented economic reforms in the 1970s to open China to global trade. His astute and measured policies of incorporating market changes into existing economic structures made China's transition not only relatively painless but ultimately hugely successful. Today, China has a huge trade surplus from its global trade, and its GDP growth of about 10 percent annually has put it on track to become the world's largest economy. Deng, who died in 1997, was largely responsible for this success.

FRIEDMAN, MILTON (1912–2006) A noted economist and Nobel Prize winner in economics (1976), Friedman advocates what is called the "monetarist" school of economics, which is based on the principle that the supply of money and interest rates have greater influence on a nation's economy than government fiscal policy does. A conservative, Friedman opposes the economic principles propounded by John Maynard Keynes and supports neoliberal laissez-faire free trade economics and globalization.

FRIEDMAN, THOMAS (1953–) A well-known writer of books on globalization, he is also a regular columnist for the *New York Times*. Through his books, including *The Lexus and the Olive Tree* and *The World Is Flat*, Friedman has argued that globalization is inevitable, and he has had a significant impact on the public perception of globalization, promoting the benefits of globalization and liberal free trade.

GORBACHEV, MIKHAIL S. (1931–) The last president of the Soviet Union, Gorbachev oversaw the demise of the communist bloc in the USSR and Eastern Europe. Though he had always been a member of the Communist Party, when he came to power in 1985, Gorbachev recognized the shortcomings of the communist system. He instituted a number of reforms, including glasnost (openness) and perestroika (restructuring). The latter reform eased the state's control over the economy and began to promote entrepreneurship and private ownership as a boost to the economy. The corruption of the Soviet economy was revealed, and many Russians were bitter about losing their far-reaching empire, as former Soviet satellite nations one by one declared their independence. The process culminated in 1989 with the fall of the Berlin Wall, which had separated communist East Berlin from democratic West Berlin. In 1990, Gorbachev was awarded the Nobel Peace Prize.

HAYEK, FRIEDICH A. VON. (1899–1992) Born in Vienna, Austria, von Hayek was a fierce defender of liberal democracy who believed that socialism, or any type of central planning, led invariably to totalitarianism. He believed that the "free price" system arose as a type of spontaneous order and that civilization arose from private property. His work in economics addressed the value of money and described his new theory of the business cycle, which he explained, arose out of central bank policies. Hayek became a British citizen after the Nazis annexed Austria. In the 1930s, his economic theories gained credence and, in 1950, he became a professor at the University of Chicago. Hayek's lifelong critique of collectivism and his belief in the noninterference of government in the economy made him a leading light among economic conservatives and neoliberals. In 1974, Hayek received the Nobel Prize in economics.

KEYNES, JOHN MAYNARD (1883–1946) Keynes is considered to be one of the world's greatest economic theorists. Often called a genius, Keynes is credited with formulating policies that helped lift the United States and Europe out of the Great Depression. In his masterwork, *The General Theory of Employment, Interest, and Money* (1936), Keynes set out his concept that the Great Depression was not caused by overproduction, as was then believed, but by inequalities in the distribution of money and thus of goods. Keynes offered several solutions to this problem, most relating to increasing employment. Keynes supported free-market capitalism, but he also believed that government actions and policies were necessary to moderate the negative effects of unfettered laissez-faire capitalism. Keynes was present at the Bretton Woods conference and was a key figure in establishing the economic policies adopted and the global economic institutions formed at Bretton Woods.

KRUEGER, ANNE O. (1934–) Krueger has been the first deputy minister of the IMF since September 1, 2001. A graduate of Stanford University in economics, Krueger was a senior fellow at the Hoover Institution and the vice president for economics and research at the WB from 1982 to 1986. She is a staunch defender of the IMF's liberalization policies.

KRUGMAN, PAUL (1953–) Krugman is a well-known and influential economist and an engrossing, witty writer on economic issues. His best-known venue is the editorial page of the *New York Times.* He is a specialist in international economics, or macroeconomics, and has written both favorably and critically about various aspects of globalization. Generally, Krugman has opposed the view that nations are like corporations that compete with one another and has supported the idea that controls are needed to rein in the worst excesses of speculative capital investments. He is the author of several books, including *Pop Internationalism* and *Market Structure and Foreign Trade.*

LULA DA SILVA, LUIZ INÁCIO *See* SILVA, LUIZ INÁCIO LULA DA

MARX, KARL (1818–1883) Marx, a German philosopher and economist, founded modern, so-called scientific, socialism, which sparked communist movements and revolutions in many parts of the world. In his most famous work, *Das Kapital,* Marx set forth his materialistic view of history and society. He argued that history is a continual process whose events are predetermined by the economic institutions that arise at regular, predictable periods in a society's development. Thus, Marx asserted that capitalism was the next-to-last stage of historical development. Capitalism would be followed by an uprising by exploited workers—the proletariat—who would overthrow the old system and institute a government and society run by and for workers—pure communism—in which everything is shared and equally distributed among all citizens.

McNAMARA, ROBERT S. (1916–) McNamara earned an MBA from Harvard Business School in 1939 and after World War II, was a successful businessman, becoming the financial officer of Ford Motor Company in 1949 and rising to chief executive (1960) and then president. In 1961, McNamara joined the administration of John F. Kennedy as secretary of defense, a post he held during most of Lyndon B. Johnson's administration, too. In 1968, Johnson named McNamara as head of the WB, where he continued until 1981. Under his leadership, the Bank became the most significant international development and lending institution in the world, lending about $12 million a day to developing countries and overseeing more than 1,600 projects, valued at about $100 billion, in more than 100 developing countries. As WB president, McNamara stressed poverty eradication as the Bank's most important mission. Out of step with neoliberal economics, McNamara left the Bank when the Washington Consensus became ascendant in the early 1980s.

MORALES, EVO (1959–) Morales was born to an indigenous Aymara family in Bolivia, who were miners in the highlands. Later, they moved to lower altitudes where they farmed the land. By the 1990s, they, like most other lowland farmers, began growing coca as the most profitable crop. President Hugo Banzer's banning of coca growing in the mid-1990s left many farmers with little or no income. Morales began organizing the coca growers, and in 1997, he was elected by his district to the Bolivian legislature. In 2002, Morales became a candidate for the Bolivian presidency. He was elected and became Bolivia's first indigenous president. Morales, like other left-wing, antipoverty Latin American leaders recently elected to their nation's highest office, opposes globalization and the FTAA. Morales has agreed to help restrict illegal coca (cocaine) trafficking to the United States, but he supports the growing of this traditional crop for domestic use.

MORGENTHAU, HENRY, JR. (1891–1969) Named secretary of the treasury by President Franklin D. Roosevelt in January 1934, Morgenthau helped Roosevelt stabilize the price of gold and managed the international exchange rate of the dollar in order to prop up the value of the federal bonds that helped fund New Deal programs. Though he supported most of Roosevelt's policies,

Morgenthau was critical of Keynesian economics and, at first, opposed much of the federal spending that funded the New Deal. Morgenthau thought that a balanced budget would have lifted the Great Depression without huge government expenditures. Viewed as a conservative, he was a an important architect of the economic policies that came out of the Bretton Woods conference, although he sometimes clashed with John Maynard Keynes and attempted to water down Keynes's influence on the conference outcome.

NIXON, RICHARD M. (1913–1994) Born and educated in California, Nixon was elected to the House of Representatives in 1947 and four years later, to the Senate. In Congress, he gained prominence for his role on the House Un-American Activities Committee. He was also notorious for the vicious smear campaigns he used against his political opponents. In 1952, he became vice president on the Republican ticket with Dwight D. Eisenhower. In 1960, he lost his bid for the presidency to John F. Kennedy, but was successful in 1968. Nixon intensified the war in Vietnam, running up huge budget deficits and increasing domestic inflation. In 1971, he devalued the U.S. dollar and delinked it from the gold standard. The pressure he exerted on other developed countries led to a total abandonment of the gold standard and to an acceptance of floating exchange rates. Despite these measures, the national debt and the rate of inflation continued to rise. Nixon resigned his presidency in August 1974 as a result of the Watergate scandal.

POLANYI, KARL (1886–1964) Born in Vienna, Austria, this Hungarian economist and historian believed that laissez-faire capitalism was merely one passing phase in the evolution of the world economy. After fleeing fascism, Polanyi taught at Oxford University in England. He was particularly interested in how different economic structures arise out of and change, for better or worse, the societies that adopt them. Polanyi thought that economists who insisted that this laissez-faire world would continue in perpetuity in more or less the same form were misguided. Polanyi thought that the rise of markets was not, as many today believe, a natural or inevitable occurrence but that it required deliberate political intervention to bring it about. He was especially interested in nonmarket economies, such as those that existed for millennia in traditional societies, as well as in removing the obstacles to world peace. In 1944, Polanyi wrote his seminal *The Great Transformation,* which analyzed the effects on traditional British society of the adoption of laissez-faire capitalism in the second half of the 19th century.

PREBISCH, RAUL (1901–1986) A renowned Argentine economist, Prebisch studied and taught at the University of Buenos Aires. As a young man, Prebisch embraced the ideas of John Maynard Keynes, but the decline in the Argentine economy during and after the 1930s caused Prebisch to reevaluate his beliefs. Prebisch was greatly influenced by David Ricardo's work, but he took it a step further. Prebisch analyzed the power structure that underlay comparative advantage and found and then elucidated the metropole-core and periphery structure that often underpins global trade. Prebisch pointed out the commodity dependency of periphery nations and showed the negative effects this dependency has on nonindustrial economies. He also showed how the importation into nonindustrial countries of value-added manufactured goods prevents these nations from developing economically. Prebisch was named director of the Economic Commission for Latin America in 1948. During this time, Prebisch became a proponent of import substitution industrialization (ISI), which encourages developing nations to resist trade and to industrialize their economies via their domestic markets. In 1964, Prebisch became the first secretary general of UNCTAD, where he supported trade pacts that included preferential treatment for developing and poor nations. The UN bureaucracy and slow or nonexistent progress did not suit Prebisch, and he resigned his post in 1969. For the rest of his life, Prebisch criticized neoclassical economics as inimical to economic growth in poor nations.

RATO Y FIGAREDO, RODRIGO DE (1949–) De Rato became the managing director of the IMF in June 2004. Previously, he had been Spain's vice president for economic affairs and minister of economy. He was also on the boards of the WB, the IMF, the European Investment Bank, and the European Bank for Reconstruction and Development.

REAGAN, RONALD (1911–2004) Reagan was a famous film actor before entering politics, first as governor of California. As president from 1981 to 1989, he supported trickle-down, or supply-side, economics, in which tax cuts that benefit the wealthy, who supposedly invest them and create jobs, are believed to eventually benefit all. Supply-side economics led to large budget deficits and an increasing wealth gap during the Reagan administration. Reagan was a neoliberal who supported untrammeled free trade and the shrinking of government and concomitant reduction in regulation and oversight.

REICH, ROBERT (1946–) Reich spent time as a Rhodes scholar at Oxford University, in England, with fellow student Bill Clinton. Later, Reich was to serve as President Clinton's secretary of labor. In the 1970s, Reich was on the Federal Trade Commission as director of policy planning and, by age 30, became the director. He taught at Harvard's Kennedy School of Government during the Reagan years. Reich is a believer in the free market and was quick to recognize the role multinational corporations play in the global economy. He understood that they would naturally move jobs and capital to those areas or nations that provided them with the best-trained and best-educated workforce and the best business environment in terms of communications, transportation, and other aspects of infrastructure. He therefore supports government support for education, training, and infrastructure improvements to attract and retain high-paying corporate jobs.

RICARDO, DAVID (1772–1823) Ricardo was an English stockbroker who became an influential economic thinker at the dawn of the Industrial Revolution. He is considered by many to be the father of scientific economics because he was the first economist to use mathematics and abstract reasoning to make his arguments. Ricardo's view of economics was generally quite pessimistic. He saw capitalism as a tripartite conflict among capitalists (industrialists), workers, and landlords (aristocrats). Ricardo believed that in the long run, capitalists and workers would inevitably lose to the more powerful aristocratic landowners, who would swallow all the profits by continually raising rents. More pertinent to the issue of globalization, Ricardo set forth the concept of "comparative advantage," which states that certain places have definite advantages over other places for the production of a good. For example, tropical areas have a comparative advantage in the production and export of bananas, and the British Isles have a comparative advantage in the production of sheep and wool. Ricardo showed that it would be economic folly for an Englishman to try to grow bananas in Yorkshire or for a wool industry to struggle for existence in the Caribbean. Each place should produce goods suited to its environment, as this confers an advantage in terms of efficiency that cannot be realized otherwise, and they should trade with other nations for goods in which they do not have a comparative advantage.

ROOSEVELT, FRANKLIN DELANO (1882–1945) Born into a rich, powerful, and political family, Roosevelt was President Woodrow Wilson's secretary of the navy and then was elected governor of New York State in 1928. He was sworn in as the 32nd president of the United States in 1933, faced with a nation suffering through the Great Depression. On March 9, 1933, Roosevelt convened a special session of Congress, which lasted 100 days, in order to hammer out a program for national economic recovery. This special congressional session passed more significant legislation than any other U.S. Congress in history. What emerged were the laws that became the New Deal. Roosevelt used his radio broadcasts ("fireside chats") to convince a desperate but still skeptical public that strong intervention by the federal government would bring relief The New Deal gave jobs to the unemployed and took the first steps toward a guaranteed minimum wage. It provided assistance to farmers and mortgage protection to homeowners. Roosevelt also enacted the Social Security Act to provide pensions to the elderly. Roosevelt devalued the dollar to enable debtors to repay loans. He regulated the U.S. banking system to prevent bank failures and restore public trust in them. The Roosevelt administration showed how strong, targeted government intervention and control can turn around economic collapse.

RUBIN, ROBERT (1938–) Rubin was President Bill Clinton's secretary of the treasury from 1995 to 1999. He then went on to chair the Executive Committee at Citigroup, one of the world's largest and most powerful financial institutions. Rubin's policies helped foster the prosperity many Americans experienced during the Clinton administration. He favors liberalized trade policies, such as NAFTA.

SALINAS DE GORTARI, CARLOS (1948–) Salinas was president of Mexico from 1988 to 1994 and leader of the Institutional Revolutionary Party, or PRI, then the most powerful (some would say only) political party in Mexico at the time. Salinas began his presidential career as a conservative who was skeptical of the forces of laissez-faire economics and unrestricted free trade. After the collapse of the Soviet Union in 1989, Salinas began to look more favorably on the free market, though he still professed opposition to liberalized trade agreements. Then, in 1990, Salinas shocked his nation by opening negotiations with the United States to formulate a trade agreement, which became the foundation of NAFTA. The economic windfall Salinas promised his constituents never materialized; by 1993, more than 70 percent of Mexicans did not earn enough to buy the food they needed. In 1994, Mexico suffered a foreign debt crisis.

SAMUELSON, PAUL (1915–) Samuelson earned graduate degrees at Harvard University and then taught at the Massachusetts Institute of Technology. He wrote extensively on economic theory, emphasizing mathematical approaches to economics. He has written textbooks and technical books on scientific economics, making him one of the best-known economists of his age. Samuelson was president of the Econometrics Society (1951) and later economic adviser to Presidents John F. Kennedy and Lyndon B. Johnson. His criticism of President Richard Nixon's economic policies landed him on the executive "enemies list." This in no way tarnished his reputation as one of the nation's leading economists.

SCHUMPETER, JOSEPH A. (1883–1950) A 20th-century Austrian economist and academic, he advanced abstract mathematical, or "pure," economic theories and wrote books for experts as well as the public on economic theory. Schumpeter's work elucidated the theory behind business cycles, entrepreneurship, and the development of capitalism.

SHIVA, VANDANA (1952–) Shiva is a trained physicist, though she has spent the better part of her career deeply engaged in issues of globalization and its effects on the poor, particularly farmers and especially farmers in India.

She has written numerous books, including *Biopiracy: The Plunder of Nature and Knowledge* and *Stolen Harvest*, both of which critique corporations' patenting of genes. She also lectures widely on the devastating effects that corporate globalization of agriculture has had on the world's farmers, both subsistence farmers in developing countries and family farmers in the West. Shiva has established the Navdanya movement in her native India to fight for farmers' rights and to preserve India's agricultural biodiversity.

SILVA, LUIZ INÁCIO LULA DA (1945–) Born to an impoverished rural family, Lula, as he is known, became an advocate for workers, helping found the Workers Party in 1980. His runs for the Brazilian presidency as a left-wing candidate in 1989, 1994, and 1998 were unsuccessful. Yet, by the early years of the new century, Brazilians were more attuned to Lula's ideas about Western exploitation and the negative effects of globalization on developing countries. In November 2002, Lula ran for president again and won with 61 percent of the popular vote. Though highly skeptical of the policies of globalization and the FTAA, Lula is attempting to lead his nation along a middle path that balances workers' rights and the eradication of poverty with industrial development and sound fiscal policy.

SMITH, ADAM (1723–1790) Smith was a Scottish philosopher and writer who penned the "bible of capitalism," *The Wealth of Nations*. Published in 1776, the book attempted to depict the ideal conditions under which capitalism best functioned. Smith envisioned a system of "perfect liberty" in which small businesses engaged in perfect competition under perfect circumstances. Smith believed that the laws that drove the free market were based solely on the individual's drive to fulfill his or her self-interest within the context of similar-minded individuals who competed to satisfy their interests. Smith stated that if left to their own devices (laissez-faire), these market forces would provide the goods that consumers want, in the amounts they want them, and at the price they were willing to pay for them. Smith called this perfectly functioning, self-correcting system of self-interest the "invisible hand" of the market. Any external interference with this perfect system would invariably cause economic disruption. When Smith wrote, however, it was of small businesses; he did not envision the role that large corporations play in today's economy. Though Smith is often considered a zealous laissez-faire economist, he wrote: "No society can surely be flourishing and happy if the greater part of the [people] are poor and miserable."

STIGLITZ, JOSEPH (1943–) In 1991, Stiglitz won the Nobel Prize in economics; he currently teaches at Columbia University. Stiglitz showed why Adam Smith's ideal free market never works, optimally because it never happens that all the players (individuals) involved in the market have equal access to the same information (equal access to information is one of the foundations of Smith's ideal laissez-faire economy). In 1993, Stiglitz left academia to join President Bill Clinton's Council of Economic Advisers. From there, he went to the WB, where he was chief economist and senior vice president. Despite his very "official" status, Stiglitz took every opportunity to write or lecture about how, in his opinion, the IMF's economic policies were misguided and harmful. In 2000, his boss, James Wolfensohn, told him to stop his criticism. Stiglitz quit. Since then he has been an even more outspoken critic of what he views as the IMF's ruinous and rigid economic policies. His best-selling book *Globalization and Its Discontents* clearly sets forth his position.

THATCHER, MARGARET HILDA (1925–) Thatcher was the Conservative prime minister of Britain from 1979 to 1990, and the first woman to hold this position in the United Kingdom. With Ronald Reagan, Thatcher supported trickle-down, or supply-side, economics. A fierce proponent of individualism, Thatcher dismantled or gravely underfunded numerous social programs in the areas of public housing, health care, and education. She privatized services that had previously been under state control or regulation, such as public utilities and airlines; she also sought to privatize the public health service to the greatest degree possible. Her proposal to introduce a poll tax in 1988 led to her downfall and loss of office.

WEBER, MAX (1864–1920) Weber is considered to be the father of modern sociology. He was a social scientist who studied the rise and characteristics of civilizations. His most famous work, *The Protestant Ethic and the Spirit of Capitalism,* showed how the Calvinist work ethic informs and supports the tenets of capitalism. Weber explained how rationalism and an emphasis on the work one did in this world led to the great improvements in the standard of living, and therefore in society, that came about as a result of the Industrial Revolution. Weber argued that this constituted a step forward for Western civilization, though he bemoaned the lack of ethics in the cutthroat capitalism he found in the United States at that time.

WHITE, HARRY DEXTER (1892–1948) Dexter was an American economist and key developer, with John Maynard Keynes, of the IMF and WB. As a major U.S. negotiator at the Bretton Woods meeting, White had enormous influence on the agreements and institutions that arose from the conference. White's economic philosophy was in tune with those of Keynes and with President Franklin D. Roosevelt's New Deal. In August 1948, White was called before Joseph McCarthy's House Un-American Activities Committee and charged with being a Soviet spy. White passionately denied the charges and died of a heart attack three days later. (New evidence indicates that White may have had some shady dealings with the USSR.)

WILLIAMSON, JOHN (1937–) Williamson is most famous as the writer who coined the name of the Washington Consensus and wrote in support of it. As an economist, Williamson has been a senior fellow at the Institute for International Economics since 1981. Between 1996 and 1999, he was chief economist for South Asia at the WB.

WOLFENSOHN, JAMES (1933–) Wolfensohn spent many years climbing the ladder of the banking industry, eventually owning his own investment banking firm. His success was rewarded in 1995 when he was named president of the WB. The Bank was struggling then, and Wolfensohn is credited with restructuring it and making it more efficient and effective. Wolfensohn worked to change the Bank's emphasis from that of funding huge infrastructural projects, such as dams, to supporting smaller projects with more direct social and environmental benefits.

WOLFOWITZ, PAUL (1943–) As a young man, Wolfowitz supported President John F. Kennedy and marched for civil rights with Martin Luther King, Jr. His time as a graduate student at the University of Chicago quickly and radically changed his worldview. He became a Republican and campaigned for Ronald Reagan in 1981. Ever since, he has used his keen intellect to further what have become known as neoconservative, or neoliberal, policies. His reputation as a neoliberal strategist grew, and in 2001, President George W. Bush named him deputy secretary of defense, in which post Wolfowitz had great influence on U.S. foreign policy. In 2005, President Bush nominated Wolfowitz to be president of the WB, where he promotes his neoliberal policies in the realm of global economics.

YELTSIN, BORIS NIKOLAYEVITCH (1931–) Born in 1931 in a poor town in rural Siberia, Yeltsin, though working class, went to university and earned a degree in engineering. Yeltsin rose through the ranks of the Soviet Communist Party, at first working closely with and supporting Mikhail Gorbachev. After Gorbachev's fall, in 1991, Yeltsin was elected president of Russia. He initiated the "shock therapy" that he believed would propel Russia into the newly global capitalist marketplace. Corruption within the government (and allegedly his family, as well) made rapid privatization of the Russian economy a disaster, leaving much of the economy in the hands of oligarchs and organized crime, while the vast majority of Russians suffered severe privation. To quell opposition to his policies, in 1993, Yeltsin dissolved the Duma, the Russian parliament. He became increasingly viewed as antidemocratic, although with the help of oligarch money, he was re-elected to the presidency in 1986. His health—and his support—deteriorated. Yeltsin left the Russian economy in a shambles, when he was succeeded in 1999 by Vladimir Putin as president.

9

Organizations and Agencies

A wide variety of information is available from the following organizations, including statistical data on globalization as it relates to regions around the world, reports on globalization activities, and links to globalization-related issues such as sustainability, freshwater, toxics, scientific studies, conservation, and policy assistance.

Africa Action
URL: http://www.africaaction.org/index.php
1634 I Street NW, #810
Washington, DC 20006
Phone: (202) 546-7961
E-mail: africaaction@ige.org

Africa Action is the oldest organization in the United States working on African affairs. Its mission is to change United States–Africa relations to promote political, economic, and social justice in Africa. It provides accessible information and analysis and mobilizes popular support for campaigns to achieve this mission.

African Development Bank
URL: http://www.afdb.org
Rue Joseph Anoma
01 BP 1387 Abidjan 01
Côte d'Ivoire
Phone: (225) 20-20-44-44
E-mail: afdb@afdb.org

The African Development Bank is the premier financial development institution of Africa, dedicated to combating poverty and improving the lives of people of the continent and engaged in the task of mobilizing resources toward the economic and social progress of its regional member countries. The bank's mission is to promote economic and social development through loans, equity investments, and technical assistance.

African Economic Research Consortium (AERC)
URL: http://www.aercafrica.org
Middle East Bank Towers Building
Third Floor
Milimani Road
PO Box 62882
00200 Nairobi, Kenya
Phone: (254-20) 273-4150
E-mail: exec.dir@aercafrica.org

The African Economic Research Consortium's principal objective is to streghthen local capacity for conducting independent and rigorous inquiry into the problems faced by the nations of sub-Saharan Africa.

Alternative Information and Development Centre (AIDC)
URL: http://www.aidc.org.za
PO Box 129 43
Mowbray 7705
Cape Town, South Africa
Phone: (27-21) 447-57-70
E-mail: info@aidc.org.za

AIDC aims to contribute to the development of national, regional, and international challenges to the currently dominant global economic system through research, information production and dissemination, popular education, campaigning, and coalition building. Through the empowerment and mobilization of progressive organizations and popular social movements, AIDC further aims to contribute to the development of alternatives that ensure fundamental socioeconomic transformation.

Asian Development Bank
URL: http://www.adb.org
PO Box 789
0980 Manila, Philippines
Phone: (632) 632-4444
E-mail: information@adb.org

The Asian Development Bank, composed of 66 regional member nations, aims to improve the welfare of Asian people living on less than $2 a day. The bank provides loans, technical assistance, grants, and investments to help member nations alleviate poverty.

Association for Sustainable Human Development (ASHD)
URL: http://users.freenet.am/~ashd/
33 Khanjyan Street, ap. 18,
Yerevan, Republic of Armenia 375010
Phone: (374-1) 522-327
E-mail: ashd@freenet.am

The mission of ASHD is to propagandize and spread the main ideas, principles, and values system of the Sustainable Human Development Concept, as well as the activities of UN structures in this sphere, and to assist in the elaboration and putting into practice of the concept and the program of sustainable development of Armenia.

Association for Women's Rights in Development (AWID)
URL: http://www.awid.org
215 Spadina Avenue, Suite 150
Toronto, Ontario MST 2C7
Canada
Phone: (416) 594-3773
E-mail: awid@awid.org

AWID's mission is to connect, inform, and mobilize people and organizations committed to achieving gender equality, sustainable development, and women's human rights.

Association of Southeast Asian Nations (ASEAN)
URL: http://www.aseansec.org
ASEAN Secretariat
70A, Jalan Sisingamangaraja
Jakarta 12110
Indonesia
Phone: (6221) 7262991 or 7243372
E-mail: public@aseansec.org

The ASEAN Declaration states that the aims and purposes of the association are (1) to accelerate the economic growth, social progress, and cultural development in the region through joint endeavors in the spirit of equality and partnership in order to strengthen the foundation for a prosperous and peaceful community of Southeast Asian nations and (2) to promote regional peace and stability through abiding respect for justice and the rule of law in the relationship among countries in the region and adherence to the principles of the United Nations Charter.

Bank Information Center (BIC) USA
URL: http://www.bicusa.org/bicusa/index.php
1100 H Street NW, Suite 650
Washington, DC 20005
Phone: (202) 737-7752
E-mail: info@bicusa.org

BIC partners with civil society in developing and transition countries to influence the WB and other international financial institutions to promote social and economic justice and ecological sustainability. BIC is an independent nonprofit, nongovernmental organization that advocates for the protection of rights, participation, transparency, and public accountability in the governance and operations of the WB, regional development banks, and the IMF.

BRAC (Bangladesh Rural Advancement Committee)
URL: http://www.brac.net
BRAC Centre
75 Mohakhali
Dhaka 1212
Bangladesh
Phone: (880-2) 9881265
E-mail: brac@brac.net

BRAC is an independent, virtually self-financed paradigm in sustainable human development with the twin objectives of poverty alleviation and empowerment of the poor.

Bretton Woods Project
URL: http://www.brettonwoodsproject.org
c/o Action Aid
Hamlyn House
Macdonald Road
London N19 5PG
United Kingdom
Phone: (44-(0)20) 7561-7610
E-mail: info@brettonwoodsproject.org

The Bretton Woods Project works as a networker, information provider, media informant, and watchdog to scrutinize and influence the WB and IMF. Through briefings, reports, and the bimonthly digest *Bretton Woods Update,* it monitors projects, policy reforms, and the overall management of the Bretton Woods institutions, with special emphasis on environmental and social concerns.

Caribbean Conservation Association (CCA)
URL: http://www.ccanet.net
The Garrison
St. Michael, Barbados
Phone: (246) 426-5373
E-mail: crepinformation@ccanet.net

The CCA exists to enhance the quality of life for present and future generations of the Caribbean by facilitating the development and implementation of policies, programs, and practices that contribute to the sustainable management of the region's natural and cultural resources.

Center for International Environmental Law (CIEL)
URL: http://www.ciel.org
1367 Connecticcut Avenue NW, Suite 300
Washington, DC 20036
Phone: (202) 785-8700
E-mail: info@ciel.org

CIEL's goals are (1) to solve environmental problems and promote sustainable societies through the use of law, (2) to incorporate fundamental principles of ecology and justice into international law, (3) to strengthen national environmental law systems and support public-interest movements around the world, and (4) to educate and train public-interest-minded environmental lawyers.

Centre for Development and Enterprise
URL: http://www.cde.org.za
PO Box 1936
Johannesburg 2000
South Africa
Phone: (27-11) 482-5140
E-mail: info@cde.org.za

CDE is an independent policy research and advocacy organization focusing on critical national development issues and their relationship to economic growth and democratic consolidation. Through examining South African realities, and looking at international experience where appropriate, CDE formulates practical policy proposals outlining ways in which South Africa can tackle major social and economic challenges.

Centre for Environment and Development for Arab Region and Europe (CEDARE)
URL: http://isu2.cedare.org.eg
CEDARE Building
2 El-Hegaz Street
PO Box 1057
Heliopolis Bahary
Cairo, Egypt
Phone: (202) 4513921
E-mail: email@cedare.org.eg

CEDARE's main mission is to build the capacity of its member countries, promoting skills in environmental management, transfer of technologies, environmental education, and development of environmental policies. CEDARE assists member countries to achieve sustainable development, particularly in the management of freshwater and land resources, and development and urban areas and human settlements. CEDARE is an "enabling" agent in support of sustainable development initiatives at national, regional and subregional levels.

Centre for Research on Multinational Corporations (SOMO)
URL: http://www.somo.nl
Keizersgracht 132
1015 CW Amsterdam
Netherlands
Phone: (31-(0)20) 639-12 91
E-mail: info@somo.nl

SOMO specializes in research on labor conditions in developing countries in cooperation with local organizations and labor unions. SOMO uses its field of expertise in international guidelines and international treaties in order to measure labor conditions.

CIVICUS: World Alliance for Citizen Participation
URL: http://www.civicus.org
CIVICUS House
24 Gwigwi Mrwebi Street (former Pim), corner Quinn Street
Newtown
2001 Johannesburg, South Africa
Phone: (27-11) 833-5959
E-mail: florence@civicus.org

CIVICUS is an international alliance of more than 1,000 members from 105 countries that have worked for more than a decade to strengthen citizen action and civil society throughout the world, especially in areas where participatory democracy and citizens' freedom of association are threatened. CIVICUS believes that the health of societies exists in direct proportion to the degree of balance between the state, the private sector, and civil society. CIVICUS provides a focal point for knowledge sharing, common interest representation, global institution building, and engagement among these disparate sectors. It acts as an advocate for citizen participation as an essential component of governance and democracy worldwide. CIVICUS seeks to amplify the voices and opinions of ordinary people and give expression to the enormous creative energy of the burgeoning sector of civil society.

Commission for Environmental Cooperation (CEC)
URL: http://www.cec.org
393 Rue St.-Jacques Ouest
Bureau 200
Montreal Quebec H2Y 1N9
Canada
Phone: (514) 350-4300
E-mail: info@cec.org

CEC is an international organization created by Canada, Mexico, and the United States under the North American Agreement on Environmental Cooperation (NAAEC). CEC was established to address regional environmental concerns, help prevent potential trade and environmental conflicts, and promote the effective enforcement of environmental law. The agreement complements the environmental provisions of NAFTA.

CorpWatch
URL: http://www.corpwatch.org
1611 Telegraph Avenue, #702
Oakland, CA 94612
Phone: (510) 271-8080
E-mail: pratap@corpwatch.org

CorpWatch counters corporate-led globalization through education, network-building, and activism. It works to foster democratic control over corporations by building grassroots globalization, a diverse movement for human rights, and dignity, labor rights, and environmental justice.

Development Group for Alternative Policies (Development GAP)
URL: http://www.developmentgap.org
927 15th Street, NW, Fourth Floor

3 McPherson Square
Washington, DC 20005
Phone: (202) 898-1566
E-mail: dgap@developmentgap.org

Since 1977, the Development GAP has worked to ensure that the knowledge, priorities, and efforts of the women and men of the Southern Hemisphere inform decisions made in the Northern Hemisphere about their economies and the environments in which they live. Through its collaboration with citizens' organizations overseas, the Development GAP is able to demonstrate practical alternatives to prevailing policies and programs.

50 Years Is Enough: U.S. Network for Global Economic Justice
URL: http://www.50years.org
3628 12th Street NE
Washington, DC 20017
Phone: (202) 463-2265
E-mail: info@50years.org

50 Years Is Enough is a coalition of more than 200 U.S. grassroots, women's, solidarity, faith-based, policy, social- and economic-justice, youth, labor and development organizations dedicated to the profound transformation of the WB and the IMF. Through education and action, the network is committed to transforming the international financial institutions' policies and practices, to ending the outside imposition of neoliberal economic programs, and to making the development process democratic and accountable. It focuses on action-oriented economic literacy training, public mobilization, and policy advocacy.

Focus on the Global South
URL: http://www.focusweb.org
CUSRI
Chulalongkorn University
Bangkok, Thailand
Phone: (66-2) 2187365
E-mail: Contact form online at http://www.focusweb.org/contact-us/view.html

Focus on the Global South is a program of development policy research, analysis, and action. Founded in 1995, Focus on the Global South currently has three offices: in Bangkok, Thailand; Mumbai, India; and Manila, Philippines. Focus on the Global South aims to consciously and consistently articulate, link, and develop greater coherence between local community-based and national, regional, and global actors for change. It strives to create a distinct and cogent link between development at the grassroots and "macro" levels.

Foreign Policy In Focus (FPIF)
URL: http://www.fpif.org
FPIF–IPS
733 15th Street NW, Suite 1020
Washington, DC 20005
Phone: (202) 234-9382
E-mail: infocus@fpif.org

FPIF is a think tank for research, analysis, and action that brings together scholars, advocates, and activists who strive to make the United States a more responsible global partner. FPIF provides timely analysis of U.N. foreign policy and international affairs and recommends policy alternatives. It aims to amplify the voice of progressives and to build links with social movements in the United States and around the world. Through these connections, FPIF advances and influences debate and discussion among academics, activists, policy makers, and decision makers.

Forum for the Future
URL: http://www.forumforthefuture.org.uk
Overseas House
19-23 Ironmonger Row
London EC1V 3QN
United Kingdom
Phone: (44-(0)20) 7324-3688
E-mail: business@forumforthefuture.org.uk

Founded in 1996, Forum for the Future is recognized as the United Kingdom's leading sustainable development charity. Its object is to promote sustainable development and to educate interested groups to accelerate the building of a sustainable way of life by using a positive solutions-oriented approach. Forum for the Future works with more than 150 companies, local authorities, regional bodies, and universities to build their capacity to overcome the many barriers to more sustainable practice.

GATSwatch
URL: http://www.gatswatch.org
Paulus Potterstraat 20
1071 DA Amsterdam
Netherlands

GATSwatch offers critiques of GATS provisions of the WTO. It criticizes GATS for its (1) negative impacts on universal access to basic services such as health care, education, water, and transport; (2) fundamental conflict between freeing up trade in services and the right of governments and communities to regulate companies in areas such as tourism, retail, telecommunications, and broadcasting; (3) absence of a comprehensive assessment of the impacts of GATS-style liberalization before further negotiations continue; and (4) one-sidedness, stressing that GATS is primarily about expanding opportunities for large multinational companies.

Global Policy Forum (GPF)
URL: http://www.globalpolicy.org
777 UN Plaza, Suite 3D
New York, NY 10017
Phone: (212) 557-3161
E-mail: globalpolicy@globalpolicy.org

GPF's mission is to monitor policy making at the United Nations, promote accountability of global decisions, educate and mobilize for global citizen participation, and advocate on vital issues of international peace and justice. GPF is a nonprofit organization with consultative status at the UN. Founded in 1993, it works with partners around the world to strengthen international law and create a more equitable and sustainable global society.

Global Trade Watch (GTW)
URL: http://www.citizen.org/trade/
1600 20th Street NW
Washington, DC 20009
Phone: (202) 588-1000
E-mail: gtwinfo@citizen.org

GTW promotes democracy by challenging corporate globalization and argues that the current globalization model is neither a random inevitability nor "free trade." Its work seeks to make the measurable outcomes of this model accessible to the public, press, and policy makers, while emphasizing that if the results are not acceptable, then the model can and must be changed or replaced. GTW works on an array of globalization issues, including health and safety, environmental protection, economic justice, and democratic, accountable governance.

Global Vision Corporation
URL: http://www.global-vision.org

Little Alders
Knockrath
Rathdrum, County Wicklow
Ireland
Phone: (353) 404-43-885
E-mail: mail@global-vision.org

Global Vision Corporation is an independent nonprofit, nongovernmental organization founded in 1982. The Global Vision Project is an international educational media campaign to promote the concept of sustainability as a global goal. The corporation has a network of international partners for which it provides a whole-systems strategic approach to combine their insights, integrate their outreach, and communicate the emerging global civil society consensus for a positive future more effectively to the global public.

Human Sciences Research Council (HSRC) of South Africa
URL: http://www.hsrc.ac.za
Pretoria Office
Private Bag X41
Pretoria, South Africa 0001
Phone: (27-12) 302-2000

The HSRC of South Africa is a statutory body established in 1968. It supports development nationally, through the Southern African Development Community (SADC), and in Africa. It primarily conducts large-scale policy-relevant, social-scientific projects for public-sector users, nongovernmental organizations, and international development agencies, in partnership with researchers globally, but particularly in Africa.

Institute for Agriculture and Trade Policy (IATP)
URL: http://www.iatp.org
2105 First Avenue South
Minneapolis, MN 55404
Phone: (612) 870-0453
E-mail: iatp@iatp.org

IATP promotes resilient family farms, rural communities, and ecosystems around the world through research and education, science and technology, and advocacy. The institute works with organizations around the world to analyze how global trade agreements impact domestic farm and food policies. Alongside a global coalition, IATP advocates for fair trade policies that promote strong health standards, labor and human rights, the environment and, most fundamentally, democratic institutions. IATP works to promote building sustainability by developing alternative economic models that include clean sources of energy that would spur rural development. It works with landowners to form cooperatives that promote sustainable forest management, as well as advocating for green businesses and farms that reduce toxic runoff into the Great Lakes and Mississippi River. IATP promotes safe food and healthy ecosystems by working to stop the overuse of antibiotics in agriculture and aquaculture, while limiting the release of mercury and other toxic pollutants that fall onto farmland and enter the food supply. IATP also monitors the impact of genetically engineered crops on the environment, human health, and farmer income.

Inter-American Development Bank (IDB)
URL: http://www.iadb.org
1300 New York Avenue NW
Washington, DC 20577
Phone: (202) 623-1000
E-mail: pic@iadb.org

A longstanding initiative of the Latin American countries, the IDB was established in 1959 as a development institution whose programs and tools proved so effective that it soon became the model on which most other regional and subregional multilateral development banks were created. Today, the IDB is the main source of multilateral financing for economic, social, and institutional development projects as well as trade and regional integration programs in Latin America and the Caribbean. The charter defined as its mission to "contribute to the acceleration of the process of economic and social development of the regional developing member countries, individually and collectively."

International Centre for Trade and Sustainable Development (ICTSD)
URL: http://www.ictsd.org
International Environmental House 2
7 Chemin de Balexert
1219 Châtelaine
Geneva, Switzerland

ICTSD was established in Geneva in September 1996 to influence the international trade system to advance the goal of sustainable development by empowering stakeholders in trade policy through information, networking, dialogue, well-targeted research, and capacity building. As an independent nonprofit and nongovernmental organization, ICTSD engages a broad range of actors in ongoing dialogue about trade and sustainable development. With a wide network of governmental, nongovernmental, and intergovernmental partners, ICTSD facilitates interaction between policy makers and those outside the system to help trade policy become more supportive of sustainable development.

International Development Association (IDA)
URL: http://www.worldbank.org/ida/
World Bank
1818 H Street NW
Washington, DC 20433
Phone: (202) 473-1000
E-mail: ksharing@worldbank.org

IDA is a subsidiary of the WB that helps the world's poorest countries reduce poverty by providing interest-free loans and some grants for programs aimed at boosting economic growth and improving living conditions. IDA funds help these countries deal with the complex challenges they face in striving to meet the Millennium Development Goals. They must, for example, respond to the competitive pressures as well as the opportunities of globalization, arrest the spread of HIV/AIDS, and prevent conflict or deal with its aftermath.

International Finance Corporation (IFC)
URL: http://www.ifc.org
2121 Pennsylvania Avenue NW
Washington, DC 20433
Phone: (202) 473-1000
E-mail: webmaster@ifc.org

IFC's mission is to promote sustainable private-sector investment in developing countries, helping to reduce poverty and improve people's lives. IFC, a member of the World Bank Group, is committed to promoting sustainable projects in its developing member countries that are economically beneficial, financially and commercially sound, and environmentally and socially sustainable. IFC believes that sound economic growth is key to poverty reduction, that it is grounded in the development of entrepreneurship and successful private investment, and that a conducive business environment is needed for the latter to thrive and contribute to improving people's lives.

International Forum on Globalization (IFG)
URL: http://www.ifg.org
1009 General Kennedy Avenue, #2
San Francisco, CA 94129
Phone: (415) 561-7650
E-mail: ifg@ifg.org

IFG is an alliance of activists, scholars, economists, researchers, and writers formed to stimulate new thinking, joint activity, and public education in response to economic globalization. Representing more than 60 organizations in 25 countries, IFG associates come together out of a shared concern that the world's corporate and political leadership is undertaking a restructuring of global politics and economics that may prove as historically significant as any event since the Industrial Revolution. It recognizes that this restructuring is happening at tremendous speed, with little public disclosure of the profound consequences affecting democracy, human welfare, local economies, and the natural world.

International Institute for Sustainable Development (IISD)
URL: http://www.iisd.org
161 Portage Avenue East, Sixth Floor
Winnipeg, Manitoba R3B OY4
Canada
Phone: (204) 958-7700
E-mail: info@iisd.ca

IISD advances policy recommendations on international trade and investment, economic policy, climate change, measurement and assessment, and natural resources management. By using Internet communications, it reports on international negotiations and brokers knowledge gained through collaborative projects with global partners, resulting in more rigorous research, capacity building in developing countries, and better dialogue between the Northern and Southern Hemispheres. Through its research and the effective communication of its findings, IISD engages decision makers in government, business, NGOs, and other sectors to develop and implement policies that are simultaneously beneficial to the global economy, the global environment, and social well-being.

International Labour Organization (ILO)
URL: http://www.ilo.org
4 Route des Morillons
CH-1211 Geneva 22
Switzerland
Phone: (41-22) 799-6111
E-mail: ilo@ilo.org

ILO is the UN agency that seeks the promotion of social justice and internationally recognized human and labor rights. It was founded in 1919 and is the only surviving major creation of the Treaty of Versailles, which brought the League of Nations into being. It became the first specialized agency of the United Nations in 1946. ILO formulates international labor standards in the form of conventions and recommendations, setting minimum standards of basic labor rights: freedom of association, the right to organize, collective bargaining, abolition of forced labor, equality of opportunity and treatment, and other standards regulating conditions across the entire spectrum of work-related issues. It provides technical assistance primarily in the fields of (1) vocational training and vocational rehabilitation, (2) employment policy, (3) labor administration (4) labor law and industrial relations, (5) working conditions, (6) management development, (7) cooperatives, (8) social security, and (9) labor statistics and occupational safety and health.

International Monetary Fund (IMF)
URL: http://www.imf.org
700 19th Street NW
Washington, DC 20431
Phone: (202) 623-4661
E-mail: publicaffairs@imf.org

The IMF is an international organization of 184 member countries that was established to promote international monetary cooperation, exchange stability, and orderly exchange arrangements; to foster economic growth and high levels of employment; and to provide temporary financial assistance to countries to help ease balance of payments adjustment.

International South Group Network (ISGN)
URL: http://www.isgnweb.org
c/o AWEPON
Plot 9, Ntinda Road
PO Box 33576
Kampala, Uganda
Phone: (256) 41-286-916
E-mail: awepon@africaonline.co.ug

ISGN is a network of individuals actively involved in social movements and centers of research and learning. ISGN advocates for peoples of the Southern Hemisphere, disseminating critical analysis of global issues, propagating people's on-the-ground struggles, conducting studies and workshops to forge unity among social movements, and enhancing efforts to discover and promote people-centered development alternatives. ISGN is an initiative of African and southern people's democratic institutions, created to respond to historical transformations taking place in the era of globalization.

MAP International
URL: http://www.map.org
2200 Glynco Parkway
Brunswick, GA 31525-6800
Phone: (800) 225-8550
E-mail: Contact form online at "Contact Us"

MAP's mission is to advance the total health (physical, economic, social, emotional, and spiritual) of people living in the world's poorest communities. That mission is carried out in the areas of community health development, disease prevention and eradication, relief and rehabilitation, and global health advocacy. It is currently focusing on three primary program activities: (1) provision of essential medicines, (2) promotion of comprehensive community health, and (3) prevention of HIV/AIDS.

Organization of Economic Cooperation and Development (OECD)
URL: http://www.oecd.org
2 Rue André Pascal
F-75775 Paris Cedex 16
France
Phone: (33-1) 45-24-82-00

The OECD consists of 30 member countries sharing a commitment to democratic government and the market economy. It has a global reach, maintaining active relationships with some 70 other countries, NGOs, and civil societies. Best known for its publications and statistics, its work covers economic and social issues from macroeconomics to trade, education, development, and science and innovation. The OECD fosters good governance in both public-service and corporate activity.

Overseas Development Institute (ODI)
URL: http://www.odi.org.uk
Public Affairs
111 Westminster Bridge Road
London SE1 7JD
United Kingdom
Phone: (44-(0)20) 7922-0300
E-mail: media@odi.org.uk

ODI is Britain's leading independent think tank on international development and humanitarian issues. Its mission is to inspire and inform policies and practices that lead to poverty reduction and the achievement of sustainable livelihoods in developing countries. It does this by linking high-quality applied research, practical policy advice, and policy-focused information. ODI's work centers on its research and policy groups and programs.

Overseas Private Investment Corporation (OPIC)
URL: http://www.opic.gov
1100 New York Avenue NW
Washington, DC 20527
Phone: (202) 336-8400
E-mail: info@opic.gov

OPIC was established as a development agency of the U.S government in 1971. OPIC helps U.S. businesses invest overseas, fosters economic development in new and emerging markets, complements the private sector in managing the risks associated with foreign direct investment, and supports U.S. foreign policy. By expanding economic development in host countries, OPIC-supported projects can encourage political stability, free market reforms, and the United States' best practices.

Oxfam International
URL: http://www.oxfaminternational.org
Oxfam America
26 West Street
Boston, MA 02111-1206
Phone: (617) 482-1211
E-mail: info@oxfamamerica.org

Oxfam Great Britain
Oxfam House
John Smith Drive
Cowley
Oxford OX4 2JY
United Kingdom
Phone: (44-1865) 473-727
E-mail: Contact form online at http://www.oxfam.org.uk/contact

Oxfam International is a confederation of 12 organizations working together with more than 3,000 partners in more than 100 countries to find lasting solutions to poverty, suffering, and injustice. With many of the causes of poverty being global in nature, the 12 affiliate members believe they can achieve greater impact through their collective efforts. Popular campaigning, alliance building, and media work are designed to raise awareness among the public of the real solutions to global poverty, to enable and motivate people to play an active part in the movement for change, to foster a sense of global citizenship, and to increase public understanding that economic and social justice are crucial to sustainable development. Oxfam also seeks to help people organize so that they might gain better access to the opportunities they need to improve their livelihoods and govern their own lives. It also works with people affected by humanitarian disasters.

ProPoor
URL: http://www.propoor.org
E-mail: Contact form online at http://www.propoor.org/contact/

ProPoor is a nonprofit organization registered in Kolkata (India), Singapore, and Atlanta, Georgia. Established in 1998, ProPoor is committed to the dissemination of information and promotion of sustainable development initiatives in response to the needs of underrepresented and marginalized sectors of society in South Asia. ProPoor has developed a comprehensive Internet portal containing information about South Asian NGOs, funding agencies, events, projects, job opportunities in social development, success stories of individuals and organizations, and other relevant links.

Rio+5 Consultation
URL: http://www.ecouncil.ac.cr/rio/
Earth Council
Apartado 2323-1002
San José, Costa Rica
Phone: (506) 256-1611
E-mail: earthnet@terra.ecouncil.ac.cr

In March 1997, the Rio+5 Forum began developing a collection of supporting instruments to help the principles of sustainable development to become widely accepted and strongly integrated into public policy and private decisions at every level, thus moving sustainable development "from agenda to action" in the spirit of the Earth Summit and in preparation for the next millennium. Its four key objectives are (1) clarification, to explore effective ways of clarifying and dealing with the complex issues and processes of sustainable development; (2) systems integration, to help move societies from the management of sustainability issues to the management of systems that address them in an integrated way, across national borders and at every economic level; (3) implementation, to advance beyond international policy dialogues on sustainability by adopting pragmatic approaches for implementing sustainability from the "ground up," at local and national levels; and

(4) cooperation, to generate multistakeholder initiatives and alliances that will build and strengthen management and governance systems for sustainable development.

Stakeholder Forum for a Sustainable Future
URL: http://www.stakeholderforum.org
3 Bloomsburg Place
London WC1A 2QL
United Kingdom
Phone: (44-(0)20) 7580-6912

Stakeholder Forum for a Sustainable Future is an international multistakeholder organization working on sustainable development and supporting the increased involvement of stakeholders in international and national governance processes. The organization played a key role in the preparations for and follow-up to the World Summit on Sustainable Development. It is the lead organization in the development and facilitating of multistakeholder processes for sustainable development.

Third World Institute (ITeM)
URL: http://www.item.org.uy
PO Box 1539
Montevideo 11000
Uruguay
Phone: (598-2) 419-6192
E-mail: item@item.org.uy

The Third World Institute (Instituto del Tercer Mundo, or ITeM) performs information, communication, and education activities on an international level concerning development and environment-related activities. It is a civil society organization, encouraging citizen involvement in global decisionmaking processes. ITeM aims to (1) contribute to the construction of democracy, supporting organizations from Third World countries to further the interests of the world's poor, of women, and of oppressed minorities; (2) promote respect for human rights, in particular freedom of speech and free access to information (ITeM has pioneered the use of electronic networks as ideal tools for these purposes); (3) promote national and international networking among citizen organizations for the exchange of experiences and the design and implementation of common interest actions; and (4) contribute to solving the problems affecting the Third World. ITeM conducts research, disseminates its findings, and furthers the adoption of policies aimed at implementing solutions.

Third World Network (TWN)
URL: http://www.twnside.org.sg
121-s Jalan Utama
10450 Penang, Malaysia
E-mail: twnet@po.jaring.my

TWN is an independent, international nonprofit network of organizations and individuals involved in issues relating to development, the Third World, and North-South (Hemisphere) issues. It conducts research on economic, social, and environmental issues pertaining to the Southern Hemisphere; publishes books and magazines; organizes and participates in seminars; and provides a platform representing broadly Southern interests and perspectives.

United Nations Children's Fund (UNICEF)
URL: http://www.unicefusa.org
UNICEF House
3 United Nations Plaza
New York, NY 10017
Phone: (212) 326-7000
E-mail: information@unicef.org

The United Nations International Children's Emergency Fund was established on December 11, 1946, by the United Nations to meet the emergency needs of children in postwar Europe and China. In 1950, its mandate was broadened to address the long-term needs of children and women in developing countries everywhere. It became a permanent part of the UN system in 1953, when its name was shortened to the United Nations Children's Fund, though it retained its original acronym, UNICEF. Its priorities are (1) child protection; (2) girls' education; (3) HIV/AIDS prevention, care, and support, including of orphaned children; (4) immunization; and (5) early childhood, to ensure the best start in life, survival, growth, and early learning.

United Nations Conference on Trade and Development (UNCTAD)
URL: http://www.unctad.org
Palais des Nations
8-14, Avenue de la Paix
1211 Geneva 10
Switzerland
Phone: (41-22) 917-5809
E-mail: info@unctad.org

Established in 1964, UNCTAD promotes the development-friendly integration of developing countries into the world economy. UNCTAD has progressively evolved into a knowledge-based institution whose work aims to help shape current policy debates and thinking on development, with a particular focus on ensuring that domestic policies and international action are mutually supportive in bringing about sustainable development. The organization works to fulfill this mandate by carrying out three key functions: (1) It serves as a forum for intergovernmental deliberations, supported by discussions with experts and exchanges of experience and aimed at consensus building; (2) it undertakes research, policy analysis and data collection for the debates of government representatives and experts; and (3) it provides technical assistance tailored to the specific requirements of developing countries, with special attention to the needs of the least developed countries and of economies in transition.

United Nations Development Program (UNDP)
URL: http://www.undp.org
One United Nations Plaza
New York, NY 10017
Phone: (212) 906-5000
E-mail: hq@undp.org

UNDP is the UN global development network, an organization advocating for change and connecting countries to knowledge, experience, and resources to help people build a better life. UNDP works in 166 countries to help them solve national development challenges. As they develop local capacity, they draw on the people of UNDP and its wide range of partners. UNDP's network links and coordinates global and national efforts to reach the Millennium Development Goals, including the goal of cutting poverty in half by 2015. Its focus is on helping countries build and share solutions to the challenges of (1) democratic governance, (2) poverty reduction, (3) crisis prevention and recovery, (4) energy and environment, and (5) HIV/AIDS. UNDP helps developing countries attract and use aid effectively. In all its activities, it encourages the protection of human rights and the empowerment of women. UNDP also produces an annual Human Development Report, commissioned by UNDP, focusing on key development issues and providing new measurement tools, innovative analysis, and policy proposals.

United Nations Educational, Scientific and Cultural Organization (UNESCO)
URL: http://portal.unesco.org
7 Place de Fontenoy
75352 Paris 07 SP
France

Phone: (33-(0)1) 45-68-10-00
E-mail: bpi@unesco.org

UNESCO, founded in November 1945, uses education, social and natural science, culture, and communication as the means to an ambitious goal: to build peace in the minds of men and women. UNESCO functions as a laboratory of ideas and a standard setter to forge universal agreements on emerging ethical issues. The organization also serves as a clearinghouse for the dissemination and sharing of information and knowledge, while helping member states build their human and institutional capacities in diverse fields.

United Nations Food and Agriculture Organization (FAO)
URL: http://www.fao.org
Vaile delle Terme di Caracalla
00100 Rome, Italy
Phone: (39) 06-57051
E-mail: FAO-HQ@fao.org

The FAO leads international efforts to defeat hunger. Serving both developed and developing countries, FAO acts as a neutral forum where all nations meet as equals to negotiate agreements and debate policy. It is also a source of knowledge and information. It helps developing countries and countries in transition modernize and improve agriculture, forestry and fishery practices, and ensure good nutrition for all. Since its founding in 1945, it has focused special attention on developing rural areas, home to 70 percent of the world's poor and hungry people. FAO's activities comprise four main areas: (1) putting information within reach, (2) sharing policy expertise, (3) providing a meeting place for nations, and (4) bringing knowledge to the field.

United Nations High Commissioner for Human Rights
URL: http://www.ohchr.org
Office of the High Commissioner for Human Rights (OHCHR)
United Nations Office at Geneva
1211 Geneva 10
Switzerland
E-mail: tb-petitions@ohchr.org

The OHCHR is a department of the United Nations secretariat that promotes and protects the enjoyment and full realization, by all people, of all rights established in the Charter of the United Nations and in international human rights laws and treaties. The mandate includes preventing human rights violations, securing respect for all human rights, promoting international cooperation to protect human rights, coordinating related activities throughout the UN, and strengthening and streamlining the UN system in the field of human rights.

United Nations Population Fund (UNFPA)
URL: http://www.unfpa.org
220 East 42nd St.
New York, NY 10017
Phone: (212) 297-5000
E-mail: dungus@unfpa.org

UNFPA is an international development agency that promotes the right of every woman, man, and child to enjoy a life of health and equal opportunity. UNFPA supports countries in using population data for policies and programs to reduce poverty and to ensure that every pregnancy is wanted, every birth is safe, every young person is free of HIV/AIDS, and every girl and woman is treated with dignity and respect.

United Nations World Food Program (WFP)
URL: http://www.wfp.org
Via C.G. Viola 68
Parco dei Medici
00148 Rome, Italy
Phone: (39) 06-65131
E-mail: wfpinfo@wfp.org

Whatever the cause, hunger is one of the first threats to survival. At the request of a local government, WFP sets its emergency response procedure in motion against hunger. First, emergency assessment teams are sent in to assess the situation. WFP then draws up a plan of action and a budget for the crisis zone. WFP launches appeals to the international community for funds and food aid. The agency relies entirely on voluntary contributions to finance its operations, with donations made in cash, food, or services. WFP transports and delivers the aid to the affected area.

United Nations World Health Organization (WHO)
URL: http://www.who.int
Avenue Appia 20
1211 Geneva 27
Switzerland

Phone: (41-22) 791-21-11
E-mail: info@who.int

The WHO is the specialized UN agency for health. It was established on April 7, 1948. WHO's objective, as set out in its constitution, is the attainment by all peoples of the highest possible level of health. Health is defined in WHO's constitution as a state of complete physical, mental, and social well-being and not merely the absence of disease or infirmity.

United States Agency for International Development (USAID)
URL: http://www.usaid.gov
Ronald Reagan Building
Washington, DC 20523-1000
Phone: (202) 712-4320
E-mail: pinquiries@usaid.gov

USAID works in agriculture, democracy and governance, economic growth, the environment, education, health, global partnerships, and humanitarian assistance in more than 100 countries to provide a better future for all. U.S. foreign assistance has always had the twofold purpose of furthering America's foreign-policy interests in expanding democracy and free markets while improving the lives of the citizens of the developing world. Spending less than one-half of 1 percent of the federal budget, USAID works around the world to achieve these goals.

World Bank (WB)
URL: http://www.worldbank.org
1818 H Street NW
Washington, DC 20433
Phone: (202) 473-1000
E-mail: askmna@worldbank.org

The WB is a vital source of financial and technical assistance to developing countries around the world. It is not a bank in the common sense. It is made up of two unique development institutions owned by 184 member countries: the International Bank for Reconstruction and Development (IBRD) and the International Development Association (IDA). Each institution plays a different but supportive role in the mission of global poverty reduction and the improvement of living standards. The IBRD focuses on middle-income and creditworthy poor countries, while IDA focuses on the poorest countries in the world. Together they provide low-interest loans, interest-free credit, and grants to developing countries for education, health, infrastructure, communications, and many other purposes.

World Conservation Union (IUCN)
URL: http://www.iucn.org
Rue Mauverney 28
Gland 1196
Switzerland
Phone: (41-22) 999-0000
E-mail: webmaster@iucn.org

The IUCN is the world's largest and most important conservation network. The union brings together 82 states, 111 government agencies, more than 800 NGOs, and some 10,000 scientists and experts from 181 countries in a unique worldwide partnership. The IUCN's mission is to influence, encourage, and assist societies throughout the world to conserve the integrity and diversity of nature and to ensure that any use of natural resources is equitable and ecologically sustainable.

World Intellectual Property Organization (WIPO)
URL: http://www.wipo.int
34 Chemin des Colombettes
Geneva, Switzerland
Phone: (41-22) 338-91-11
E-mail: publicinf@wipo.int

WIPO is an international organization, with 182 nations as member states, dedicated to promoting the use and protection of works of the human spirit. These works—intellectual property—are expanding the bounds of science and technology and enriching the world of the arts. WIPO administers 23 international treaties dealing with different aspects of intellectual property protection. Through its work, WIPO plays an important role in enhancing the quality and enjoyment of life, as well as creating real wealth for nations.

World Resources Institute (WRI)
URL: http://www.wri.org
10 G Street NE, Suite 800
Washington, DC 20002
Phone: (202) 729-7600
E-mail: pmackie@sri.org

WRI is an environmental think tank that goes beyond research to create practical ways to protect the Earth and improve people's lives. Its mission is to move human society to live in ways that protect Earth's environment for current and future generations. WRI's programs work to catalyze public and private action: (1) to reverse damage to ecosystems by protecting the capacity of ecosystems to sustain life and prosperity, (2) to expand participation in environmental decisions, (3) to avert dangerous climate change by promoting public and private action to ensure a safe climate and sound world economy, and (4) to increase prosperity while improving the environment by challenging the private sector to grow by improving environmental and community well-being.

World Trade Organization (WTO)
URL: http://www.wto.org
Centre William Rappard
Rue de Lausanne 154
CH-1211 Geneva 21
Switzerland
Phone: (41-22) 739-51-11
E-mail: enquiries@wto.org

The WTO is the only global international organization dealing with the rules of trade between nations. At its heart are the WTO agreements, negotiated and signed by the bulk of the world's trading nations and ratified in their parliaments. The goal is to help producers of goods and services, exporters, and importers conduct their business.

Worldwatch Institute
URL: http://www.worldwatch.org
1776 Massachusetts Avenue NW
Washington, DC 20036-1904
Phone: (202) 452-1999
E-mail: worldwatch@worldwatch.org

Founded by Lester Brown in 1974, the Worldwatch Institute offers a unique blend of interdisciplinary research, global focus, and accessible writing that has made it a leading source of information on the interactions among [illegible]y environmental, social, and economic trends. Its work revolves around the transition to an environmentally sustainable and socially just society—and how to achieve it. Nonpartisan and independent, its research is funded primarily by donations from private foundations and individuals, as well as by sales of its publications, such as its annuals *State of the World* and *Vital Signs.*

World Wildlife Fund (WWF)
URL: http://www.wwf.org
WWF International
Avenue du Mont-Blanc 1196
Gland, Switzerland
Phone: (41-22) 364-91-11

The WWF's mission is to stop the degradation of the planet's natural environment and to build a future in which humans live in harmony with nature by conserving the world's biological diversity, ensuring that the use of renewable natural resources is sustainable, and promoting the reduction of pollution and wasteful consumption. WWF's work encompasses sustainability, forests, freshwater, marine conservation, species conservation, and toxics. For each of these areas, WWF helps with scientific research, conservation research, and policy assistance.

Wuppertal Institute for Climate, Environment and Energy
URL: http://www.wupperinst.org
PO Box 10 04 80
D-42004 Wuppertal, Germany
Phone: (49-202) 2492-0
E-mail: info@wupperinst.org

The Wuppertal Institute intends to contribute to the public debate on causes, forms, and effects of economic globalization. It publishes "Sustainable Globalisation," research that explores the strained relationship between the rising transnational economy and goals of public policy, such as sustainability and equity. Studies identify options for shaping globalization according to these goals.

10

Annotated Bibliography

The following annotated bibliography focuses on many aspects of globalization. Entries are grouped into the following seven categories:

Globalization

Human Rights, Democracy, and Poverty

Sustainable Development, Environment, and Agriculture

Economics, Finance, and Multinational Corporations

The International Monetary Fund, the World Bank, and the World Trade Organization

Trade

Labor and the North American Free Trade Agreement

Each category is subdivided into two sections: Books (and Book Chapters) and Articles and Papers. A list of Nonprint Resources, such as films and videos, and of Web sites and Documents close the chapter.

GLOBALIZATION

Books and Book Chapters

Baylis, John, and Steve Smith, eds. *The Globalization of World Politics: An Introduction to International Relations.* Oxford: Oxford University Press, 1997. An introduction to world politics explaining the history, the major theories, the structures and processes by which it operates, and the top issues nowadays, the major feature being globalization. Arguments, pro and con, are presented.

Benyon, John. *Globalization: The Reader.* New York: Routledge, 2001. An overview of globalization's effects on culture, technology, and the media.

Bhagwati, Jagdish. *In Defense of Globalization.* New York: Oxford University Press, 2004. A clear-eyed view of globalization's benefits, including its provision of jobs to the poor and unemployed in the developing world, which are often overlooked by its critics.

Buck, Susan J. *The Global Commons: An Introduction.* Washington, D.C.: Island Press, 1998. The author examines Antarctica, the oceans, the atmosphere, outer space, and telecommunications from the perspective of law and international relations.

Chatterjee, Pratap, and Matthias Finger. *The Earth Brokers: Power, Politics and World Development.* London and New York: Routledge, 1994. A history of the preparations, meetings and results of the United Nations Conference on Environment and Development. The book criticizes the process and analyzes the documents as well as the players.

Compton, Robert W., Jr. *East Asian Democratization: Impact of Globalization, Culture, and Economy.* Westport, Conn.: Praeger, 2000. Compton studies the Asian financial crisis, emphasizing the cases of Japan, South Korea, and Thailand with a view to their culture and economics, and concludes that patterns of government around the world are not becoming ever more similar, despite globalization.

Cusimano, Maryann K. *Beyond Sovereignty: Issues for a Global Agenda.* New York: Bedford/St. Martin's Press, 2000. Textbook on the problems between nations that have arisen as a result of globalization. The new roles of NGOs and MNCs are considered, as well as potential resolutions to current conflicts.

Escobar, Arturo. *Encountering Development: The Making and Unmaking of the Third World.* Princeton, N.J.: Princeton University Press, 1995. Escobar criticizes the way in which capitalism reduces human and social experiences to economic categories, which in turn shape the response of international institutions to questions of development in the Third World.

Friedman, Thomas. *The Lexus and the Olive Tree: Understanding Globalization.* New York: Anchor Books, 2000. Argues that globalization has the potential to improve human life around the world, though it causes cultural conflict.

———. *The World Is Flat: A Brief History of the Twenty-first Century.* New York: Farrar, Straus and Giroux, 2005. Friedman argues that the world has qualitatively "flattened" as a result of globalization.

Giddens, Anthony. *Runaway World: How Globalization Is Reshaping Our Lives.* New York: Routledge, 2000. A brief, thoughtful book that examines how globalization affects most aspects of life.

Gilpin, Robert. *The Challenge of Global Capitalism: The World Economy in the 21st Century.* Princeton, N.J.: Princeton University Press, 2000. How technology and politics affect globalization.

———. *Global Political Economy: Understanding the International Economic Order.* Princeton, N.J.: Princeton University Press, 2001. An overview and explanation of the forces guiding globalization of economies and the political significance of these forces.

Gray, John. *False Dawn: The Delusions of Global Capitalism.* New York: New Press, 1998. How globalization developed and who benefits.

Harriss-White, Barbara, ed. *Globalisation and Insecurity: Political, Economic, and Physical Challenges.* London and New York: Palgrave, 2002. Globalization brings new threats to physical, political, and economic security. The articles in this collection examine the responses in terms of politics, the environment, finance, industry, labor, social security, and the military.

Hutton, Will, and Anthony Giddens, eds. *Global Capitalism.* New York: New Press, 2000. Essays on globalization and its effects on culture and poverty, as well as the impact of technology.

———. *On the Edge: Living with Global Capitalism.* London: Vintage, 2001. Eminent contributors, including George Soros, weigh in on the debate over globalization.

International Development: Pro/Con. Vol. 14. Danbury, Conn.: Grolier, 2004. A group of essays that present the proglobalization and antiglobalization positions.

Kaul, Inge, Isabelle Grunberg, and Marc A. Stern, eds. *Global Public Goods: International Cooperation in the 21st Century.* New York: Oxford University Press, 1999. International public goods include efficient markets, justice, and a healthy environment. Case studies suggest that the world needs more and better public goods.

Keck, Margaret E., and Kathryn Sikkink. *Activists Beyond Borders: Advocacy Networks in International Politics.* Ithaca, N.Y.: Cornell University Press, 1997. The authors study the transnational "advocacy networks" that take up issues of human rights, the environment, and violence against women.

Keohane, Robert O., and Elinor Ostrom, eds. *Local Commons and Global Independence: Heterogeneity and Cooperation in Two Domains.* London: Sage Publications, 1995. Arrangements for sharing resources and international relations both involve alliances that depend on cooperation and self-enforcement to endure. This book examines their structures from the perspectives of economics, policy, and international relations to determine the conditions under which these arrangements work well or fail.

Klein, Naomi. *Fences and Windows: On the Front Lines of the Globalization Debate.* New York: Picador, 2002. Firsthand accounts of the effects of globalization, as well as description and analysis of worldwide demonstrations against it.

———. *No Logo.* London: Flamingo, 2000. Klein reveals the downsides of consumer capitalism and brand fetishism. She also demonstrates how globalization has led to human rights abuses.

Langhorne, Richard. *The Coming of Globalization: Its Evolution and Contemporary Consequences.* New York: St. Martin's Press, 2001. Explains globalization in terms of underlying economic, political, and cultural processes.

Leys, Colin. *Market-Driven Politics: Neoliberal Democracy and the Public Interest.* London: Verso Books, 2001. Leys examines how global corporate forces are shaping politics and government.

Luttwak, Edward. *Turbo Capitalism: Winners and Losers in the Global Economy.* New York: HarperCollins, 1999. Shows how unregulated capitalism leads to economic inequality.

Maiguashca, Bice. "The Transnational Indigenous Movement in a Changing World Order." In *Global Transformation: Challenges to the State System.* Edited by Sakamoto Yoshkazu. Tokyo, New York, and Paris: United Nations University Press, 1994 Global capitalist expansion has threatened indigenous groups' land, and assimilationist policies of governments have threatened their culture. However, there are now international laws on indigenous populations, who have learned to use Western legal concepts such as nondiscrimination and self-determination to defend themselves.

McMurtry, John. *The Cancer Stage of Capitalism.* Sterling, Va.: Pluto Press, 1999. McMurtry describes how the system of money and capital developed within an already existing market system but then began to grow and spread without restraint.

Micklethwaite, John, and Adrian Wooldridge. *A Future Perfect: The Challenge and Hidden Promise of Globalization.* New York: Times, 2003. Overview of globalization with an emphasis on how it benefits humanity.

Mishra, R. *Globalization and the Welfare State.* London: Edward Elgar, 1999. Under a globalized world order standards have fallen in the United States and Great Britain but much less so in the rest of Europe and Japan. Thus, globalization is not a purely objective economic force; it is also political and ideological.

Mittelman, James H. *The Globalization Syndrome.* Princeton, N.J.: Princeton University Press, 2000. Mittelman studies globalization not only theoretically but also from an observational approach, analyzing the experiences of people who are impacted by it and injured by it. The book calls for a challenge to the Washington Consensus.

———. *Whither Globalization? The Vortex of Knowledge and Ideology.* New York: Routledge, 2004. Mittelman proposes that globalization is not just a matter of markets, power, and culture but involves the very concept and representation of the world. The question is not whether to be for it or against it, but how it is to be implemented.

Mosler, David, Bob Catley, and Robert Catley. *Global America: Imposing Liberalism on a Recalcitrant World.* Westport, Conn.: Praeger, 2000. The authors argue that liberalism is the essence of the order that the United States, with the strongest economy and mightiest military, is imposing on the whole world; however, the very nature of liberalism makes it uncontrollable, even for the United States.

O'Connor, David E. *Demystifying the Global Economy.* Westport, Conn.: Greenwood Press, 2002. An easily understood introduction to many aspects of the global economy.

O'Meara, Patrick, and Howard D. Mehlinger, eds. *Globalization and the Challenges of the New Century: A Reader.* Bloomington: Indiana University Press, 2000. Scholars, businesspeople, and government leaders examine globalization from different sides.

O'Rourke, Kevin H., and Jeffrey G. Williamson. *Globalization and History: The Evolution of a Nineteenth-Century Atlantic Economy.* Cambridge, Mass.: MIT Press, 2001. The history of globalization as it began in the 1800s.

Phillips, Lynne, ed. *The Third Wave of Modernization in Latin America: Cultural Perspectives on Neoliberalism.* Wilmington, Del.: Scholarly Resources, 1998. The book consists of studies of how neoliberalism has played out in Argentina, Bolivia, Brazil, Guatemala, Mexico, Nicaragua, and Peru. It turns out to take very different forms in different places.

Robertson, Robbie. *The Three Waves of Globalization: A History of a Developing Global Consciousness.* London: Zed Books, 2003. A historian asserts that globalization has earlier roots than are usually acknowledged.

Rodrik, Dani. *Has Globalization Gone Too Far?* Washington, D.C.: Institute for International Economics, 1997. While governments in both the industrial and the developing world appear committed to globalization, the protests against it around the world are growing and themselves becoming more integrated. The authors uses case studies to suggest that the "winners" may be risking as much as the "losers."

Rosenau, James N. *Distant Proximities: Dynamics Beyond Globalization.* Princeton, N.J.: Princeton University Press, 2003. People inhabit different "worlds" depending on their conception of what goes on in other places. The author analyzes how this plays out in human rights, government, and economics.

Sandler, Todd. *Global Challenges: An Approach to Environmental, Political and Economic Problems.* Cambridge: Cambridge University Press, 1997. The concept of global public goods provides the framework for considering an economic and policy approach to world environmental, political, and economic problems.

Saul, John Ralston. *The Collapse of Globalism and the Reinvention of the World.* New York: Overlook Press, 2005. While at first it was predicted that globalization would bring an end to nation-states, this has not happened. Instead, nationalism and racism are on the rise, and countries such as China and India have grown phenomenally by following their national interest rather than the agenda of globalism.

Scholte, J. A. *Globalization: A Critical Introduction.* London: Palgrave, 2000. The author analyzes globalization, showing what has changed and what has not in production, law, community, and science. He explores how a more humane, just, secure, and democratic future could be achieved.

Schoonover, Thomas. *Uncle Sam's War of 1898 and the Origins of Globalization.* Lexington: University Press of Kentucky, 2003. How the push for economic growth and new markets in the 19th century led to wars and eventually to a globalized economy.

Soros, George. *George Soros on Globalization.* New York: Public Affairs, 2002. The multimillionaire businessman talks about why globalization as it is today does not work and how it can be made better for everyone, including the poor.

Sousa-Santos, B. de. *Toward a New Common Sense: Law, Science and Politics in the Paradigmatic Transition.* New York: Routledge, 1995. "Common heritage of mankind" has become the legal terminology that expresses the concept of the global commons. It is one of the four main manifestations of globalism that has mobilized people.

Stiglitz, Joseph. *Globalization and Its Discontents.* New York: Norton, 2003. The Nobel Prize winner in economics offers a succinct and cogent argument against the policies and theories of the IMF, offering illustrative case studies.

Thurow, Lester. *Fortune Favors the Bold: How to Build a New and Lasting Global Prosperity.* New York: HarperCollins, 2003. Analysis of globalization's effects, both good and bad, and cogent suggestions for how the process can be changed to benefit all.

Van der Pijl, K. *Transnational Classes and International Relations.* London: Routledge, 1998. The authors says that intensified capital accumulation has begun to wear down the "social and natural substratum," leading to conflict. People will have to resist if they are to survive.

Wolf, Martin. *Why Globalization Works.* New Haven, Conn.: Yale University Press, 2004. Wolf uses conventional economic market theory to demonstrate that globalization will be beneficial as long as markets are free of government-imposed distortions. Developed economies requires less capital per worker, so jobs will not be lost in those countries, even as they are gained in the less developed ones.

Articles and Papers

Centre for Economic Policy Research. "Making Sense of Globalization: A Guide to the Economic Issues." *CEPR Policy Paper,* no. 8 (July 2002). This is a European report on the economic costs and benefits of globalization. It tries to meet the concerns of opponents of globalization with recommendations for improving the position of developing nations.

Galbraith, James K. "The Crisis of Globalization." *Dissent* 46, no. 3 (1998): 12–16. Galbraith argues that the Washington Consensus of faith in free markets, privatization, deregulation, and open capital markets for economic development has proven wrong and damaging to development. Those countries such as Japan, earlier, Korea, and Taiwan that grew fastest had strong governments, mixed economies, and weak capital markets.

Lagon, Mark P. "Visions of Globalization: Pretexts for Prefabricated Prescriptions—and Some Antidotes." *World Affairs* 165, no. 3 (Winter 2003): 142. The term *globalization* may focus on capital flow, labor mobility, or information, but it always implies a situation qualitatively different from that of the past. Proponents see a growing world economy raising standards for all, leading to more democracy, and creating interdependence that fosters peace. Opponents see growing inequality and environmental harm, terrorism, drug trafficking, and piracy.

Lipschutz, Ronnie E. "Reconstructing World Politics: The Emergence of Global Civil Society." *Millennium: Journal of International Studies* 21, no. 3 (1992): 389–420. The author sees global civil society rising to respond to individual rights being privileged over governmental rights, decreased ability of government to address human welfare, and new identities that have overtaken nationality.

McKay, Bonnie J., and Sven Jentoft. "Market or Community Failure? Critical Perspectives on Common Property Research." *Human Organization* (Spring 1998): 21–29. The authors take an ethnographic and historical approach to exploring models of the commons, communities, and collective institutions. They explore embeddedness versus disembeddedness.

Monbiot, George, and Helena Norberg-Hodge. "Globalization: Use It or Lose It?" *The Ecologist* 33, no. 7 (September 2003): 24. The authors debate globalization. One argues that it takes trade to move wealth from rich to poor countries, while the other says that localized production can mean both wealth and local economic self-reliance.

Phillips, Nicola, and Richard Higgott. "Global Governance and the Public Domain: Collective Goods in a 'Post–Washington Consensus' Era." *Centre for the Study of Globalisation and Regionalisation (University of Warwick, Coventry) Working Paper,* no. 47/99 (November 1999). The financial crises of 1997–99 showed just how unsustainable and harmful an unregulated globalized market can be. Now both Asia and Latin America are looking for a safety net of public goods in times of crisis.

Shaw, Martin. "Civil Society and Global Politics: Beyond a Social Movements Approach." *Millennium: Journal of International Studies* 23, no. 3 (1994): 647–667. Martin claims that the actions of social movements reflect national concern, and therefore social movements cannot be effective in international work. On the other hand, civil society can be internationally effective.

Smith, Jackie. "Transnational Political Processes and the Human Rights Movement." *Research in Social Movements, Conflict and Change* 18 (1995): 185–219. Smith suggests that the end of the cold war, the rise of UN institutions, and expansion of the role of NGOs in international bodies has created political opportunities for transnational social movements.

Uphoff, Norman. "Grassroots Organizations and NGOs in Rural Development: Opportunities with Diminishing States and Expanding Markets." *World Development* 21, no. 4 (1993): 607–622. Popular collective organizations and NGOs are working in a changing relationships with governmental agencies in developing countries.

Watkins, Kevin. "Globalisation and Liberalisation: Implications for Poverty, Distribution and Inequality." *UNDP: HDR Occasional Paper* 32 (1997). Watkins considers globalization and associated forces and how they affect poverty, inequality, and development. He discusses whether international trade agreements should include a social clause and looks at other policies that can foster more equitable globalization.

Williams, Heather L. "Planting Trouble: The Barzón's Debtors Movement in Mexico." *Center for US-Mexican Studies, University of California, Current Issues Brief Series,* no. 6 (1996). The crisis of the Mexican peso in 1994 caused widespread discontent, which gave rise to a broad protest movement. People from different classes joined to criticize and resist how the Mexican government was colluding with multinational financial institutions.

HUMAN RIGHTS, DEMOCRACY, AND POVERTY

Books

Alvarez, Sonia E., and Arturo Escobar, eds. *The Making of Social Movements in Latin America: Identity, Strategy and Democracy.* Boulder, Colo.: Westview Press, 1992. The papers in this book, taken together, constitute an interdisciplinary study of Latin American social movements. Identity and strategy are the main themes that shape the analysis.

Anderson, Walt. *All Connected Now: Life in the First Global Civilization.* Boulder, Colo.: Westview Press, 2001. This book on globalization goes beyond economics to consider culture, politics, and biology. The author claims that we have moved from a world of closed systems to one of open systems so that the future global civilization will have problems but also offering with more complex experiences and richer meaning to our lives.

Bello, Walden, Shea Cunningham, Bill Rau, et al. *Dark Victory: The United States and Global Poverty.* Oakland, Calif.: Food First Books, 1999. Demonstrates how structural adjustment pushed by the IMF and WB have led to worse debt and greater poverty in developing nations. Meanwhile, inequality is increasing and real wages are falling in the industrial world as well—part of the same process.

Bodley, John H. *Victims of Progress.* Menlo Park, Calif.: Cummings Publishing, 1999. Bodley examines how government policies of the past destroyed indigenous cultures and whole peoples, either accidentally or on purpose. Modern land and economic development policies are having similar recults. The author advocates policies that would allow tribal cultures to continue and suggests that they may be more viable than the ones they replace.

Chomsky, Noam, and Edward S. Herman. *The Political Economy of Human Rights.* Vol. 1: *The Washington Connection and Third World Fascism.* Boston: South End Press, 1979. The authors discuss the effects of U.S. foreign policy, which has established dictatorial client states around the world that support the interests of local and foreign business and military elites. The United States touts democracy and human rights as a cover, but American military and economic aid correlates with human rights abuses, while the media fails to cover this.

Chossudovsky, Michel. *The Globalization of Poverty and the New World Order.* Shanty Bay, Ontario: Global Outlook, 2003. Data showing how globalization increases world poverty and destabilizes governments in the developing world.

Chua, Amy. *World on Fire: How Exporting Free Market Democracy Breeds Ethnic Hatred and Global Instability.* New York: Doubleday, 2003. How the free market tends to favor certain ethnic groups in developing nations and how this fuels ethnic hatred and generates instability (and war) in these countries.

Falk, Richard. *Human Rights Horizons: The Pursuit of Justice in a Globalizing World.* New York: Routledge, 2000. Falk traces the history of the growth of the concept and pursuit of human rights since World War II. He then describes the emergence of new challenges and new global aspirations.

Frank, T. *One Market Under God: Extreme Capitalism, Market Populism, and the End of Economic Democracy.* London: Vintage, 2002. Frank examines the contradictions in the prevailing view that markets and democracy are inextricably linked. He concludes that corporate globalization cannot be reformed from within but must be met by outside forces.

Giroux, H. A. *Stealing Innocence: Corporate Culture's War on Children.* New York: Palgrave, 2000. Giroux examines the myth that democracy is linked to the market, the myth that power does not affect children, and the myth that education has no role in improving the world. He then argues that teaching could be done in ways to benefit the public rather than corporations.

Griffin, Keith. *Studies in Development Strategy and Systemic Transformation.* New York: St. Martin's Press, 2000. These studies consider the human side of economic development: culture, human development, wealth inequality, and transition to markets.

Hurrell, Andres, and Ngaire Woods, eds. *Inequality, Globalization, and World Politics.* Oxford: Oxford University Press, 1999. The gap between rich and poor is widening in developing countries. These essays ask whether globalization can be harnessed to slow this process.

Kane, Joe. *Savages.* New York: Alfred A. Knopf, 1995. Kane lived and worked with the Huaorani peoples of Ecuador while they struggled for their land against multinational petroleum companies. Missionaries and environmentalists from outside meant well but did not always help.

Khan, A. R., and C. Riskin. *Inequality and Poverty in China in the Age of Globalization.* Oxford: Oxford University Press, 2001. Data collected separately in 1988 and 1995 form the basis for analysis of changes in poverty and inequality in China.

Nye, Joseph, and John D. Donahue, eds. *Governance in a Globalizing World.* Washington, D.C.: Brookings Institution, 2000. Discusses the importance of government action in protecting citizens' culture and economic well-being in the face of globalization.

Palast, Greg. *The Best Democracy Money Can Buy: An Investigative Reporter Exposes the Truth About Globalization, Corporate Cons, and High Finance Fraudsters.* London: Pluto Press, 2002. A wry and outraged exposé of MNCs, banks, and other miscreants in the globalization game. How globalization actually undermines democracy.

Tabb, William K. *The Amoral Elephant: Globalization and the Struggle for Social Justice in the Twenty-first Century.* New York: Monthly Review Press, 2001. Tabb describes the present-day capitalist system, globalization, and American domination. Globalization is not an inevitable force; it requires the support of governments, and people who understand it can and should resist it, as they began to do in Seattle.

Tran, Van Hoa, ed. *The Social Impact of the Asia Crisis.* Houndmills, UK, and New York: Palgrave, 2000. These papers look at how the Asian financial crisis affected human beings and how the situation could have been handled better. Discussions focus on Indonesia, Vietnam, and China.

Articles and Papers

Amnesty International. "Globalise This: Human Rights." *The OECD Observer* 231/232 (May 2002): 38–39. Since 2001, Amnesty International has moved from focusing solely on prisoners to a new focus on human rights, including economic, social, and cultural rights. The campaign will take up the effect of globalization on human rights.

"Bottom of the Barrel: East Africa's Oil Boom Displays the Most Extreme Examples of Misery Amidst Plenty." *Energy* 28, no. 3 (Summer 2003): 31. African and Northern (Hemisphere) governments have joined with oil companies to develop African oil very quickly. While the oil revenues raise promise for Africa's poor, it will take major structural changes if the poor are to benefit from the boom.

Bowles, Samuel. "Globalization and Redistribution." Paper given at Stiglitz Summer Research Workshop on Poverty. Washington, D.C., July 6–8, 1999. Bowles examines whether globalization hinders the attempts of governments and labor unions to alleviate poverty.

Brysk, Alison. "Globalization: The Double-Edged Sword." *NACLA Report on the Americas* 34, no. 1: 29–33. While globalization poses a threat to human rights in Latin America, the Latin American human rights movement has globalized. Both transnational legal proceedings, such as those against Augusto Pinochet of Chile, and global information outreach, such as that of the Mexican Zapatistas, represent new means for defending human rights.

Buckley, Ross P. "The Essential Flaw in Globalisation of Capital Markets: Its Impact on Human Rights in Developing Countries," *California Western International Law Journal* 32, no.1 (2000): 119–131. The globalization of capital markets, which made capital easily available to developing countries, turned sour in a series of financial crises. These new international markets have had a deleterious effect on the human rights and human condition of poor people in these countries.

Deaton, Angus. "Measuring Poverty in a Growing World (or Measuring Growth in a Poor World)." *Review of Economics and Statistics* 87, no. 1 (February 2005): 1. It is still controversial whether growth reduces world poverty. The author argues that today's statistical procedures understate poverty reduction at the same time that they overstate growth.

Deininger, Klaus, and Lyn Squire. *Economic Growth and Income Inequality: Re-Examining the Links.* Washington, D.C.: World Bank Finance and Development, March 1997. Some economists argue that inequality increases in the early stages of development; others show that income inequality slows growth. The authors examine the evidence.

Department for International Development, United Kingdom. *Eliminating World Poverty: Making Globalization Work for the Poor.* London: White Paper on International Development, December 2000. This White Paper analyzes the nature of globalization in the light of accepted international development goals. It advocates how to manage globalization so that the wealth, technology, and progress it generates will reduce poverty and benefit people.

Dollar, David. "Globalization, Poverty and Inequality since 1980." *World Bank Policy Research Working Paper,* no. WPS 3333 (June 2004). Dollar argues that in the recent era of globalization, poor countries have grown more swiftly than rich ones, poverty has decreased worldwide, and so has inequality both within and between countries. Nevertheless, wage inequality is increasing, but it is not the whole picture for many people.

Dollar, David, and Aart Kraay. *Growth Is Good for the Poor.* Washington, D.C.: World Bank, April 2001. A rise in average income brings a proportionate rise in the average incomes in the poorest fifth. This much is true even in different areas and times, as well as at different income levels and rates of growth. However, the share of income that the poorest fifth get varies greatly with time and place, and the reasons for this are not well understood.

Annotated Bibliography

Howard-Hassmann, Rhoda E. "Culture, Human Rights, and the Politics of Resentment in the Era of Globalization." *Human Rights Review* 6, no. 1 (October–December 2004): 5. Political leaders have been using the politics of resentment to control their societies and protect their own interests, and this policy has intensified in the face of globalization. However, globalization also means that human rights activists come ever more into contact with people everywhere, spreading their ideals and threatening established leaders.

Kanbur, Ravi, and Nora Lustig. "Why Is Inequality Back on the Agenda?" Paper prepared for the Annual Bank Conference on Development Economics, World Bank. Washington D.C., April 28–30, 1999. Inequality has been changing within developing countries and between countries. This paper looks at growth and distribution and analyzes efficiency and equity.

Krasner, Stephen D. "Sovereignty." *Foreign Policy* 122 (January–February 2001): 20–29. International pressure on governments to improve treatment of their citizens is not new, but globalization is giving it new meaning. Unfortunately, the United Nations is ill equipped to enforce human rights.

Kufour, Edward. "South Refuses to Compromise Sovereignty." *Earth Island Journal* 7, no. 3 (Summer 1996): 8–10. This is a statement delivered on behalf of the Group of 77 less developed nations before the Earth Summit of 1992. It asserts that "the global commons" hides an attempt to allow more developed nations to get control of the resources of the less developed ones.

Lindgren Alves, José A. "The Declaration of Human Rights in Postmodernity." *Human Rights Quarterly* 22, no. 2 (2000): 478–500. The UN Declaration of Human Rights has gradually changed the concept of human rights, making them more than a matter of national choice. It has led to the International Law of Human Rights. As it applies universally, it relates to globalization in fundamental ways.

McCarthy, Joseph R. "The Third United Nations World Conference on the Least Developed Countries: A Global Agenda for the New Millennium." *New York Law School Journal of Human Rights* 18, no. 3 (2002): 487–497. The LDCs have severe poverty and lack the capacity to provide basic necessities. The UN has begun a "Programme of Action" to improve both physical and social infrastructure and, in turn, health care, education, and social services, as well as to expand trade.

McCorquodale, Robert, and Richard Fairbrother. "Globalization and Human Rights." *Human Rights Quarterly* 21, no. 3 (1999): 735–766. Globalization has brought technological and communications advances that create rising expectations, but development strategies have ignored the people whose countries are targeted for economic development.

Moore, Rebecca R. "Globalization and the Future of U.S. Human Rights Policy." *Washington Quarterly* 21, no. 4 (1998): 193–212. Moore asserts that recent U.S. administrations have overused punitive means against human rights violators, while failing to build democracy and civil society. Globalization can provide new opportunities to defend human rights.

Norberg-Hodge, Helena. "The Consumer Monoculture." *International Journal of Consumer Studies* 27, no. 4 (2003): 258–261. Global trade and advertising that promote Western culture are destroying cultural diversity. The author urges measures be taken to protect national cultural identity.

"A Rigged Game." *Canada and the World Backgrounder* 70, no. 5 (March 2005): S14. The Make Poverty History group demonstrates how the rules of international trade are ruinous for the poorest people of the world. Allegedly "free" trade is in fact governed by rules that favor the wealthiest nations and the most powerful corporations. The WTO, WB, and IMF are now feeling pressure to change these rules.

Shiva, Vandana. "New Emperors, Old Clothes." *The Ecologist* 35, no. 6 (July–August 2005): 22–23. Theories differ as to what causes poverty and what role the IMF, WB, and other international monetary agencies play. The very system used by the rich countries to create wealth at the same time removes resources from the poor; ending this system would be an effective way to end poverty.

Short, Clare, and Edward Goldsmith. "Does Development Create or Mitigate Poverty?" *The Ecologist* 35, no. 3 (April 2005): 28–32. Proponents of development hold that there are fair international rules on trade, the environment, and conflict resolution that will resolve problems of poverty. Opponents state that economic development floods the world with the exports of the industrial world, driving small traditional farmers and producers into deeper poverty.

Suryahadi, Asep, Sudarno Sumarto, Yusuf Suharso, et al. *The Evolution of Poverty during the Crisis in Indonesia, 1996–99.* Washington, D.C.: World Bank, September 2000. The economic crisis in Indonesia caused a relative increase in the price of food. Hence, estimates of the rate of poverty are very dependent on the weight given to food in the calculations.

World Bank. "Globalization, Growth and Poverty: Building an Inclusive World Economy." *World Bank Policy Research Report,* no. 23,591 (December 2001). This report examines the anxieties about impoverishment and cultural homogenization that globalization has provoked. It concludes that countries that have become part of the global industrial world have seen reduced poverty and suggests policy for bringing more countries into this sphere.

Yao, Shujie. "Economic Growth, Income Inequality and Poverty in China under Economic Reforms." *Journal of Development Studies* 35, no. 6 (August 1999): Despite China's quadrupled GDP between 1978 and 1996, tripled urban incomes, and nearly quadrupled rural incomes, massive inequality kept poverty from being reduced proportionally. Rural areas and some geographic areas are particularly impoverished.

Zhang, Zongyi, and Shujie Yao. "Regional Inequalities in Contemporary China Measured by GDP and Consumption." *Economic Issues* 6, no. 2 (September 2001): The study looks at consumption and GDP over a nearly 50-year period to evaluate the results of economic reforms in China. Inequality between regions has been growing steadily, both before and after the reforms. Inequality in per capita GDP is greater than inequality in consumption.

Annotated Bibliography

SUSTAINABLE DEVELOPMENT, ENVIRONMENT, AND AGRICULTURE

Books

Bhaskar, V., and Andrew Glyn, eds. *The North, the South and the Environment: Ecological Restraints and the Global Economy.* New York: St. Martin's Press, 1995. Addresses negotiations about global warming, the ozone layer, and biodiversity in the perspective of the North-South (Hemisphere) conflict. Alain Lipietz, author of one chapter, suggests that "global enclosure" may address the crisis of the "global commons."

Cowell, Adrian. *The Decade of Destruction: The Crusade to Save the Amazon Rainforests.* New York: Henry Holt, 1990. Cowell filmed the Amazon rain forest over a period of 30 years and watched it being burned to clear the land. However, he sees hope in the work of grassroots groups such as the rubber tappers to save this environment by using it for a sustainable livelihood.

The Ecologist. Whose Common Future? Reclaiming the Commons. Philadelphia: New Society Publishers, 1993. In the wake of the Earth Summit in Rio de Janeiro, *The Ecologist* brought out this book introducing the concept of the "commons," defined broadly to include air, water, habitats, and land, as well as streets, the airwaves, contraception, language, and time. It shows how dismantling and privatizing the commons has led to environmental crises.

French, Hillary. *Vanishing Borders: Protecting the Planet in the Age of Globalization.* New York: Norton, 2000. Globalization's effects on the environment and on people's efforts to protect it.

Gedicks, Al. *The New Resource Wars: Native and Environmental Struggles Against Multinational Corporations.* Boston: South End Press, 1993. Indigenous people and environmentalists have allied in many places to resist MNCs. Opposition to mining in northern Wisconsin, hydroelectric dams in Quebec, logging in Malaysia, and drilling for oil in Ecuador makes for enlightening comparison.

Goldman, Michael, ed. *Privatizing Nature: Political Struggles for the Global Commons.* London: Pluto Press, 1998. Once a familiar political concept, the commons has been overtaken by a wave of privatization but is making a comeback. The book provides case studies of local and international social movements that are trying to make societies' approaches to nature less exploitative, more socially just, and sounder for the environment.

Gray, Andrew, Alejandro Parellada, and Hellen Newing, eds. *From Principles to Practice: Indigenous People and Biodiversity Conservation in Latin America.* Copenhagen, Denmark: International Work Group for Indigenous Affairs, 1997. Excluding indigenous people from conservation areas is not a viable solution. Rather, indigenous territory must be protected so that the people there can preserve the local biodiversity.

Lipschutz, Ronnie D., and Ken Conca, eds. *The State and Social Power in Global Environmental Politics.* New York: Columbia University Press, 1993. These essays examine global environmental change from the viewpoint of international relations. The roles of both governmental and nongovernmental actors in the disputes around these changes are described.

Lomborg, Bjorn. *The Skeptical Environmentalist: Measuring the Real State of the World.* Cambridge: Cambridge University Press, 2001. Lomborg holds that the debate about the environment has been hampered by myths spread by the media. His book is intended to turn the discussion toward a factual basis.

Peet, Richard, and Michael Watts, eds. *Liberation Ecologies: Environment, Development and Social Movements.* London and New York: Routledge, 1996. Social movements that challenge environmental policy may actually have a different concept of both environment and development than the dominant paradigm in their society.

Princen, Thomas, and Matthias Finger, eds. *Environmental NGOs in World Politics: Linking the Local and the Global.* London and New York: Routledge, 1994. The world environmental crisis has given rise to the "NGO phenomenon," for NGOs are not limited by national borders. They can combine local and global issues better than multinational financial actors can. Their role in the Great Lakes Water Quality Agreement and several other such cases is detailed.

Revkin, Andrew. *The Burning Season: The Murder of Chico Mendes and the Fight for the Amazon Rain Forest.* Boston: Houghton Mifflin, 1990. Chico Mendes organized rubber tappers to resist the destruction of the Amazon rain forest of Brazil. The book tells about his life, work, and assassination in 1988.

Rich, Bruce M. *Mortgaging the Earth: The World Bank, Environmental Impoverishment, and the Crisis of Development.* Boston: Beacon Press, 1994. Rich was himself a participant in many WB projects and witnessed the environmental problems they frequently caused. He advocates more attention to the valuable local knowledge of grassroots actors as the key to preserving the environment and gives examples of sound projects where outside collaborators listened to the locals.

Shiva, Vandana. *Stolen Harvest: The Hijacking of the Global Food Supply.* Boston: South End Press, 1999. Shiva brings environmentalism, agriculture, spirituality, and women's rights to bear on the question of the world's food supply. Globalization does not bode well for it.

Wapner, Paul. *Environmental Activism and World Civic Politics.* Albany: State University of New York Press, 1996. Wapner studies Greenpeace, the World Wildlife Fund, and Friends of the Earth and concludes that world environmental issues should not be framed in terms of governments. There are other strategies, both global and local in scope.

Articles and Papers

Conca, Ken. "Rethinking the Ecology-Sovereignty Debate." *Millennium: Journal of International Studies* 23, no. 3 (1994): 701–711. It has been asserted both that international environmentalist pressure undermines national sovereignty and that it enhances it. Conca responds both that sovereignty must be understood in a more comprehensive way and that the role of environmentalists must be seen in a more complex way, for the issues themselves are very complicated.

Annotated Bibliography

Finnegan, William. "Leasing the Rain: The World Is Running Out of Fresh Water, and the Fight to Control It Has Begun." *The New Yorker* 78, no. 7 (April 8, 2002): 43. In the water wars of Cochabamba, Bolivia, citizens successfully resisted an attempt by Bechtel Corporation, with the cooperation of the Bolivian government, to privatize the public water supply. However, the world's supply of freshwater is limited and will ever more become a source of conflict.

Hardin, Garrett. "The Tragedy of the Commons." *Science* 162 (December 1968): 1,243–1,248. Hardin argues that the very concept of the commons is fundamentally unsustainable. Individuals will always gain more from overuse of the commons than they will lose from the eventual degradation of the resource.

Hart, Stuart L. "Beyond Greening: Strategies for a Sustainable World." *Harvard Business Review* 75, no. 1 (1997): 66–76. Hart views MNCs, as the potential saviors of the environment, for they have the capital to carry out their plans. He points out that while rich nations consume more resources, they also emit less pollution.

Jeffrey, Paul. "Depressed Coffee Prices Yield Suffering in Poor Countries." *National Catholic Reporter* 39, no. 14 (February 7, 2003): 12. Before 1989, the International Coffee Agreement kept coffee wholesale prices stable to ward off unrest that might lead to communism, but then the United States pulled out of the agreement, and prices fell. Low prices, caused also by high production and falling coffee consumption in the United States, have brought about a situation in which coffee farmers cannot earn a living.

Kane, Joe. "With Spears from All Sides." *The New Yorker* 69, no. 31 (September 1993): 54–79. Kane tells the story of an Ecuadorean tribe struggling against a multinational oil company for control of the land. Outside environmentalists, academics, and missionaries do not always help, nor do other indigenous groups, whose interests do not always coincide.

Kates, Robert W., Thomas M. Parris, and Anthony A. Leiserowitz. "What Is Sustainable Development? Goals, Indicators, Values, and Practice." *Environment* 47, no. 3 (April 2005): 8. Sustainable development is a commonly cited goal, but in fact it has not been clearly defined. There is an ambiguous but constructive definition: development that "meets the needs of the present without compromising the ability of future generations to meet their own needs."

Keck, Margaret E. "Social Equity and Environmental Politics in Brazil: Lessons from the Rubber Tappers of Acre." *Comparative Politics* 27, no. 4 (July 1995): 409–424. Keck describes the movement of the rubber tappers in western Brazil. Their struggles have come to symbolize how environmental and human rights are linked and how there is indeed a way to sustainable development.

Kneen, Brewster. "Size Is Everything." *The Ecologist* 33, no. 3 (April 2003): 48–51. Cargill, Inc. is the world's largest privately owned corporation. This survey of its economic, social, political, and environmental impacts worldwide demonstrate how it puts obstacles in the way of sustainable development and sound agricultural practices.

Pollan, Michael. "A Flood of US Corn Rips at the Heart of Mexico's Farms: The Effect of Free Trade in Corn Is the Decimation of the Farming Communities South of the Mexican Border." *The Ecologist* 34, no. 5 (June 2004): 6. NAFTA, by forcing

Mexico to lower tariffs in 1994 that had protected corn, made it possible for U.S. farmers to sell the staple corn very cheaply in Mexico. Unable to compete, Mexican farmers were forced off the land and became unemployed. Some take low-wage manufacturing jobs; others in desperation immigrate to the United States.

Rich, Bruce M. "The Emperor's New Clothes: The World Bank and Environmental Reform." *World Policy Journal* (Spring 1990): 305–329. In 1987, the WB announced reforms that were to address environmental concerns. Rich asserts that these were merely a cover for continued environmental destruction.

———. "The Multilateral Development Banks, Environmental Policy and the United States." *Ecology Law Quarterly* 12, no. 4 (1985): 681–745. The U.S. government has attempted to influence how foreign aid affects the environment, focusing first on USAID and then in the 1980s on multilateral institutions. To the extent that the latter have been concerned about the environment, it is mainly thanks to U.S. actions.

Sassen, Saskia. "The Ecology of Global Economic Power: Changing Investment Practices to Promote Environmental Sustainability." *Journal of International Affairs* 58, no. 2 (Spring 2005): 11. The concentrated power of corporate capital and the huge population concentration of large cities are two major sources of problems for the environment. However, their very concentration could provide the opportunity to change their direction into one that promotes environmental sustainability.

Silva, Eduardo. "Thinking Politically about Sustainable Development in the Tropical Forests of Latin America." *Development and Change* 25 (1994): 697–721. The article examines case studies from Brazil, Mexico, and Peru. Local groups have banded together with international allies to force governments to support sustainable development.

Smith, Mick. "Against the Enclosure of the Ethical Commons: Radical Environmentalism as an 'Ethics of Place.'" *Environmental Ethics* 18 (Winter 1997): 339–353. Smith suggests that modern ethical systems, whether utilitarian or based on rights, tend to break down duties and obligations into privatized bundles. An example of a challenge to this way of thinking is to be found in the "ethics of place," exemplified by protests against road building in the United Kingdom.

Stanley, Denise. "Demystifying the Tragedy of the Commons: The Resin Tappers of Honduras." *Grassroots Development* 15, no. 3 (1991): 26–33. Theoreticians have insisted that property held in common will inevitably be overused and environmentally degraded; however, Honduran resin tapper organizations have found ways to maintain a healthy forest that is held in common.

Vaughn, Scott. "How Green Is NAFTA? Measuring the Impacts of Agricultural Trade." *Environment* 46, no. 2 (March 2004): 26–43. NAFTA agricultural policy is damaging the environment in Mexico. The articles explains the mechanisms.

World Conference on Global Commons. "Tokyo Declaration on Global Commons." *Environmental Policy and Law* 29, no. 5 (November 1999): 249–250. This conference convened by Global Environmental Action in cooperation with UNCED issued these recommendations for managing the global environmental commons in a way consistent with sustainable development. The recommendations cover finance, international organizations, science and technology, information and communications, resource management and energy science, the urban environment, and regional cooperation.

ECONOMICS, FINANCE, AND MULTINATIONAL CORPORATIONS

Books and Book Chapters

Anderson, Sarah, et al. *Field Guide to the Global Economy.* New York: New Press, 2000. Analyzes the primarily negative effects of globalization as practiced by MNCs.

Barnet, Richard, and John Cavanaugh. *Global Dreams: Imperial Corporations and the New World Order.* New York: Simon and Schuster, 1994. An in-depth look at MNCs and their tremendous influence on the global economy and the world's working people.

Bates, Robert H. *Open-Economy Politics: The Political Economy of the World Coffee Trade.* Princeton, N.J.: Princeton University Press, 1997. This book gives the history of the International Coffee Organization. While it lasted, it regulated the price of coffee by setting quotas, discouraging competition among exporters, and fostering cooperation. It also protected consumers.

Callinicos, Alex. *Against the Third Way.* Cambridge, Oxford, and Boston: Polity Press, 2001. Callinicos argues that the "Third Way" politics of Tony Blair, Bill Clinton, and Gerhard Schröder have in fact put conservative, neoliberal policies in place and worked in the interest of MNCs. What is needed is an international movement against global capitalism, such as that begun in Seattle and Prague, one that challenges the market.

Cohen, Benjamin. "Balance of Payments Financing: Evolution of a Regime." In *International Regimes.* Edited by Stephen Krasner. Ithaca, N.Y.: Cornell University Press, 1983. International financial institutions were created to extend balance-of-payments financing. They evolved into powerful institutions capable of shaping the policies of the borrowers.

Danaher, Kevin, ed. *Corporations Are Gonna Get Your Mama: Globalization and the Downsizing of the American Dream.* Monroe, Maine: Common Courage Press, 1996. Business and media together have created a myth that globalization is a force for betterment, but in fact American jobs are being lost. New alternative institutions are needed to resist corporate domination.

Friedman, Milton. *Capitalism and Freedom: Fortieth Anniversary Edition.* Chicago: University of Chicago Press, 2002. This is the classical economic theory of capitalism. It argues that capitalism is at the root of both economic and political freedom and that government should promote capitalism.

Gabel, Medard, and Henry Bruner. *Globalinc: An Atlas of the Multinational Corporation.* New York: New Press, 2003. The authors present new and unexpected data about MNCs. They find them to be neither entirely evil nor always a force for prosperity.

George, Susan. *The Lugano Report: On Preserving Capitalism in the Twenty-first Century.* London and Sterling, Va.: Pluto Press, 1999. George wrote this fictitious report, taking the viewpoint of the capitalists, to lay out what it would take to preserve capitalism in the face of the ecological and human damage it does to the world. The book distinguishes between the reforms that would curb the excesses of the system and thus ultimately strengthen it and those that would actually challenge its essence.

Gilpin, Robert, and Jean M. Gilpin. *The Challenge of Global Capitalism.* Princeton, N.J.: Princeton University Press, 2000. Gilpin holds that capitalism is the best system ever for creating wealth, but it is threatened by those who have less and want more. Globalization may have raised the stakes, making necessary a world monetary, trade, and investment regime that can convince or force people everywhere to accept it.

Graham, Edward M. *Fighting the Wrong Enemy: Antiglobal Activists and Multinational Enterprises.* Washington, D.C.: Institute for International Economics, 2000. Examining the opposition to globalization, Graham asks whether the MAI negotiations failed because of labor and NGO opposition or because of differences among the negotiating countries. He reassesses whether MNCs are negatively affecting workers in industrial and developing nations.

Hutton, Will, and Anthony Giddens, eds. *Global Capitalism.* New York: New Press, 2000. Capitalism dominates the world order, and for the first time it has become truly global, thanks to advances in technology and the new financial regime. Capitalism, seen both as an economic system and as a culture, makes for new opportunities but also for risks to the environment and social justice and the problem of privately owned transnational media.

Keynes, John Maynard. *The General Theory of Employment, Interest, and Money.* New York: Prometheus Books, 1997. Controversial when it first appeared during the Great Depression, this theory has become commonly accepted. Keynes pointed out that putting more money in the hands of the poor and unemployed gives rise to greater demand for goods and services and stimulates prosperity throughout the economy.

Krugman, Paul. *Peddling Prosperity: Economics Sense and Nonsense in an Age of Diminishing Expectations.* New York: W. W. Norton, 1995. A leading economist discusses how the ways in which we think about economics has led to a raft of misguided governmental policies.

———. *Pop Internationalism.* Cambridge, Mass.: MIT Press, 1996. Essays on economics in the age of globalization.

Kuttner, Robert. *The End of Laissez-Faire: National Purpose and the Global Economy after the Cold War.* New York: Knopf, 1991. A look at the rise of globalization and how it affects governance and development, with suggestions for giving capitalism a more "human face."

Lindsey, Brink. *Against the Dead Hand: The Uncertain Struggle for Global Capitalism.* New York: John Wiley and Sons, 2001. The desire for top-down control and central planning has dominated the economy for a century and still shapes the world. Globalization has a long way to go before there is real change.

Lipson, Charles. "Banker's Dilemmas: Private Cooperation in Rescheduling Sovereign Debts." In *Cooperation Under Anarchy.* Edited by Kenneth Oye. Princeton, N.J.:

Princeton University Press, 1986. What allows creditors to cooperate or prevents them from doing so? The IMF has facilitated creditor cooperation greatly.

Madeley, John. *Big Business, Poor Peoples: The Impact of Transnational Corporations on the World's Poor.* New York: Zed, 1999. Reveals how MNCs perpetuate poverty and why regulations are necessary.

McKinley, Terry, ed. *Macroeconomic Policy, Growth and Poverty Reduction.* New York: Palgrave, 2001. The studies in this collection are empirically based and often critical of standard theory and practice. The criticisms and observations are now being incorporated in the latest development policies.

Monbiot, George. *Captive State: The Corporate Takeover of Britain.* London: Pan, 2000. Monbiot describes the expansion of corporate power and globalization. He demonstrates that their influence over government is undermining democracy.

Pettifor, Ann, ed. *Real World Economic Outlook: The Legacy of Globalization: Debt and Deflation.* New York: Palgrave Macmillan, 2003. Essays in this collection examine policies of the WB and IMF and the debt they exacerbate, as well as deflation and increasing unemployment, underemployment, and poverty. The authors conclude that economic liberalization, that is, free trade, contributes to these problems.

Polanyi, Karl. *The Great Transformation.* Boston: Beacon Press, 2001. Polanyi combines economic history, anthropology, and political theory to demonstrate that "free" markets will not solve our problems, for there is nothing natural or even free about these markets. The book brings much insight to bear on issues surrounding not only globalization and the IMF and WB but also the debate over privatization.

Ricardo, David. *Principles of Political Economy and Taxation.* New York: Prometheus Books, 1996. This was the book that originally laid out the principles of market economics. Its innovations included the theory of comparative advantage in international trade.

Rosenberg, Justin. *The Follies of Globalisation Theory.* New York and London: Verso Books, 2001. Rosenberg critiques modern globalization theory. It has been obsessed with "spatiality" and has stood in the way of understanding actual globalization.

Schumpeter, Joseph A. *Capitalism, Socialism, and Democracy.* New York: Harper Perennial, 1962. Schumpeter takes Marx seriously and proposes a socialism that has similarities with that of Marx. But he also seriously disagrees with Marx. He argues that if capitalism fails, it will be because it succeeds too well and leads to overly concentrated monopolies that end up destroying competition.

Smith, Adam. *Wealth of Nations.* Amherst, N.Y.: Prometheus Books, 1991. Smith's book laid the foundations for modern economics, although without the extensive mathematics that is de rigeur nowadays. He demonstrated how labor had to be specialized, how supply and demand determine the prices of commodities in markets, how capital works, and the need for "unproductive" as well as "productive" labor. He also established the role of government in the economy.

Articles and Papers

Ames, Brian, Ward Brown, Shanta Devarajan, et al. "Macroeconomic Policy and Poverty Reduction." *IMF Poverty Reduction Strategy Sourcebook* (April 2, 2001). Macroeconomic stability is needed for strong and sustainable growth, and growth is what most affects poverty. Therefore, macroeconomic stability is a key factor in poverty reduction.

Bognanno, Mario F., Michael P. Keane, and Donghoon Yang. "The Influence of Wages and Industrial Relations Environments on the Production Location Decisions of U.S. Multinational Corporations." *Industrial and Labor Relations Review* 58 (January 2005): 171–200. Low wages and nonunion workforces are attractive to American-based MNCs. However, their decisions to relocate are in the end based more on the size of the market where they locate. The authors also conclude that reduction of tariffs leads to less job loss than had previously been supposed.

Cashin, Paul, Paolo Mauro, Catherine Pattilo, et al. "Macroeconomic Policies and Poverty Reduction: Stylized Facts and an Overview of Research." *IMF Working Papers,* 01/135 (September 2001). The authors briefly summarize work on the connection between macroeconomic policy and reduction of poverty. They correlate rising standards in 100 nations with macroeconomic factors and suggest avenues for future inquiry.

Cobham, Alexander. "Capital Account Liberalisation and Poverty." *Working Paper,* no. 70. Finance and Trade Policy Research Centre, Queen Elizabeth House, University of Oxford, April 2001. Multilateral institutions, seeking to reduce poverty, have focused mainly on growth. Capital account regulation also needs attention; it appears that capital controls need to be kept as an instrument of antipoverty policy.

Dailami, Mansoor, and Nadeem ul Haque. "What Macroeconomic Policies Are 'Sound?'" *World Bank Workpapers* (October 1998). Volatility is an inevitable aspect of the globalized financial market in which developing countries must operate. This paper suggests principles to guide their macroeconomic policies.

Drummonds, Henry H. "Transnational Small and Emerging Business in a World of Nikes and Microsofts." *Journal of Small and Emerging Business Law* 4 (2000): 249. Drummonds surveys labor market globalizations and concerns for international labor standards. He concludes that private, not public, mechanisms will prevail.

Ellwood, Wayne. "The Great Privatization Grab." *New Internationalist,* 9, no. 4 (April 2003): 9. Ellwood argues that privatizing public assets is tantamount to stealing. The notion of the public good and public goods needs to be restored.

Ferreira, Francisco, Giovanna Prennushi, and Martin Ravallion. *Protecting the Poor from Macroeconomic Shocks.* Washington, D.C.: World Bank, Washington, 1999. Policies including a public safety net should be in place even before a macroeconomic shock hits. If there is a shock, interest rates should be reduced as soon as possible and public spending restored, jobs should be created building infrastructure, investment in public goods should not be reduced, the social fabric must be protected, and accurate information should be put out.

Annotated Bibliography

Galeano, Eduardo H. "The Waters of October." *New Internationalist,* no. 376 (March 2005): 5. In October 2004, Uruguay held an election in which the Left won for the first time ever, and people explicitly rejected the proposed privatization of water in a plebiscite. The United States has failed to notice these events.

"Globalisation with a Third-World Face: Economics Focus." *The Economist* (U.S.) 375, no. 8,421 (April 9, 2005): 66. MNCs based in industrial nations that invest in Third-World countries are well known, but now the investment often flows from Third World countries. Companies based in India, Brazil, Malaysia, South Africa, and China have at times bought First World companies or put their plants in still poorer, lower-wage lands, rather than investing at home.

Knowles, James C., Ernesto M. Pernia, and Mary Racelis. "Social Consequences of the Financial Crisis in Asia: The Deeper Crisis." Paper presented at the Manila Social Forum, Manila, Philippines, November 9–12, 1999. Survey data and participatory methods were used in Indonesia, the Republic of Korea, Laos, Malaysia, the Philippines, and Thailand to assess the social impact of the recent financial crisis. It affected prices, property, employment, income distribution and poverty, education, health, and the environment.

Morley, Samuel A. *The Impact of the Macroeconomic Environment on Urban Poverty.* Washington, D.C.: World Bank, January 1999. Macroeconomic policies and conditions can set the stage for the success or failure of programs intended to address poverty, especially urban poverty. Morley examines this in light of growth rates, minimum wages, unemployment rates, and exchange rates.

Prahalad, C. K., and Allen Hammond. "Serving the World's Poor, *Profitably.*" *Harvard Business Review* (September 2002): 48–59. The authors suggest that the industries of the developed world could find a profitable market among the poor of the whole world by offering low-priced goods and services, such as cell phones that can be used for a fee. The poor are already paying more for such goods and services, so there is room for better-targeted products.

Sahay, Ratna, Paul Cashin, and Paolo Mauro. "Macroeconomic Policies and Poverty: The State of Play and a Research Agenda." Asian Development Bank (February 3, 2001). Research into how macroeconomic policies affect poverty has been extensive but not deep. This paper looks at 100 countries in the last quarter of the 20th century, estimates well-being, suggests which factors are key, and suggests further research.

Sala-I-Martin, Xavier. "The World Distribution of Income (Estimated from Individual Country Distributions)." *National Bureau of Economic Research Working Paper,* no. 893 (May 2002). This economist has examined income data for 125 countries, at several points in time, breaking the population into centiles. He concludes that inequality and poverty have been reduced, but certain regions, such as sub-Saharan Africa, have experienced economic disaster.

Sikkel, Marinus. "A Reinvigorated Instrument for Global Investment." *The OECD Observer* 225 (March 2001): 29–30. In 2000, the OECD issued new Guidelines for Multinational Enterprises, addressing concerns such as environmental protection and human rights, the latter newly added. The guidelines are not binding but encourage the governments of the industrial nations to enforce them.

THE INTERNATIONAL MONETARY FUND, THE WORLD BANK, AND THE WORLD TRADE ORGANIZATION

Books

Bandow, Doug, and Ian Vasquez. *Perpetuating Poverty: The World Bank, the IMF, and the Developing World.* Washington, D.C.: Cato Institute, 1994. How the economic policies of these international agencies creates poverty in developing countries.

Cockburn, Alexander, Jeffrey St. Clair, and Allan Sekula. *Five Days That Shook the World: The Battle for Seattle and Beyond.* New York: Verso Books, 2000. The authors hail the challenge to global capitalism that burst forth in Seattle, Washington, D.C., and Los Angeles and caused people to question the system and the free trade that it sought. They document the trend toward criminalizing protest and use of paramilitary forces to suppress it.

Empty Promises: The IMF, The World Bank, and the Planned Failure of Global Capitalism. Washington, D.C.: 50 Years Is Enough, 2003. A series of essays illustrating the failure of its major global proponents to make free-market capitalism work for people around the world.

Fox, Jonathan A., and L. David Brown, eds. *The Struggle for Accountability: The World Bank, NGOs and Grassroots Movements.* Cambridge, Mass.: MIT Press, 1998. The book studies cases of NGO advocacy aimed at WB projects or at broader WB policy. Both the effectiveness of the campaigns and their accountability to grassroots organizations are studied.

George, Susan, and Fabrizio Sabelli. *Faith and Credit: The World Bank's Secular Empire.* Boulder, Colo.: Westview Press, 1994. The WB has grown greatly and become more influential, even though in terms of its own mission and its own data it has failed. The authors explain this as a question of secular faith.

Heredia, Carlos, and Mary Purcell. *The Polarization of Mexican Society: A Grassroots View of World Bank Economic Adjustment Programs.* Washington, D.C.: The Development Gap and Equipo Pueblo, 1994. Southern and Northern (Hemisphere) NGOs worked together to produce this study of how structural adjustment has worsened income inequality and damaged the environment. Both rural producers and urban consumers were examined.

Hockman, Bernard, Aaditya Mattoo, and Philip English, eds. *Development, Trade, and the WTO: A Handbook.* Washington, D.C.: World Bank, 2002. The WB declares that those developing countries that have integrated into the global economy have done better than those that have remained outside. Integration typically involves policies that attract investment and involve impoverished citizens in the new industrialization.

Nelson, Paul. *The World Bank and Non-Governmental Organizations: The Limits of Apolitical Development.* New York: St. Martin's Press, 1995. The WB has been collaborating more and more with NGOs, but the role of the NGOs remains small and uninfluential. Unfortunately, the Bank tends to use NGOs as cover to take the blame for suffering caused by structural adjustment, while the Bank hides behind the claim that it is apolitical.

Paul, Samuel, and Arturo Israel, eds. *Nongovernmental Organizations and the World Bank: Cooperation for Development.* Washington, D.C.: World Bank, 1991. This is the WB's own study of the role of NGOs in the development projects it sponsors. It finds both positive aspects and limitations.

Reddaway, Peter, and Dmitri Glinski. *The Tragedy of Russia's Reforms.* Herndon, Va.: U.S. Institute of Peace Press, 2001. An analysis of how the policies of globalization's organizations affected Russia and its people.

Schwartzman, Stephan. *Bankrolling Disaster: International Development Banks and the Global Environment.* San Francisco: Sierra Club Books, 1986. The book describes some environmentally disastrous projects financed by the WB and describes how such projects are proposed and carried out. It is designed to help activists understand how to influence such projects for greater environmental sensitivity.

Wallach, Lori, and Michelle Sforza. *The WTO: Five Years of Reasons to Resist Corporate Globalization.* New York: Seven Stories Press, 1999. Analysis, with examples, to show why the WTO as presently constituted harms local economies.

Articles and Papers

Ala'i, Padideh. "A Human Rights Critique of the WTO: Some Preliminary Observations." *George Washington International Law Review,* 33, nos. 3–4 (2001): 537–553. A recent UN report has criticized the WTO for representing globalization of trade and commerce without regard for economic, social, and cultural rights. However, such rights are gaining new recognition and could affect the interpretation of WTO requirements.

Alben, Elissa. "GATT and the Fair Wage: A Historical Perspective on the Labor-Trade Link," *Columbia Law Review* 101 (October 2001): 1,410. When GATT was first negotiated, fair labor standards were seen as a matter of wages. Now they are seen as a matter of human rights. Nevertheless, there is no good precedent for separating labor issues from trade agreements.

Bal, Salman. "International Free Trade Agreements and Human Rights: Reinterpreting Article XX of the GATT." *Minnesota Journal of Global Trade* 10 (Winter 2001): 62. Bal argues that labor rights cannot be separated from international trade policy. He examines GATT and the WTO agreement and concludes that they can be used to protect human and labor rights.

Bird, Graham. "The IMF and Developing Countries: A Review of the Evidence and Policy Options." *International Organization* 50, no. 3 (1996): 477–513. Bird reviews the existing literature on the role of the IMF in developing countries. As a financial institution that extends credit, it has power, and it has used its power to shape economic policies of the borrowing nations.

Birdsall, N., and J. L. Londono. "Asset Inequality Matters: An Assessment of the World Bank's Approach to Poverty Reduction." *American Economic Review* 87, no. 2, AEA Papers and Proceedings (1997): 32–37. Asset inequalities as well as income inequalities are important in dealing with poverty, and the WB needs to take asset inequalities into account.

Davis, Bob. "IMF Wants Further Economic Liberalization in Latin America." *Wall Street Journal* (Eastern Edition), February 9, 2005, p. A9. The IMF is disappointed that despite economic growth, Latin American countries have not liberalized their economies, repealed their labor laws, and ended corruption.

Diamond, Stephen F. "Bridging the Divide: An Alternative Approach to International Labor Rights after the Battle of Seattle." *Pepperdine Law Review* 29 (2001): 115–146. Diamond analyzes the issues between labor and the Clinton administration during the WTO 2001 meeting and the debate over trade relations with China. He advocates using the WTO to discuss issues of wages, hours, and working conditions.

Dillon, Sara Ann. "A Deep Structure Connection: Child Labor and the World Trade Organization." *ILSA Journal of International and Comparative Law* 9, no. 2 (Spring 2003): 443–456. The WTO at this time is in no way capable of responding to even the worst of child labor, nor are trade sanctions and import restrictions effective. The WTO would have to set specific goals based on internationally agreed upon principles and reorient the IMF and WB if child labor is to be effectively combatted on a worldwide basis.

DiMatteo, Larry A. "The Doha Declaration and Beyond: Giving a Voice to Non-Trade Concerns Within the WTO Trade Regime." *Vanderbilt Journal of Transnational Law* 36 (January 2003): 95–160. The author examines the environmental, labor, and consumer concerns that the WTO does not take into account at present. The Doha Declaration has taken up some of these nontrade concerns, but not labor standards.

Easterly, William. *The Effect of IMF and World Bank Programs on Poverty.* Washington, D.C.: World Bank. October 31, 2000. Structural adjustment loans by the WB and IMF have little effect on growth and particularly little effect on the poor. The poor appear to be isolated both from the sectors that expand with adjustment loans and from the sectors that may lose the protection they had before the loan programs were carried out.

"Globalization Under Siege," *America* 182 (2000): 3. Demonstrators against the WB and IMF in April 2000 protested against policies that were impoverishing people, causing environmental destruction, putting wealth in the hands of the already rich, and stoking social and political conflict. They were arguing that the transnational institutions should adopt the transparency they advocate, that the working poor should not bear the burden of repaying debts they never requested, and that governments must protect their own people.

Healy, Mark Alan, and Ernesto Seman. "The Costs of Orthodoxy: Argentina Was the Poster Child for Austerity and Obedience to the IMF Formula. Not Surprisingly, Its Economy Tanked." *The American Prospect* 13, no. 1 (January 1, 2002): A34. In the 1990s, Argentina carefully followed the orders of the IMF and had a period of privatization, decreased social spending, stable currency, and swift economic growth. Then everything fell apart, and the authors argue that it was predictable that austerity policies would ruin the Argentine economy.

Howse, Robert. "Back to Court after Shrimp/Turtle? Almost but Not Quite Yet: India's Short Lived Challenge to Labor and Environmental Exceptions in the European Union's Generalized System of Preferences." *American University International Law Review* 18, no. 1333 (2003): 1,333–1,381. The author argues that a WTO panel's ruling that allowed exporting countries to restrict imports on policy grounds set a precedent. There can now be new debate about labor and environmental preferences at the WTO.

Josephs, Hilary K. "Upstairs, Trade Law; Downstairs, Labor Law." *George Washington Law Review* 33, nos. 3–4 (2001): 849–872. Josephs investigates the lack of labor law and labor aspects of immigration law in GATT and the WTO. Labor issues could be advanced through side agreements, by giving the ILO a formal role with the WTO, or better yet through WTO dispute settlement.

Mallaby, Sebastian. "Saving the World Bank." *Foreign Affairs* 184, no. 3 (May–June 2005): 75. The WB is huge and prosperous, pouring more money into the developing world than does the United States in foreign aid, and moreover its responses to crises have been very swift. However, the author fears that if it listens to critics, it may change its practices and lose its effectiveness.

Mitro, Mathew T. "Outlawing the Trade in Child Labor Products: Why the GATT Article XX Health Exception Authorizes Unilateral Sanctions." *American University Law Review* 51 (2002): 1,223. GATT's Article 20 is designed to protect human health. Mitro argues that it could be used to defend sanctions against goods produced by child labor.

Moorman, Yasmin. "Integration of ILO Core Rights Labor Standards into the WTO." *Columbia Journal of Transnational Law* 39, no. 2 (2001): 555–583. The ILO has issued a Declaration on Fundamental Principles and Rights at Work, and now scholars are looking at how it could be enforced under WTO dispute settlement. Moorman argues that WTO procedures are ill-suited for this purpose; innovative approaches are needed instead.

Palast, Greg. "Resolved to Ruin: The World Bank/IMF Takeover, in Four Easy Steps." *Harper's Magazine* 306, no. 834 (March 2003): 48. While the mainstream has ridiculed protesters for claiming that there are secret agreements between the WB, IMF, and finance ministers, Palast has actually found one, between Argentina and the WB, with IMF involvement. Dated June 2001, it was a very damaging agreement that required the Argentine government to cut spending during a severe economic crisis, which led to a 2.6 percent decline in the Argentine GDP.

Polaski, Sandra. "In Agricultural Trade Talks, First Do No Harm." *Issues in Science and Technology* 22, no. 1 (Fall 2005): 27. The concerns of developing nations over their agriculture threaten to scuttle the latest round of trade talks. These countries fear with good reason that if they are no longer allowed to protect their agriculture with tariffs, industrial nations will flood them with the cheaply produced goods of agribusiness, often itself the recipient of government subsidies, and the small farmers of the developing world, unable to compete, will be driven off the land.

Rosen, Ellen Israel. "The Wal-Mart Effect: The World Trade Organization and the Race to the Bottom." *Chapman Law Review* 8 (Spring 2005): 261–282. The WTO's elimination of textile and apparel quotas will not benefit developing countries.

Rather, it will drive retailers, led by Wal-Mart, to go where they can get largest volume at lowest cost, namely China and India, and working conditions will be worsened.

Savona, Paolo. "Can Economic Growth Coexist with Social Justice in Globalization? Reflections on the Failure of the WTO Summit in Seattle." *Banca di Roma Review of Economic Conditions in Italy,* no. 1 (2000). Savona argues that globalization can reduce poverty and the resulting social problems. However, it is not enough to open markets, for they are subject to many distortions and abuses. There must be provisions in the bilateral and multilateral agreements to protect markets from monetary distortions, for instance.

Shaffer, Gregory. "WTO Blue-Green Blues: The Impact of U.S. Domestic Politics on Trade-Labor, Trade-Environment Linkages for the WTO's Future." *Fordham International Law Journal* 24 (November 2001): 608–651. U.S. labor and social protections are the weakest in the industrial world. Meanwhile, Americans criticize the WTO for failing to allow trade restrictions to be used to defend the environment and labor rights. Clearly, internal U.S. politics could have an effect on the future shape of the WTO.

Stevenson, Benjamin James. "Pursuing an End to Foreign Child Labor through U.S. Trade Law: WTO Challenges and Doctrinal Solutions." *UCLA Journal of International Law and Foreign Affairs* 7 (Spring 2002): 129. Stevenson argues that the United States could in fact invoke trade sanctions against goods produced by child labor. The WTO would very likely back such measures as needed to protect human life.

Summers, Clyde. "The Battle in Seattle: Free Trade, Labor Rights, and Societal Values." *University of Pennsylvania Journal of International Economic Law* 22 (Spring 2001): 61. There is a dispute within the WTO as to whether to link trade agreements to the core labor standards of the ILO. While developing countries have argued that such measures would cost them their comparative advantage, the author finds that core labor standards alone would not increase wages.

TRADE

Books

Barfield, Claude E. *Free Trade, Sovereignty, Democracy: The Future of the World Trade Organization.* Washington, D.C.: American Enterprise Institute Press, 2001. Barfield, a conservative, argues strongly on the side of free trade and the WTO. Nevertheless, even he finds that to be truly effective the organization may need to make some changes in its structure.

Castells, Manuel. *The Rise of the Network Society.* Oxford and Malden, Mass.: Blackwell Publishers, 2000. Castells sets out to do for global informational capitalism what Marx and Weber did for industrial capitalism. In the space between sociology and business analysis, he describes changes in information technology, conditions of employment, corporate responsibility, and MNCs.

Gowa, Joanne. *Allies, Adversaries, International Trade.* Princeton, N.J.: Princeton University Press, 1994. Since free trade gives a country more resources, it benefits it militarily as well. Therefore countries are more likely to trade with allies than with enemies, especially in a situation where there are only two blocs, so that the temptation to trade outside the bloc is reduced. Statistics back this up historically.

Gray, John. *False Dawn: The Delusions of Global Capitalism.* London: Granta, 1999. Gray reviews the debates over globalization and argues against the attempt at a global free market.

Kuttner, Robert. *Everything for Sale: The Virtues and Limits of Markets.* Chicago: University of Chicago Press, 1996. The globalized world economy affects everything in our lives, our work, and our consumption. Only those with a strong faith in markets will be convinced that it is all for the best.

Petras, James, and Henry Veltmeyer. *System in Crisis: The Dynamics of Free Market Capitalism.* Winnipeg, Manitoba: Zed Books, 2003. The authors examine how modern capitalism functions in the world economy and in the politics of countries everywhere, but particularly in Latin America. They find that technology, at least under capitalism, will not solve the world's problems, and they propose how globalization could be made more democratic, more beneficial to people, and less environmentally damaging.

Prestowitz, Clyde. *Three Billion New Capitalists: The Great Shift of Wealth and Power to the East.* New York: Basic Books, 2005. Prestowitz examines the swift growth of China and India, marking a massive shift of economic power away from the United States. Americans can no longer take their hegemonic position of the past for granted.

Ross, John. *The Annexation of Mexico: From the Azecs to the IMF.* Monroe, Maine: Common Courage Press, 1998. Ross examines U.S.-Mexican relations, taking into account history, economics, and current social movements in Mexico. Together these explain Mexican popular opposition to the U.S. strategy of globalization.

Williams, Heather L. *Social Movements and Economic Transition: Markets and Distributive Conflict in Mexico.* Cambridge: Cambridge University Press, 2001. Williams explores how groups in Mexico whose economic survival has been threatened by neoliberal policies have organized and mobilized politically.

Articles and Papers

Bartlett, Christopher A., and Sumantra Ghoshal. "Going Global: Lessons for Late Movers." *Harvard Business Review* 78, no. 3 (2000): 132–142. Being a late entrant into international trade can actually be a competitive advantage, the basis for a company's business strategy. The author presents evidence from 12 new MNCs in previously poor developing nations.

Guzman, Andrew T. "Trade, Labor, Legitimacy." *California Law Review* 91, no. 3 (May 2003): 885–902. At present, the WTO represents trade interests and therefore is not suited to protecting labor interests. Moreover, its dispute resolutions process is not as useful as a political process of negotiation to establish labor standards. Separating trade and labor departments within the WTO would be a useful first step.

Hoekman, Bernard, Constantine Michalopoulos, Maurice Schiff, et al. "Trade Policy Reform and Poverty Alleviation." *World Bank Poverty Reduction Strategy Sourcebook.* Washington, D.C.: World Bank, 2001. How can trade liberalization become part of a strategy for reducing poverty in developing economies? Policy instruments, institutions, sectors, adjustment reforms, and safety nets must all be taken into account.

Kanter, Rosabeth Moss. "Thriving Locally in the Global Economy." *Harvard Business Review* 73, no. 4 (1995): 119–127. Globalization can benefit local economies and businesses if these companies create a loyal customer base, network, and meet international standards. Kanter advises businesses how to carry this out.

Oxfam International. "Rigged Rules and Double Standards: Trade, Globalisation, and the Fight Against Poverty." *Make Trade Fair Report* (April 3, 2002). Oxfam urges developed countries to import more agricultural products, textiles, and other goods produced in less developed countries by reducing tariffs and regulations that protect the workers of the industrial world. The report has proven controversial.

Prahalad, C. K., and Kenneth Lieberthal. "The End of Corporate Imperialism." *Harvard Business Review* 76, no. 4 (1998): 69–79. As corporations go global, they have to modify their business practices to adapt to the countries where they are seeking to sell. The emerging markets of China, India, and Brazil are large enough to affect the range of goods that multinationals can offer.

Simms, Andrew. "Free Market Economics for Dummies." *The Ecologist* 33, no. 7 (September 2003): 17. Governments and corporations and their representatives claim that a free market will raise standards of living for people and countries in poverty. However, experience shows that free trade impacts negatively on their social, political, and economic conditions.

———. "Think Small." *The Ecologist* 33, no. 5 (June 2003): 45. Simms advocates returning to local production for local consumption instead of globalized trade. This would be particularly beneficial in that it would make developing nations more self-sufficient.

Weisbrot, Mark, and Dean Baker. "The Relative Impact of Trade Liberalization on Developing Countries." *Center for Economic and Policy Research Briefing Paper* (June 11, 2002). Weisbrot and Baker use economic models to show problems with globalization and trade liberalization. They make unusual suggestions such as to repeal copyright and patent protections and to restructure the international financial system.

LABOR AND THE NORTH AMERICAN FREE TRADE AGREEMENT

Books and Book Chapters

Bales, Kevin. *Disposable People: New Slavery in the Global Economy.* Berkeley: University of California Press, 2000. Discusses the impact of globalization on workers, particularly those in developing nations.

Annotated Bibliography

Brown, Sherrod. *Myths of Free Trade: Why American Trade Policy Has Failed.* New York: New Press, 2003. A U.S. congressman analyzes the effects of NAFTA and globalization on American workers and the U.S. economy.

Carr, Barry. "Crossing Borders: Labor Internationalism in the Era of NAFTA." In *Neoliberalism Revisited: Economic Restructuring and Mexico's Political Future.* Edited by Gerardo Otero. Boulder, Colo.: Westview Press, 1996. As the cold war ended, it seemed that the slogan "Workers of the world unite!" had lost its appeal, but NAFTA swiftly made it clear that the interests of Canadian, U.S., and Mexican labor were closely tied. Now people are reaching across the borders to work together on questions of democracy, human rights, and the environment, as well as on labor issues.

Compa, Lance, and Fay Lyle. *Justice for All: A Guide to Worker Rights in the Global Economy.* Washington, D.C.: American Center for International Labor Solidarity/AFL-CIO, 2003. The authors survey labor law and labor rights clauses in trade agreements and the work of international financial institutions. They give the history and case studies of protection of labor rights and standards and look at the effectiveness of corporate codes of conduct and international solidarity campaigns.

Cook, María Elena. "Regional Integration and Transnational Politics: Popular Sector Strategies in the NAFTA Era." In *The New Politics of Inequality in Latin America: Rethinking Participation and Representation.* New York: Oxford University Press, 1997. Cook combines data and theory to demonstrate that integrated North American trade has created a continent-wide political arena. This has given networks of labor activists new resources and more political influence in their own countries.

Foley, Connor. *Global Trade, Labour, and Human Rights.* London: Amnesty International United Kingdom, 2000. This handbook on human rights, globalization, and labor gives case studies of human rights abuses related to economic interests and Third World development. It presents both the institutions that can address such abuses and the international trade regime under which they take place.

Gordon, David. *Fat and Mean: The Corporate Squeeze of Working Americans and the Myth of Managerial "Downsizing."* New York: Free Press, 1996. Gordon challenges standard economic teachings. He demonstrates that labor policies designed to extract the most value at lowest cost may work for a time, but eventually the long-term costs will appear.

Gross, James A., ed. *Workers' Rights as Human Rights.* Ithaca, N.Y.: ILR Press, 2003. This collection of articles gives both the employers' and labor side of the debate around U.S. labor law. Does it violate core ILO labor standards? Are human rights universal? Should health and saftey standards be part of the international labor law? Is international labor solidarity the solution?

Hepple, Bob, ed. *Social and Labor Rights in a Global Context: International and Comparative Perspectives.* Cambridge: Cambridge University Press, 2002. The articles in this collection address questions of social rights and labor rights in different countries as well as in regional and international frameworks. Such rights appear to conflict with economic regimes that stress flexibility and competitiveness.

La Botz, Dan. *Democracy in Mexico.* Boston: South End Press, 1995. The book embraces both the struggle of the maquiladora workers near the U.S. border and that of the peasants of southern Mexico. It summarizes the recent history of the official unions and workers' attempts to form independent unions.

———. *Mask of Democracy: Labor Suppression in Mexico Today.* Boston: South End Press, 1992. LaBotz sketches labor law and labor rights in Mexico and outlines the history of the labor movement there. He explains how most Mexican unions work together with the ruling party and corporations and not for the workers.

MacArthur, John R. *The Selling of Free Trade: NAFTA, Washington and the Subversion of American Democracy.* New York: Hill and Wang, 2000. The book reveals how Congress was manipulated into passing NAFTA.

Michel, Lawrence, Jared Bernstein, and John Schmitt. *The State of Working America, 1996–1997.* Washington, D.C.: Economic Policy Institute, 1997. This book, like others in its series, gives a comprehensive guide to changes in the labor market, compiled with a view to the needs of working people.

Mutti, John H. *NAFTA: The Economic Consequences for Mexico and the United States.* Washington, D.C.: Economic Strategy Institute, 2000. How the two economies are affected by NAFTA.

New York Times. The Downsizing of America. New York: Random House, 1996. The *New York Times* reworked and expanded a series of articles to create this book. It combines statistics with accounts of individuals, especially managers and professionals, caught up in the processes of globalization.

Sheshabalaya, Ashutosh. *Rising Elephant: The Growing Clash with India over White Collar Jobs and Its Challenge to America and the World.* Monroe, Maine: Common Courage Press, 2004. Middle-class American jobs are indeed being outsourced to India in a profound and far-reaching process. The Indian middle class is growing, to become larger than the whole American population, whose position in the world is in fact threatened.

Sims, Beth. *Workers of the World Undermined: American Labor's Role in U.S. Foreign Policy.* Boston: South End Press, 1991. Sims criticizes the foreign policy of the AFL-CIO and exposes how the labor federation collaborated with the CIA in Latin America to the benefit of corporate rather than labor interests.

Articles and Papers

Alben, Elissa. "GATT and the Fair Wage: A Historical Perspective on the Labor-Trade Link." *Columbia Law Review* 101 (October 2001): 1,410. When GATT was first negotiated, fair labor standards were seen as a matter of wages. Now they are seen as a matter of human rights, but nevertheless, there is no good precedent for separating labor issues from trade agreements.

Anderson, Gordon. "Labour Law in a Globalising World." *Modern Law Review* 66, no 4 (July 2003): 640–649. Anderson summarized the pessimistic results of a 2001 convergence that sees little hope for labor rights under the pressure of international capital. The WTO has not been willing to work with the ILO.

Annotated Bibliography

Anderson, Sarah. "A Decade of NAFTA in the United States and Mexico." *Canadian Dimension* 38, no. 12 (March–April 2004): 36. NAFTA was controversial when it passed Congress in 1993, and the record in the decade since has borne out the critics. Transnational corporations profited handsomely, both from increased trade and from their new ability to challenge local regulations, but jobs were lost, and Mexican agriculture was devastated.

Basu, Kaushik. "Compacts, Conventions, and Codes: Initiatives for Higher International Labor Standards." *Cornell International Law Journal* 35, no. 3 (2001): 487. Basu argues that the WTO is not suited to enforcing labor standards; the task is better left to individual nations. Only if the WTO is first democratized could it become a vehicle for enforcement of international labor standards.

Beachy, Debra. "A Decade of NAFTA," *Hispanic Business* 26, nos. 7–8 (July–August 2004): 42. NAFTA, after 10 years in effect, has become controversial. Certainly, it increased trade and investment across borders and benefited business, but the benefits have been uneven, and thousands of jobs have been lost.

Bognanno, Mario F., Michael P. Keane, and Donghoon Yang. "The Influence of Wages and Industrial Relations Environments on the Production Location Decisions of U.S. Multinational Corporations." *Industrial and Labor Relations Review* 58 (January 2005): 171–200. Low wages and nonunion workforces are attractive to American-based MNCs. However, their decisions to relocate are in the end based more on the size of the market where they locate. The authors also conclude that reduction of tariffs leads to less job loss than had previously been supposed.

Burtless, Gary. "Workers' Rights: Labor Standards and Global Trade." *Brookings Review* 19, no. 4 (2001): 10–13. While it is argued that workers' rights must be protected to avoid unfair advantage in international trade, there are no agreed-upon universal labor standards, nor are there adequate enforcement mechanisms. Even the issue of child labor has not been resolved.

Diamond, Stephen F. "Bridging the Divide: An Alternative Approach to International Labor Rights after the Battle of Seattle." *Pepperdine Law Review* 29 (2001): 115–146. Diamond analyzes the issues between labor and the Clinton administration during the WTO 2001 meeting and the debate over trade relations with China. He advocates using the WTO to discuss issues of wages, hours, and working conditions.

Finkin, Matthew W. "International Governance and Domestic Convergence in Labor Law as Seen from the American Midwest." *Indiana Law Journal* 76 (Winter 2001): 143. Finkin looks at possible ways to achieve international labor standards: common markets, the ILO, domestic law applied to other countries, trade agreements that call for partners to observe labor standards or that call for the home country to obey its own laws, and corporate codes of conduct. He is pessimistic because he observes that American courts do not even respect precedents set in other states.

Garrett, Geoffrey. "Globalization's Missing Middle." *Foreign Affairs* 83, no. 6 (November–December 2004): 84. Much of the argument over globalization has focused on whether it benefits both rich and poor or benefits the rich at the expense of the poor. In fact, it is the middle classes that lose, and also the middle-income countries.

Hubbard, Glenn. "CAFTA: A Win-Win Case." *Business Week*, no. 3,941 (July 4, 2005): 102. The business press argues for CAFTA, asserting that this regional free trade agreement will improve economic conditions by removing tariffs, promoting more trade, and strengthening the hand of business against governments. Moreover, the feasibility of further trade agreements may hang on the success of this one.

Josephs, Hilary K. "Upstairs, Trade Law; Downstairs, Labor Law." *George Washington Law Review* 33, nos. 3–4 (2001): 849–872. Josephs investigates the lack of labor law and labor aspects of immigration law in GATT and the WTO. Labor issues could be advanced through side agreements, by giving the ILO a formal role with the WTO, or better yet through WTO dispute settlement.

LaSala, Barry. "NAFTA and Worker Rights: An Analysis of the Labor Side Accord After Five Years of Operation and Suggested Improvements." *Labor Lawyer* 16, no. 3 (2001): 319–348. LaSala examines the recent record of labor law enforcement in Mexico under the North American Agreement on Labor Cooperation (NAALC), a NAFTA side agreement. He concludes that Mexico has good labor law but poor enforcement mechanisms and suggests an arbitration system be established in the NAALC.

Lee, Thea. "How Should the Left Respond to Globalization?" *Dissent* 48, no. 1 (2001): 12–13. Organized labor calls on governments and corporations to respect workers' rights, human rights, and the environment as conditions for economic growth. U.S. labor will reach out to existing allies worldwide, pressure governments, and create new mechanisms to defend the rights of labor everywhere.

Lindsey, Brink. "Offshore Trade: Making Sense of the Arguments." *Current*, no. 465 (September 2004): 3. The author claims that it is not true that offshoring of jobs or world trade is causing job loss and a race to the bottom. He claims that through changes in jobs and new high-paying jobs the standard of living is now higher.

Magnusson, Paul. "States' Rights vs. Free Trade: As Trade Pacts Proliferate, States Start to Howl About Lost Sovereignty." *Business Week*, no. 3,923 (March 7, 2005): 102. Utah had outlawed gambling more than 100 years ago, but now the WTO has ruled that Utah may not forbid Internet gambling based in Antigua. Such rulings have states concerned that their power is being lost to international trade agreements, and they are starting to oppose globalization.

Meils, Hannah L. "A Lesson from NAFTA: Can the FTAA Function as a Tool for Improvement in the Lives of Working Women?" *Indiana Law Journal* 78, no. 2 (Summer 2003): 877–897. NAFTA and its NAALC side agreement have failed to protect women workers adequately. The future FTAA should be negotiated so as to do a better job.

Mitro, Mathew T. "Outlawing the Trade in Child Labor Products: Why the GATT Article XX Health Exception Authorizes Unilateral Sanctions." *American University Law Review* 51 (2002): 1,223. GATT's Article 20 is designed to protect human health. Mitro argues that it could be used to defend sanctions against goods produced by child labor.

Mordecai, Adam. "Anti-Offshoring Legislation: The New Wave of Protectionism: The Backlash Against Foreign Outsourcing of American Service Jobs." *Richmond Journal of Global Law and Business* 5 (Winter 2005): 85–105. As trade agreements have lowered tariffs, other legal requirements have been enacted to discourage outsourcing to lower-wage countries. Mordecai argues that such outsourcing is beneficial because profits rise and prices for services go down.

Sen, Amartya. "Work and Rights." *International Labour Review* 139, no. 2 (2000): 119–128. Globalization can be made to work for people rather than against them. The ILO aims to abolish child labor, slavery, forced prostitution, and trafficking and to enable workers worldwide to achieve decent working conditions.

Smith, Geri, and Cristina Lindblad. "Mexico: Was NAFTA Worth It?" *Business Week,* no. 3,863 (December 22, 2003): 66. NAFTA has led to the creation of some better manufacturing jobs in Mexico; the article gives an example of one of the better ones. But free trade cannot overcome low wages and poverty in Mexico.

Stone, Katherine Van Wezel. "To the Yukon and Beyond: Local Laborers in a Global Labor Market." *Journal of Small and Emerging Business Law* 3, no. 1 (Summer 1999): 93–130. Both hard (that is, legal) and soft consumer-based approaches have been tried to protect labor rights in world markets. The author proposes that both types be combined in a new approach to protecting basic labor rights.

Strang, David, and Patricia Mei Yin Chang. "The ILO and the Welfare State: Institutional Effects on National Welfare Spending, 1960–80." *International Organization* 47, no. 2 (1993): 235–263. The ILO has had an effect on recent thinking about the welfare state. This is an example of how international and domestic bodies can mutually influence each other.

Udombana, N. J. "The Third World and the Right to Development: Agenda for the Next Millennium." *Human Rights Quarterly* 22, no. 3, 753–787. How can Third World countries combine economic growth with human needs in the modern global market? Udombana gives the historical and theoretical background to the question.

Weiss, Marley. "Two Steps Forward, One Step Back—or Vice Versa: Labor Rights under Free Trade Agreements from NAFTA, Through Jordan, via Chile, to Latin America, and Beyond." *University of San Francisco Law Review* 37, no. 689 (2003): NAFTA and its NAALC side agreement have set the pattern for the labor aspects of trade agreements that the United States negotiates. The article explores how future agreements could do a better job of supporting labor rights.

Wishnie, Michael J. "Immigrant Workers and the Domestic Enforcement of International Labor Rights." *University of Pennsylvania Journal of Labor and Employment Law* 4, no. 3 (Spring 2002): Wishnie explores how international labor law approaches can protect immigrant household workers and migrant farmworkers in the United States. He concludes that both the Alien Torts Claims Act and the NAALC have the potential to make a difference.

NONPRINT RESOURCES

American Jobs. 62 min. Directed by Greg Spotts. 2004. DVD. A 19-city tour of America that reveals the true cost of the "jobless" recovery in the United States. Background and interviews with politicians on both sides of the aisle, as well as with both blue- and white-collar workers, most of whom lost their jobs to low-wage workers overseas, many through NAFTA.

"Asian Values Devalued." 40 min. Princeton, N.J.: Films for the Humanities and Sciences, 1998. VHS. The policy errors and weaknesses in the Asian economy that led to the Asian economic crisis of 1997–98 are explored and analyzed.

Between Midnight and the Rooster's Crow. 66 min. Directed by Nadja Drost. 2005. VHS. A study of the cultural and environmental effects of the extraction practices of a multinational oil corporation in Ecuador's rainforest.

Bill Moyers Reports: "Trading Democracy." 58 min. Princeton, N.J.: Films for the Humanities and Sciences, 2002. VHS and DVD. Moyers, a respected investigative journalist, looks at NAFTA in terms of its effects on democracy, calling it an "end run around the Constitution," as corporations use its more obscure provisions to undermine laws, regulations, and the rights of American citizens.

"The Bottom Line: Privatizing the World." 53 min. Princeton, N.J.: Films for the Humanities and Sciences, 2002. VHS and DVD. An unflinching look at corporations' bold attempts to commodify, own, and profit from the world's resources, including water and the genes in plants, animals, and humans.

"Business and Commerce: A Perspective on the 20th Century." 49 min. Princeton, N.J.: Films for the Humanities and Sciences, 1996. VHS. An overview of the enormous changes trade has undergone in the last century, including the liberalized free market and globalization. Also reviews the economic history that led to the Bretton Woods agreement.

"Business Ethics: A Twenty-first Century Perspective." 19 min. Princeton, N.J.: Produced by Meridian Productions. Films for the Humanities and Sciences, 1994. VHS. Looks at the conflicts and ambiguities in the ethics of doing business for MNCs.

"Business Is Blooming: The International Floral Industry." 53 min. Princeton, N.J.: Films for the Humanities and Sciences, 2003. VHS and DVD. A comprehensive look at the globalized flower industry, from the poorly paid workers who tend the blooms in developing countries to the upscale florist shops where pricey flowers are sold in developed nations.

"Cappuccino Trail: The Global Economy in a Cup." 50 min. Princeton, N.J.: Films for the Humanities and Sciences, 2001. VHS. Coffee is one of the most widely traded commodities in the world. This follows coffee beans from the poor farmers who grow them (and are paid $50 per 150-pound bag) to the coffee shops in Western countries, where that same bag of beans makes 10,000 cups of coffee worth more than $20,000.

Case Studies from the Multinational Marketplace. Princeton, N.J.: Films for the Humanities and Sciences, 2005. VHS and DVDs. A five-part series (each lasting 180–200 minutes) that examines how several multinational corporations market products and trade globally.

China: Unleashing the Dragon. 200 min. Miracle Pictures/Channel 4 TV/UK. London: 1995. VHS. A four-part series that looks at the astounding development and increasing prosperity of China as it enters, and in some cases begins to dominate, the global marketplace. The economic and cultural transformations currently taking place in China are revealed.

Choropampa: The Price of Gold. 75 min. Brooklyn, N.Y.: First Run/Icarus Films, 2002. VHS. How a gold-mining multinational, supported by the World Bank, destroyed a pristine Andean environment in Peru after spilling 151 Kilograms of liquid mercury that covered a 25-square-mile area.

City Life: A Series about Globalization. Oley, Pa.: Bullfrog Films, 2001. VHS. A multipart series (each film 22–27 minutes long) about globalization's effects on urban areas and city-dwellers around the world. Covers trade, health, sustainability, violence, democracy, homelessness, and many other relevant issues.

"Coca-Cola: The History of an American Icon." 145 min. Orland Parkl, Ill.: Mpi Home Video, 2001. DVD. A close look at how the soft drink company became an icon of American culture and how it has been exported around the world.

Commanding Heights: The Battle for the World Economy. 360 min. Directed by Greg Barker and William Cran. Boston PBS/WGBH, 2002. DVD. This three-part documentary explains macroeconomics and reveals its impacts on the global economy. The film covers the history of modern economic theory, the consequences of deregulation in the 1980s, and the effects of globalization on developed and developing economies and the people who live in them.

The Corporation. 145 min. Directed by March Achbar and Jennifer Abbott. New York: Zeitgeist Films, 2004. DVD. An in-depth look at the history of the corporation, the development of its "persona," and how that persona imposes itself upon the world. All aspects of globalization are examined, from transnational corporations, to privatization, intellectual property, and the externalization of all things that do not add profits to the bottom line.

The Debt Crisis: An African Dilemma. 20 min. Directed by Steve Whitehouse. Produced by the United Nations. First Run/Icarus Films, 1988. VHS. An unblinking look at how foreign debt affects poor African nations, with a focus on Zambia and how this nation attempted to rebuild its economy after refusing to adopt austerity measures imposed by the IMF and WB.

A Decent Factory. 79 min. BBC London: Directed by Thomas Balmes. 2004. VHS. The issue of outsourcing jobs to low-wage countries is described using the example of Nokia, the Finnish electronics company, which hires ethics advisers to monitor their overseas manufacturing facilities.

"Economic Recovery in Africa: The Role of the IMF." Princeton, N.J.: Films for the Humanities and Sciences, 1996, 1998. VHS. Examines how liberalization of the global economy is affecting poor African nations and the effect of IMF policies on their economic development.

"Fast Forward: Life Inside Our Ever-Shrinking World." 80 min. Boston: PBS, 1999. VHS. Explores the roles of globalization and technology on a world that seems to be getting smaller and more interconnected. It also looks at how the forces of globalization affect people's lives around the world.

"A Feast Amid Famine: The World Food Paradox." 60 min. Beacon, N.Y.: Guidance Associates, 1990. VHS and DVD. Looks at the problems of hunger and starvation in a globalized world that is supposed to be improving the lives of all.

Fishing in the Sea of Greed. 45 min. Directed by Anand Patwardhan. 1998. VHS. How industrial fishing, funded by international finance institutions, is ruining the lives of people in traditional fishing communities in the developing world.

"Free Market Economics: The Commanding Heights." 16 min. Princeton, N.J.: Films for the Humanities and Sciences, no date. VHS. How liberalized markets and the fall of communism have benefited people in both developed and developing nations.

Free Markets for Free Men. 52 min. Brooklyn, N.Y.: First Run/Icarus Films, 1986. VHS. Shows how the fluctuations in the global prices for commodities negatively affects commodity-producing nations, such as Brazil.

"Free Trade." 28 min. Princeton, N.J.: Films for the Humanities and Sciences, 1993. VHS Overview of the benefits of global free trade.

"Free Trade: Slaves." 57 min. Princeton, N.J.: Films for the Humanities and Sciences, 1999. VHS. Shows how free trade zones sometimes lead to the exploitation of workers.

"Global Capitalism and the Moral Imperative." Princeton, N.J.: Films for the Humanities and Sciences, 1998. VHS. How the world should respond to the growing inequalities arising from globalization.

"Globalization and Human Rights." 57 min. New York: Globalvision, 1998. VHS. Explores whether human rights can coexist with the irresistible drive for increased profits realized through human exploitation in a globalized economy.

"Globalization Is Good." 50 min. Princeton, N.J.: Films for the Humanities and Sciences, 2003. VHS and DVD. Writer Johan Norberg presents his forthright arguments in support of globalization and its universal benefits.

"Globalization: Winners and Losers." 40 min. Princeton, N.J.: Films for the Humanities and Sciences, 2000. VHS. How globalization affects the developing world and, in particular, the world's poorest nations. Looks at the benefits, as well as the costs, of the globalization of the economy.

"The Global Trade Debate." 42 min. Princeton, N.J.: Films for the Humanities and Sciences, 2001. VHS and DVD. A balanced look at both antiglobalization activists' issues and the views of MNCs. Attempts to explain the paradox of a 12-fold increase in world trade that has accompanied considerable impoverishment of local communities in both the developed and developing world.

"The International Monetary Fund: Financial Cure or Catastrophe?" 35 min. Princeton, N.J.: Films for the Humanities and Sciences, 1998. VHS. A close look at the IMF and its policies and approaches to stabilizing economies in crisis, with an emphasis on the Asian crisis of 1997–98.

"International Trade." 30 min. Princeton, N.J.: Films for the Humanities and Sciences, 1999. VHS and DVD. An overview of global trade and its benefits, as well as its drawbacks. Includes a discussion of the WTO.

"An Introduction to the IMF." 18 min. Princeton, N.J.: Films for the Humanities and Sciences, 2000. VHS and DVD. An overview of the IMF, its origins, its original mandate, and how it has changed over the years. Includes interviews with IMF officials.

Life and Debt. 86 min. New York: Directed by Stephanie Black. New Yorker Films, 2003. DVD. The decline of the Jamaican economy is used as an example of the effects of globalization. The documentary looks at the history of Jamaica and how the conditionalities set by the IMF have led to unemployment and reduced wages, crushing foreign debt, and a dismal economic future for Jamaicans.

"Malawi: A Nation Going Hungry." 26 min. Princeton, N.J.: Films for the Humanities and Sciences, 2004. VHS and DVD. A sobering look at the poverty, poor governance, instability, and resultant hunger in this African nation. Reviews how the policies of the IMF and the WTO might contribute to Malawian starvation (for example, austerity measures that prohibit the government from subsidizing agriculture).

Maquila: A Tale of Two Mexicos. 55 min. Directed by Saul Landau and Sonia Angula. New York: Cinema Guild, 2000. VHS. Contrasts the living and working conditions in the free-trade-zone industrial areas, or maquiladoras, near the U.S. border and those in the Mexican countryside.

Millennium: The IMF in the New Century. Princeton, N.J.: Films for the Humanities and Sciences, 2000. VHS. Through four installments (each 16–19 minutes in length), this study follows the evolution of the IMF from its inception to the role it currently plays in the global economy. Analyzes its policies in regard to economic stabilization, with emphasis on Korea and Argentina.

"Money Never Sleeps: Global Financial Markets." 53 min. Princeton, N.J.: Films for the Humanities and Sciences, 1999. VHS and DVD. How today's financial markets work and how money travels the world at the speed of an electron; the effects on currencies, including currency speculation, the stock market, and nations' economies and people.

The New Global Economics: A Real World Guide. Princeton, N.J.: Films for the Humanities and Sciences, 1999. VHS. Consisting of 10 videos (each lasting 30 minutes), this offers a wide-ranging exploration of many aspects of the global economy, including basic economics, investment, international trade, and others.

The New Rulers of the World. 53 min. Directed by Alan Lowery. Oley, Pa.: Bullfrog Films, 2001. VHS and DVD. The role of MNCs and their backers, the IMF, and the WB is investigated by John Pilger. How these financial institutions affect the lives of poor people, with a focus on Indonesia, whose globalized economy collapsed in 1998.

Not for Sale. 31 min. Directed by Mark Dworkin and Melissa Young. Oley, Pa.: Bullfrog Films, 2002. VHS and DVD. Examines the modern corporate practice of patenting life-forms in developing nations, particularly the genes of rain forest organisms and indigenous crops.

Our Friends at the Bank. 85 min. Directed by Peter Chappell. Brooklyn, N.Y.: First Run/Icarus Films. 1997. VHS. Using Uganda as its focus, this film analyzes how the WB's large-scale development projects affect ordinary people and the economy they struggle to survive in. Shows how financial crises force nations to accept ruinous conditionalities in order to get loans to keep afloat financially.

"Outsourcing: White Collar Exodus." 51 min. Princeton, N.J.: Films for the Humanities and Sciences, 2005. VHS and DVD. Highlights the emotional and financial devastation that afflicts white-collar workers when their jobs are outsourced to cheaper labor overseas. With an in-depth look at this type of outsourcing to India, the film presents the pros and cons of outsourcing from both perspectives.

"Planet Earth: Fate of the Earth." 57 min. Claremont, Calif.: Southern California Consortium, 1986. VHS. Looks at the conflict between global economic growth and the conservation of the natural world and its resources.

"Russia in Ruins: Can the Nation Survive?" 18 min. Madison, Wis.: Knowledge Unlimited, 1998. VHS. An overview of the transitional economy of this once-communist nation and an analysis of the challenges it faces in its move toward democracy and the free market.

"Sick Economics: The IMF Prescription." 15 min. Princeton, N.J.: Films for the Humanities and Sciences, no date. VHS and DVD. A clear-eyed view of the conditionalities imposed by the IMF before loans are offered to nations experiencing financial crisis. The example of Ruritania is used to show how the austerity measures were implemented and their effects.

"Stolen Childhoods." 20 min. Princeton, N.J.: Films for the Humanities and Sciences, 2005. VHS and DVD. An uncompromising look at the exploitation of child labor, from an ABC News program. Using examples from developing nations around the world, the film exposes the often terrible exploitation of children for cheap labor—and the general indifference of Western consumers.

The Take. 87 min. Directed by Avi Lewis. Brooklyn, N.Y.: First Run Features, 2004. DVD. A David-and-Goliath story about how 30 unemployed auto-parts workers in Brazil during its economic meltdown (due mostly to austerity measures imposed by the IMF) took matters into their own hands, stared down the liberal economists, and took over and restarted their business as a worker-owned enterprise.

Thirst. 62 min. Directed by Alan Snitow and Deborah Kaufman. Brooklyn, N.Y.: Bullfrog Films, 2004. VHS. Visits communities in the United States as well as in the developing world to document how corporations are buying up and privatizing the water supply.

Trinkets and Beads. 52 min. Directed by Christopher Walker. Brooklyn, N.Y.: First Run/Icarus Films, 1996. VHS. How the oil company MAXUS attempted to convince the indigenous Huaorani of the Ecuadorean Amazon to allow them to drill for oil on their ancestral lands. After experiencing the devastating pollution of their land by Texaco and Shell, the Huaorani organize to fight the new MNC.

Understanding Free Market Economics: Lessons Learned in the Former Soviet Union. Princeton, N.J.: Films for the Humanities and Sciences, 1994, 1995. VHS. A six-part (30 minutes each) examination of the role of the IMF and its policies as they played out in the transition from a command economy to a free market economy in Russia and Eastern Europe.

"Voices of Disposable People." 53 min. Princeton, N.J.: Films for the Humanities and Sciences, 2003. VHS and DVD. There are more than 300 million men, women, and children working as virtual slaves in the global economy. When they can no longer work, they are simply "discarded" and left to fend for themselves. This film looks unflinchingly at the plight of such "disposable" people in several developing countries.

Wall Street: A Wondering Trip. 50 min. Directed by Andreas Hoessli. Brooklyn, N.Y.: First Run/Icarus Films, 2004. VHS. A behind-the-scenes look at how "the Street" operates, with forays onto the floor of the New York Stock Exchange. Explains how bond traders, speculators, hedge fund operators, and other Wall Street insiders operate, what they do, and how it affects economies everywhere.

Wal-Mart: The High Cost of Low Price. Directed by Robert Greenwald. Culver City, Calif.: Brave New Films, 2005. DVD. Using the personal stories of employees and former employees, this documentary provides an in-depth look at how Wal-Mart's policy of low wages and few or no benefits affects Americans. Globalization's role in providing the company with low-cost goods made overseas sweatshops is examined.

"Witness to History II: The New Deal." 15 min. Beacon, N.Y.: Guidance Associates, no date. VHS and DVD. A broad overview of the Great Depression and the New Deal policies implemented to turn it around; includes eyewitness accounts regarding the passage of New Deal legislation.

"The World Bank: The Great Experiment." 100 min. Princeton, N.J.: Films for the Humanities and Sciences, 1997. VHS. The role of the World Bank in economic development is explored using Uganda as an example of its policies and their consequences.

WEB SITES AND DOCUMENTS

Some of the listings below cite particular reports on a specific Web site. Others refer to Web sites that contain permanent collections of some of the official documents pertinent to globalization. Additionally, some Web sites contain a constantly updated list of articles, analyses, news reports, and data regarding current or ongoing globalization issues or meetings. Some sites retain an archive of commentary, news, and articles; others do not. The general content of each Web site is described below, but because of the timeliness of the content of some Web sites, it is advisable to visit the sites to see "what's new," as well as to search their archives for archival material.

Alliance for Responsible Trade. Available online. URL: http://www.art-us.org. Accessed on January 4, 2006. Contributors to this Web site analyze and critique global trade agreements, including NAFTA, CAFTA, and FTAA. With their focus on sustainable development, the Web site offers constantly updated articles, official government reports, and opinion relevant to international trade agreements and their impact on people and society. The general content of each Web site is described below, but because of the timeliness of the content of some Web sites, it is advisable to visit the sites to see "What's New," as well as to search their archives for more dated material.

Avalon Project. "Bretton Woods Agreements." Available online. URL: http://www.yale.edu/lawwweb/avalon/decade/decade047.htm. Accessed on January 4, 2006. Yale's Avalon Project provides the text of the original agreements. Other legal documents relating to trade and international issues are also available.

Basu, Parantap, and Alessandra Guariglia. "Foreign Direct Investment, Inequality, and Growth." Leverhulme Centre, Nottingham University, United Kingdom. Available online. URL: http://www.nottingham.ac.uk/economics/leverhulme/research_papers/05_41.pdf. Accessed on January 4, 2006. This paper examines how FDI affects unequal income distribution within and among nations and their people. It addresses the paradoxical finding that FDI seems to promote economic growth while at the same time increasing poverty and inequality.

Bello, Walden. "The Real Meaning of Hong Kong: Brazil and India Join the Big Boys' Club." The Transnational Institute. Available online. URL: http://www.tni.org.

British Library for Development Studies (BLDS), Institute for Development Studies. Available online. URL: http://blds.ids.ac.uk/blds/. Accessed on January 4, 2006. This Web site claims to be "Europe's largest research collection on economic and social change in developing countries." The claim is not without merit. The Web site allows you to search for journal articles, reports, working papers of governments, NGOs, and economic institutions; a database is also available for searching for particular statistics. You can also read the latest news about economic development and the social impacts of globalization. Country-specific reports and data, as well as comprehensive subject guides, round out the enormous amount of useful information available.

Brookings Institution, Global Economics. "Free Trade in the New Global Economy: A Discussion on the State of U.S. Trade Policy." Available online. URL: http://www.brookings.edu/comm/events/20040107.pdf. Accssed on January 4, 2006. This paper is a transcript of a discussion on free trade held at the Brookings Institution in 2004. Four panelists, including U.S. senators, debate the effects of free trade and globalization on the American economy and the nature of U.S. free trade policies in light of these effects.

Bureau of Economic Analysis, U.S. Available online. URL: http://www.bea.gov. Accessed on January 5, 2006. If you're looking for economic data about the United States and its economy, this is the Web site to visit. It also contains comparisons of the U.S. economy and the economies of other nations, as well as written explanations of some of the key issues in national and global economics.

Census Bureau, U.S. "Foreign Trade Statistics." Available online. URL: http://www.census.gov/foreign-trade/www/statistics.htm#online/. Accessed on January 3, 2006. Recent monthly reports on U.S. international trade are available here, as are historical data on U.S. trade. Here you can find information about the United States's largest trading partners and the U.S. trade balance with each of the countries with which it trades.

Center for Globalization and Policy Research. Available online. URL: http://www.sppsr.ucla.edu/cgpr/. Accessed on January 9, 2006. This Web site of the School of Public Policy and Social Research at the University of California at Los Angeles, offers cogent analysis of many issues relating to globalization and its effects on society. Many working papers on numerous globalization issues can also be found (http://www.sppsr.ucla.edu/cgpr/wpaperspage.htm). Note that most of these working papers are available only as Word documents.

Annotated Bibliography

Central Intelligence Agency, U.S. "Handbook of International Economic Statistics." Available online. URL: http://www.cia.gov/cia/di/products/hies/index.html. Accessed on January 10, 2006. In-depth economic analyses of and information about every major nation and region on earth.

Centre for Economic Policy Research. Available online. URL: http://www.cepr.org. Accessed on January 6, 2006. A wealth of economic information is available at this Web site, including articles and issue briefs. Click on the "Hot Topics" button to access its pages on "Globalization, Regionalism, and Trade" and "IMF, World Bank, and WTO." Both contain up-to-date articles and information on these topics, as well as background information.

Centre for Research on Globalisation. Available online. URL: http://globalresearch.ca. Accessed on January 6, 2006. This openly antiglobalization site offers news, opinion, articles, and reports on the ill effects of globalization. The content changes frequently.

CI: Corporate Information. Available online. URL: http://www.corporateinformation.com. Accessed on January 3, 2006. Just about anything you want to know about corporations can be found on this Web site. Corporations in the United States and in countries around the world are listed, and information about what they do is included.

Critical Theory Institute, University of California, Irvine. "The Forces of Globalization." Available online. URL: http://www.humanities.uci.edu/critical/html/Projects%20+%20Events/Forces%20Full/Forces Full1Intro.html. Accessed on January 10, 2006. An in-depth look at the forces that propel globalization. From the Introduction, you can access detailed information about globalization's effects on the environment, culture, technology, and corporations.

Economic Policy Institute. Available online. URL: http://epinet.org. Accessed on January 9, 2006. This Washington D.C.–based, left-leaning Web site offers reports and information that cast a fairly critical eye on globalization and its effects. See especially the "Datazone" on the site, which offers an overview of world economic data. Clicking on the .pdf or .xls buttons near each line of data will get you more detailed information about employment, investment, trade, and many other issues.

ELDIS: Gateway to Development Information. Available online. URL: http://www.eldis.org/. Accessed on January 5, 2006. This Web site offers tens of thousands of documents on numerous issues relating to globalization and economic development. Many globalization issues are explained in the sites issue-specific resource guides. The constantly updated site provides reports and news about various aspects of globalization. You can also search its extensive collection of articles and reports or its databases for further information.

Foreign Trade Information Service. "North American Free Trade Agreement (NAFTA)." Available online. URL: http://www.sice.oas.org/trade/nafta/naftatce.asp. Accessed on January 4, 2006. This Web site, part of the Organization of American States (OAS), provides the full text of the NAFTA trade agreement. The document is accessible by chapter or by article.

Free Trade. Available online. URL: http://www.freetrade.org. Accessed on January 5, 2006. This proglobalization and pro–free trade Web site offers constantly updated articles and reports in favor of economic liberalization. It also supplies extensive links to other sites with a similar bent.

Friends of the Earth. Available online. URL: http://www.foe.org. Accessed on January 10, 2006. FOE's international program emphasizes globalization and its relationship to the environment. Reports and articles change frequently, but look for "Goldman Sachs Leads Investment Banks on Environmental Commitments" (URL: http://www.foe.org/new/releases/november/goldmansachs.html).

GATSwatch. Available online. URL: http://gatswatch.org. Accessed on January 4, 2006. This Web site addresses economic and social issues regarding GATS, which is part of the WTO. The site is generally critical of the impact of GATS. What GATS is and why it is opposed are both extensively and clearly explained here. The site's "News" link provides visitors with up-to-date reports about GATS negotiations and GATS effects on various aspects of people's lives and society.

Globalization 101. Available online: URL: http://www.globalization101.org. This Web site offers an invaluable, easy-to-understand introduction to globalization and the many issues surrounding it. It also has a constantly updated news column and information about upcoming globalization events, both official and nonofficial. Highly recommended. Accessed on January 3, 2006.

Global Trade Negotiations, Center for International Development at Harvard University. Available online. URL: http://www.cid.harvard.edu/cidtrade/issues/labor.html. This Web site, maintained by Harvard University, offers basic overviews of various issues related to international trade and development. Each issue page provides a link to "Papers," or articles and reports, that explain many different aspects of the trade issue. This is a highly respected and valuable site for clear and dependable analysis of many trade issues. See especially its report on NAFTA (URL: http://www.cid.harvard.edu/cidtrade/topics/nafta.pdf) and its valuable report on "Trade and Conflict" (URL: http://www.cid.harvard.edu/cidtrade/features/tradeconflict.pdf). Accessed on January 7, 2006.

Goldin, Claudia. "The Development of the American Economy." National Bureau of Economic Research. Available online. URL: http://www.nber.org/reporter/fall05/index.html. Accessed on January 7, 2006. Examines the history and prospects for the U.S. economy in a globalized world.

Harvard Business School. "Working Knowledge Newsletter." Available online. URL: http://hbsworkingknowledge.hbs.edu/topic.jhtml't=globalization. Accessed on January 7, 2006. A business perspective on globalization, with articles, opinion pieces, and other features in this constantly updated newsletter.

Heritage Foundation. Available online. URL: http://www.heritage.org. Accessed on January 7, 2006. A conservative U.S. think tank, the Heritage Foundation offers reports and research on many issues supportive of economic liberalization. You can research many economic topics on the site, but see especially its *2006 Index of Economic Freedom*, its major annual economic publication. (URL: http://www.heritage.org/index).

Institute for Development Studies. Available online. URL: http://www.ids.ac.uk/ids/global/index.html. Accessed on January 9, 2006. The Globalisation Team at the institute offers extensive information on the Web site. Click on "Projects and Outputs" to access reports and research on trade, finance, values, macroeconomics, and more.

Institute of International Economics. Available online. URL: http://www.iie.com. Accessed on January 9, 2006. This Web site is an invaluable resource for research, working papers, and other documents about all economic issues. An extensive list of working papers is available (URL: http://www.iie.com/publications/pubs_type.cfm?ResearchTypeID=1). A section containing speeches and other primary documents is also available (URL: http://www.iie.com/publications/pubs_type.cfm?ResearchTypeID=3).

Intellectual Property Rights Online. Available online. URL: http://iprsonline.org. Accessed on January 9, 2006. This Web site gives you all you need to know about the controversies over intellectual property rights as stipulated by the WTO and other trade agreements. How intellectual property rights affects a variety of social issues—from health care to education—are explained, as are the TRIPS, WIPO, and other relevant provisions of the WTO. Documents on this issue from governments, the UN, NGOs, Bretton Woods institutions, corporations, and other significant players are also available on a timely and updated "News" service. Resource books, regional profiles and data, and articles and reports are also accessible on this Web site.

International Council for Free Trade Unions. Available online. URL: http://www.icftu.org. Accessed on January 10, 2006. This Web site offers reports and articles that examine the role and fate of unions and workers in the face of globalization. Extensive coverage of related news is frequently updated on the council's home page, which also offers links to analyses of many labor- and globalization-related issues.

International Institute for Labour Studies. "The Future of Work, Employment, and Social Protection." International Labour Organisation. Available online. URL: http://www.ilo.org/public/english/bureau/inst/papers/confrnce/annecy2001/index.htm. Accessed on January 10, 2006. An ILO report on how globalization is affecting work and social "safety nets" that came out of the Annecy Conference of 2001. Through this page you can also access speeches, documents, and conference papers, which all address this issue that is vital to workers in both developed and developing nations.

International Labor Organization, home page. Available online: URL: http://www.us.ilo.org. Accessed January 4, 2006. The texts of the ILO's statements on the rights of the world's workers can be found here, as can extensive information and data about labor-related issues.

"Globalization Failing to Create New, Quality Jobs or Reduce Poverty." Available online. URL: http://www.ilo.org/public/english/bureau/infpr/2005/48.htm. Accessed on January 3, 2006. This 2005 report explains why globalization is failing to live up to its promise of providing new jobs at good wages to workers in both the developed and developing world. The promise that globalization will "lift all boats" is shown to be false, and reasons for that failure are explained and supported with data.

"Report of the World Commission on the Social Dimension of Globalization: A Fair Globalization—Creating Opportunities for All." Available online. URL: http://www.ilo.org/public/english/fairglobalization/report/index.htm. Accessed on January 10, 2006. This 2004 report reviews the shortcomings of today's globalization policies and makes recommendations about how global institutions can change their policies to improve the lives of ordinary working people around the world.

International Monetary Fund, home page. Available online. URL: http://www.imf.org. Accessed January 6, 2006. The IMF offers a slew of documents, statistics, and other useful information. Most can be accessed from the organization's main Web page.

"Articles of Agreement." Available online. URL: http://www.imf.org/external/pubs/ft/aa/index.htm. Accessed on January 6. 2006. Voluminous original documents that established the IMF. These documents, though written largely in "legalese," describe the original mandate of the IMF.

Bretton Woods Conference: Birth of a Monetary System. Available online. URL: http://imfsite.org/origins/confer.html. Accessed on January 4, 2006. The IMF's story of its own birth, with quotations and anecdotes from the conference.

Independent Evaluation Office. Available online. URL: http://www.imf.org/external/np/ieo/index.htm. Accessed on January 6, 2006. Contains news and information about the reexamination of the IMF, its policies, and the role it plays, or should play, in the international financial arena. The site explains why the IMF is moving toward greater transparency in its decision-making process, provides access to documents, and has news updates related to this issue.

Poverty Reduction Strategy Papers (PRSP). Available online. URL: http://www.imf.org/external/np/prsp/prsp.asp. Accessed on January 6, 2006. Constantly updated papers provide the latest news and efforts regarding the IMF's Poverty Reduction program. The program itself is described, and you can read about the program and its effects by nation, with chronological progress reports for each. All IMF PRSPs and reports can be accessed here. Links to the IMF's Debt Relief Initiative and to similar programs at the WB are also provided.

"World Economic Outlook." Available online. URL: http://www.imf.org/external/pubs/ft/weo/2005/02/index.htm. Accessed on January 6, 2006. The IMF's annual report about the world economy is published online. The above address will take you to the 2005 report. The IMF's home page will have a link to all subsequent reports, which contain descriptions and data about the world economy.

International Trade/Import-Export Web Portal. Available online. URL: http://fita.org. Accessed on January 10, 2006. You can search the extensive database on this Web site to find information on imports and exports for countries around the world.

It also lists chambers of commerce, trade associations, and other organizations involved in international trade.

Paul Krugman's home page. Available online. URL: http://web.mit.edu/krugman/www/. Accessed on January 3, 2006. Krugman is a professor of international economics and a widely read economics columnist for the *New York Times,* among other venues. Here you can access many of his informative and highly readable articles, written for the *Times, Fortune, Slate,* and other publications. "What Happened to Asia" is of particular interest in that it cogently analyzes the causes of the Asian economic crisis of 1997–98. It is just one of many articles available on this Web site that a student of globalization will find interesting and pertinent.

London School of Economics Centre for the Study of Global Governance. "Global Civil Society 2005/6." Available online. URL: http://www.lse.ac.uk/Depts/global/yearbook 05.htm. Accessed on January 9, 2006. This 2005 publication, available online, examines trends in many aspects of globalization and its effects on society and democracy. Issues of gender, citizenship, infrastructure, the role of government, and many others are covered in the report.

Make Trade Fair (Oxfam). "Rugged Rules and Double Standards: Trade, Globalisation, and the Fight Against Poverty." Available online. URL: http://www.maketradefair.com/en/index.php?file=03042002121618.htm. Accessed on January 3, 2006. This extensive article discusses in depth the double standard that developed countries often insist upon in their trade dealings and negotiations with developing nations; for example, demanding that developing countries eliminate tariffs and subsidies while developed nations maintain them. In addition to this illuminating report, the Make Trade Fair Web site also links to an extensive report on international trade, offers various views in the debate about fair trading practices, and provides an analysis of the problem as it relates to the trade in coffee.

Monbiot, George. "I'm with Wolfowitz: Have We Forgotten What the Bank Is for?" Centre for Research on Globalisation. Available online. URL: http://globalresearch.ca/index.php?context=viewArticle&code=MON20050405&articleID=-191. Accessed on January. 6, 2006. Examination of how the WB's new head will likely carry out his role, and what effects this will have on poor nations.

National Bureau of Economic Research. Available online. URL: http://www.nber.org. A treasure trove of statistics and research about all things economic. Reports, articles, and research papers are frequently updated.

New York University Law Library. Available online. URL: http://law.nyu.edu. Within this Web site are pages offering reports, documents, and so on related to international trade.

United Nations Research. Available online, URL: http://www.law.nyu.edu/library/unguide.html. Accessed on January 9, 2006. This page of the NYU Law Library gives you instant access to many, if not all, United Nations documents and reports. The UN Charter and subsequent resolutions are available, as are links to the General Secretariat, the International Court of Justice, the Economic and Social Council, and many other agencies and commissions, and the documents, reports, and statistics many of them provide.

WTO and GATT Research. Available online. URL: http://www.law.nyu.edu/library/wtoguide.html. Accessed on January 4, 2006. Provides numerous legal documents, reports, and commentary regarding the WTO. It also offers useful information on tariffs, dispute settlement reports, the legislative history of the WTO, U.S. government documents and sources, statistics, and research guides for more information. It links to the many WTO Web sites where you can find further information and documentation.

Organization for Economic Cooperation and Development (OECD). Available online. URL: http://www.oecd.org. Accessed on January 9, 2006. This site offers a wealth of information and data (some restricted) on worldwide trade and globalization. Surveys, reports, country economic outlooks and surveys, and statistics can be found on the site. A very useful resource.

Policy Network.Available online. URL: http://www.policynetwork.org. Accessed on January 10, 2006. Policy centers and think tanks that support globalization and free trade are represented on this Web site. The site offers reports, scholarly studies, and papers, all with a pro–free trade slant. To access the papers, click on "Publications;" most reports are in .pdf format.

The South Centre. Available online. URL: http://www.southcentre.org. Accessed January 6, 2006. As its name suggests, this Web site offers information on globalization from the point of view of the less developed nations. Speeches, articles, reports, and policy papers explain the effects of globalization from a generally non-Western perspective. Though the articles change over time, see especially "State of Play in the WTO Agriculture Negotiations," which offers various positions on this key controversial issue.

Trade Observatory. Available online. URL: http://www.tradeobservatory.org. Accessed on January 3, 2006. This Web site (formerly Corpwatch) offers up-to-the-minute news on all things related to international trade issues, as well as corporations and MNCs. Though it is critical of globalization as currently practiced, this site offers the full text of official trade documents, such as WTO documents, draft agendas for WTO ministerial meetings, and other official texts. It also provides articles and reports that are generally cogent critiques of globalization from NGOs, economists, and others. The site has a searchable database on treaties and issues relating to trade and development.

The Transnational Communities Programme. Available online. URL: http://www.transcomm.ox.ac.uk. Accessed on January 10, 2006. This Web site, from Oxford University, provides research reports and newsletters about the globalizing economy. Content changes, but see especially "Final Report to the Economic and Social Research Council" (URL: http://www.transcomm.ox.ac.uk/Director'sFinalReport2003b.pdf).

The Transnational Institute. Available online. URL: http://ww.tni.org. Based in Amsterdam, the Netherlands, this site offers a wealth of viewpoints from around the world on globalization, mostly critical, though all insightful.

United for a Fair Economy. Available online. URL: http://www.faireconomy.org. Accessed on January 9, 2006. This site offers articles, opinion, reports, and news about the worldwide struggle to create fair economies out of globalized economies. The site is especially good on the issues of poverty, corporate accountability, taxation, trade, and similar issues.

United Nations home page. Available online. URL: http://www.un.org. Accessed on January 4, 2006. The United Nations and its many agencies provide a variety of useful Web sites with information pertaining to globalization. Some links to the UN's many agencies and reports follows.

United Nations Commission on Trade and Development. Available online. URL: http://www.unctad.org/en/pub/pubframe.htm. Accessed on January 4, 2006. This trade-related Web site contains reports, surveys, and statistics about world trade and development. Click on the "Digital Library" button at the top of the page to access reports, data, and other publications regarding globalization and development.

United Nations Development Programme. "Human Development Report." Available online. URL: http://hdr.undp.org/reports/global/2005/. Accessed on January 4, 2006. A treasure trove of 2005 data and descriptive information about the status of human development in the world. These reports are released annually.

United Nations Development Programme. "Poverty Report, 2000." Available online. URL: http://www.undp.org/povertyreport/. Accessed on January 4, 2006. An in-depth look at the issues of global poverty, with information on the effects of globalization on the world's poor.

United Nations Global Compact. Available online. URL: http://www.unglobalcompact.com. Accessed on January 4. 2006. The text and general overview of the United Nations Global Compact and reports, surveys, and updates about its implementation in nations around the world can be found on this Web site. The compact is intended to blend universal human values into the business sector in order to humanize economic development.

The Whirled Bank. Available online: URL: http://www.whirledbank.org. Accessed on January 5, 2006. This site, a spoof of the World Bank, offers a changing menu of insightful and sometimes satirical articles, most guaranteed to raise a smile, about the Bank and globalization. Good information with a light touch.

World Bank home page. Available online: URL: http://www.worldbank.org. Accessed on January 5, 2006. The World Bank has numerous Web sites, each with different types of information.

"Global Economic Prospects, 2006: Economic Implications of Remittances and Migration." Available online. URL: http://econ.worldbank.org/external/default/main?menuPK=476823&pagePK=64165236&piPK=44165141+?theSitePK=469372. Accessed on January 5, 2006. This report on the World Bank's Data and Research Web page examines how migration can be managed to promote economic growth and greater prosperity for migrants. The report also forecasts a slowdown in economic growth in 2006 and gives reasons for this rather gloomy forecast. This Web page also provides links to other World Bank Policy Research reports on various global issues.

JOLIS: the Joint Libraries of the World Bank Group. Available online. URL: http://jolis.worldbankimflib.org/index.html. Accessed on January 5. 2006.

PovertyNet. Available online. URL: http://Web.worldbank.org/WBSITE/EXTERNAL/TOPICS/EXTPOVERTY/0,,menuPK:33698~pagePK:149018~4piPK:149093~theSitePK:336992.00.html. Accessed on January 5, 2006. This is the WB site that covers its work in helping to fight poverty in the world. The Bank's Poverty Reduction Strategy is explained, as is the means of monitoring an achieving these goals. The site is also frequently updated with studies, reports, and articles relating to world poverty and its relief. Various topics relating to poverty reduction are explained, data and statistics are available, and regional and country reports are also provided. News, updates, and feature articles round out the site.

Publications. Available online. URL: http://publications.worldbank.org/ecommerce/. Accessed on January 5, 2006.

Regional and Country Information. Available online. URL: http://www.worldbank.org/html/extdr/regions.htm. Accessed January 5, 2006.

"World Development Indicators." Available online. URL: http://www.worldbank.org/data/. Accessed on January 5, 2006.

World Business Council for Sustainable Development. Available online. URL: http://www.wbscd.ch. Accessed January 5, 2006. This Web site offers businesses' perspective on globalization issues, though it emphasizes the importance of corporate accountability. Its online publications include reports about corporations, the environmental effects of corporate globalization, agriculture, human resources, sustainable development, climate change, among many other issues. The menu of publications changes, but notable among them are "Business for Development: Business Solutions in Support of the Millennium Goals" and "Driving Success: Marketing Sustainable Development."

World Economic Forum. Available online. URL: http://www.weforum.org. Accessed on January 7, 2006. This site offers news, articles, reports, and opinion pieces that support the corporate viewpoint in the globalization debate. If you click on the "Knowledge Navigator" button, you will find worldwide national economic profiles, with an emphasis on each nation's "competitiveness" in the global economy.

World Growth. Available online. URL: http://worldgrowth.org. Accessed on January 10, 2006. This Web site offers a continually updated menu of articles and reports on issues related to globalization. Its policies and analyses are generally proglobalization and science based and offer an excellent balance to the globalization debate.

World Institute for Development Economics Research. Available online. URL: http://www.wider.unu.edu. Accessed on January 7, 2006. This site contains a vast collection of working papers, research reports, and lectures on many topics relevant to globalization.

World Trading Organization (WTO) home page. Available online. URL: www.wto.org. Accessed on January 7, 2006. Like the other Bretton Woods institutions, the WTO offers a huge number of Web sites, each containing different types of information. More specialized WTO site follow.

The Doha Declaration Explained. Available online. URL: http://www.wto.org/english/tratop_e/dohaexplained_e.htm. Accessed January 7, 2006. This Web site contains the full text of the Doha Ministerial Declaration and other official documents related to the Doha Round of WTO trade negotiations. Primarily, this site is an "unofficial" (nonlegalese) document that explains why the Doha Round and Doha declaration are important. It explains what the Doha declaration is and what it mandates in the various areas it deals with (for example, agriculture, environment, investment, etc.).

Gateway to Documents. Available online. URL: http://www.wto.org/english/docs_e/docs_e.htm. Accessed on January 7, 2006. This is your entry into the voluminous world of WTO documents. The site contains links to Web pages where you can find all types of WTO and trade-related documents, including news, publications, NGO documents, and many other relevant texts.

Understanding the WTO. Available online. URL: http://www.wto.org/english/thewto_e/whatis_e/tif_e/tid_e.htm. Accessed January 7, 2006. This Web site provides a general overview of the WTO, from its inception to its current policies. It is written, of course, from the point of view of the WTO itself, yet it contains useful information about the evolution of this organization from GATT to the present.

WTO Legal Texts. Available online. URL: http://www.wto.org/english/docs_e/legal_e/legal_e.htm. Accessed January 7, 2006. The portal for accessing all the legal documents pertaining to the WTO, including its organizing articles, agreements, reports and agendas from ministerial meetings, negotiations, and WTO decisions.

WTO Trade Topics. Available online. URL: http://www.wto.org/english/tratop_e/tratop_e.htm. Accessed January 7, 2006. This Web site is the starting point for locating information about the WTO's councils, committees, and its trade agreements. The site is divided into three sections, which provide information on the topic and/or link to more information on the issue: Services, Intellectual Property, and Other Topics (including environment, regional trade agreements, and more). This site also has a search capability to help you access online WTO documents on a wide range of topics.

Chronology

First Century B.C.E.

China opens the Silk Road to permit trade with the West.

1271 C.E.

Marco Polo travels from Venice, Italy, to China. In 1295, he writes a book about his travels.

c. 1400

The Silk Road is essentially abandoned when ships become the primary means of transportation in trade with the East.

1492

Christopher Columbus reaches the New World, landing on Hispaniola.

c. 1500–1800

Mercantilism reigns in Europe as the organizing economic principle.

1500

The Netherlands becomes Europe's center of trade, favoring the free flow of goods between nations.

1685

The English establish their first trading outpost in Sumatra, in the East Indies.

1690s

England imposes some of its first protectionist policies to protect its infant woolen industry.

Chronology

1700s

The French physiocrats formulate a complete system of economics based on the principles of laissez-faire, an expression used ever after to describe unfettered free trade and capitalism.

1773

- *December 16:* The Boston Tea Party. American colonists dump imported British tea into Boston Harbor to protest the tax imposed on it by Great Britain.

1776

Adam Smith publishes *The Wealth of Nations,* one of the most important and influential books in economics. The book advocates free trade and noninterference by government in economic life, which, Smith argues, is self-correcting via the invisible hand of enlightened self-interest.

1776

- *July 4:* American colonists adopt the Declaration of Independence from Britain.

1789

U.S. Congress puts in place the first high tariff to protect infant industries and deter imported goods from entering the country.

1798

Thomas Malthus publishes *An Essay on the Principle of Population,* which sets forth the proposition that the human population will grow until the land can no longer sustain it. Malthus's ideas had a great influence on David Ricardo, Karl Marx, and other economists.

1815

In Britain, the Corn Laws, which prohibit grain imports, are passed by Parliament.

1816

U.S. Congress renews the tariffs of 1789 with the Tariff Act, which extends the tariff to more manufactured goods in order to protect the nation's fledgling industries.

1817

David Ricardo publishes *Principles of Political Economy and Taxation,* in which he sets forth his concept of comparative advantage, an idea that is key to the pursuit of free trade.

GLOBALIZATION AND FREE TRADE

1821

James Mill publishes *Elements of Political Economy,* which criticizes the protectionism of the mercantile system.

1828

U.S. Congress passes what has come to be called the "Tariff of Abominations" in order to increase the price of goods imported into the country from Britain. The measure helped industry in the north, but angered southerners, who suffered when Britain retaliated and reduced its imports from this region.

1832

The British Parliament repeals the Corn Laws, opening the way for the dominance in Britain of free trade and laissez-faire capitalism.

1839–1842

Britain fights China in the First Opium War in an attempt to force China to accept opium as payment for trade. Britain is triumphant.

1840s

Irish potato famine results in the starvation of more than 1 million Irish citizens; at least a million more emigrate, primarily to the United States. Though Britain had sufficient food, its laissez-faire policies inhibited it from removing food from the more profitable open market and providing it to the starving Irish.

1856–1860

Britain and France fight China in the Second Opium War. China is routed and forced to accept the legal importation of opium in payment for trade.

1873

The Panic of 1873 is triggered by a financial crisis in Austria; the economic crisis affects most of the Western world, including the United States, which suffers an economic depression that lasts until 1878. Protectionist tariffs are largely to blame for the intensity, duration, and extent of the depression.

1882

A second panic and depression hit the United States; this is the second economic crisis in the Long Depression, which lasts, on and off, from 1873 to 1898.

1890

The McKinley Tariff Act is passed, levying a tax of about 50 percent on most goods imported into the United States. This tariff is often blamed for the Panic of 1893.

Chronology

1893

The Panic of 1893, caused by a run on gold, is the worst economic downturn in U.S. history to that time. It lasts until 1898, when the Long Depression ends.

1894–1895

The Japanese win the Sino-Japanese War against China and begin to establish administrative and trading systems in defeated and weakened China.

1897

The Dingley Act is passed by the U.S. Congress; it increases tariffs on a wider range of goods. It is passed in the hope that it will cure the depression, even though high tariffs were partly to blame for the depression's onset.

1898

- ***April:*** The United States begins its war against Spain. The Spanish-American War is fought in the Caribbean and the Philippines in order to wrest these colonies away from Spain and bring them under the economic control of the United States. The United States gains control of Hawaii, Guam, Wake Island, Cuba, and Puerto Rico. It also gains a long-term lease on the coveted Panama Canal Zone across the isthmus of Central America, which will prove to be a hugely profitable trade route to Asia.

1899–1902

United States fights the Philippine War against Filipino rebels who had previously fought for independence for their nation against the Spanish. Though the Filipino rebels had helped U.S. forces defeat the Spanish, they were crushed by the U.S. military in this bloody war. A violent insurgency continued in the Philippines for decades.

1914–1918

World War I is fought between the Central Powers and the Allies, who are victorious. A defeated Germany is forced to pay reparations, despite its ruined economy, and this leads to hyperinflation.

1917

The Bolsheviks are victorious in the revolution in Russia; Russia becomes the communist Union of Soviet Socialist Republics.

1922

U.S. Congress passes the Fordney-McCumber Act, which raises the average tariff on imported goods to 40 percent.

1929

- *October 29:* The New York stock market crashes, ushering in the Great Depression. Economies around the world go into steep decline, with massive unemployment. The depression lasts until World War II.

1929–1932

Trade between the United States and Europe falls about 60 percent, due to "beggar-thy-neighbor" tariffs.

1930

- *June 13:* President Herbert Hoover signs the Smoot-Hawley Tariff Act, imposing a punitive tariff, the highest in U.S. history, on thousands of products; soon after, more than 20 nations retaliate by imposing similarly high tariffs against U.S. exports.

1933

Franklin D. Roosevelt becomes president of the United States and begins implementing his New Deal policies, in which government takes an active role in helping to lift the country out of depression.

1939

- *September 1:* German leader Adolf Hitler's army invades Poland; Britain declares war on Nazi Germany. World War II begins.

1941

- *December 7:* Japan bombs Pearl Harbor in Hawaii, and the United States enters World War II on the side of the Allies.

1942–1943

John Maynard Keynes and Harry Dexter White negotiate the outline of a world economic system.

1944

Karl Polanyi publishes *The Great Transformation: The Political and Economic Origins of Our Time.* It is a highly influential book that examines how economics evolves from being embedded within a society to a society being shaped by and embedded within an economic system.

1944

- *July 1–22:* More than 700 delegates from 44 countries meet at Bretton Woods, New Hampshire, to formulate a new economic order for the world that will hopefully ensure peace and prosperity. The final agreement is a compromise between the mixed economy supported by Keynes and White and the more laissez-faire capitalism promoted by the United States. Two Bretton Woods institutions are created: the International Bank for Reconstruction and Development (later part of the World Bank) and the International Monetary Fund.

1945

World War II ends with the defeat of Germany in Europe. After the United States drops two atomic bombs on Japan, the war in the Pacific comes to an end and all hostilities are over.

1948

Fifty-four nations meeting in Havana, Cuba, become signatories to the International Trade Organization. The U.S. Congress will not ratify the agreement, so the less radical General Agreement on Tariffs and Trade is adopted by member nations instead. (It later becomes the World Trade Organization.) With the reduction or elimination of many trade barriers, international trade increases, and economic conditions improve.

1948–1951

The United States implements the Marshall Plan to help rebuild Europe and Japan, which are viewed as key trading partners and security against communist power.

1949

Chinese Communists are victorious in that nation's civil war. The new People's Republic of China establishes a closed, command economy.

1951

- ***April:*** European nations form the European Coal and Steel Community to promote free trade in these goods.

1957

The Treaty of Rome establishes the European Economic Community, the initial form of the trade bloc the European Union.

c. 1963–1973

United States is engaged in fighting the Vietnam War; the cost of the war leads to increased deficit spending and inflation in the United States.

1964

The Group of 77 developing nations forms to advocate for policies favorable to developing and least developed countries.

1964–1967

The Kennedy Round of GATT talks reduces tariffs on trade in certain goods.

1967

The Association of Southeast Asian Nations is formed.

1968

Robert S. McNamara is named head of the World Bank, and he changes its focus to concentrate more on alleviating poverty.

1968

All tariffs and customs duties, as well as most quotas, are eliminated among all members of the EU.

1971

- ***August 15:*** U.S. president Richard M. Nixon devalues the dollar and abandons the gold standard.

1971

- ***December:*** Developed nations accept the abandonment of the gold standard, signing the Smithsonian Agreement.

1973

Nations of the Organization of Petroleum Exporting Countries reduce their oil production, causing a worldwide shortage and a tripling of oil prices. This is the first oil crisis of the 1970s.

1973–1979

The Tokyo Round of GATT talks reduces tariffs and nontariff barriers to trade.

1976

Developed nations agree to flexible international exchange rates at the Jamaica Conference.

1977

The Chinese government begins instituting gradual capitalist reforms as outgrowths of its domestic economic institutions. The reforms are hugely successful and are expanded from agriculture to industry.

1979

OPEC again reduces exports of oil, leading to the second oil crisis.

Chronology

1986–1994

The Uruguay Round of GATT trade talks leads to the establishment of the WTO.

1989

The Berlin Wall falls, signaling the end of communist rule in Eastern Europe and the breakup of the Soviet Union.

1991

The Maastricht Treaty establishes the euro as the currency for those EU member nations wishing to adopt it, who become part of the "eurozone."

1991

ASEAN nations form the Southeast Asian Free Trade Area, or AFTA. The trade bloc reduces tariffs and quotas among member nations.

1991

South American nations form MERCOSUR, a trade bloc that works to eliminate barriers to trade and tariffs among member nations.

1991

The IMF, the U.S. Treasury, and international banks impose "shock therapy" to transform the Russian economy from a command economy to a free market, capitalist economy.

1992

- ***August 12:*** President George H. W. Bush signs the North American Free Trade Agreement.

1994

- ***January 1:*** NAFTA enters into force.

1994

- ***December:*** Western Hemispheric nations meet in Miami, Florida, to try to establish the Free Trade Area of the Americas. No agreement is reached.

1995

- ***January 1***: The WTO officially comes into existence.

1997

- ***July 2:*** The Thai currency, the baht, collapses as a consequence of currency speculation and investment.

1997–1998

The East Asia economic crisis causes severe economic decline in this region, and contagion carries the downturn to nations around the world.

1998

Hyperinflation and economic chaos lead the Russian government to devalue the ruble. A worldwide financial crisis ensues.

1999

- ***November:*** Tens of thousands of antiglobalization protesters demonstrate in Seattle, Washington, during a WTO meeting there. The size and diversity of the demonstration makes globalization a worldwide issue.

2000

- ***September:*** Officials from 189 nations sign on to the Millennium Development Goals in order to halve extreme poverty throughout the world by 2015.

2000

The people of Cochabamba, Bolivia, become the first to organize and successfully undo the privatization of their water system.

2001

Western Hemispheric nations meet in Quebec City, in Quebec, Canada, for further talks on establishing the FTAA. Huge antiglobalization protests occur. No agreement is reached.

- ***December 11:*** China admitted as member of WTO.

2003

The Group of 20 developing nations forms at the WTO meeting in Cancún, Mexico. The G-20 refuses to accede to Western pressure, and their delegates walk out of the meeting.

2005

- ***July 27:*** U.S. Congress ratifies the Central American Free Trade Agreement.

2005

After years of astounding economic growth, with GDP rising at about 10 percent per year, China becomes the world's third largest exporter. It is on track to becoming the world's largest economy.

2006

- ***June:*** Member nations of the WTO fail to reach any agreement at their meeting in Geneva, Switzerland. Issues of agricultural subsidies and biopiracy sink the negotiations. The WTO therefore faces the real possibility of collapse.

2006

- ***July:*** Pascal Lamy, director general of the WTO, postpones indefinitely any attempts at revising trade agreements and provisions, or reviving negotiations, that might serve to save the WTO. The Doha Round of trade talks has failed, and no new round of negotiations is scheduled.

Glossary

This chapter presents a glossary of terms relevant to issues of globalization.

austerity measures The conditions that are imposed by an international lending agency, such as the IMF, that force a borrowing government to curtail spending and contract the economy, which often hurt the standard of living of citizens.

balance of payments A statement of a nation's global economic transactions over a given time period, usually a year; includes all the goods, services, and other economic transfers the economy received from or provided to the rest of the world, as well as its capital transfers and the changes that occurred in its financial claims and liabilities.

balance of trade The difference between a nation's total imports and its total exports.

bilateral agreement An agreement between two parties or governments.

biopiracy A corporation's entering a nation, removing one or more of its life-forms, altering the life-form in some way, and then patenting the life-form. After the organism is patented, native people can no longer use the life-form as they have always done because traditional use becomes a patent infringement.

Bretton Woods Conference (1944) The international conference of 44 nations at which groundrules for the stability of global economics and monetary policy were set. The Bretton Woods institutions were created at this conference.

Bretton Woods institutions The global economic organizations created at the Bretton Woods Conference in 1944: the World Bank (WB) and the International Monetary Fund (IMF), later joined by the General Agreement on Tariffs and Trade (GATT), which became the World Trade Organization (WTO).

bubble What occurs when an asset's increasing price is based on expectations that it will increase further in value; often, this does not happen, and the bubble bursts, resulting in economic losses or even recession.

Glossary

capital Anything that is used to yield or produce other goods and services, such as money.

capital account The total amount of capital that flows into a country in a given time period minus the total amount of capital that flows out of the country in the same period of time.

capital account liberalization The dismantling of regulations on the free movement of capital across national borders.

capital flight The removal of savings kept in one country that are transferred to another country deemed to be a safer or more profitable investment.

capitalism The economic system in which a large part of a nation's resources are held privately by individuals or businesses, which are free to use and trade them for profit.

capital market liberalization A nation's opening its financial sector to investment by foreign banks and other financial institutions, as well as currency speculators.

cartel An organization of businesses or nations that produce the same product and that control the supply of that product through a formal organizational agreement.

Central America Free Trade Agreement (CAFTA) The open trade treaty between the United States and the nations of Central America, some of which have not yet ratified the treaty.

central bank A nation's main financial institution, charged with managing the money supply and the value of the country's currency on the foreign-exchange market.

cold war The post–World War II nonmilitary conflict between communist nations and capitalist democratic nations.

command economy An economy in which all production is owned and run by the state, as in a communist country.

communism An economic system in which the government owns the means of production and controls the production of goods. Often called a command economy.

comparative advantage A principle elucidated by David Ricardo that states that a product should be produced in an area or country that is best suited to produce it most efficiently or that has an advantage in its production when compared with other areas.

conditionalities The terms a borrowing nation must comply with before it can get an IMF loan; conditionalities often include trade liberalization, raising interest rates, and so on.

contagion The spreading of an economic downturn, or crisis, from one nation to another.

convergence The economic idea that by following neoliberal economic policies, a poor, developing nation will over time become like an industrial, developed nation.

current account The balance of trade (exports minus imports) plus the flow of interest payments, profits, and labor costs. The current account and the capital account together make up a country's balance of payments.

customs duties Tariffs, or taxes, imposed on imported goods.

deflation A general fall in prices, often due to a fall in wages.

deflation A general fall in prices, often due to a fall in wages.

democracy A political system in which the people elect their government representatives.

depression A severe and prolonged economic downturn in which a nation's GDP and level of investment drop, unemployment increases, and businesses fail.

developed nations Richer, more industrially and technologically advanced countries that generally have a sophisticated and efficient financial infrastructure.

developing nations Poorer nations that are less industrialized and technologically advanced than the developed nations; these countries often do not have the financial infrastructure in place that helps them control their economies.

development economics An area of economic study that accepts that poor countries are fundamentally different from developed nations and addresses why poor nations stay poor and what policies will help them prosper.

dumping Refers to a company selling a product or service to a foreign country for less than it charges domestically for the same product or service.

East Asia crisis (1997–98) The financial crisis that began in Thailand and spread throughout East Asia.

economic globalization The policy—pursued by governments or corporations—of increasing the flow of goods, services, and money across national borders to create an integrated global economy.

economic sanctions The restriction of trade with a particular nation as punishment for its actions or to coerce it to act in a certain way.

economies of scale The principle that producing goods and buying goods in bulk results in a lower per-unit cost and is therefore more efficient.

efficiency The most effective and least wasteful means of production, of providing services, or of accumulating profits.

entrepreneurship Taking an economic risk in order to start a business.

euro The new common currency used by member nations in the EU.

eurodollars Foreign currency that is deposited in international or U.S. banks in U.S. dollars.

European Union (EU) The regional trade organization that includes the nations of Austria, Belgium, Cyprus, Czech Republic, Denmark, Estonia, Finland,

France, Germany, Greece, Hungary, Ireland, Italy, Latvia, Lithuania, Luxembourg, Malta, the Netherlands, Poland, Portugal, Slovakia, Slovenia, Spain, Sweden, and the United Kingdom.

exchange rate The exact value of one currency in relation to another currency.

export Goods and services sent out of one country and sold to other countries.

export processing zone (EPZ) An area, often near a port, that is set aside by special arrangements to promote exports.

expropriation The taking over of a private company by a government that does not compensate the nationalized business.

externalities Those factors that corporations do not consider and refuse responsibility for in the course of their operations; for example, environmental pollution, resource depletion, and so on.

fast track In the United States, the executive's authority to negotiate trade pacts without consulting Congress, which must then vote on the pact in an up or down vote.

Fed, the The U.S. Federal Reserve Bank; the central bank of the United States.

fiat money Paper and nongold coins that are the currency of a nation and that are backed by gold reserves.

financial contagion The rapid spread of a financial crisis from one nation to others, due largely to the globalization of financial markets.

financial market speculation Foreign short-term investors taking advantage of the volatility of foreign currencies by buying the currency when its value goes down and then selling it when its value goes up.

flexible exchange rate A system in which supply and demand affect the rate at which currencies are valued against each other.

foreign aid The money or other help one nation or group of nations provides to another.

foreign debt The amount of money a nation owes to foreign nations.

foreign direct investment (FDI) Cross-border investment made primarily by transnational corporations, which may include building factories and manufacturing facilities in a nation and/or investing in or taking over businesses in a nation.

foreign exchange markets A network of commercial and investment banks, as well as other financial institutions, that promote and facilitate international trade by converting currencies, though today these markets are dominated mostly by the trading of currency itself.

foreign exchange trading The buying and selling of nations' currencies in the global market.

foreign portfolio investment (FPI) Investment that is easily traded (unlike FDI, which often takes the form of factories and other tangibles) and does not represent a long-term stake in a business, such as stocks or bonds.

free trade The abolition or reduction of barriers to trade, such as tariffs, customs duties, and quotas.

Free Trade Area of the Americas (FTAA) The proposed regional trade association that would include the 34 democratic countries in the Western Hemisphere.

gangster economy An economy that is largely controlled by organized crime.

General Agreement on Tariffs and Trade (GATT) The institution created by the Bretton Woods Conference in 1944 to promote free and fair global trade; superseded in 1995 by the WTO

globalization The process in which countries of the world become more closely integrated economically, usually via unrestricted mobility of capital and free trade.

global warming The increase in globally averaged temperatures resulting from the burning of fossil fuels.

gold standard A system in which the value of a nation's currency, and the amount of its currency in circulation, is tied to how much gold it has in its reserves; the gold standard tends to limit a nation's monetary supply.

greenfield investment A kind of FDI in which a transnational corporation builds a completely new production facility in a country.

gross domestic product (GDP) A measure of the value of all the goods and services produced in a nation by both domestic and foreign companies in a particular year.

gross national product (GNP) A measure of the value of all the goods and services produced by a country's businesses within the nation's borders and overseas in a particular year.

Group of 8 (G-8) An organization of the world's most economically powerful and wealthy nations, including Canada, France, Germany, Italy, Japan, the United Kingdom, the United States, and, more recently, Russia.

Group of 77 (G-77) A group of mainly developing countries and LDC that advocate for trade rules and economic policies favorable to its members.

harmonization The creation of uniform, worldwide standards for goods produced by MNCs involved in FDI; controversial because the global standards are usually very low and are intended to override any nation's more stringent standards.

hot money Short-term, speculative investment, especially currency speculation, that enters a nation to make the investor a quick profit and is then pulled out of the country.

human capital Another term for labor.

human development A measure of the quality of life for individuals around the world; it includes human rights, freedom from poverty, reduction of income inequality, and conservation of the natural world and its resources.

hyperinflation A runaway inflation rate that generally increases by double digits every month.

import The goods and services brought into a country from another nation.

import quota The limits set on the amount of goods and services that can be brought into a country.

infant industry A newly developing industry in a country that is just beginning to industrialize; historically, infant industries have been protected by tariffs in order to allow them the time to grow and mature until they can compete successfully in the free market.

inflation A general rise in prices, often due to deficit spending, or borrowing.

intellectual property Refers to the creations of the human mind and includes books, music, inventions, artworks, commercial designs, trademarks and copyrights, patented pharmaceuticals, and so on.

international financial institution (IFI) A financial institution, such as the WB and IMF, that is responsible for regulating the behavior of nations and businesses involved in the global economy.

International Labour Organization (ILO) The well-respected and well-known organization, part of the UN, that promotes the rights of workers around the world.

International Monetary Fund (IMF) A Bretton Woods institution that was created to help stabilize the global economy and promote economic development through technical and financial aid, as well as surveillance.

laissez-faire French for "to leave alone." An economic doctrine introduced by the French physiocrats of the 18th century, which promoted the absolute noninterference of government in trade, or in other economic matters, which, the physiocrats felt, were best left to market forces.

least developed country (LDC) One of the poorest nations in the world, generally having a large population living in poverty (less than $1/day).

macroeconomics Economics that have to do with the overall economy, such as monetary policy, inflation, total output, and so on.

maquiladora A foreign-owned factory where duty-free goods are produced for export to member nations in a trade bloc; the word comes from the Spanish term referring to such manufacturers in Mexico, which is part of NAFTA.

mercantilism An economic system prevalent among Western nations from the 15th to the 18th centuries, in which it was believed that a nation's strength came from having lots of gold (bullion) and being self-sufficient, which entailed expanding exports and limiting imports to the greatest degree possible.

MERCOSUR A South American regional trade bloc whose members include Argentina, Bolivia, Brazil, Chile, Colombia, Ecuador, Paraguay, Peru, Uruguay, and Venezuela.

metropole (state) An industrialized nation that takes control of a periphery state; the metropole state appropriates the periphery's raw materials and forces the periphery state to import the metropole's manufactured goods.

microeconomics Economics that have to do with smaller parts of an economy, such as businesses, labor unions, and so on.

moral hazard The incentive for investors to make ill-conceived loans because they know that the IMF will bail them out if the loan goes bad.

most favored nation (MFN) A global trade designation that grants trade concessions, or benefits, to a country that are denied to other (non-MFN) countries. MFN status is automatically applied to all member nations in the WTO.

multilateral agreement An agreement between more than two parties or governments.

multinational corporation (MNC) A corporation that controls or owns businesses or has affiliates in many nations around the world, though its home base is in a particular country.

nationalization The government takeover of a private company doing business in the country in which compensation is paid to the company.

neoliberalism An economic, as well as political, philosophy that states that markets should have a dominant and controlling role in all, or nearly all, aspects of life; it promotes privatization and economic efficiency above other values, such as wealth redistribution, conservation, and social justice.

nongovernmental organization (NGO) An organization that disseminates information, advocates for a policy or group, provides air, or otherwise is involved in the affairs of nations though it is not affiliated with a government.

North, the The developed nations of the Northern Hemisphere.

North American Free Trade Agreement (NAFTA) The open trade agreement between the United States, Canada, and Mexico, creating a regional trade bloc.

oligopoly Economic control by one or more large corporations.

outsourcing Hiring workers in foreign countries to do the work that domestic workers once did.

panic An economic crisis that occurs when citizens lose confidence in a bank's ability to return their savings in cash. During a panic, so many people try to withdraw their bank savings that the bank cannot cover the withdrawals and begins to call in its loans. If outstanding loans cannot be repaid to the bank, the bank will fail. (This occurred before the U.S. federal government insured bank deposits as part of the New Deal.)

periphery (state) A weak, disorganized, and unindustrialized nation that is taken over by a metropole state and is forced to export its raw materials to the metropole, while importing large amounts of the metropole's manufactures.

Ponzi finance A mode of financing, named after Charles Ponzi, that entails paying for old liabilities with newly created liabilities.

precautionary principle A globally accepted principle that states, "where there are threats of serious or irreversible damage, lack of full scientific certainty shall not be used as a reason for postponing cost-effective measures to prevent environmental degradation."

privatization The selling of state-owned services and industries to for-profit corporations.

protectionism The erection of trade barriers or limits by governments to protect one or more of a country's industries from competition from imports.

purchasing power parity (PPP) Measurement, or adjustment, made in foreign exchange rates to allow for the differences in the cost of living in different countries.

quota A government restriction on the quantity of a specific good or service that can be imported into a country.

race to the bottom The phrase that aptly describes what happens when corporations seek to locate facilities in nations with the lowest wages and weakest labor laws and the fewest environmental and business regulations; as poor nations compete for foreign investments, they vie with one another to eliminate all regulations and protections that might interfere with corporate profits, thus generating a downward spiral in the hope of luring investment.

real capital Actual things, such as factories, buildings, and the machines and equipment used by workers to produce goods.

regional trade agreement An agreement made by the nations in a particular area or region to reduce tariffs among member nations.

relocalization A movement to reinstate the primacy of local, small-scale community production and control of resources.

round A periodic meeting of all members of the WTO, at which global trade issues are discussed and rules made.

sequence and pacing Making structural adjustments to a developing economy in the correct order and at a reasonable pace; for example, establishing a jobs program before unemployment rises due to imposed privatization.

shock therapy The extremely rapid liberalization of an economy.

Smoot-Hawley Tariff Act (1930) A highly protectionist law passed by the U.S. Congress that levied harsh taxes on imports, initiated a trade war with the United States's trade partners, and worsened the Great Depression.

social capital Capital, often in the form of social services and infrastructure, that a government provides to its people, including roads, sewers, schools, and so on.

social imperialism The economic system in which a metropole nation takes over a periphery nation to use it for its own economic benefit, including the appropriation of raw materials and the maintenance of high employment in the metropole state.

South, the The poorer, developing nations of the Southern Hemisphere.

stagflation Coined in the 1970s, the term refers to a condition in which slow economic growth (stagnation) occurs at the same time as inflation.

structural adjustment program (SAP) The neoliberal program imposed on borrowing nations by the IMF and international banks that follow the Washington Consensus.

sustainable development The economic improvement in a country that is built on the wise use and conservation of resources and the fair treatment of labor, which results in a continuous improvement in people's standard of living because resources are not thoughtlessly exploited and depleted.

tariff A tax on imports that is a type of trade barrier among nations.

technology transfer The movement of innovative technologies (manufacturing, information, research, or other) by an MNC to a less technologically advanced nation in which it is doing business.

trade barrier A restriction on trade imposed by a government against imports from other nations; may be a tariff or quota that limits the quantity of certain imports.

trade bloc A group of nations most often in the same geographic region that joins together to reduce or eliminate tariffs and promote free trade among members.

trade deficit A situation in which the value of the goods and services a nation imports exceeds the value of the goods and services it exports.

trade liberalization Policies that free up trade, such as the removal of trade barriers, elimination of tariffs, and so on.

Trade-Related Aspects of Intellectual Property (TRIPS) An agreement arising from the Uruguay Round of GATT that sets global standards for the protection of intellectual property, such as patents on computer software, drugs, books, and so on.

trade surplus A situation in which the value of the goods and services a nation exports exceeds the value of the goods and services it imports.

transitional economy A nation whose economy is changing from a communist command economy to a capitalist free trade economy.

transparency The idea that the decisions, and the processes that lead to these decisions, made by the Bretton Woods institutions should be open and made available to governments and the general public; often also implies that those affected by these decisions should also have input into the decision-making process.

unsustainable debt A condition in which a nation's foreign debt is so great that it cannot be paid off without doing serious damage to the country's economy.

Washington Consensus The neoliberal policies promoted primarily by the IMF and international lending banks, including free trade, capital market deregulation, and privatization, and noninterference in the economy by government.

World Bank (WB) A Bretton Woods institution that provides development loans for projects in developing nations.

World Trade Organization (WTO) An organization that evolved in 1995 from GATT and that is charged with promoting global trade and making it freer and fairer for all nations; it also resolves international trade disputes.

Index

Page numbers in **boldface** indicate major treatment of a subject. Page numbers followed by *f* indicate figures. Page numbers followed by *b* indicate biographical entries. Page numbers followed by *c* indicate chronology entries. Page numbers followed by *g* indicate glossary entries.

A

acquired immunodeficiency syndrome (AIDS) 51–52
addiction 13
AERC. *See* African Economic Research Consortium (AERC)
Africa 46, 47, 49, 51–52, 61, 62. *See also specific headings, e.g.:* Nigeria
Africa Action 296
Africa Group Initiative 56
African Development Bank 296–297
African Economic Research Consortium (AERC) 297
African Group (of 41 nations) 56
AFTA. *See* Southeast Asian Free Trade Area (AFTA)
"... After Seattle?" (Korten) **147–151**
Age of Exploration 6
Age of Imperialism 14, 60
Agreement on Agriculture (AoA) **48–49,** 55
agricultural subsidies 48–49, 55, 88, 89
agriculture 117–118
Aguas del Turnari 104, 105
AIDC. *See* Alternative Information and Development Centre (AIDC)
AIDS. *See* acquired immunodeficiency syndrome
air pollution 123
Allied Reparations Committee 16
Allies 14–16, 375*c*
Alternative Information and Development Centre (AIDC) 297
American colonists 373*c*
"America's Win-Win-Win Trade Relations with China" (Griswold) **159–163**
antiglobalization advocates v
antiglobalization protest 88, 380*c*
anti-inflation monetary policy 33, 103
anti-trust laws 72
Appellate Body of the DSB 53
Arab Maghreb 270*f*
Article XX of GATT 53, 54
ASEAN. *See* Association of Southeast Asian Nations (ASEAN)
ASHD. *See* Association for Sustainable Human Development (ASHD)
Asia 12, 52, 74, 75
Asian Development Bank 297–298
assembly plants (in Mexico) 85
Association for Sustainable Human Development (ASHD) 298
Association for Women's Rights in Development (AWID) 298
Association of Southeast Asian Nations (ASEAN) 270*f*, 298–299, 378*c*, 379*c*
austerity measures 23, 56, 82
Austria 12, 374*c*
Austria-Hungary 14
AWID. *See* Association for Women's Rights in Development (AWID)

B

baht (Thai currency) 95, 97–99, 379*c*
bailout loan 99
Baker, James A., III 33, 283*b*
Baker Plan 33
balanced budget 90, 100
balance of payments
- and East Asia crisis 100
- and gold standard 15
- and John Maynard Keynes 20
- and mercantilism 7
- and NAFTA **85–86**
- and U.S. 89, 90

Bank Information Center (BIC) USA 299
banking (banks)
- and East Asia crisis 99, 101
- and eurodollars 28, 80–81
- failure of 72
- and Mexican financial crisis 32–33
- and New Deal 76
- run on 73
- in Russia 109, 112, 113
- in South Korea 97–98
- in Thailand 97
- and U.S. policy 80–81

bankruptcy 72, 99, 100

Index

Barfield, Claude E. 54–55
Bechtel Corporation 103, 104
"beggar-thy-neighbor" tariffs 17, 376*c*
benefit/cost analysis vii
Bergsten, C. Fred **141–147, 239–247**
Berlin Wall falls 108, 379*c*
Bhagwati, Jagdish vii, 46, 55, 283*b*
BIC. *See* Bank Information Center (BIC) USA
big business 72
"Big Pharma" 51–52
"Big Push" 22
billionaires 112
biopiracy 52, 55
blacklisting 24
black markets 108, 110, 113, 115
Bolivia vii, 24, 88, 89, 102–106, 380*c*
Bolshevik Revolution of 1917 18, 107, 375*c*
Boston Tea Party 373*c*
BRAC. Bangladesh Rural Advancement Committee (BRAC) 299
Brazil 52, 56, 57
bread 110
Bretton Woods 25, 41
Bretton Woods Agreement **179–189**
Bretton Woods conference 20–21
Bretton Woods Institutions 21–27. *See also specific headings, e.g.:* GATT
- developing nations 26–27
- GATT 25–26
- IMF **22–24**
- ITO **24–25**
- World Bank **21–22**

Bretton Woods Project 299–300, 376*c*–377*c*
Brezhnev, Leonid 108
briberization 35
Brown, Sherrod 85–86
budget deficit 79–80
Bush, George H. W. 83, 283*b*, 379*c*
Bush, George W. 88, 284*b*
businesses 109, 111, 119–120

C

CAFTA. *See* Central America Free Trade Agreement (CAFTA)
Camdessus, Michel 101, 284*b*
Canada 83, 85, 86, 380*c*
capital 383*g*
capital account 383*g*
capital account liberalization 383*g*
capital flight 383*g*
capitalism 11–12, 18, 383*g*
capitalist class 108
capitalist reforms 378*c*
capital market liberalization 31, 36–37, **38–40,** 41, 95–96, 110, 383*g*
Caribbean 74, 75
Caribbean Community and Common Market (CARICOM) 270*f*
Caribbean Conservation Association (CCA) 300
cartel 27, 383*g*
casualties 15, 17
CCA. *See* Caribbean Conservation Association (CCA)
CCC. *See* Civilian Conservation Corps (CCC)
CEC. *See* Commission for Environmental Cooperation (CEC)
CEDARE. *See* Centre for Environment and Development for Arab Region and Europe (CEDARE)
Center for International Environmental Law (CIEL) 300
Central America Free Trade Agreement (CAFTA) 86–87, 380*c*, 383*g*
Central American Common Market 270*f*
central bank(s) 39, 58, 95, 383*g*
central planning 33
Central Powers 375*c*
Centre for Development and Enterprise 300
Centre for Environment and Development for Arab Region and Europe (CEDARE) 301
Centre for Research on Multinational Corporations (SOMO) 301
Chapter 11 (NAFTA) **86**
Chávez, Hugo 88, 284*b*–285*b*
Chenery, Hollis 22
Chiang Kai-shek 117
chickens 36
child labor 44, 45
Chile 34, 37, 41, 57
China vii, 116–125
- agricultural reform 117–118
- background on **117**
- challenges for **122–125**
- communism 116, 117, 377*c*
- contract responsibility program **119,** 120
- and East Asia crisis **121**
- economic growth of 57
- exports of 380*c*
- and FDI 43, 44–45
- historical background for **13–14**
- and import of kerosene 13
- local initiative/innovation in **119–120**
- market pricing 118–119
- Opium Wars 13, 374*c*
- Marco Polo 372*c*
- PRC established 377*c*
- reforms in **117–118, 122,** 378*c*
- and silk trade 3, 13
- Sino-Japanese War 375*c*
- and trade liberalization 37, 56
- trade zones **119–120**
- and U.S. debt 82
- and WTO 56, 380*c*

"China: Just Say No to Monetary Protectionism" (O'Driscoll and Hoskins) **255–258**
Chinese Communists 377*c*
CIEL. *See* Center for International Environmental Law (CIEL)
CIVICUS: World Alliance for Citizen Participation 301–302
Civilian Conservation Corps (CCC) 77
Civil Works Administration 77
classical liberal economics 29
Clausen, Alden Winship 46, 285*b*
Clinton, William (Bill) Jefferson 83, 163–170, 285*b*
coal 377*c*
Cochabamba, Bolivia vii, 102–106, 380*c*
coffee 49, 62
Cohen, Stephen 116
cold war 77–78, 383*g*
cold war, economic 7
collective bargaining 44
collective interest 30
collectivization 117, 118
Colombia 34
colonialism **6,** 7, 13–14, 21
Columbus, Christopher 6, 372*c*
command economy 106–108, 111, 118–119, 123, 377*c*, 383*g*
Commission for Environmental Cooperation (CEC) 302

commodification" of the world 50, 52
commodities 7, 48, 55, 62, 99, 102
Common Market for Eastern and Southern Africa (COMSEA) 271*f*
communications 12
communism 383*g*. *See also* Soviet Union
- Berlin Wall falls 108, 379*c*
- in China 116, 117, 377*c*
- and Marshall Plan 18, 77
- and Karl Marx 10, 287*b*–288*b*, 373*c*
- in Russia 107–108, 116
- and transitional economies 40, 106–107

companies 100, 102, 103, 112, 119
comparative advantage 9–11, 57–59, 63, 373*c*, 383*g*
competition 35, 40, 47, 49, 64
competitive advantage 64, 90
compound interest 61
computers 95–96
COMSEA. *See* Common Market for Eastern and Southern Africa (COMSEA)
conditionalities 383*g*
- capital market liberalization **38–40**
- definition of 23
- and East Asia crisis 99–100
- historical background on 32–40
- and IMF 23–24
- interest rates **36**
- market liberalization **36–37**
- privatization **33–36**
- trade liberalization **37–38**
- and transitional economy **40**
- and U.S. 23
- and Washington Consensus **32–33**
- and World Bank 46

confidence 112
confidential information 51
Congress, U.S.
- and CAFTA 86–87, 380*c*
- Dingley Act 375*c*
- fast-track trade 82–83
- Fordney-McCumber Act 375*c*
- and ITO 25
- and NAFTA 83
- tariffs 373*c*, 374*c*

consensus basis 47
conservation 103, 106
consumption 90, 91
contagion vii, 41, 98–99, 101, 113, 383*g*
containment policy 77–78
contract responsibility program **119,** 120
convergence **59–60,** 63, 384*g*
Cooke & Co. 72
La Coordinadora de Defensa del Agua y la Vida 105
copyrights 51
core (state) 30, 60. *See also* metropole (state)
Corn Laws (Great Britain, 1832) 11, 373*c*, 374*c*
corporations 9, 47, 51, 86. *See also* multinational corporations
Corp Watch 302
corruption
- in China 116, 123
- in poorer countries 35
- and privatization 34
- in Russia 40, 109–114
- in Soviet Union 108

Costa Rica 87
cotton 48, 57, 58
creditors, U.S. 91
crime 40, 115
criminalized markets 115
Cuba 74–75, 87, 375*c*, 377*c*
currency(-ies)
- and capital market liberalization 39
- and China 122
- devaluing of 22, 27, 80, 98, 99, 103, 113–114
- dollar 20, 27, 73, 79, 80, 378*c*
- and East Asia 95, 96, 100
- eurodollars 28
- and gold standard 15
- and IMF loan quotas 23
- stabilization of 110
- strong 95, 96
- Thai 95, 97–99, 379*c*

currency reserves 122
currency speculation 28, 39–40, 95
current account 384*g*
customs duties 3–4, 378*c*, 384*g*

D

dams 46, 103
Dawes Plan 16
debt
- in 1970 61
- in 2002 61
- in China 121
- and developing countries 24, **61–62**
- and East Asia crisis 100
- foreign 385*g*
- and IMF conditionalities 24
- increasing 29
- and least developed countries 29, **61–62,** 275*f*
- Mexican 32
- need to address 65
- Nigerian 61, 62
- as percent of exports 275*f*
- personal 90, 91
- and Russia 114
- unsustainable 275*f*, 391*g*
- of U.S. 82, 90, 91
- and World War I 15

debtor-nation participation 46
debtor nations 82
debt relief 103
decision making 47
Declaration of Independence (U.S.) 373*c*
deficit spending 16, 17, 27, 79–80, 100
deflation 16, 384*g*
deforestation 124
Dell 44
delocalization 4–5
DeLong, Brad 30
democracy 23, 46, 50, 54, 65, 120, 384*g*
"democratic deficit" 54, 60–61
Deng Xiaoping 117, 285*b*–286*b*
Department of Agriculture, U.S. 87
depression (economic) 384*g*
- of 1890s **12–13**
- and Dingley Act 375*c*
- and gold standard 16
- Great Depression **16–17, 75–77**
- Long Depression **72–73,** 374*c*, 375*c*
- New Deal policy 376*c*
- and old economic order 18
- Panic of 1873 374*c*
- and protectionism 12, 374*c*

deregulation 32, 39, 60, 81, 98
desertification 123
Detroit, Michigan 64
devaluing of currency 22, 27, 80, 98, 99, 103, 113–114
devaluing of exports 38
developed nations 57–59, 384*g*
- and agricultural subsidies 48–49
- and comparative advantage 57–59

Index

and Doha Round 55
and new economic theories 65
and protectionism 57–58
wealthbuilding of 57–59
and WTO 47
developing nations 384*g*
assertiveness of 26–27
biopiracy in 52
and conditionalities 24
and confidence in IMF 41
and debt 24, **61–62**
and Doha Round 55, 56
and GATT 26
and industrialization 59
and ITO 25
and new economic theories 65
and oil shocks of 1970s 29
and pharmaceutical patents 51–52
prospering of 59
and trade liberalization 63
and WTO 47, 89
development economics 22, 384*g*
Development Group for Alternative Policies (Development GAP) 302–303
digging wells 104
Dillon Round of GATT talks 272*f*
Dingley Act 73, 375*c*
dislocation from privatization 34
Dispute Resolution Body (DSB) 48–49, **52–54**
Dispute Resolution Panel (DSP) 53
Dixit, Avinash 64
Doctors Without Borders 41–42
Doha Round (WTO trade talks) **55–56,** 272*f*, 381*c*
dollar, U.S. 20, 27, 73, 79, 80, 378*c*
dolphins 53, 54
domestic companies 35
domestic competition 45
domestic content 86
domestic food production 33
domestic food security 55
Dominican Republic 87
drinking water 124
drug traffickers 106
DSB. *See* Dispute Resolution Body
DSP (Dispute Resolution Panel) 53
dumping 384*g*
dust storms 123

E

East Asia vii, 94–102
capital liberalization **95–96**
growth of **94–95**
speculation, financial market **95–96**
and trade liberalization 37
East Asia crisis (1997-98) vii, 96–102, 384*g*
background on 94–96
and capital market liberalization 38–39
causes of **96–102,** 380*c*
and China **121**
and confidence in IMF 40–41
and contagion **98–99**
and IMF 40–41, **99–101**
results of **101–102**
and Russia 113
and South Korea **97–98**
and Thailand **96–97**
and U.S. policies 82
Eastern European countries 108
East Indies 372*c*
EC. *See* European Commission (EC)
economic collapse **113–114,** 114–116
Economic Community of West African States (ECOWAS) 271*f*
Economic Consequences of Peace, The (Keynes) 18
economic crisis 31–33, 41, 374*c*
economic decline 380*c*
economic development 26, 32, 43–44
economic globalization 384*g*
economic growth
and China 122
and comparative advantage 10
and conditionalities 24
in East Asia 94
and gold standard 16
and government intervention 45–46, 58
and ITO 24
and John Maynard Keynes 19
of second-tier nations 57
economic policies **80**
Economic Policy Institute 84–86
economics 30, 31, 373*c*, 376*c*
economic sanctions 53, 384*g*
economic theories 63–65. *See also* Keynesian economics; neoliberalism
economies of scale 384*g*
economists vii
economy 18–21, 89–92, 110, 122, 377*c*
ECOSOC. *See* UN Economic and Social Council (ECOSOC)
ECOWAS. *See* Economic Community of West African States (ECOWAS)
education
in East Asia 94
and economic growth 57
and endogenous grow theory 63
free 79
funding of 24
and GATS 50
and IMF conditionalities 24
efficiency 34, 111, 112, 384*g*
elderly 115
electric power projects 21
Elements of Political Economy (Mill) 7, 374*c*
El Salvador 87
emergency loans 22
employment 44, 90, 125. *See also* jobs
endogenous growth theory **63**
England 372*c*
entrepreneurship 384*g*
environmental degradation 61, 123, 124
environmental laws 50, 53, 54, 61, 83, 86
EPZs. *See* export processing zones (EPZs)
Essay on the Principle of Population, An (Maltus) 373*c*
ethanol 87
Ethiopia 49
EU. *See* European Union (EU)
euro 91, 379*c*, 384*g*
eurodollars 28, 29, 80–81
Europe
after World War II 77
and "beggar-thy-neighbor" tariffs 376*c*
Berlin Wall falls 108, 379*c*
and China 14
and exchange rates 28
and gold standard 27, 28
and Great Depression 17
and Marshall Plan 17–18, 377*c*
social democracies in **78–79**
and social imperialism 13, 14
European Coal and Steel Community 377*c*
European Commission (EC) 102

European Economic Community 377*c*
European social democracies **78–79**
European Union (EU) 270*f*, 377*c*, 384*g*–385*g*
 and agricultural subsidies 48–49, 55
 and commodification 102
 growing dominance of 82
 and pan-European federalism 78
 and tariffs/customs duties/quotas 378*c*
"eurozone" 379*c*
exchange rate(s) 15, 28, 32, 122, 378*c*, 385*g*
expansion 20, 100
expansionism 14, 73–75
expenditures, U.S. 90
exploration, European 6
export(s) 385*g*
 to Asia 75
 and CAFTA 87
 in China 121, 122, 380*c*
 of coffee 49
 and creditors 91
 devaluation of 38
 and East Asia crisis 100, 101
 growth of 279*f*
 and John Maynard Keynes 20
 and Marshall Plan 78
 and mercantilism 7
 to Mexico 85–86
 James Mill on 7
 and NAFTA 85–86
 and poverty 62, 276*f*
 of raw materials 57
 and social imperialism 13
 and trade liberalization 38
 and unsustainable external debt 275*f*
 and U.S. 16, 80, 90, 91
export processing zones (EPZs) 44, 120–121, 385*g*
expropriation 86, 385*g*

F

factories 43–44
famines 41–42, 107
FAO. *See* United Nations Food and Agriculture Organization (FAO)
farmers 48, 87, 104, 105, 117, 118
farm subsidies 48–49, 55, 88
fast track 82–83, 385*g*
FDI. *See* foreign direct investment (FDI)
Fed, the 75, 79, 385*g*
federal debt, U.S. 91
Federal Deposit Insurance Corporation (1933) 76
Federal Reserve, U.S. 75
fiat money 15, 385*g*
50 Years Is Enough: U.S. Network for Global Economic Justice 303
Figes, Orlando 107
Filipino rebels 375*c*
films, pirated 51
financial contagion 385*g*. *See also* contagion; financial crisis
financial crisis 19–20, 380*c*. *See also* East Asia crisis; Mexican financial crisis
financial infrastructure 95
financial market speculation vii, 19, 20, 72, 73, 95–97, 385*g*
Fireside Chats **131–137**
fiscal discipline 32
flexible exchange rate 385*g*
flood-control projects 21
Focus on the Global South 303–304
food imports 280*f*
food policies 41–42, 101
food production 125
food self-sufficiency 123
Ford Motor Company 44
Fordney-McCumber Act 75, 375*c*
foreign aid 22, 279*f*, 385*g*
foreign companies 35, 50, 52
foreign debt 385*g*
foreign direct investment (FDI) **43–46**, 385*g*
 and capital market liberalization 39
 in China 120, 121
 in East Asia 96
 and endogenous grow theory 63
 in Europe 79
 and least developed countries 43, 278*f*
 and outsourcing 90
 in Russia 116
foreign exchange 122
foreign exchange markets 385*g*
foreign exchange trading 385*g*
foreign investment 28
Foreign Policy In Focus (FPIF) 304
foreign portfolio investment (FPI) 96, 385*g*
Forum for the Future 304
FPI. *See* foreign portfolio investment (FPI)
FPIF. *See* Foreign Policy In Focus (FPIF)
France 7–8, 13–15, 373*c*, 374*c*
free markets 8, 11, 31, 33
free trade 386*g*
 criticisms of v
 definition of 3
 and "democratic deficit" 61
 and development economics 22
 European Coal and Steel Community formed 377*c*
 in France 373*c*
 and John Maynard Keynes 18, 19
 and Marshall Plan 78
 and poverty 62
 and Adam Smith vi, 9
 as WTO principle 47
Free Trade Area of the Americas (FTAA) 87–89, 379*c*, 380*c*, 386*g*
free trade zones 44
Friedman, Milton 29, 42, 286*b*
Friedman, Thomas 286*b*
Frye, William P. 74
FTAA. *See* Free Trade Area of the Americas (FTAA)

G

gangster economy 386*g*
GATS. *See* General Agreement on Trade in Services (GATS)
GATSwatch 304–305
GATT. *See* General Agreement on on Tariffs and Trade (GATT)
GDP. *See* gross domestic product (GDP)
General Agreement on Tariffs and Trade (GATT) 25–26, 47, 59, 377*c*–379*c*, 386*g*. *See also* World Trade Organization (WTO)
General Agreement on Trade in Services (GATS) **49–50**, 102
General Electric 44
generic drugs 52
genetically modified plants 51
Germany
 Berlin Wall falls 108, 379*c*
 and China 14
 Adolf Hitler 376*c*
 hyperinflation in 16, 17, 375*c*
 invades Poland 376*c*
 rebuilding of 18
 reparations paid by 16
 and U.S. debt 82

and World War I 14, 15, 375*c*
and World War II 17, 376*c*, 377*c*
Ghana 46
Gilpin, Robert 54
"Giving Aid Effectively" (Stokey) vii
glasnost 108
globalization 386*g*
benefits of 57
and convergence **59–60**
criticisms of v
at the crossroads 56–63
definition of vi, **4–5**
and developed nations 57–59
drawbacks of **60–63**
early evolution of 6–15
lack of results from 56
need for "human face" for 65
new type of **64–65**
unpopularity of 56
and U.S. economic policies **80**
as worldwide issue 380*c*
"Globalization" (Greenspan) **152–159**
Global Policy Forum (GPF) 305
global trade 17, 26
Global Trade Watch (GTW) 305
Global Vision Corporation 305–306
global warming 386*g*
G-90 group 89
GNP. *See* gross national product
gold 6, 7, 13, 80, 375*c*
Goldman Environmental Prize for Sustainable Development 106
gold standard **15–16,** 386*g*
abandonment of 17, 27–28, 38, **79–80,** 378*c*
and depressions 12, 16–17, 75
and John Maynard Keynes 20
in U.S. 73, 79–80
Gorbachev, Mikhail S. 108, 112, 286*b*
government expenditures 33
government intervention
and China 122
developing nations view of 41
in East Asia 95
and East Asia crisis 100
and endogenous grow theory 63
and growth 45–46
and IMF 60
and ITO 25
in Japan 80
and John Maynard Keynes 19
and neoliberalism 29, 30
and New Deal policy 76–77
and new economic theories 63–65
pressure for less 59
prohibition on 59
in South Korea 80
and Structural Adjustment Program 33
and WTO 60
government investment 64
government regulation
of big business 72
and East Asia crisis 99
and economic growth 58
financial 39
and GATS 50
Adam Smith on 9
and South Korea 98
and Thailand 97
governments, dwindling power of 60
government subsidies 63, 64, 71
GPF. *See* Global Policy Forum (GPF)
grain imports 373*c*
Gray, John 4–5, 107
Great Britain
and China 13, 14
and colonization 6
Corn Laws 11, 373*c*, 374*c*
Irish potato famine 374*c*
and ITO 24, 25
laissez-faire capitalism in 11
and Opium Wars 374*c*
protectionism in 57–58
and World War I 14, 15
and World War II 17, 376*c*
Great Depression **16–17,** 18, 75–77, 376*c*
Great Leap Forward 117
Great Transformation 11
The Great Transformation(Polanyi) 376*c*
greenfield investment 43, 386*g*
Greenspan, Alan **152–159**
Griswold, Daniel T. **159–163**
gross domestic product (GDP) 386*g*
in China 120–122, 125
devoted to social services 79
and East Asia crisis 101
in Europe 79
growth of 279*f*
in Russia 115, 116
in South Korea 37
and trade liberalization 37, 38
in U.S. 82, 89
Grossman, Gene 64
gross national product (GNP) 386*g*
Group A/B stocks 121
Group of 8 (G-8) 386*g*
Group of 77 (G-77) 26, 377*c*, 386*g*
Group of 20 (G-20) 56, 192–194, 239–247, 271*f*, 380*c*
G-7 countries 99
GTW. *See* Global Trade Watch (GTW)
Guam 74, 375*c*
guilds 6

H

Hamilton, Alexander 58
hands-off policy 59
harmonization 45, 386*g*
Havana negotiations (ITO) 25
Hawaii 375*c*, 376*c*
Hawley, Willis 76
Hayek, Friedich A. von. 29, 286*b*–287*b*
health 53, 54, 61
health care 24, 50, 79, 115
hedge funds 95
"herd mentality" 96
high inflation 277*f*
high interest rates 29, 61, 91, 100
highway building projects 21, 121
Hispaniola 372*c*
historical background vi, 6–40
Bretton Woods conference 20–21
capitalism in late 1800s **11–12**
capital market liberalization **38–40**
on China **12–13, 117**
colonization **6**
conditionalities 32–40
depression of 1890s **12–13**
East Asian crisis 82
European social democracy **78–79**
expansionist policies of U.S. **73–74**
GATT 25–26
gold standard **15–16, 79–80**

Great Depression **16–17, 75–77**
IMF **22–24,** 80, 81
interest rates **36**
ITO **24–25**
Keynesian economics **18–19,** 20
laissez-faire **11**
Long Depression in U.S. **72–73,** 374*c*, 375*c*
market liberalization **36–37**
Marshall Plan **75–77**
mercantilism **6–7**
neoliberalism, 1980s-1990s 29–40
oil shocks, 1970s **27–28,** 29, 80–81
post–World War II economy **18–21**
privatization **33–36**
protectionism **15–18**
David Ricardo **9–11**
of Russia **107–108**
Adam Smith vi, **8–9**
southern assertiveness **26–27**
trade liberalization **37–38**
transitional economy **40**
of U.S. vi, 71–72
Washington Consensus **32–33**
World Bank **21–22**
World War II **17–18**
WTO 80
Hitler, Adolf 376*c*
Honduras 87
Hoover, Herbert 76, 376*c*
Hoskins, Lee **255–258**
host nation participation 46
hot money 39, 97, 386*g*
hours, working 44
housing 109, 123–124
"How Trade Liberalization Impacts Employment" (Moore) **235–238**
HSRC (Human Sciences Research Council) of South Africa 306
human capital 60, 386*g*
human development 386*g*
Human Sciences Research Council (HSRC) of South Africa 306
Hume, David 7
hyperinflation 387*g*
in Bolivia 24, 103
in Germany 16, 17, 375*c*
in Russia 110, 114, 380*c*
and worldwide financial crisis 380*c*

I

IATP. *See* Institute for Agriculture and Trade Policy (IATP)
IBRD. *See* International Bank for Reconstruction and Development (IBRD)
ICTSD. *See* International Centre for Trade and Sustainable Development (ICTSD)
IDA. *See* International Development Association (IDA)
IDB. *See* Inter-American Development Bank (IDB)
IFC. *See* International Finance Corporation (IFC)
IFG. *See* International Forum on Globalization (IFG)
IFI. *See* international financial institution (IFI)
IISD. *See* International Institute for Sustainable Development (IISD)
ILO. *See* International Labor Organization (ILO)
IMF. *See* International Monetary Fund (IMF)
"The IMF View on IMF Reform" (Rato) **202–207**
imperfect competition 64
imperialism 14, 18, 60, 71
import(s) 387*g*
from Asia 75
and East Asia crisis 100, 101
of food/machinery 280*f*
Fordney-McCumber Act 75
growth of 279*f*
and ITO 24
and John Maynard Keynes 20
in least developed countries 280*f*
James Mill on 7
in Russia 113
and social imperialism 13
tariffs on 27, 72
and trade liberalization 37
of tuna 53
in U.S. 90
import quota 387*g*
incentive programs 119–120
income 34, 44, 62
income inequality 43, 115
incrementalism 5
indebtedness 98
independence (national) 21
India
biopiracy in 52
economic growth of 57
and FDI 43
and generic drugs 52
imports from 58
opium from 13
stagflation in 37
and trade liberalization 37
and WTO 56
Indonesia 101
industrialization
in 1890s–1918 11–12
in China 125
and colonization 6, 21
and economic growth 57
and World Bank 21
during World War I 14–15
industrialized countries 26
industrial jobs, loss of 84
industrial output 113
industrial plants 111–112
industrial production 58–59, 107, 115
Industrial Revolution 57
"industrial tourists" 85–86
industries 113, 118
industry lobbyists 51
infant industry 57–59, 387*g*
inflation 387*g*. *See also* hyperinflation
in Bolivia 103
in China 119, 121
and East Asia crisis 100
and gold standard 15, 16
and high interest rates 36
IMF philosophy on 32
and interest rates 29, 36
during oil crisis 28
and reparations 16
20 Nations with highest, 2003 277*f*
in U.S. 79
and Vietnam War 27, 80, 377*c*
infrastructure 21, 58, 71, 78, 121
innovation 63, 119–120
Institute for Agriculture and Trade Policy (IATP) 306–307
insurgency 375*c*
intellectual property 51, 52, 83, 88, 104, 387*g*
Inter-American Development Bank (IDB) 307
interest rates
and East Asia crisis 99, 100

Index

and the Fed 75–76
during Great Depression 17
high 29, 61, 91, 100
and inflation 29, 36
for least developed countries 114
liberalization of 39
lowering 75
and monetarist school of economics 29–30
and privatization **36**
raising 75–76
and Russia 113
and U.S. 81, 91
of World Bank 21
International Bank for Reconstruction and Development (IBRD) 20, 21, 377*c*. *See also* World Bank (WB)
International Centre for Trade and Sustainable Development (ICTSD) 307–308
international clearing union 19, 20, 22
International Development Association (IDA) 22, 308
International Finance Corporation (IFC) 43–44, 308
international financial institution (IFI) v, vi, 80–81, 387*g*
international financial speculation 19
International Forum on Globalization (IFG) 308–309
International Institute for Sustainable Development (IISD) 309
International Labour Organization (ILO) 309–310, 387*g*
International Labour Organization Declaration on Fundamental Principles and Rights at Work **219–221**
International Monetary Fund (IMF) **22–24,** 310, 387*g*
and Bolivia 103
Bretton Woods Project 377*c*
creation of 20
crisis of confidence in **40–46,** 102
and East Asia 97
and East Asia crisis **99–101**
excerpts from the Agreement of **189–192**
and FDI **43–46**
as lender of last resort 22
and market fundamentalism 32
and market liberalization 36–37
and Mexican financial crisis 33
and MNCs **43–45**
neoliberal policies of **31–32**
and Niger famine 41–42
and oil crises 29
and privatization 33, 35, 36
and Russia 108–111, 114, 379*c*
sequencing/pacing of **40**
and South Korea 98
and trade liberalization 37
U.S. veto power at 80
"The International Monetary Fund and the National Interests of the United States" (Bergsten) **141–147**
international monetary system 28
International South Group Network (ISGN) 310
International Trade Organization (ITO) **24–25,** 377*c*
Interstate Commerce Act of 1887 72
interstate highway system 71
investment 83, 91
"investor state" clause 86
"invisible hand" 8–9
Iran 91
Irish potato famine (1840s) 11, 374*c*
iron 58
"iron law of wages" 10
irrationality of markets 102
irrigation 21
Irwin, Douglas A. 37
ISGN. *See* International South Group Network (ISGN)
isolationism 17, 71, 78
Israel 28
ITeM. *See* Third World Institute (ITeM)
ITO. *See* International Trade Organization (ITO)
IUCN. *See* World Conservation Union (IUCN)

J

Jamaica Conference (1976) 28, 378*c*
Japan
and China 14, 117
economic model in 80
exports from 80
and Marshall Plan 377*c*
and Pearl Harbor 17, 77, 376*c*
rebuilding of 18
Sino-Japanese War 375*c*
U.S. bombs 377*c*
and U.S. debt 82
and World War II 17
Jay Cooke and Company 72
Jiang Jieshi. *See* Chiang Kai-shek
job creation 36, 40, 43
job losses
layoffs 34, 35
to Mexico 90
and NAFTA 83–86
and privatization 34
in Russia 111, 115
in U.S. 90
jobs. *See also* employment
high-paying 90
and NAFTA **84–85**

K

Kennedy Round of GATT talks 272*f*, 378*c*
Kernaghan, Charles **221–225**
kerosene 13
Keynes, John Maynard 18–20, 137–141, 287*b*, 376*c*
Keynesian economics **18–19,** 19–21, 25, 29, 76, 78, 108–109
kickbacks 35, 110, 111
Kirchner, Néstor 88
klepto-capitalists 113, 114
Kletzer, Lori G. **170–178**
Korean War 98
Korten, David C. **147–151**
Krueger, Anne O. 42, 287*b*
Krugman, Paul 31, 63, 64, 82, 287*b*

L

labor 6, 10, 12
labor conditions 4
labor laws 50, 84
labor standards 61, 87
labor theory of value 10
labor unions 44, 45
laissez-faire v, 387*g*
and Age of Imperialism 14
beginnings of 11
and booming economy 78
and China 122
and Corn Laws 11, 373*c*, 374*c*
and development economics 22
and distribution of wealth 12–13

and France 7–8, 373*c*
and IMF conditionalities 23
and John Maynard Keynes 18, 19
and Marshall Plan 78
and neoliberalism 80
outcomes of 18
radical policies of 29
in U.S. 58
Lamy, Pascal 55, 381*c*
land 10, 117
land-grant colleges 71
"late-late" syndrome 22
Latin America 24, 34, 56, 87–89
"Latin American Adjustment: How Much Has Happened?" (Williamson) 32
Latin American Free Trade Association 270*f*
layoffs 34, 35
LDCs. *See* least developed countries (LDCs)
"Learning from East Asia's Woes" (Williamson) **247–255**
least developed countries (LDCs) 387*g*
and agricultural subsidies 48
and capital market liberalization 39–40
and coffee export 49
and conditionalities 24
and debt 29, **61–62,** 275*f*
and development economics 22
and Doha Round 55, 56
economic trends in selected 279*f*
and endogenous grow theory 63
and FDI 43, 278*f*
and GATS 50
imports of food/machinery in 280*f*
interest rates on loans for 114
lack of benefits of globalization for 57
and loans 21–22
and new economic theories 65
and oil crises 81
and pharmaceutical patents 51–52
and poverty 62, 276*f*
and privatization 35, 36
and proglobalization economists 57
and repayment of World Bank loans 21–22
stagnation of 59–60
and trade liberalization 37–38
UNCTAD data on poverty in 62
unsustainable debt of 275*f*
and WTO 47, 89
"least trade restrictive" rule 50
liberal (economic) 29
liberalization policies 94–95
life expectancy 115
Lincoln, Abraham 71
living conditions 84, 121
loans
bailout 99
in East Asia 99, 101
emergency 22
during Great Depression 76
IMF 22–24, 32, 80–82
to least developed countries 21–22, 114
and Mexican financial crisis 33
and oil crises 29
and privatization 102
and Russia 112–114
and South Korea 98
and World Bank 21
and World War I 15
"loans-for-share" program **112–113**
lobbyists 83
local control 65
local initiative programs **119–120**
Lodge, Henry Cabot 74
logos 51
Long Depression (1873–1898) **72–73,** 374*c*, 375*c*
lowest common denominator standards 45, 50

M

Maastricht Treaty 379*c*
machinery imports 280*f*
macroeconomics 31, 33, 387*g*
mafia. *See* organized crime
Malawi 61–62
Malaysia 43
Maltus, Thomas 10, 373*c*
managers 119
manufactured goods 4–5, 373*c*
manufacturing sector 84
Mao Zedong 117
MAP International 311
maquiladora 84–85, 387*g*
market fundamentalism 32
market liberalization **36–37**
market pricing 118–119
market reforms 116–120
Marrakesh Agreement establishing the World Trade Organization, excerpts from the **207–211**
Marshall, George C. 77
Marshall Plan 17–18, **75–77,** 377*c*
Marx, Karl 10, 287*b*–288*b*, 373*c*
McKinley Tariff Act 73, 374*c*
McNamara, Robert S. 22, 46, 288*b*, 378*c*
"Measuring the Costs of Trade-Related Job Loss" (Kletzer) **170–178**
meat 123
median income 90
medicinal plants 52
mercantilism vi, **6–7,** 8, 372*c*, 374*c*, 387*g*
MERCOSUR 271*f*, 379*c*, 387*g*
Metalclad 86
metropole (state) 13, 14, 60, 63, 388*g*
Mexican financial crisis (1982) 32–33
Mexico 34, 53, 83–86
MFN. *See* most favored nation (MFN)
microeconomics 31, 388*g*
Microsoft 44
middle class 6, 85, 115
Middle East 27, 28
Midway 74
military industry 115
milk 110
Mill, James 7, 374*c*
Millennium Development Goals 65, 380*c*
millionaires 111
minimum labor standards 83
Misicuni Dam 103
MNCs. *See* multinational corporations (MNCs)
modern economic system 28
monetarist school of economics 29–30
money in circulation 30
monopolies 9, 34, 35, 72
Monroe Doctrine (1823) 73–74
Moore, Mike **235–238**
Morales, Evo 88–89, 288*b*
moral hazard 114, 388*g*
Morgenthau, Henry, Jr. 288*b*–289*b*
Morocco 36
most favored nation (MFN) 25, 50, 388*g*

Index

MTBE (gasoline additive) 86
multilateral agreement 388*g*
multilateral economic organizations 270*f*–271*f*
multinational corporations (MNCs)
- in Age of Imperialism 14
- definition of 43
- expansion of 5
- and FDI **43–45,** 388*g*
- and GATS 49–50
- hands-off policies toward 60
- and privatization 36

music, pirated 51
mutual funds 95

N

NAFTA. *See* North American Free Trade Agreement (NAFTA)
Naim, Moses 33
NAMA. *See* Non-Agricultural Market Access (NAMA)
National Cordage Company 73
national debt, U.S. 82
Nationalist forces (Chinese) 117
nationalization 89, 388*g*
National Recovery Act (1933) 76
Native populations 6
NATO. *See* North Atlantic Treaty Organization (NATO)
natural resources 110, 112
Nazi Germany 376*c*
NEG theory. *See* new economic geography (NEG) theory
neoliberalism 29–40, 388*g*
- and capital market liberalization **38–40**
- and convergence 59–60
- criticisms of v, 30–31
- and East Asia 95
- and government intervention 29, 30
- and IMF policies **31–32,** 40
- and interest rates 36
- and laissez-faire 80
- and Latin America 88, 89
- and market liberalization **36–37**
- origins of 29
- and privatization 30, **33–36**
- and Russia 108–109, 116
- and Adam Smith 9
- and trade liberalization **37–38**
- and transitional economies **40**
- two tenets of 30
- and Washington Consensus **32–33,** 43

Netherlands 372*c*
New Deal policy 76–77, 376*c*
new economic geography (NEG) theory **63–64**
New International Economic Order (NIEO) 26
New York Stock Exchange 72, 101
New York Times, The 88–89
New York Tribune, The 74
NGO. *See* nongovernmental organization (NGO)
Nicaragua 87
NIEO. *See* New International Economic Order (NIEO)
Niger 41–42
Nigeria 61, 62
Nike 44
Nixon, Richard M. and administration 27, 38, 82, 289*b*, 378*c*
Noland, Marcus **211–219**
Non-Agricultural Market Access (NAMA) 55
Non-Aligned Movement 26
nongovernmental organization (NGO) 388*g*
North, the 26, 388*g*
North American Free Trade Agreement (NAFTA) 388*g*
- and balance of payments **85–86**
- George H. W. Bush signs 379*c*
- Chapter 11 **86**
- Bill Clinton on side agreements **163–170**
- enters into force 379*c*
- and jobs **84–85**
- side agreements 83, **163–170**
- and U.S. **83–86**

North Atlantic Treaty Organization (NATO) 78
Northern Pacific Railroad 72

O

Obasanjo, Olusegun 61–62
oblasts 112
The Observer 42
ODI. *See* Overseas Development Institute
O'Driscoll, Gerald P. **255–258**
OECD. *See* Organization for Economic Cooperation and Development (OECD)
oil 91, 99, 110
oil crises 28, 29, 32, 81, 378*c*
oil prices 113, 116
oligarchies 108
oligarchs 112–114
oligopoly 63, 64, 388*g*
Olivera, Oscar 105, 106
"one-size-fits-all" policy 42
OPEC. *See* Organization of Petroleum Exporting Countries (OPEC)
"open door" policy (in China) 120
OPIC. *See* Overseas Private Investment Corporation (OPIC)
opium 13, 374*c*
Opium Wars 13, 374*c*
opponents of globalization 9
organisms, patenting of 52
Organization for Economic Cooperation and Development (OECD) 78, 98, 311
Organization of Petroleum Exporting Countries (OPEC) 27, 28, 82, 91, 378*c*
organized crime 107, 108, 111, 115
outsourcing 90, 388*g*
overgrazing 123
"overproduction" 12
Overseas Development Institute (ODI) 311–312
Overseas Private Investment Corporation (OPIC) 312
Oxfam Great Britain 312–313
Oxfam International 312

P

Panama Canal Zone 74, 375*c*
pan-European federalism 78
panic 388*g*
Panic of 1873 374*c*
Panic of 1893 73, 374*c*, 375*c*
panic selling 99
paper money 15, 16
Parliament (Great Britain) 11, 373*c*, 374*c*
patents 51–52
"path dependence" 64
Pax Americana 78
Pearl Harbor 17, 77, 376*c*
pension funds 95
pensions 114, 115
People's Republic of China 117, 377*c*. *See also* China
perestroika 108
perfect competition v, 8, 30, 31
perfect information 30–31

periphery (state) 388*g*
China as 13
exploitation of 14
and neoliberalism 30
and new economic geography theory 63
reverting back to 60
and social imperialism 13, 14
personal debt 90, 91
Peru 34
"petrodollars" 28
pharmaceutical patents 51–52
Philadelphia and Reading Railroad 73
Philippines 74, 75
Philippine War 75, 375*c*
Pinochet, Augusto 41
pirated music/films 51
Pliny the Elder 3, 4
Poland vii, 17, 376*c*
Polanyi, Karl 11, 289*b*, 376*c*
police 105
Polo, Marco 372*c*
Ponzi finance 89–90, 389*g*
the poor 104–106
population 10, 373*c*
population growth 124–125
positive feedback loop 64
postwar economy **18–21**
poverty
based on export specialization 276*f*
in Bolivia 103, 104
in East Asia 95
and East Asia crisis 101
and FDI 43
and least developed countries 62, 276*f*
in Mexico 84
and Millennium Development Goals 380*c*
need to address 65
in Russia 114–115
in South Korea 98
and World Bank 22, 28, 378*c*
"Poverty and Globalisation" (Shiva) **225–235**
powdered milk 48
PPP (purchasing power parity) 389*g*
Prebisch, Raul 26, 289b–290*b*
precautionary principle 389*g*
price controls 110
price liberalization **110–111**
prices 9, 109, 110, 118–119
Principles of Political Economy and Taxation (Ricardo) 10, 373*c*
private enterprise 8
private property 118
privatization **33–36,** 389*g*
in Bolivia 103–104
and CAFTA 87
in China 118, 123
in Cochabamba, Bolivia **102–106**
and "democratic deficit" 61
and GATS 50
as IMF conditionality 33–36
and interest rates **36**
"loans-for-share" program **112–113**
and MNCs 43
and neoliberalism 30, **33–36**
and Russia 35, 109, **111–113**
and unemployment 34, 35, 40
of water systems 35, **102–106,** 380*c*
and John Williamson 32
problem solving vii
profits 95, 96, 119
property rights 32
proponents of globalization 9
ProPoor 313
"protection" 115
protectionism **15–18,** 389*g*
and Age of Imperialism 14
and depressions 12, 374*c*
and developed nations 57–58
and economic depression 374*c*
and England 372*c*
in Great Britain 57–58
and Great Depression 17, 76
and John Maynard Keynes 19
outcomes of 18
and trade liberalization 63
in U.S. 57, 58, 71, 73, 76
and wealth of developed nations 57
and WTO 59
public participation 54. *See also* transparency
Public Works Administration 76
Puerto Rico 74, 375*c*
purchasing power parity (PPP) 389*g*

Q

Quebec, Canada 88, 380*c*
quota 23, 118, 119, 378*c*, 387*g*, 389*g*

R

race to the bottom 10, 44, 60, 389*g*
railroads 71–73, 121
rain water 104, 105
random factors 64
rapid liberalization 108–110
rate increase 104
Rato y Figaredo, Rodrigo de 41, 89–91, **202–207,** 290*b*
raw materials 5, 26, 57, 59
Reagan, Ronald 30
real capital 389*g*
real estate bubble 97
"real" investments 96
recession 91, 99, 100
reconstruction 78
redistribution of wealth 32
"red menace" 78
reform policies 110, 117–118, 122
Regan, Ronald 290*b*
regional trade agreements 389*g*
CAFTA **86–87**
FTAA **87–89**
NAFTA **83–86**
Reich, Robert 290*b*–291*b*
re-importation 59
relocalization 389*g*
reparations 15, 16
repayment 21–22
reserve currency 20, 27, 121
reserve gold 73, 80
resident staff 46
revenues 33, 59, 90
Ricardo, David **9–11,** 291*b*, 373*c*
rice 52
Rio+5 Consultation 313–314
riots 101
road-building projects 21
robber barons 12, 113
Rockefeller, John D. 72
Roman Empire 3–4
Rome, Treaty of 377*c*
Romer, Paul 63
Roosevelt, Frankllin Delano 18, 76–77, 131–137, 291*b*–292*b*, 376*c*
Roosevelt, Theodore 74
round 389*g*
Rubin, Robert 292*b*
ruble 110, 113–114, 380*c*
Russia vii, **106–116**. *See also* Soviet Union
background on **107–108**
banking in 109, 112, 113
Bolshevik Revolution 18, 107, 375*c*
and China 14

Index

communism in 107–108, 116
corruption in 40, 109–114
economic collapse in **113–114,** 114–116
emergency stabilization in **110**
and FDI 116
and GDP 115, 116
hyperinflation in 110, 114, 380*c*
and IMF 108–111, 114, 379*c*
"loans-for-share" program **112–113**
and neoliberalism 108–109, 116
poverty in 114–115
price liberalization in **110–111**
privatization in 35, 109, **111–113**
prospects for **116**
ruble devalued 380*c*
shock therapy for 40, **108–110,** 111, 114–116, 379*c*
as transitional economy vii, 40, **107–108**
and World War I 14, 15

S

safety net 34, 79, 95, 123
Salinas de Gortari, Carlos 292*b*
Samoa 74
Samuelson, Paul 292*b*
sanctions. *See* economic sanctions
sanitation 44
SAPs. *See* structural adjustment programs (SAPS)
savings
in China 119, 120
in East Asia 94, 95
in Russia 110
in South Korea 97
in U.S. 89, 90
school fees 24
schools 60
Schumpeter, Joseph A. 292*b*
Schurz, Carl 75
science 53
SDR. *See* Special Dra ng Rights (SDR)
sea turtles 53–54
second tier nations 37, 57
secrecy 53, 54
self-interest (individual) 8–9, 30
Seneca the Younger 3–4
sequence and pacing 36, **38–40,** 94, 389*g*
services 49–50, 88
service sectors 87
Seward, William 11–12
SEZs. *See* Special Economic Zones (SEZs)
"shares" (company) 111–112
Sherman Anti-Trust Act of 1890 72
Shiva, Vandana **226–235,** 292*b*–293*b*
shock therapy 389*g*
in Bolivia 103
for Russia 40, **108–110,** 111, 114–116, 379*c*
social costs of **114–116**
and transitional economies 40
short selling 96
shrimp 53–54
side agreements 83, **163–170**
silk 3–4, 13, 58
Silk Road (China) 3, 372*c*
Silva, Luiz Inácio Lula da 88, 293*b*
silver 7, 13, 73
Sino-Japanese War 14, 375*c*
skilled workers 43
small business 64
Smith, Adam vi, **8–9,** 29, 293*b*, 373*c*
Smithsonian Agreement 27, 378*c*
Smoot, Red 76
Smoot-Hawley Tariff Act (1930) 17, 76, 376*c*, 389*g*
social capacity 63
social capital 60, 389*g*
social democracies (European) **78–79**
social imperialism 13–14, 389*g*–390*g*
social inequality 89
Social Security Act (1935) 77
social services 24, 33, 35
SOEs. *See* state-owned enterprises (SOEs)
SOMO. *See* Centre for Research on Multinational Corporations (SOMO)
South, the 26–27, 29, 390*g*
South America 49, 379*c*. *See also specific headings, e.g.:* Brazil
Southeast Asian Free Trade Area (AFTA) 379*c*
Southern Common Market. *See* MERCOSUR
South Korea
East Asia crisis **97–98,** 100, 101
economic growth of 57
economic model in 80
and FDI 43
and trade liberalization 37
Soviet Union (USSR)
breakup of 108, 379*c*
collapse of 29
containment policy towards 77–78
creation of 107, 375*c*
and Europe 79
and Marshall Plan 18, 77
Spain 375*c*
Spanish-American War 71, 74, 75, 375*c*
Special Drawing Rights (SDR) 23
Special Economic Zones (SEZs) 120–121
specialization 10
speculation, currency. *See* currency speculation
speculation, financial market. *See* financial market speculation
spending 23, 99, 100, 103
spending cuts 33
"spillovers" 64
stabilization, emergency **110**
"stabilization fund" 19
stagflation 28, 29, 37, 390*g*
Stakeholder Forum for a Sustainable Future 314
standard of living 26, 85
Standard Oil Company 13, 72
starvation 11, 117
State Department, U.S. 25
state-owned enterprises (SOEs) 34–36, 120, 122–123
steam engines 58
steamships 12
steel 377*c*
steel industry 58
Stiglitz, Joseph vii, 293*b*–294*b*
on austerity measures 56
on capital market liberalization 39
on East Asia 95
on East Asia crisis 99–101
on FDI 45
on market fundamentalism 32
on privatization 36
stock market crash of 1929 16, 76, 376*c*
stock market crash of 1998 101
stocks (in China) 121
Stokey, Nancy L. vii
strategic trade theory (STT) **64**
stripping assets 35

structural adjustment programs (SAPs) 33, 46, 390*g*
structuralism 26
STT. *See* strategic trade theory (STT)
sub-Saharan Africa 62
subsistence farming 55
sugar 48
sugar growers 87
suicide 115
Sumatra 372*c*
Sun Yat-sen 117
supply and demand 7, 9
sustainable development 61, 65, 390*g*
"Sweatshop Blues: Companies Love Misery" (Kernaghan) **221–225**
sweatshops 44
Switzerland 381*c*
synthetic raw materials 26

T

Taiwan 82, 117
Talbott, Strobe 40
Tanzania 46
tariff(s) 390*g*
    AFTA formed 379*c*
    agricultural 55
    "beggar-thy-neighbor" 17, 376*c*
    and CAFTA 87
    and Congress 373*c*, 374*c*
    Dingley Act 375*c*
    European Union eliminates 378*c*
    in export processing zones 44
    Fordney-McCumber Act 375*c*
    and FTAA 88
    and GATT 26
    and Great Depression 17, 75
    import 27, 72
    and ITO 24, 25
    Kennedy Round of GATT talks 378*c*
    Abraham Lincoln on 71
    during Long Depression 72, 73
    McKinley Tariff Act 374*c*
    and mercantilism 7
    and NAFTA 83
    Smoot-Hawley Tariff Act 376*c*
    Tokyo Round of GATT talks 378*c*
    in U.S. 27, 58
    and WTO 47
Tariff Act of 1816 58, 373*c*
Tariff Act of 1913 58
"Tariff of Abominations" 374*c*
taxation 23, 44, 90, 119
tax policy 82
tear gas 105
technology 53, 60, 63, 86
technology transfer 65, 390*g*
TEDS. *See* turtle escape devices
teenagers 44
telegraph 12
textile industry 87
textile manufacturing 57–58
Thailand 43, 96–99, 101, 379*c*
Thatcher, Margaret Hilda 30, 294*b*
Third World Institute (ITeM) 314
Third World Network (TWN) 315
"Three World Empires" theory 14
thrift 120
Tokoyo Round of GATT talks 272*f*, 378*c*
totalitarianism 29
towns 119–120
toxic waste dump 86
trade balance 22, 62
trade barrier 88, 379*c*, 390*g*
trade bloc 82, 83–89, 270*f*–271*f*, 390*g*
trade deficit 20, 85, 390*g*
trade liberalization **37–38,** 390*g*
    and China 37, 56
    and comparative advantage 58
    and GATS 50
    as IMF conditionality 36–37
    and John Maynard Keynes 19
    and protectionism 63
    and Structural Adjustment Program 33
    UNCTAD report on impact of 62–63
    and unemployment 40
    and John Williamson 32
    WTO report on 56
trademarks 51
Trade-Related Aspects of Intellectual Property (TRIPS) **51–52,** 55, 390*g*
trade surplus 20, 79–80, 84, 100, 101, 390*g*
trade zones **119–120**
trading outpost 372*c*
trading partners 6
transitional economy **40,** 390*g*. *See also* China
    background on Russian **107–108**
    collapse, economic **113–114**
    contract responsibility program **119,** 120
    emergency stabilization **110**
    local initiative/innovation in **119–120**
    market pricing 118–119
    price liberalization **110–111**
    privatization of **111–113**
    Russia vii, 40, 106–116
    shock therapy **108–110, 114–116**
    trade zones **119–120**
transparency **54–55,** 390*g*
Treasury, U.S.
    and balance of payments 90
    and IMF policy 81
    notes held by foreign nations 82
    and Russian economy 108, 379*c*
    and South Korea 98
    and transitional economies 40
Treasury bills, U.S. 27, 91
Treatise on Money (Keynes) 18
"trickle-down economics" 30
TRIPS. *See* Trade-Related Aspects of Intellectual Property (TRIPS)
tuna import ban 53
Turkey 14
turtle escape devices (TEDS) 53–54
TWN. *See* Third World Network (TWN)
two-tiered pricing 119, 121

U

UNCTAD. *See* United Nations Conference on Trade and Development (UNCTAD)
underconsumption 12
"Understanding the World Trade Organization" (Noland) **211–219**
UNDP. *See* United Nations Development Program (UNDP)
unemployment. *See also* job losses
    in China 14, 123
    and East Asia crisis 100, 101
    and Great Depression 376*c*